SOUTHERN CALIFORNIA
CABINS & COTTAGES

FOGHORN OUTDOORS®

SOUTHERN CALIFORNIA
CABINS &
COTTAGES

Great Lodgings with Easy Access
to Outdoor Recreation

Second Edition

Ann Marie Brown

AVALON
TRAVEL

FOGHORN OUTDOORS SOUTHERN CALIFORNIA CABINS & COTTAGES
Great Lodgings with Easy Access to Outdoor Recreation

Second Edition

Ann Marie Brown

Printing History
1st edition—2002
2nd edition—April 2005
5 4 3 2 1

Avalon Travel Publishing
An Imprint of
Avalon Publishing Group, Inc.

AVALON
publishing group incorporated

ISBN: 1-56691-588-0
ISSN: 1538-0548

Editor: Sabrina Young
Series Manager: Ellie Behrstock
Acquisitions Editor: Rebecca Browning
Copy Editor: Wendy Taylor
Graphics Coordinator: Justin Marler
Production Coordinators: Darren Alessi, Tamara Gronet
Cover and Interior Designer: Darren Alessi
Map Editor: Kevin Anglin
Cartographers: Kat Smith, Mike Morgenfeld
Indexer: Judy Hunt

Front cover photo: © Fern Valley Inn

Printed in the United States of America by Malloy Inc.

About the Author

The author of 12 outdoors guidebooks, Ann Marie Brown is a dedicated California outdoorswoman. She hikes, bikes, and camps more than 150 days each year in a committed effort to avoid routine, complacency, and getting a real job.

Ann Marie's work has appeared in *Sunset, VIA,* and *Backpacker* magazines. As a way of giving back a little of what she gets from her experiences in nature, she writes and edits for several environmental groups, including the Sierra Club and Natural Resources Defense Council. When not enjoying a Southern California retreat, Ann Marie can be found at her home near Yosemite National Park.

Ann Marie's other guidebooks include:

Foghorn Outdoors 101 Great Hikes of the San Francisco Bay Area
Foghorn Outdoors 250 Great Hikes in California's National Parks
Foghorn Outdoors Bay Area Biking
Foghorn Outdoors California Hiking (with Tom Stienstra)
Foghorn Outdoors California Waterfalls
Foghorn Outdoors Easy Biking in Northern California
Foghorn Outdoors Easy Camping in Southern California
Foghorn Outdoors Easy Hiking in Northern California
Foghorn Outdoors Easy Hiking in Southern California
Foghorn Outdoors Northern California Biking
Moon Handbooks Yosemite

For more information on these titles, visit Ann Marie's website at www.annmariebrown.com.

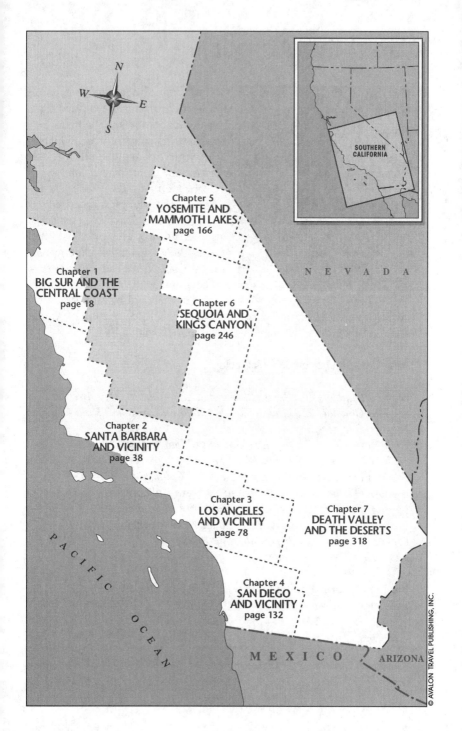

Chapter 5
**YOSEMITE AND
MAMMOTH LAKES**
page 166

Chapter 1
**BIG SUR AND THE
CENTRAL COAST**
page 18

Chapter 6
**SEQUOIA AND
KINGS CANYON**
page 246

N E V A D A

Chapter 2
**SANTA BARBARA
AND VICINITY**
page 38

Chapter 3
**LOS ANGELES
AND VICINITY**
page 78

Chapter 7
**DEATH VALLEY
AND THE DESERTS**
page 318

Chapter 4
**SAN DIEGO
AND VICINITY**
page 132

P A C I F I C   O C E A N

M E X I C O   ARIZONA

SOUTHERN
CALIFORNIA

N
W E
S

© ANN MARIE BROWN

Contents

Defining *Cabins and Cottages* x

How to Use This Book xi
   About the Cabin Profiles • About the Icons • About the Ratings • About the Maps

Introduction 2
   Questions to Ask When Reserving a Cabin 3
   About the National Forest Adventure Pass 4
   Traveling with Pets 5

Best Cabins and Cottages 6
   Best for Hiking 6
   Best for Fishing 7
   Best for Horseback Riding 7
   Best for Boating & Water Sports 8
   Best for Winter Sports 9
   Best for Families 10
   Most Unusual 11
   Best in the Desert 11
   Best Value 11
   Most Luxurious 12
   Best for Beach Activities 12
   Most Secluded 13

Chapter 1—Big Sur and the Central Coast 15
Chapter 2—Santa Barbara and Vicinity. 35
Chapter 3—Los Angeles and Vicinity 75
Chapter 4—San Diego and Vicinity. 129
Chapter 5—Yosemite and Mammoth Lakes 163
Chapter 6—Sequoia and Kings Canyon. 243
Chapter 7—Death Valley and the Deserts 315

Index. 335

Our Commitment

We are committed to making *Foghorn Outdoors Southern California Cabins & Cottages* the most accurate, thorough, and enjoyable guide to cabin and cottage rentals in Southern California. With this second edition you can rest assured that every cabin and cottage in this book has been carefully reviewed and is accompanied by the most up-to-date information. Be aware that with the passing of time some of the fees listed herein may have changed, facilities may have been upgraded (or downgraded), and changes in weather may close cabins or the roads leading to them. With these possibilities in mind, or if you have a specific need or concern, it's best to call the location ahead of time.

If you would like to comment on the book, whether it's to suggest a cabin or cottage we overlooked, or to let us know about any noteworthy experience—good or bad—that occurred while using *Foghorn Outdoors Southern California Cabins & Cottages* as your guide, we would appreciate hearing from you. Please address correspondence to:

Foghorn Outdoors Southern California Cabins & Cottages, 2nd edition
Avalon Travel Publishing
1400 65th Street, Suite 250
Emeryville, CA 94608

email: atpfeedback@avalonpub.com
If you send us an email, please put "Southern California Cabins & Cottages" in the subject line.

Defining *Cabins and Cottages*

The foremost purpose of this book is to provide a hearty resource of cabins and cottages for a successful overnight or weeklong getaway. The secondary goal is to provide enough information about nearby outdoors attractions to jump-start your interest in beachcombing for sea shells, hiking a summit trail, fishing for trout, or soaking in mineral hot springs. This book therefore caters to those who welcome outdoor recreation by day *and* a roof over their head by night—whether that roof is constructed of pine logs, canvas, or fiberglass.

. . . *Fiberglass?* Yes, you read right. The range of materials used to construct the "cabins and cottages" featured in this book is due to our broad definition of a cabin: a self-contained, stand-alone lodging. That is why the cabins and cottages that fill this guidebook range from rustic tent cabins to luxurious vacation home rentals. They may be part of a resort, lodge, ranch, campground, or rental company. Each lodging is a separate building or unit, and would be suitable for couples, families, or singles who want more privacy and personality than a typical hotel or motel room provides.

Each lodging in *Foghorn Outdoors Southern California Cabins & Cottages* is located in or near a major outdoor recreation area, including seven national parks: Joshua Tree, Death Valley, Mojave, Devils Postpile, Yosemite, Sequoia, and Kings Canyon. Also included are cabins and cottages along the length of the Southern California coast from San Diego to Big Sur, and throughout the southern and central Sierra Nevada mountains. Because these cabins and cottages are located near major recreation areas, general information on nearby outdoor activities, such as hiking, fishing, snow skiing, and bicycling, is provided.

Foghorn Outdoors Southern California Cabins & Cottages provides everything you need for an enjoyable weekend getaway or a week-long vacation centered around outdoor recreation and a cabin or cottage (or yurt, chalet, or yacht) that's right for you.

How to Use This Book

Foghorn Outdoors Southern California Cabins & Cottages is divided into seven chapters: Big Sur and the Central Coast, Santa Barbara and Vicinity, Los Angeles and Vicinity, San Diego and Vicinity, Yosemite and Mammoth Lakes, Sequoia and Kings Canyon, and Death Valley and the Deserts. Although that is a lot of territory to cover in one book, navigating this guide can be done easily in two ways:

1. If you know the name of the lodging facility you want to stay at, or the name of the surrounding geographical area or nearby feature (town, national or state park or forest, mountain, lake, river, etc.), look it up in the index beginning on page 335 and turn to the corresponding page.

2. If you know the general area you want to visit, turn to the map at the beginning of that chapter. You can then determine which cabins are in or near your destination by their corresponding numbers. Opposite the map will be a chapter table of contents listing each lodging in the chapter by map number and the page number it's profiled on. Then turn to the corresponding page for the cabin you're interested in.

About the Cabin Profiles

Each featured cabin profile includes an introduction to the lodging facility and what it has to offer. This usually includes an overview of the grounds, units, facilities, and amenities. There is also a discussion of the recreation opportunities available on-site or within a short drive. These range from horseback riding to kayaking and from hiking to fishing. The practical information you need to have an enjoyable trip is broken down further into the following categories:

Facilities

This section conveys the number of cabins or cottages available, whether kitchen facilities are available, whether linens and towels are provided, and if not, what you should bring to sleep comfortably, and whether private or communal bathrooms and showers are available. Amenities inside the cabins (such as fireplace, hot tub, and air-conditioning) as well as on the property (such as swimming pool, restaurant, and picnic area) are also mentioned here.

Reservations and Rates
This section notes whether reservations are required or recommended. It also discusses the rates for each cabin, which often range due to cabin size, amenities, time of week, and time of year. If there are additional fees for extra persons or pets, this will be noted here. If there are package deals, that will also be noted. If a cabin is open during part of the year, those dates will be mentioned.

Contact information, including address, phone number, and website address, if available, for the featured cabin will be included.

Directions
This section provides mile-by-mile driving directions from the nearest major town.

About the Icons
The icons in this book are designed to provide at-a-glance information on activities that are available on-site or nearby a cabin. Some icons have been selected to also represent facilities available or services provided. They are not meant to represent every activity or service, only the ones that the majority of our readers would be interested in.

 — Hiking trails are available.

 — Biking trails or routes are available. Usually this refers to mountain biking, although it may represent road cycling as well. Refer to the text for that cabin for more detail.

 — Swimming opportunities are available.

 — Fishing opportunities are available.

 — Boating opportunities are available. Various types of vessels apply under this umbrella activity, including motorboats, canoes, kayaks, sailboats, personal watercrafts, and row boats. Refer to the text for that cabin for more detail, including mph restrictions and boat ramp availability.

 — Beach activities are available. This general category may include activities such as beachcombing, surfing, and volleyball. Refer to the text for that cabin for more detail on what's allowed.

— Winter sports are available. This general category may include activities such as downhill skiing, cross-country skiing, snowshoeing, snow mobiling, snowboarding, and ice skating. Refer to the text for that cabin for more detail on which sports are available.

 — Hot or cold springs are available.

 — Pets are permitted. Lodging facilities that allow pets may require a deposit, nightly fee, or for the pet to be on a leash. Cabins may also restrict pet size. Refer to the text for that cabin for more specific instruction or call the cabin in advance.

 — The cabin or cottage is especially popular with families. Typically that is because it has activities nearby that are suitable for children. These include a playground or play area, swimming pool, ocean beach, lake with a wading or swimming beach, or family-oriented skiing or snow play. At these kid-friendly cabins, you won't have to travel far to keep the kids entertained.

 — Wheelchair access is provided. Not all cabins at a facility may be wheelchair accessible, but if at least one is, the cabin will receive this icon. Refer to the text for that cabin for more detail or call the cabin in advance.

About the Ratings

Every lodging option in this book is rated on two scales.

Luxury rating

This scale of 1 to 5 stars rates the comfort level of the cabin. We expect that users of this guidebook will have different requirements for cushy living, but in general, a place with more amenities will get a higher ranking. For example, a tent cabin without bathrooms or running water may receive 1 or 2 stars. That doesn't mean that you can't have the perfect vacation here. All it means is you might have to carry your water from a nearby fountain and be prepared to use chemical toilets. Likewise, a cottage with fireplace, hot tub, king-size bed, and down comforters will probably rank 4 or 5 stars. But, that doesn't guarantee the perfect vacation; the cabin may be close to a noisy highway, the management may not be friendly, or the recreation options may be an hour's drive away.

Recreation rating

This scale of 1 to 5 stars rates the accessibility of on-site or nearby activities. We expect that users of this guidebook are interested in the outdoors and seek a cabin experience that is coupled with recreation opportunities. This scale does not rate the number of activities available, nor the level of expertise needed to participate in them. Rather, it rates how *accessible* they are. For example, if you can access a trailhead or launch your boat within a two-minute walk of your cabin, the recreation rating will likely be 5 stars. On the other hand, if fishing or downhill skiing requires a one-hour drive, the cabin may be rated 1 star. That doesn't mean you can't have the same quality vacation . . . it just means you'll need more than your feet for transportation.

Rank

Each cabin and cottage that appears in this guide is carefully selected from myriad options, so we like to think that each of the cabins profiled in this book is special. But those places that are extra-special may receive a ranking in one or more of the "Best Cabins and Cottages" categories. For the complete list of the categories and the cabins that have made it to the top ranks, turn to page 6.

About the Maps

Each chapter in this book begins with a map of the area. Every cabin profile in the chapter is noted by a number on the map. These points are placed as precisely as possible, but the scale of these maps often makes it difficult to pinpoint a cabin's exact location. We advise that you purchase a detailed map of the area, especially if it is new to you.

Introduction

© ANN MARIE BROWN

Introduction

Over and over, traveling around California teaches me to be flexible and adaptable. It's a lesson for which I'm grateful, because these seem to be critical life skills. In travel writing, as in the rest of life, things just don't always go as you plan.

In the course of researching this book, for example, a major rainstorm on the Central Coast closed the cabin where I was scheduled to stay. But a series of detours on a flooded road took me to another cabin resort—one I never would have found otherwise. With a fire roaring in the fireplace and rain splashing on the windowpanes, I spent a cozy, wonderful night in a place I would ordinarily have passed by.

On another occasion, noisy neighbors in the cottage next door caused me to give up my attempt at slumber and go for a drive before dawn. At four in the morning, I stopped my car along a Mojave Desert highway and was awestruck by a horizon-to-horizon sky blanketed with glittering stars.

Yet another day, I drove many miles from my rental cabin to hike a peak in the San Gabriel Mountains. When I arrived at the trailhead, I found the trail was closed due to a forest fire. Sorely disappointed, I settled for hiking to the summit of another peak instead. As I neared the mountaintop, I saw my first bighorn sheep close-up. He was only a few feet ahead of me on the trail, displaying remarkable spiraling antlers.

During my travels for this book, there were days when it snowed in the middle of the desert, or when rain poured down just after the day had dawned clear and blue. But each time, what seemed like an obstacle turned out to be a blessing in disguise. I wound up making new friends, discovering new places, or witnessing a sight I would have otherwise missed.

Kurt Vonnegut Jr. wrote that "peculiar travel suggestions are dancing lessons from God." If you travel around Southern California and stay at any of this book's cabins, cottages, ski huts, fire lookouts, boat-and-breakfasts, or guest ranches, you'll probably learn to dance. At the very least, you'll have a great time trying.

—Ann Marie Brown

Questions to Ask When Reserving a Cabin

The majority of these questions are addressed in the cabin and cottage write-ups that follow. But resort owners change, policies change, and times change, so it's wise to ask a few questions. The best advice: Know before you go.

- Are pets allowed in the cabin? Is there any extra charge for pets?
- Does the cabin have a private bathroom and shower, or do I use a shared bathroom facility on the grounds?
- Does the cabin have electricity and heat? Should I bring flashlights and lanterns?
- Does the cabin have a fireplace or woodstove? Should I bring my own firewood?
- Does the cabin have a kitchen, and are all dishes, pots, pans, and utensils provided? What about paper towels, toilet paper, soap, trash bags, and cleaning supplies?
- Does the cabin have a barbecue or fire grill where I can cook outside?
- Is there a grocery store nearby, or should I bring all my own food?
- Is there a restaurant or café nearby?
- Does the cabin have all linens provided, or should I bring sleeping bags, pillows, and towels?
- Is the cabin a single unit or duplex-style? Is it situated very close to other cabins, where I might hear my neighbors?
- Is the cabin close to the road, so I might hear road noise?
- Does the cabin have a view?

About the National Forest Adventure Pass

Beginning in 1997, a fee policy was instituted in Angeles, San Bernardino, Cleveland, and Los Padres National Forests as a way of raising revenue to cover the costs of recreation on national forest land.

The policy is as follows: Any vehicle that is parked in the Angeles, San Bernardino, Cleveland, and Los Padres National Forests must display a national forest adventure pass. You are free to drive through national forest land without a pass, but if you park your car, you must display one. The cardboard pass hangs from your rearview mirror.

Passes are available for a fee of $5 per day or $30 per year, and the same pass is valid in all four national forests. When you purchase a yearly pass, you receive an extra pass for use on a second vehicle, such as a motorcycle or trailer. Passes can be purchased at all Angeles, San Bernardino, Cleveland, and Los Padres National Forest visitor centers and ranger stations. They are also available at many commercial establishments, such as grocery stores and mini-marts located on or near national forest land.

Traveling with Pets

Many of the cabins and cottages in this book allow pets in some or all of their units. Look for the 🐄 symbol to easily identify these places. However, before packing your pet's suitcase, please alert the resort's management of your intentions. At many places, dogs are permitted only in some cabins; you'll need to reserve one of these dog-friendly cabins in advance. Also, some resorts charge a nightly fee for dogs, while others insist on a one-time fee or a doggy cleaning deposit. If you have more than one dog with you, the fee is usually per dog. Find out the specifics before you go.

Also, most cabin and cottage owners agree that dog owners must not leave their dogs unattended. That means that if you leave your cabin or cottage, your dog goes with you, even for short stints like meals or drives to the store. It's unfair to your dog to leave him or her alone in a strange place, and it's even more unfair to other cabin or cottage guests who get stuck listening to an upset, barking dog. If you bring your dog to a cabin or cottage resort, be prepared to have him or her at your side at all times. And it goes without saying that when you're around other people (as you will be at any resort), your dog must be leashed, no matter how well-behaved he or she is.

Please remember that in general, if you are vacationing in or near a national or state park, your dog will not be allowed to hike on trails with you. Dogs are permitted on roads and in picnic areas and campgrounds in these parks, but not on hiking trails. However, if you are vacationing in or near national forest land, your dog will be allowed to hike with you on most trails. Before you leave on your trip, contact the parks where you are heading for updated information regarding dog policies.

Best Cabins and Cottages

Of the hundreds of cabins and cottages in this book, here are my favorites in the following categories:

Best for Hiking

Yosemite High Sierra Camps, Yosemite and Mammoth Lakes, p. 195. The High Sierra Camp loop allows you to stay at five tent cabin camps spaced 5.7–10 miles apart—the perfect distance for day hiking.

Tuolumne Lodge, Yosemite and Mammoth Lakes, p. 197. These 59 tent cabins are located within 100 yards of the John Muir Trail and the Pacific Crest Trail, and they're within a stone's throw of the trailheads at Tuolumne Meadows.

Rock Creek Lakes Resort, Yosemite and Mammoth Lakes, p. 238. These cabins are only one mile from the Mosquito Flat trailhead, at 10,300 feet in elevation, with trails leading into spectacular Little Lakes Valley and Mono Pass.

Grant Grove Lodge, Sequoia and Kings Canyon, p. 280. These cabins provide ready access to dozens of trails in Kings Canyon, Sequoia National Parks, and Giant Sequoia National Monument.

Bearpaw High Sierra Camp, Sequoia and Kings Canyon, p. 289. You have to hike 11 miles to reach this tent-cabin camp, and once you're there, many more day trips are possible.

Silver City Resort

Silver City Resort, Sequoia and Kings Canyon, p. 299. The only cabin resort in Mineral King, Silver City gives you the chance to explore the spectacular high country of Sequoia National Park without sleeping in a tent at night.

Best for Fishing

Lake San Antonio South Shore Resort, Santa Barbara and Vicinity, p. 40. Just steps from these 17 cabins, you can fish for striped bass, largemouth bass, catfish, crappie, and bluegill; don't be surprised if you catch and release up to 100 bass per day.

Alpers Owens River Ranch, Yosemite and Mammoth Lakes, p. 211. At this fly-fishing ranch near Mammoth, you can choose between a trophy trout pond, the Owens River, and Alpers Creek—all within a few feet of your rustic cabin.

Hot Creek Ranch, Yosemite and Mammoth Lakes, p. 232. For dedicated fly fishers, Hot Creek Ranch offers luxurious cabins along a stretch of Hot Creek in the Owens River valley.

Convict Lake Resort, Yosemite and Mammoth Lakes, p. 234. Fishing for brown and rainbow trout is the main task of vacationers staying at Convict Lake's 23 cabins.

Bishop Creek Lodge, Sequoia and Kings Canyon, p. 274. This resort makes no pretenses; it's a base camp for anglers heading to South Lake or Sabrina Lake to fish for trout all day.

Parchers Resort, Sequoia and Kings Canyon, p. 275. Located only one mile from South Lake in Bishop Creek Canyon, these 10 cabins are perfectly situated for rainbow and brown trout fishing.

Best for Horseback Riding

Circle Bar B Guest Ranch, Santa Barbara and Vicinity, p. 56. Ride Old Paint through the coastal hills of Santa Barbara after a good night's rest in one of Circle Bar B's seven cabins.

Hunewill Guest Ranch, Yosemite and Mammoth Lakes, p. 179. At this Bridgeport ranch, 120 horses are waiting to be ridden, so pack up your cowboy boots and a bag of apples and carrots.

Red's Meadow Resort, Yosemite and Mammoth Lakes, p. 224. Stay at these rustic cabins in Devils Postpile and take guided rides into the John Muir and Ansel Adams Wilderness Areas.

Bonnie B Ranch, Sequoia and Kings Canyon, p. 255. Rent this 3,000-square-foot ranch house and the 440 acres surrounding it, then ride the ranch's horses for a week.

Golden Trout Wilderness Pack Trains Cabins, Sequoia and Kings Canyon, p. 304. Saddle up and ride into the Golden Trout Wilderness after a night in these rustic cabins.

Red's Meadow Resort

Rankin Ranch, Sequoia and Kings Canyon, p. 312. A taste of old California, Rankin Ranch is all about cowboys, cattle ranching, hayrides, and horseshoes.

Best for Boating & Water Sports

Lake San Antonio South Shore Resort, Santa Barbara and Vicinity, p. 40. The Paso Robles foothills heat up in summer, which makes long and narrow Lake San Antonio an obvious choice for waterskiing and boating.

Shore Acres Lodge, Los Angeles and Vicinity, p. 97. This cabin resort on the shore of Big Bear Lake is near Holloway's Marina, where you can rent personal watercrafts as well as boats for sailing, waterskiing, and fishing.

The Forks Resort, Sequoia and Kings Canyon, p. 252. Bass Lake is the Sierra foothills' most popular water-skiing lake, and the Forks Resort provides easy access to it.

Miller's Landing, Sequoia and Kings Canyon, p. 254. These cabins are located right across the road from Miller's Landing Marina at Bass Lake, where you can rent patio boats, ski boats, Waverunners, fishing boats, kayaks, and canoes.

Shaver Lake Lodge, Sequoia and Kings Canyon, p. 257. Twenty cabins overlook Shaver Lake, where sailors, water-skiers, and jet skiers share the water with anglers and kayakers.

Lakeshore Resort, Sequoia and Kings Canyon, p. 265. These Huntington Lake cabins give you easy access to waterskiing, fishing, and especially sailing; this lake is considered the premier high-altitude sailing lake in the United States.

Best for Winter Sports

Snowcrest Lodge, Los Angeles and Vicinity, p. 84. Located a half mile from the chairlift at Mount Baldy, the six rustic cabins at Snowcrest Lodge are a throwback to the 1930s.

Giant Oaks Lodge, Los Angeles and Vicinity, p. 92. Located only five miles from Snow Valley Ski Resort and a half hour from San Bernardino, Giant Oaks Lodge makes a weekend ski trip simple.

Our Secret Garden Mountain Retreat, Los Angeles and Vicinity, p. 104. Take the "back" way to the lifts at Big Bear's Snow Summit and Bear Mountain ski areas from this cabin resort.

Pinecrest Chalet, Yosemite and Mammoth Lakes, p. 173. The closest lodging to Dodge Ridge Ski Area, Pinecrest Chalet's 23 cabins and townhouses provide easy access to skiing and snowboarding.

Tioga Pass Resort, Yosemite and Mammoth Lakes, p. 186. The road to the resort isn't plowed in winter, but if you're willing to ski in six miles, you'll have a warm cabin in a private winter wonderland.

Mammoth Mountain Chalets, Yosemite and Mammoth Lakes, p. 222. These A-frame chalets are literally across the street from the chairlifts at Mammoth Mountain ski area.

Tamarack Lodge Resort, Yosemite and Mammoth Lakes, p. 226. Cross-country ski and snowshoe right from your cabin door on more than 45 kilometers of groomed track.

Rock Creek Lodge, Yosemite and Mammoth Lakes, p. 239. Founded in the 1920s as one of the first ski resorts in America, Rock Creek Lodge is the perfect base camp for a cross-country skiing vacation.

Big Bear Lake at Shore Acres Lodge

Rock Creek Lodge

Best for Families

The Alisal Guest Ranch and Resort, Santa Barbara and Vicinity, p. 54. The Alisal has tons of organized activities for children, from horseback riding and fishing lessons to art classes and even a petting zoo.

Rancho Oso Guest Ranch, Santa Barbara and Vicinity, p. 58. Spend the night in the "Saloon" or in one of 10 covered wagons at this campground in the Santa Ynez Mountains.

Pinecrest Lake Resort, Yosemite and Mammoth Lakes, p. 172. This resort caters to families with nightly movies, paddleboat rentals, guided nature hikes, and two- and three-bedroom housekeeping cabins near Pinecrest Lake.

Virginia Creek Settlement, Yosemite and Mammoth Lakes, p. 181. Kids will love staying in these covered wagons and tiny Old West–style cabins near Bodie State Historic Park.

Yosemite Lakes, Yosemite and Mammoth Lakes, p. 190. These cabins and yurts along the South Fork Tuolumne River attract families who want to swim and fish.

Montecito Sequoia Lodge, Sequoia and Kings Canyon, p. 285. This resort is run like a High Sierra Club Med for families, with nonstop organized activities for kids.

Rankin Ranch, Sequoia and Kings Canyon, p. 312. If your children are budding cowboys or cowgirls, take them on a cabin vacation at Rankin Ranch.

Most Unusual

White Lotus Foundation, Santa Barbara and Vicinity, p. 59. Sleep in a yurt and be a yogi for a few days at this yoga retreat center in the mountains above Santa Barbara.

Castlewood Theme Cottages, Los Angeles and Vicinity, p. 102. Spend the night in one of 10 theme cabins in Big Bear, and live out your *Antony and Cleopatra* or *Gone with the Wind* fantasies.

Mono Hot Springs Resort, Sequoia and Kings Canyon, p. 266. These cabins are way out in the middle of nowhere, existing only for the hedonistic pleasure of bathing in soothing hot springs.

Oak Flat Lookout Tower, Sequoia and Kings Canyon, p. 310. Spend the weekend in a fire lookout tower perched 40 feet above the ground on a mountaintop near Bakersfield.

Best in the Desert

La Casa del Zorro Desert Resort, San Diego and Vicinity, p. 140. These luxurious cottages are just steps from the trailheads at Anza-Borrego Desert State Park.

29 Palms Inn, Death Valley and the Deserts, p. 324. Located just outside the entrance to Joshua Tree National Park, many of these adobe bungalow and wood-frame cabins were built in 1928.

Two Bunch Palms, Death Valley and the Deserts, p. 328. Leave the real world behind at this luxurious hot-springs oasis in Desert Hot Springs.

Best Value

Green Valley Lake Cozy Cabins, Los Angeles and Vicinity, p. 94. A week at this small fishing and swimming lake in the San Bernardino Mountains will cost you less than $750 for 4–6 people.

Two Harbors Cabins, Los Angeles and Vicinity, p. 110. Available in the off-season (from October to April) only, these mobile home–style cabins on Catalina Island are offered for $40–50 a night. If you want to visit in the summer, rent a tent cabin for $40.

William Heise County Park Cabins, San Diego and Vicinity, p. 146. A family of four can stay in a wooden cabin at this popular San Diego mountain park for only $35 per night.

Virginia Creek Settlement, Yosemite and Mammoth Lakes, p. 181. Less than $25 buys you a night for two in these tiny, Old West cabins.

KOA Yosemite-Mariposa, Yosemite and Mammoth Lakes, p. 213. Where can you stay near Yosemite for $55 a night? Right here at the KOA log cabins.

Grant Grove Lodge, Sequoia and Kings Canyon, p. 280. For just over $100, stay inside the border of Kings Canyon National Park at a cabin for two—and it comes with its own bathroom!

Catalina Cabins at Two Harbors

Most Luxurious

Simpson House Inn, Santa Barbara and Vicinity, p. 63. Victorian elegance
  is the order of the day at Simpson House Inn.

San Ysidro Ranch, Santa Barbara and Vicinity, p. 66. Your name is branded in
  block letters on a wooden plaque outside your cottage at this exclusive resort.

Four Seasons Biltmore, Santa Barbara and Vicinity, p. 67. Situated right on
  Butterfly Beach, the Biltmore is the grand old dame of Santa Barbara.

Chateau Marmont, Los Angeles and Vicinity, p. 80. Bette Davis and Greta
  Garbo slept in these cottages, and you can too.

Double Eagle Resort, Yosemite and Mammoth Lakes, p. 207. For a mountain resort, this place has plenty of "city" amenities, like a health spa and
  a gourmet restaurant.

Two Bunch Palms, Death Valley and the Deserts, p. 328. Getting past the guards
  at the entrance gate is a challenge, but once you're in, you will be pampered.

Best for Beach Activities

Cayucos Vacation Rentals, Santa Barbara and Vicinity, p. 46. The little
  town of Cayucos is the quintessential beach town, where all recreation activities center on the coast.

The Tides Motel, Santa Barbara and Vicinity, p. 51. Only 90 steps separate
  your cottage from the sands of Pismo Beach.

Four Seasons Biltmore, Santa Barbara and Vicinity, p. 67. Butterfly Beach
  is only a few steps from your cottage at the Biltmore.

La Paloma Cottages, Los Angeles and Vicinity, p. 112. Situated in Avalon, on Catalina Island, these cottages offer access to every imaginable ocean and beach activity.

Manzanita Cottages, Los Angeles and Vicinity, p. 119. You can walk to the lovely white sands of Laguna Beach from these cottages.

Crystal Pier Hotel, San Diego and Vicinity, p. 154. Located in Pacific Beach, these cottages on the historic Crystal Pier don't just overlook the ocean, they sit on top of it.

The Beach Cottages, San Diego and Vicinity, p, 155. These 17 cottages are just inches from the sand in Pacific Beach, San Diego's beach party town.

Most Secluded

Lucia Lodge, Big Sur and Central Coast, p. 29. Get away from it all at one of the 10 cabins at Lucia Lodge, where it will be just you, your sweetheart, and your ocean view.

Seven Oaks Mountain Cabins, Los Angeles and Vicinity, p. 106. Close to Los Angeles but hidden three miles off the main highway, the six cabins at Seven Oaks keep guests sequestered from the crowds.

Muir Trail Ranch, Sequoia and Kings Canyon, p. 270. Because you rented the whole ranch and had to hike five miles to reach it, you probably won't have a lot of neighbors.

Paradise Canyon Cabins, Sequoia and Kings Canyon, p. 297. Situated behind a locked gate on the lonely, winding road to Mineral King, the two cabins at Paradise Canyon are a hidden paradise.

© ANN MARIE BROWN

The Tides Motel

Chapter 1

© ANN MARIE BROWN

Big Sur and the Central Coast

Big Sur and the Central Coast

I t wouldn't be easy to choose the most spectacular stretch of California coastline, but if pressed, most beach connoisseurs would agree there is nothing quite as visually stunning as the 90 miles of cliffs, rocks, and waves that run from Carmel to just north of San Simeon. Tourists and Sunday drivers have flocked to this section of Highway 1 ever since the road was first built in the 1930s. Along the way, they stop at the top of 300-foot-high bluffs to admire the crashing surf far below, cross over concrete bridges spanning precipitous river gorges, and experience mile after mile of postcard-quality coastal scenery.

There's nothing not to like here, from the mild climate to the wild seascape. Much of this area is isolated, undeveloped, and difficult to access, with high cliffs and few roads. Visiting this land means wandering along gravel beaches, pausing to watch sunsets over glimmering seas, and walking in the shadows of giant redwoods. Stores, services, and other hints of civilization are clustered in a few small towns: Big Sur, Lucia, Gorda, and San Simeon. In between are silence, solitude, and the sea.

Whereas towns are few and onshore traffic is light, a different story unfolds out at sea. Every winter and spring, like clockwork, thousands of gray whales pass by on their long migrations. Traveling from their summer home in Alaska's Bering Sea to their winter breeding grounds in Baja, then back again a few months later, the whales display occasional flashes of fins or tails and leave hundreds of frothy spouts as their calling cards. Whale-watching is at its best from December to May, on days when the sea is flat and deep blue, with no wind or whitecaps.

Neighboring this region's coastal splendor is a mountainous area of deeply carved canyons and steep escarpments, where the Santa Cruz Mountains in the north gives way to the Santa Lucia Mountains in the south. Here, dense redwood forests thin out, and the forest transitions to drier groves of oaks and pines. Visitors can explore these mountains on the hiking trails of the famous Ventana Wilderness and its lesser-known neighbor, Silver Peak Wilderness.

This is a landscape where you will want to linger; most visitors find themselves wanting to go nowhere in a hurry. Since lodgings are relatively few on this lonesome stretch of coast, make sure you reserve in advance, especially on weekends. Cabin and cottage accommodations run the gamut from the homey cottages at Carmel River Inn to the fun and funky Deetjen's Big Sur Inn. No matter where you decide to stay, remember that the coast commonly experiences "sweater weather" all year round. Pack along a few extra layers so that you can enjoy whatever this dramatic landscape throws at you—sun, wind, fog, and even winter rain. Along this stretch of the sand and sea, it's all good.

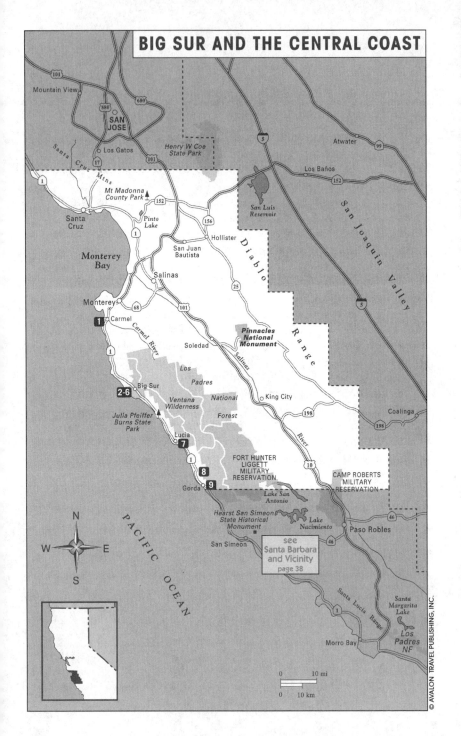

BIG SUR AND THE CENTRAL COAST

Contents

1. Carmel River Inn 20

2. Ripplewood Resort 21

3. Glen Oaks Motel 23

4. Big Sur Campground and Cabins 24

5. Big Sur Lodge 26

6. Deetjen's Big Sur Inn 27

7. Lucia Lodge 29

8. Treebones Resort 31

9. Gorda Springs Cottages 32

1 CARMEL RIVER INN
off Highway 1 in Carmel

Luxury rating: ★ ★ ★ ☆ ☆   **Recreation rating:** ★ ★ ★ ★ ☆

The Carmel River Inn is very un-Carmel in that it is neither overpriced nor stuffy in any way. Its 24 cottages are adorable—some are even surrounded by white picket fences—but they don't call attention to themselves unnecessarily. They are located on 10 acres of peaceful gardens only a mile away from the crowds thronging the shops in downtown Carmel. Everything is serene once you enter the grounds of the inn, and it's reasonably priced to boot (the antithesis of the Carmel tourist area).

The inn is all about relaxing, not about doing. Swim long, slow laps in the heated pool, hang out on your cottage's deck and read a novel, or watch a log burn in the fireplace. If you want a little more activity, take a stroll to the historic Carmel Mission, built in 1771, or to the Carmel River Beach to watch the sunset.

And get this: Your dog can accompany you for a stay at the Carmel River Inn for only a nominal fee. As many dog-lovers know, Carmel is a very dog-friendly town. The main street, Ocean Avenue, even has little hitching posts for dogs, so you can browse the shops while your four-legged friend waits patiently outside. He or she will have to wear a leash when you visit Carmel River Beach, but at nearby Carmel City Beach, Rover can run free.

Most of the Carmel River Inn's cottages are named after famous people who visited or lived in the area, like the author Henry Miller, the photographer Ansel Adams, or the explorer Gaspar de Portola. Each is surrounded by mature landscaping, including huge cypress, cottonwood, and sycamore trees and carefully tended flowers. The cottage's interiors are graciously appointed with attractive (but not pretentious) furnishings. When you walk into the room and your eyes scan the decor, you just relax.

© ANN MARIE BROWN

While you're staying at Carmel River Inn, don't miss a visit to Point Lobos State Reserve, just 2.5 miles south off Highway 1. This park contains one of California's most stunning stretches of coastline, with myriad aquamarine coves, white sand beaches, and plentiful sea otters—and it can be easily visited by walking any of several short and easy trails.

Facilities
There are 24 cottages in various configurations that can accommodate two to six people, plus 19 motel-style rooms. Some of the accommodations have kitchens. Linens and towels are provided.

Reservations and Rates
Reservations are recommended. Fees are $105–295 per night. Pets are permitted for a $25 fee per night. Contact Carmel River Inn, Highway 1 at Carmel River Bridge, P.O. Box 221609, Carmel, CA 93922, 831/624-1575 or 800/882-8142, website: www.carmelriverinn.com.

Directions
From San Luis Obispo, drive north on U.S. 101 for 24 miles to the Highway 46 exit, near Templeton. Turn west on Highway 46 and drive 23 miles to Highway 1. Turn north on Highway 1 and drive 100 miles to Carmel. Just after crossing the highway bridge over the Carmel River, turn left on Oliver Road. The inn is on the left.

2 RIPPLEWOOD RESORT
off Highway 1 in Big Sur

Luxury rating: ★ ★ ★ ☆ ☆   Recreation rating: ★ ★ ★ ★ ☆

A stay at Ripplewood Resort is a classic Big Sur experience, a back-to-nature getaway with just the right amount of creature comforts. Nine of the resort's sixteen cabins are a few feet from the Big Sur River in a secluded grove of redwoods; five others are on the hillside above Ripplewood's store and cafe, and the least desirable two are close by the highway. Although all the cabins are simply furnished, some have a few memorable extras like wood-burning stoves, or windows overlooking the river. The nine riverside cabins are the most desirable, for obvious reasons; there's nothing like the sound of a flowing stream to help you get a good night's sleep. The best of the hillside cabins is number 15, with its stone fireplace and hand-hewn ceiling beams.

Some of the cabins have kitchens, and some do not, so make sure you ask for what you want. And if you plan to cook in your cabin, pack along

© ANN MARIE BROWN

some pots, pans, and spatulas, or you'll have to rent a "kitchen kit" from the management for $10. Bring your groceries too—the little store at Ripplewood, as well as a few other small stores in Big Sur, will be of aid if you forget one or two items, but they aren't big enough to stock your larder.

Surely you will eat at the Ripplewood Café for at least one of your meals. The café serves breakfast and lunch only. They stick to what they know, and they do it well. The buttermilk pancakes and breakfast burritos will fill you up for an entire day, and there are also homemade sticky buns. If you still have room for dinner, head across the street to the Big Sur Roadhouse for California-style cuisine with a Mexican flair.

While in Big Sur, do as the locals do. Spend a lazy afternoon on the windblown sands at Pfeiffer Beach. Visit the Henry Miller library and learn all about the controversial author's life. Have a South Coast margarita at Nepenthe. Watch for whales. Visit the Coast Gallery, where prominent Big Sur artists display their works (many of Henry Miller's watercolor paintings are for sale as prints here). Sign up for a massage or a meditation class at the Esalen Institute. Or go for a hike at one of three nearby state parks: Julia Pfeiffer Burns, Pfeiffer Big Sur, or Andrew Molera. With all this to choose from, you better reserve a cabin for a week.

Facilities

There are 16 cabins in various sizes and configurations that can accommodate up to five people. Some of the cabins have kitchens but no cooking utensils; bring your own, or rent a "kitchen kit" for $10. A small store and café are on-site. Linens and towels are provided.

Reservations and Rates

Reservations are recommended. Fees are $85–135 per night. Pets are not permitted. Contact Ripplewood Resort, Highway 1, Big Sur, CA 93920, 831/667-2242, website: www.ripplewoodresort.com.

Directions

From San Luis Obispo, drive north on U.S. 101 for 24 miles to the Highway 46 exit, near Templeton. Turn west on Highway 46 and drive 23 miles to Highway 1. Turn north on Highway 1 and drive 75 miles to Big Sur. Ripplewood Resort is on the east side of the highway.

3 GLEN OAKS MOTEL
off Highway 1 in Big Sur

Luxury rating: ★ ★ ★ ☆ ☆   **Recreation rating:** ★ ★ ★ ★ ☆

There are plenty of cabin resorts in Big Sur, but one of my favorites doesn't even call itself a cabin resort. The Glen Oaks Motel looks just like a basic motel to passersby on Highway 1, because all you can see from the road are its side-by-side rooms. But just 100 yards away, tucked into the redwood forest, are two cute and cozy cottages that frequently have availability when the better-known Big Sur cabins are filled up.

Both cottages have one queen bed each, so they are only suited for singles or couples. Both are built of redwood and have workable kitchens and bathrooms, plus gas fireplaces that you turn on with a flip of a switch. Archie's Cottage is set up with a studio floor plan; it is smaller than the plainly named The Cottage, which consists of two rooms—a bedroom and a living room/kitchen. The Cottage's biggest selling point is its spacious deck, where you will likely spend most of your morning hours drinking coffee while you gaze out at the redwood trees.

A note about both cottages' kitchens: Although they are adequate for cooking most meals, you might want to bring a cooler along, because the refrigerators are only half-sized. Then again, you might just want to forget cooking and instead have dinner at the Big Sur Roadhouse, situated right across the highway. The restaurant, which serves fresh and flavorful Mexican food, is owned by the same folks who run the motel and cottages.

Don't miss the grilled tiger prawns. Ripplewood Resort (see the previous listing) is right next door to Glen Oaks, so you can always nab an omelet for breakfast or a sandwich for lunch at the café over there.

Besides gazing at the azure coastline, the most popular activity by far at Big Sur is going for a hike. Even the aerobically challenged can take the easy .25-mile walk to McWay Falls, at Julia Pfeiffer Burns State Park. You'll recognize the waterfall when you see it; it drops over a 200-foot-high cliff onto brayed tan sands and then pours into the sea. McWay Falls has been pictured on more calendars and book covers than any other waterfall in California, except perhaps Yosemite Falls. If you'd rather go for a longer hike, from the same parking lot you can start on Ewoldsen Trail, a six-mile loop under a dense canopy of redwoods that climbs to a spectacular overlook of the Big Sur coast.

Facilities

There are two cottages that can accommodate two people each, plus 15 motel rooms. Both cottages have kitchens and fireplaces. Linens and towels are provided.

Reservations and Rates

Reservations are recommended. Fees are $145–160 per night. Pets are not permitted. Contact Glen Oaks Motel, Highway 1, Big Sur, CA 93920, 831/667-2105, website: www.glenoaksbigsur.com.

Directions

From San Luis Obispo, drive north on U.S. 101 for 24 miles to the Highway 46 exit, near Templeton. Turn west on Highway 46 and drive 23 miles to Highway 1. Turn north on Highway 1 and drive 75 miles to Big Sur. Glen Oaks Motel is on the east side of the highway, just south of Ripplewood Resort.

4 BIG SUR CAMPGROUND AND CABINS
off Highway 1 in Big Sur

Luxury rating: ★ ★ ★ ☆ ☆   **Recreation rating: ★ ★ ★ ★ ☆**

Why do people stay at this private campground in Big Sur when Pfeiffer Big Sur State Park is practically across the road? One big reason: The cabins at Big Sur Campground are right on the Big Sur River, at a lovely bend where you can swim, fish, or just watch the water roll by.

You have several accommodation options at Big Sur Campground. Besides regular tent and RV sites, the camp has 12 cabins (all with fireplaces) and four tent cabins, available in summer only. The tent cabins are great if you

© ANN MARIE BROWN

want to save money, but remember that they are minimalist by design. You have to walk to a public bathhouse and do your cooking over a barbecue or camping stove. The 12 regular cabins are all slightly different. Many visitors prefer the A-frame cabins, which have full kitchens, bathrooms, fireplaces, and an upper loft that serves as an extra bedroom. These can house four to six people, but unfortunately, they are not right next to the river (although they are only a few steps away). The rest of the cabins are spread out in the big redwoods on the campground's south side, with Nos. 101 and 102 right at the river's edge. These two are the best of the lot. For vacationers on a budget, No. 65 is a duplex unit and costs a few bucks less. Keep in mind that none of these cabins are the best place to plan a romantic getaway; this place is heavily family-oriented and isn't great for solitude, especially on summer weekends.

Besides fishing and swimming in the Big Sur River, a favorite thing to do here is to rent an inner tube from the camp managers and float around all day. If you need more exercise, all of Big Sur's trails await you. And if you just want to plop down in the sand, you can always pay a visit to the coast at Andrew Molera State Park (to the north) or Pfeiffer Beach (to the south).

Facilities
There are 12 wooden cabins and 4 tent cabins that can accommodate up to six people, as well as numerous RV and tent sites. Some of the accommodations have kitchens. Linens and towels are provided in all cabins except the tent cabins.

Reservations and Rates
Reservations are recommended. Fees are $50–200 per night. Pets are permitted in the tent cabins only, for a $10 fee per night. Contact Big Sur Campground and Cabins, Highway 1, Big Sur, CA 93920, 831/667-2322, website: www.bigsurcamp.com.

Directions
From San Luis Obispo, drive north on U.S. 101 for 24 miles to the Highway 46 exit, near Templeton. Turn west on Highway 46 and drive 23 miles to Highway 1. Turn north on Highway 1 and drive 75 miles to Big Sur. Big

Sur Campground and Cabins is on the west side of the highway, just past Pfeiffer Big Sur State Park.

5 BIG SUR LODGE
off Highway 1 in Big Sur

Luxury rating: ★ ★ ★ ☆ ☆   **Recreation rating:** ★ ★ ★ ★ ☆

In the summer, Big Sur's campgrounds are like small tent cities. It's hard to have even a moment's peace among the majestic redwood trees, and even harder to get a good night's sleep. That's why the cottages at Big Sur Lodge are a godsend. The moment you step inside, you will experience serenity, and one night spent in one of these cottages will put you in the right frame of mind to truly enjoy the beauty of Big Sur.

If possible, book a cottage with both a fireplace and a kitchen; it doesn't cost much more than a standard unit, and a fireplace creates the perfect ambience in the misty, damp redwood forest. All of the cottages have decks or balconies, and none of them have phones, televisions, radios, or any other electronic junk.

If you don't want to cook, you can have your meals at the lovely Trail's Head Café, the lodge's casually elegant dining room, which has big picture windows that look out on the ferns and redwoods. The food is casual, delicious, and surprisingly affordable.

Pfeiffer Big Sur State Park's showpiece trail is the 1.6-mile Pfeiffer Falls and Valley View Loop, which begins near the park's nature center. You hike up Redwood Creek's canyon, crossing the stream on little footbridges, until you reach 60-foot Pfeiffer Falls, which streams down a vertical rock face. Then you backtrack a short distance and pick up the Valley View Trail, which climbs above the canyon to a wide overlook of the Big Sur Valley and Point Sur.

Another excellent view hike, and one that is less traveled, is the Buzzards Roost Trail. It begins near the park's bridge over the Big Sur River, and a healthy two-mile climb brings you to the Buzzards Roost Overlook, offering wide vistas of the Pacific Ocean and the Big Sur gorge.

A nice feature of your stay at Big Sur Lodge is that you are given an access pass that lets you into all the nearby parks for free: Andrew Molera State Park, Julia Pfeiffer Burns State Park, and Point Lobos State Reserve. Andrew Molera State Park is just four miles north on Highway 1. Families enjoy the easy walk from the parking lot to Molera Point, where you can look down on a large colony of sea lions. Many longer hikes are possible by linking together the park's trails.

Facilities
There are 61 cottages ranging in sizes that can accommodate two to six people. Some accommodations have kitchens and/or fireplaces. A restaurant and general store are on-site. Linens and towels are provided.

Reservations and Rates
Reservations are recommended. Fees are $99–229 per night. Pets are not permitted. Contact Big Sur Lodge, Pfeiffer Big Sur State Park, 47225 Highway 1, Big Sur, CA 93920, 831/667-3100 or 800/424-4787, website: www.bigsurlodge.com.

Directions
From San Luis Obispo, drive north on U.S. 101 for 24 miles to the Highway 46 exit, near Templeton. Turn west on Highway 46 and drive 23 miles to Highway 1. Turn north on Highway 1 and drive 75 miles to Big Sur. Pfeiffer Big Sur State Park is on the east side of the highway.

6 DEETJEN'S BIG SUR INN
off Highway 1 in Big Sur

Luxury rating: ★ ★ ★ ☆ ☆   **Recreation rating:** ★ ★ ★ ★ ☆

It's hard to know what to say about Deetjen's that hasn't already been said. Despite being decidedly rustic and determinedly unpretentious, it has been written up by just about every travel magazine and guidebook ever published. This homey, cozy place has an enigmatic appeal that attracts attention.

The Deetjen's story began when Helmuth Deetjen moved to Big Sur from Norway in the 1930s, back when Highway 1 was a dirt road. Deetjen and his wife, Helen, welcomed travelers along the exhausting coastal route to their

© ANN MARIE BROWN

property in Castro Canyon. Over the years, as more people came to enjoy their hospitality, they added guest rooms and cabins made out of scavenged, locally milled redwood. The buildings were constructed in Helmuth's native Norwegian style. When Helmuth died in 1972, a decade after Helen passed away, he willed the inn to a public trust, and it has been run by a nonprofit preservation foundation ever since.

The inn is within a few feet of Highway 1, yet because it is set in a dense, dark grove of redwoods, it feels very secluded. The cabin buildings are famous for their paper-thin walls, but a stream runs through the property and creates a marvelous white noise to drown out much of what you don't want to hear. The cabins are simply decorated with a mix of antiques, homemade furniture, and "funky treasures" (their description). One of the biggest surprises to first-time guests is that there are no locks on the outside of the doors (although you can lock them from the inside). You might think you shouldn't leave your wallet in an unlocked building, but the attitude is "Hey, relax, this is Big Sur."

Many of the cabin units here are duplexes or triplexes, but there are a couple stand-alone units (a favorite is the Castro Cabin) for those who don't want to share walls with anyone. If you choose to stay in a duplex, try to get the upstairs unit so you don't have to hear footsteps above you. If you must have a private bathroom, request it. Many of the units have shared baths.

Pfeiffer Big Sur State Park is three miles north, so you'll want to spend at least one day exploring its trails. The famous Big Sur restaurant Nepenthe is practically right across the highway from Deetjen's; plan a stop here for a sunset and a margarita. The view from Nepenthe's deck should not be missed by any Big Sur traveler.

Be sure to eat breakfast or dinner at Deetjen's restaurant while you are here. The tiny, intimate dining room is a great setting for the fabulous food they serve. While you chew on roasted New Zealand rack of lamb, consider that this building was the Deetjen's original barn; it housed a few goats and the Norwegian builder's workshop.

Facilities

There are 16 single, duplex, and triplex cabins that can accommodate two to four people. None of the accommodations have kitchens. Some units have private bathrooms; others have shared bathrooms. Linens and towels are provided.

Reservations and Rates
Reservations are recommended. Fees are $110–195 per night for units with private baths; shared bath units cost less. There is a two-night minimum on weekends. Pets are not permitted. Contact Deetjen's Big Sur Inn, 48865 Highway 1, Big Sur, CA 93920, 831/667-2377, website: www.deetjens.com.

Directions
From San Luis Obispo, drive north on U.S. 101 for 24 miles to the Highway 46 exit, near Templeton. Turn west on Highway 46 and drive 23 miles to Highway 1. Turn north on Highway 1 and drive 75 miles to Big Sur. Deetjen's Big Sur Inn is on the east side of the highway.

Other Cabins and Cottages Nearby
Riverside Campground and Cabins, Highway 1, Big Sur, CA 93920, 831/667-2414, website: www.riversidecampground.com.
Big Sur Retreat Cabins, (no mailing address), 831/624-9220, website: www.bigsurretreat.com.

7 LUCIA LODGE
off Highway 1 south of Big Sur

Luxury rating: ★ ★ ★ ☆ ☆   **Recreation rating:** ★ ★ ★ ★ ☆
Rank: Most Secluded

If you've driven Highway 1 along the spectacular Big Sur coast, you've probably seen Lucia Lodge clinging precariously to the cliffs. Then again, you might have missed it completely if, like most drivers, you were preoccupied with gaping at the view and trying to keep your car on the road.

The 1930s-era cabins at Lucia Lodge are perched 300 feet above Lucia Bay, on steep cliffs that descend with wild abandon to the breaking waves. Each cabin has an open-beamed ceiling and old-fashioned furnishings, and each is surrounded by flower-laden gardens. Stand-alone cabins Nos. 7–10 are the nicest of the lot, each with a gas fireplace, four-poster bed, and ocean view. If you are on a budget, go for Nos. 1–4, which are really more like side-by-side motel rooms. They are without fireplaces but still offer that

enchanting location and a full
helping of romance. Only two
cabins, Nos. 5 and 6, do not
face the ocean, but it doesn't
take a lot of effort to walk 10
feet from your door to take in
the marvelous coastal vista.

The lodge owners want you to
eat at their restaurant, so there
are no kitchens in the cabins.
Even if you don't have all your
meals at the restaurant, at least be sure to have one breakfast outside on the
deck (open in summer only). You'll never drink coffee that tastes this good
again, and it's not high-quality beans or special brewing that makes it so extraordinary. It's the view.

Another nice feature at Lucia Lodge is that it is right across the highway from Limekiln Creek State Park, with its beautiful limestone waterfall
that cascades over pads of thick moss and slick rock. Only one trail exists
in the park; it runs from the campground to a set of old lime kilns that
were used to make bricks at the start of the 20th century. A right fork off
this trail takes you upstream to the waterfall.

If you want to go to the beach, don't think you can beat a path from
your cabin door. Lucia Bay is inaccessible from land because of its steep
surrounding cliffs. But if you drive only a few miles north or south, you
can access the public beaches of Los Padres National Forest. The most
remarkable of these is Sand Dollar Beach (to the south) and neighboring
Jade Cove, where one of the largest pieces of jade ever seen was discovered. Rock hounds are on the beach almost every day, trying to repeat
(or top) the experience.

Facilities
There are 10 cabins that can accommodate up to four people. None of the
accommodations have kitchens. A restaurant and small store are on-site.
Linens and towels are provided.

Reservations and Rates
Reservations are recommended. Fees are $125–250 per night. Pets are not
permitted. Contact Lucia Lodge, 62400 Highway 1, Big Sur, CA 93920,
831/667-2391 or 866/424-4787, website: www.lucialodge.com.

Directions
From San Luis Obispo, drive north on U.S. 101 for 24 miles to the High-

way 46 exit, near Templeton. Turn west on Highway 46 and drive 23 miles to Highway 1. Turn north on Highway 1 and drive 50 miles to Lucia Lodge, on the west side of the highway.

8 TREEBONES RESORT
off Highway 1 in Gorda

Luxury rating: ★ ★ ★ ☆ ☆   **Recreation rating:** ★ ★ ★ ★ ☆

Treebones Resort is a newcomer on the southern Big Sur coast, having just opened in November 2004. It is a completely unique lodging concept compared to its neighbors to the north and south. Instead of older, rustic redwood cabins such as those at Deetjen's or Ripplewood Resort, and instead of posh resort-style lodging like at some of the newer Big Sur facilities, Treebones Resort consists of 16 yurts, five campsites, and a 3,500-square-foot guest services building. Perched on a grassy bluff about 500 feet above the Pacific Ocean, Treebones has knockout views in every direction. This is some piece of real estate.

For those who are new to the yurt concept, a yurt is basically a very well-constructed tent cabin that is built around a circular wooden lattice frame on top of a wooden platform. The canvas-sided structures have a skylight, windows made of heavy plastic, and wooden French doors. The windows are particularly important at Treebones, because most of the yurts have either an ocean or mountain view—or both, since the structures are circular. The yurts, which are 20 feet in diameter, are equipped with hot and cold running water, sink only, no toilets or showers, electric lights, and space heaters. Communal restrooms are a few steps away. Although yurts are basically close cousins to tents, these are

© ANN MARIE BROWN

as well built and nicely furnished as many people's homes. You gotta stay in one to believe it.

The idea at Treebones was to build a lodging resort for travelers that works in harmony with the natural landscape of the Big Sur coast. The resort describes itself as being "perched lightly on the edge of the world." Sure, it sounds like something right out of the 1960s, but Treebones is quite modern in style and attitude. The owners hope to cater to corporate retreats and other large groups that would take over all 16 yurts and use the large guest services building for events, conferences, or meetings. But most of the time, the yurts will be available to Big Sur travelers for nightly or longer stays. One thing is for sure, this place is like no other on the Big Sur coast.

Facilities
There are 16 yurts that can accommodate up to four people, as well as five campsites. None of the accommodations have kitchens. A pool and spa are on-site. Linens and towels are provided.

Reservations and Rates
Reservations are recommended. Fees are $105 per night for two people plus $10 for each additional person. Pets are not permitted. Contact Treebones Resort, Town of Gorda, Highway 1, Big Sur, CA 93920, 877/424-4787, website: www.treebonesresort.com.

Directions
From San Luis Obispo, drive north on U.S. 101 for 24 miles to the Highway 46 exit, near Templeton. Turn west on Highway 46 and drive 23 miles to Highway 1. Turn north on Highway 1 and drive 39 miles to Gorda. Continue one mile farther north on Highway 1 to Treebones Resort, on the east side of the highway.

9 GORDA SPRINGS COTTAGES
off Highway 1 in Gorda

Luxury rating: ★ ★ ★ ☆ ☆   **Recreation rating:** ★ ★ ★ ★ ☆

The tiny coastside hamlet of Gorda is just far enough north that it feels like it's in Northern California. It's not just Gorda's location, 35 miles north of San Simeon and 30 miles south of Big Sur, or the long drive on winding Highway 1 required to reach it. It's more that Gorda has a Northern California feel to it, like the kind of town you might find in Mendocino County. But luckily, Gorda is a mere two hours from San Luis Obispo and four hours from Santa Barbara—perfect for a weekend getaway.

Gorda Springs Cottages are on the inland side of Highway 1, right behind the Whale Watcher's Café and General Store. This tiny complex of buildings is the only commercial enterprise in Gorda. Otherwise, there are only endless ocean views and the sound of the waves.

To reach any one of the six sweet little cabins here, you drive up a dirt driveway on the hill behind the general store. The cabins vary in size; all have fully equipped kitchens, and most have fireplaces. Flowers bloom all over the grounds, and you may be surprised to find that you have a couple llamas for neighbors. They like to be petted. You're likely to see other wildlife too—most notably, gray whales out at sea and elephant seals lounging along the coastline.

Most visitors spend their Gorda vacation at the local beaches. Far and away the best strip of sand around is at Sand Dollar Beach; a short trail leads from the picnic-area parking lot down to its brayed tan sands. Sand Dollar has some of the Central Coast's most consistently beautiful waves, which attract hordes of surfers on weekends. Surf fishing is also excellent here, but swimming is a really bad idea. The beach is famous for riptides.

If it's foggy at the beach, you can always turn your attentions inland and do a little hiking. At Gorda, you're in perfect position to access the trailheads of nearby Ventana and Silver Peak Wildernesses. Five miles south of Gorda on Highway 1 is the start of the Soda Springs Trail; two miles farther south is the start of the Salmon Creek Trail. With only a couple miles of hiking on either trail, you will see waterfalls, cascading streams, giant boulders, and big Douglas fir trees. If you head north on Highway 1 instead, the Kirk Creek and Vicente Flat trailhead can be found across from Kirk Creek Campground, six miles north of Gorda. Check out the views of the coast from the first couple miles of this path. For updated trail information, drive 10 miles north of Gorda on Highway 1 to the Los Padres National Forest Pacific Valley Ranger Station.

Facilities

There are six cabins that can accommodate up to six people. Most of the accommodations have kitchens. A restaurant and small store are on-site. Linens and towels are provided.

Reservations and Rates

Reservations are recommended. Fees are $175–500 per night. Pets are not permitted. Contact Gorda Springs Cottages, Box 1, Town of Gorda, Highway 1, Big Sur, CA 93920, 805/927-4600 or 805/927-3918, website: www.bigsurgordasprings.com.

Directions

From San Luis Obispo, drive north on U.S. 101 for 24 miles to the Highway 46 exit, near Templeton. Turn west on Highway 46 and drive 23 miles to Highway 1. Turn north on Highway 1 and drive 39 miles to Gorda. The café and cottages are on the east side of the highway.

Chapter 2

© ANN MARIE BROWN

Santa Barbara
and Vicinity

Santa Barbara and Vicinity

The Santa Barbara region—which extends 200 miles from the artsy town of Cambria and the terraced vineyards of Paso Robles to the white sands of Ventura—encompasses what many consider to be Southern California's finest stretch of coast. Santa Barbara County's shoreline, curving up the coast from Carpinteria to Point Conception, has a southern, not western, exposure, which results in exceptionally mild weather. To the south, Ventura County's coast offers 40 miles of fine sandy beaches.

Lest you think the Santa Barbara region is all sun and sand, note that it also contains more than a million acres of national forest land in the Santa Barbara and Ojai backcountry—the southern section of Los Padres National Forest. This landscape is a conglomeration of pine-clad high mountain peaks, river-cut canyons, and chaparral-covered hillsides, all of which offer myriad hiking and mountain biking opportunities. The Santa Ynez Mountains, a centerpiece of southern Los Padres National Forest, are part of the unique Transverse Range, a system of mountains that defies the rules of California geography: It runs from east to west, rather than north to south.

Several recreation lakes and horse ranches are found in or near the mountains and foothills. Lake San Antonio and Lake Nacimiento, near Paso Robles, are large bodies of water for water-skiing, bass fishing, swimming, and kayaking. If you're spending more than a few days at the lakes, you'll probably want to take a road trip to go wine-tasting in the burgeoning Paso Robles wine country.

The Alisal, Circle Bar B, and Rancho Oso guest ranches all provide opportunities for horseback riding within steps of their cabins and cottages. Each ranch has its own flavor, from the luxurious Alisal to the one-step-above-camping Rancho Oso.

The Santa Barbara region also contains its share of oddities and wonders, including the architecturally marvelous Hearst Castle, the Danish town of Solvang, and the rugged and remote islands of Channel Islands National Park. Hearst Castle can be visited with a stay at one of several cottage resorts in Cambria, Cayucos, or Paso Robles. Solvang can be explored from the enchanting Wine Valley Inn downtown. However, no accommodations are found on the Channel Islands—only campgrounds. A stay at a cottage resort in Ventura or Santa Barbara gives visitors the opportunity to visit two of the nearest islands, Anacapa and Santa Cruz, on day trips.

When most people think of Santa Barbara proper, they think of whitewashed, Spanish-style buildings, palm trees, and luxury resorts. And that image is largely accurate, as reflected in the cottages at the Four Seasons Biltmore, El Encanto Hotel, and San Ysidro Ranch. It takes some serious money to spend a night at one of these places, but few would say it's not worth it. In the same class, but of a different genre, are the quaint bed-and-breakfast cottages in downtown Santa Barbara, such as the Simpson House Inn and Cheshire Cat Inn.

Whereas the coast around the city of Santa Barbara has been densely developed, many miles of sand to the north, from Goleta to Cayucos, retain a remote feel or small-town beach atmosphere. The quiet coastal towns of Cambria, San Simeon, and Cayucos are a foreshadowing of the remote Big Sur coast to the north. Several cottage resorts and vacation rentals in the area provide the ideal setting for a small-town vacation at the coast.

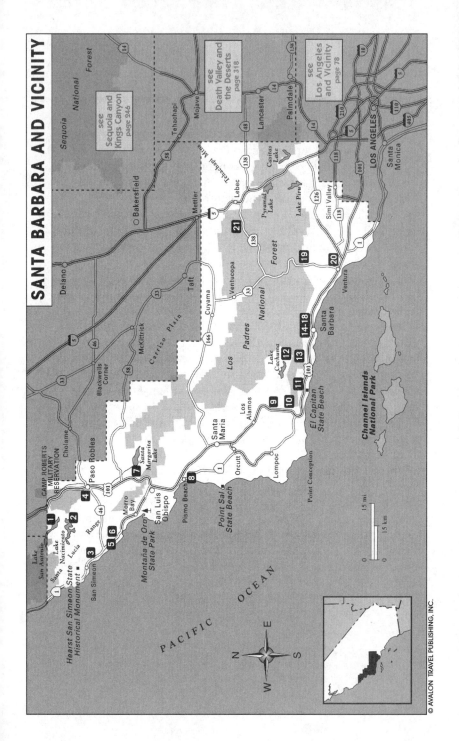

© AVALON TRAVEL PUBLISHING, INC.

Contents

1. Lake San Antonio South Shore Resort 40

2. Lake Nacimiento Resort. 41

3. Cambria Pines Lodge 43

4. Orchard Hill Farm 45

5. Cayucos Vacation Rentals. 46

6. Cottontail Creek Ranch. 48

7. KOA Santa Margarita Lake. 49

8. The Tides Motel 51

9. Wine Valley Inn & Cottages 52

10. The Alisal Guest Ranch & Resort 54

11. Circle Bar B Guest Ranch. 56

12. Rancho Oso Guest Ranch & Stables 58

13. White Lotus Foundation 59

14. El Encanto Hotel & Garden Villas 61

15. Simpson House Inn. 63

16. Cheshire Cat Inn & Cottages 64

17. San Ysidro Ranch 66

18. Four Seasons Biltmore 67

19. Emerald Iguana Cottages 69

20. The Pierpont Inn 70

21. Mountain Properties Vacation Rentals. 72

1 LAKE SAN ANTONIO SOUTH SHORE RESORT
off U.S. 101 near Paso Robles

Luxury rating: ★ ★ ★ ☆ ☆   **Recreation rating:** ★ ★ ★ ★ ☆

Rank: Best for Boating & Water Sports, Best for Fishing

It's rare that a Southern California reservoir offers more than just water-skiing, bass fishing, and power boating, but Lake San Antonio does. Located in the Central Coast grasslands east of San Simeon and west of U.S. 101, Lake San Antonio has 5,700 surface acres of water—enough to keep boaters and anglers busy all summer long. But the lake is also a major habitat area for eagles, both bald and golden. Eagle Watch boat tours are an excellent reason to come to Lake San Antonio in winter.

Whatever the season, start your trip by booking a cabin at the lake's South Shore Resort—a busy place with a restaurant, grocery store, gas station, and marina. The resort rents one-, two-, and three-bedroom cabins with fully stocked kitchens and nice views of the lake. Don't expect cute log cabins; these are more in the order of mobile homes. They won't make the cover of *Architectural Digest,* but they serve their purpose.

Water sports are plentiful at Lake San Antonio, including all boating activities and fishing for striped bass, catfish, crappie, largemouth bass, and bluegill. The largemouth bass fishing can be exceptional, with catches of up to 100 per day not uncommon. Simultaneously, Lake San Antonio is far and away the most popular waterskiing lake on the Central Coast. You don't have your own boat? No problem: You can rent boats, motors, personal watercrafts, waterskiing equipment, and fishing tackle at the South Shore Marina. You can even rent a kayak or paddleboat and just

paddle around in the lake's quiet coves.

If eagle-watching strikes your fancy, plan your stay for a weekend in late December to early March. On Friday, Saturday, and Sunday, the Monterey County Parks Department offers Eagle Watch tours aboard *Eagle One,* a 56-foot tour boat. On Sunday, you can pay a few bucks extra and have brunch aboard the boat while you scan the skies for big birds.

Mountain biking and hiking are also possible activities, but save these for winter and spring, when the temperatures are cooler. Summertime bakes out here in the foothills, although nobody cruising around the lake seems to care.

Facilities
There are 17 cabins ranging in size from one to three bedrooms; each can accommodate 6 to 10 people. All cabins have fully equipped kitchens. A store and café are on-site. Linens and towels are provided.

Reservations and Rates
Reservations are recommended. Fees are $150–300 per night; weekly rentals are discounted. Fees are reduced from October to March. Pets are not permitted. Contact Lake San Antonio South Shore Resort, Star Route, Box 2620, Bradley, CA 93426, 805/472-2313 or 800/310-2313, website: www.lakesanantonioresort.com.

Directions
From U.S. 101 in Paso Robles, take the Highway 46 East exit (24th Street or G-14 West). Drive west on G-14 for approximately 14 miles, then turn right on Lake Nacimiento Road. Cross the dam at Lake Nacimiento, then turn left on Interlake Road. Drive seven miles to Lake San Antonio Road and turn right. Drive three miles to the South Shore entrance to the lake.

2 LAKE NACIMIENTO RESORT
off U.S. 101 near Paso Robles

Luxury rating: ★ ★ ★ ★ ☆   **Recreation rating:** ★ ★ ★ ★ ☆

Lake Nacimiento and Lake San Antonio are practically side-by-side water bodies in the grassy foothills west of Paso Robles. Both are about the same size (5,000-plus acres), but whereas San Antonio is a long, narrow lake, Nacimiento has a large number of coves and arms that give it a more complex shape. The lake's varied outline allows plenty of room for waterskiers, anglers, swimmers, and kayakers to share the water without getting in each other's way.

The lake is quite busy on summer weekends. The air temperature is usually hot, and the water temperature is about 70°F. As a result, the majority of people put on their bathing suits as soon as they get out of bed and don't wear anything else all day.

© ANN MARIE BROWN

Fishing is for bass, primarily, although sunfish, crappie, and catfish are sometimes caught. Nacimiento's big catch is white bass; it's the only lake in California that is stocked with these feisty little fish. In fact, the lake has so many white bass that there is no limit on how many you can catch. Largemouth bass are also stocked. The best action is usually in late spring and early summer.

Lake Nacimiento Resort is the only commercial facility on the lake, and in addition to its boat rentals, marina, and the Lakeshore Cafe, the resort rents cabins on a hill overlooking the lake. Technically, the cabins are called lodges. They are modern, fancy affairs that look like townhouses. A dozen are clustered together and surrounded by a perfectly tended lawn, which seems otherworldly in these dry foothills.

The lodges come in three configurations: large units that sleep 10, small units that sleep 4, and combination units that sleep 14. The combo units, as you probably guessed, are a large and small unit, with opening doors in between. All units come with everything you need for daily living, with one exception: The kitchens have a range and microwave, but no oven. (Most people barbecue on the outside deck anyway.) Some units have a dishwasher, fireplace, and private deck, so make sure you request the features you want. The views are so lovely from the cabins' high vantage point that you shouldn't miss getting a lake-view deck.

If you need more choices, mobile homes and 30-foot camp trailers are also for rent.

Facilities

There are 19 cabins that can be configured for 4, 10, or 14 people, plus mobile-home and trailer rentals. All cabins have fully equipped kitchens. A store and restaurant are on-site. Linens and towels are provided.

Reservations and Rates

Reservations are recommended. Fees are $195–425 per night. Weekly rentals are discounted. Fees are reduced from November to February. Pets are not permitted. Contact Lake Nacimiento Resort, Box 2770, 10625

Nacimiento Lake Drive, Bradley, CA 93426, 805/238-3256 or 800/323-3839, website: www.nacimientoresort.com.

Directions

From U.S. 101 in Paso Robles, take the Highway 46 East exit (24th Street or G-14 West). Drive west on G-14 for approximately 14 miles (it becomes Lake Nacimiento Road). Just before reaching the dam at Lake Nacimiento, turn left to reach the resort.

3 CAMBRIA PINES LODGE
off Highway 1 in Cambria

Luxury rating: ★ ★ ★ ★ ☆   **Recreation rating:** ★ ★ ★ ☆ ☆

Cambria Pines Lodge is a large resort and conference center in the artsy, coastal town of Cambria, not far from Hearst Castle and San Simeon. Most people know Cambria for its shopping and art galleries, or as a place to have lunch after touring William Randolph Hearst's megamansion. But outdoor lovers will also find plenty to do in Cambria.

For starters, there's San Simeon State Beach, accessible via a five-minute drive from Cambria Pines. Beachcombing and whale-watching are common activities. The gray whales are spotted most often from late November to January, when they migrate south. (On their springtime return, they are farther offshore and harder to see.) Poking around tidepools can

be excellent at the state beach, especially during winter minus tides. The easiest beach access from Cambria Pines Lodge is at Leffingwell Landing on Moonstone Beach Drive, where blufftop nature trails head both north and south.

San Simeon State Beach is also a fine place to try your hand at surf fishing. Barred surf perch can be caught in December and January, and walleye surf perch are available in any season. For larger fish, head out on a commercial boat to catch kelp bass, Pacific macker-el, and California halibut. Pier fishing is also possible off Hearst Memorial State Beach.

Cambria Pines' beautifully decorated cottages have king beds and fire-places and are a few steps away from an enclosed indoor pool. Only one unit, the Honeymoon Suite, is freestanding. The rest are duplexes but are still very quiet and private. The lodge is set in 25 acres of Monterey pines, with lovely gardens and landscaping. A walking path runs through the property and to the beach; the trailhead is alongside unit No. 810. A long set of stairs raises your heart rate on the first stretch, then you turn right on Burton Drive, left on Main Street, and cross Highway 1 to the beach. It's a nice way to explore Cambria Village and gain access to the ocean at the same time.

The cottages lack kitchen facilities, but it's not the end of the world. Breakfast is included in the room rate—a huge buffet with pancakes, eggs, potatoes, granola, orange juice, and coffee. For other meals, you can choose from a wide variety of restaurants in the town of Cambria, or eat at the lodge's restaurant.

Facilities
There are 16 one-bedroom cottages, plus numerous townhouse-style ac-commodations and motel rooms. The cottages do not have kitchens. Breakfast is included and a restaurant is on-site. There is an indoor pool. Linens and towels are provided.

Reservations and Rates
Reservations are recommended. Fees range $99–239 per night, which in-cludes breakfast. Pets are not permitted. Contact Cambria Pines Lodge, 2905 Burton Drive, Cambria, CA 93428, 805/927-4200 or 800/445-6868, website: www.cambriapineslodge.com.

Directions
From San Luis Obispo at U.S. 101, take the Highway 1 exit and drive north through Morro Bay for 33 miles to Cambria. Just north of the downtown Cambria exit, take the Burton Drive exit east. Drive a quarter mile and Cambria Pines Lodge is on your left.

Other Cabins and Cottages Nearby
Cambria Vacation Rentals, 784 Main Street, Suite A, Cambria, CA 93428, 805/927-8200.

4 ORCHARD HILL FARM
off Highway 46 in Paso Robles

Luxury rating: ★ ★ ★ ★ ☆   **Recreation rating: ★ ★ ★ ☆ ☆**

Orchard Hill Farm is set on 36 acres in the rolling hills of Paso Robles. Surrounded by ancient oaks, grassy hillsides, and miles of vineyards, the bed-and-breakfast offers the utmost in privacy. Only one guest house is available for rent, and guests take over the whole building. They are then free to enjoy the pastoral scenery of this country ranch, the joie de vivre of neighboring wineries, and numerous recreational opportunities.

The guest house—or carriage house, as the owners call it—is a lovely Tudor-style building about 150 feet from the main house. It is beautifully appointed with leather armchairs, colorful fabrics, and tasteful antiques. Its two bedrooms each have their own full bath. A kitchen, dining area, and living room with fireplace separate the bedrooms. The house's best feature is its large deck, on which you can sit and look out over the countryside from your hilltop location.

The owners are willing to rent each of the house's bedrooms separately, but then you'd be sharing the kitchen and living area with strangers. It only makes sense to gather four people together—two couples or a family—and take over the entire house. Because the farm is in the center of Paso Robles' burgeoning wine country, the guest house is frequently rented by two couples or a group of friends, who spend their days driving or cycling from winery to winery, tasting as they go. More than 50 wineries and over 200 vineyards around Paso Robles grow premium wine grapes.

Other area attractions are the lovely drive on Highway 46 to the beaches at Cambria, or the architecturally marvelous Hearst Castle at San Simeon. A day of boating and fishing can be had at nearby Lakes Nacimiento and San Antonio.

Facilities

There is one two-bedroom guest house with a fully equipped kitchen, a dining room, a living area, and a fireplace. Linens and towels are provided.

Reservations and Rates

Reservations are required. Fees are $155–175 per night for each of two rooms; most guests rent both rooms together. Pets are not permitted. Contact Orchard Hill Farm, 5415 Vineyard Drive, Paso Robles, CA 93446, 805/239-9680, website: www.orchardhillbb.com.

Directions

From U.S. 101 in Paso Robles, take the Highway 46 West exit and drive west for five miles. Turn right on Vineyard Drive and drive about 2.5 miles to Orchard Hill Farm, on the left.

Other Cabins and Cottages Nearby

Country House Inn, 91 Main Street, Templeton, CA 93465, 805/434-1598.

5 CAYUCOS VACATION RENTALS
off Highway 1 near Morro Bay

Luxury rating: ★ ★ ★ ★ ☆   **Recreation rating:** ★ ★ ★ ★ ☆

Rank: Best for Beach Activities

The little town of Cayucos is quintessential Central Coast, and that's why it's so likable. Located 13 miles south of Cambria and 10 miles north of Morro Bay, Cayucos is a seaside hamlet that hasn't been overdeveloped, like most other coastal towns. All recreation revolves around the ocean—surfing, beachcombing, windsurfing, swimming, kayaking, and fishing—which is exactly the way it should be.

More than 50 private homes in Cayucos are for rent through Cayucos Vacation Rentals, including many that are oceanfront or ocean-view, or within walking distance of the beach. All rentals are fully furnished, including linens, so you only need to pack your clothes. Grocery stores, shops, and restaurants are available in town.

Most visitors rent a place in Cayucos for a few days—rates are discounted according to the number of nights you reserve. In summer, most places have a weeklong minimum; they are typically rented out to families on a week's vacation.

Note that if you sign up for an ocean-view house, your view could be from the east side of Highway 1. It's wise to pay more for a house on the west side so you have beach access without crossing the highway. What the heck, if you're going on a beach vacation, you might as well be on oceanfront property. "Near-oceanfront" just isn't the same thing.

Cayucos's two state beaches—Cayucos State Beach and Morro Strand State Beach—provide long stretches of sand for all beach activities. Cayucos's other big attraction is its historic pier, which was built in 1875. Anglers can fish without a license from the pier; it is lit up for night fishing. Many people just stroll along it, enjoying the views and the seagulls.

If you feel like taking a side trip, Morro Bay State Park is only a short drive away. Visit its great blue heron rookery in spring, or hike on one of the nine dome-shaped, volcanic hills, or *morros,* in the area (but not Morro Rock itself). You can even rent a kayak and paddle around Morro Bay, or take a harbor cruise. Bike trails are plentiful, from level cruises to challenging hill climbs.

If you've never been there, another great side trip is a tour of Hearst Castle, only 20 miles to the north. Whatever else you want to say about it, it's a fascinating place—the opulent estate of newspaper magnate William Randolph Hearst, with 165 palatial rooms containing an outrageous display of art and artifacts.

Facilities
There are 52 private homes for rent, ranging in size from one to four bedrooms, all with fully equipped kitchens. Linens and towels are provided.

Reservations and Rates
Reservations are required. Fees range from $85–350 per night. In summer, a weeklong minimum is required. In winter, there is a two-night minimum. Pets are permitted in some rentals with prior approval. Contact Cayucos Vacation Rentals, 177 North Ocean Avenue, Cayucos, CA 93430, 805/995-2322 or 800/995-2322, website: www.cayucosvacationrentals.com.

Directions
From San Luis Obispo at U.S. 101, take the Highway 1 exit and drive

north through Morro Bay for 18 miles to Cayucos. Stop at the rental office for Cayucos Vacation Rentals; they will give you a key and directions to your vacation rental.

6 COTTONTAIL CREEK RANCH
off Highway 1 in Cayucos

Luxury rating: ★ ★ ★ ★ ☆   **Recreation rating:** ★ ★ ★ ☆ ☆

There aren't too many places around like Cottontail Creek Ranch. It's an 850-acre ranch in the coastal hills above Cayucos, with panoramic views of the Pacific coast from its ridge tops, trails for hiking and wildlife viewing, seasonal creeks, and fish ponds. You and a bunch of your best friends can rent it for a few days or a week.

You won't be staying in the horse corral, either. The ranch house at Cottontail Creek is a 4,200-square-foot, five-bedroom, four-bath house. Yes, you read that right. It features a massive stone fireplace in the living room, open beam ceilings, a gourmet kitchen, and three lofts, one of which houses a library.

Cottontail Creek Ranch's owners, the Lyon family, live on another part of the working ranch. In addition to raising cattle, they grow oranges, avocados, and kiwis. They'll gladly take you on a tour of the groves.

The ranch is most frequently rented by families holding reunions or celebrating special occasions, but a group of friends could use it as well, for no other reason than to have a good time. A week's stay doesn't come cheap; it costs $3,300 in summer, but that buys you a special kind of experience you won't get anywhere else. And for 10 people, the weekly fee works out to less than 50 bucks a night per person. Summer rentals are by the week only; the rest of the year there is a three-night minimum.

You want something to do at the ranch besides admire the place and wish you owned it? A large pond is available for catch-and-release fishing and kayaking. Horse owners can bring their own horses and ride around the 850 acres. Bikers and hikers can wander as they wish, or head over to Montana de Oro State Park.

If you want to spend a day swimming in the ocean or soaking up rays on white sand, you can do so with just a 10-minute drive to Cayucos. Hearst Castle is a half-hour away, and the charming waterfront of Morro Bay, with its harbor cruises and bike trails, is 15 minutes away.

Facilities

There is one ranch house with five bedrooms and four bathrooms that can accommodate up to 12 people. It has a fireplace and a fully equipped kitchen. Linens and towels are provided.

Reservations and Rates

Reservations are required. Fees are $3,300 per week from June to September, and $490 per night the rest of the year (with a three-night minimum). Pets are not permitted. Contact Cottontail Creek Ranch, 1885 Cottontail Creek Road, Cayucos, CA 93430, 805/995-1787, website: www.cottontail-creek.com.

Directions

From U.S. 101 in San Luis Obispo, take the Morro Bay/Highway 1 exit and drive 18 miles to Old Creek Road. Turn right and drive 3.1 miles, past Whale Rock Reservoir, to Cottontail Creek Road. Turn left and drive 3.4 miles (road turns to gravel) to Cottontail Creek Ranch's gate. Continue another quarter mile to the house on your left.

7 KOA SANTA MARGARITA LAKE

off Highway 58 near San Luis Obispo

Luxury rating: ★★☆☆☆   **Recreation rating:** ★★★☆☆

The first time I stayed in a KOA cabin, I felt a little funny. The cute little log cabins with their front-porch swings looked a lot like children's playhouses, and there I was, trying to act like a serious guidebook writer.

But two nights in a cabin at KOA Santa Margarita Lake turned me into a believer. After a day of exploring around Santa Margarita Lake and the Santa Lucia Wilderness, I returned to my cabin for a hot shower, clean clothes, and a barbecue dinner outside on the porch. It rained later that night, but I was warm and dry in my cabin with electric heat and lights. It sure beat the heck out of eating freeze-dried lasagna, wearing dirty socks, and fussing with the zipper on my flimsy tent.

KOA Santa Margarita Lake is only one mile from the lake, where you can rent boats, fish, and hike. In fact, you can do anything at the lake except touch the water, which means no swimming, windsurfing, or waterskiing. Most people don't complain about the rules, however, because they come here to fish. Rainbow trout are stocked in winter and spring, and bass fishing is good in the summer. The lake is fair-sized—nearly 800 acres—and more scenic than you'd expect in this low-elevation foothill country. Tall, rocky crags form the backdrop behind the lake.

The KOA has 10 cabins, all partially shaded by canyon oaks. Each one has its own barbecue grill and picnic table out front. The camp has a small store where you can buy basic groceries and supplies. The Rinconada Store is a mile down the road, where you can buy tackle and bait.

If hiking is your bag, an overnight at the KOA puts you in a good position for exploring. Take a drive down U.S. 101 to Arroyo Grande and then head east to Lopez Lake, where you can access the trails at Lopez Lake Recreation Area. The best of these are the Duna Vista and Two Waters Trails (check out the spring wildflowers). Or drive past Lopez Lake and into the backcountry to reach the Santa Lucia Wilderness trailheads along Lopez Creek, including those leading to popular Big Falls and Little Falls. The Santa Lucia Ranger District in Santa Maria can provide you with trail information and maps.

Facilities

There are 10 cabins that can accommodate up to five people, plus 54 campsites for tents or RVs. The cabins do not have kitchens. Restrooms and showers are located nearby. Linens and towels are not provided.

Reservations and Rates

Reservations are recommended. Cabin fees are $45–60 per night. Pets are permitted. Contact KOA Santa Margarita Lake, 4765 Santa Margarita Lake Road, Santa Margarita, CA 93453, 805/438-5618 or 800/562-5619, website: www.koakampgrounds.com.

Directions

From San Luis Obispo, drive eight miles north on U.S. 101 to the Highway 58/Santa Margarita exit. Drive through the town of Santa Margarita on Highway 58. Turn right and follow the signs for Santa Margarita Lake. In eight miles, you will reach the KOA on the right, one mile before the lake.

8 THE TIDES MOTEL
off U.S. 101 in Pismo Beach

Luxury rating: ★ ★ ★ ☆ ☆   **Recreation rating:** ★ ★ ★ ★ ☆

Rank: Best for Beach Activities

There are a few places left on the Southern California coast that haven't been turned into condominiums or chain hotels, and The Tides Motel is one of them. Located in the town of Pismo Beach, The Tides is the ideal place to wake up to the sound of the ocean, play at the beach all day, then return home to a clean, comfortable cottage.

Most of The Tides' cottages come with a serviceable kitchen, including the basic dishes and utensils you'll need for cooking. A few cottages are duplexes; make sure you request a single unit if you want one. The rooms come equipped with televisions, which you can ignore. The only telephone is the pay phone at the motel office.

Many visitors to The Tides do nothing but hang out on the beach all day. It's easily accessible from your cottage, as long as you don't mind walking the 90 steps down to the sand and 90 steps back up.

The watery adventures possible in Pismo Beach are unlimited, including fishing, swimming, surfing, and exploring its 23 miles of coastline. Although the town has suffered from recent urbanization, there's still some of the old Pismo left, including a long fishing pier and wide, sandy beaches. Bustling seafood restaurants and coffee shops neighbor the surf shops and tackle stores, but they don't outnumber them.

Even if you don't fish, be sure to walk along the 1,250-foot Pismo Pier. If you are lucky enough to time your visit for an evening with a full moon and clear skies, you'll witness one of the world's greatest sights—moonlight on ocean waves. I suppose it doesn't look like this every night in Pismo Beach, but it made my trip unforgettable.

Although clamming at Pismo Beach isn't what it was in the late 19th century, when clams were so abundant that local farmers used them for animal feed and harvested them by plowing the sand, you can still dig for the tasty bivalves. The 1990s saw a

© ANN MARIE BROWN

resurgence in the clam population along the area's beaches; hopefully, the 21st century will see a complete comeback. To go clamming, you'll need a special shovel (available for rent at the hardware store in town) and your California fishing license.

If you need something else to do, surfboards, wetsuits, boogie boards, and bicycles are for rent in town. That should be enough to keep you busy.

Facilities
There are five cottages that can accommodate two to eight people, plus 16 motel rooms. Most cottages have fully equipped kitchens. Linens and towels are provided.

Reservations and Rates
Reservations are recommended. Fees are $120–260 per night in summer; winter rates are discounted. Pets are not permitted. Contact The Tides Motel, 2121 Price Street, Pismo Beach, CA 93449, 805/773-2493 or 888/234-2892, website: www.thetidesmotel.com.

Directions
From U.S. 101 in Santa Maria, drive north for 17 miles to Pismo Beach. Take the Price Street exit and drive west to The Tides Motel.

Other Cabins and Cottages Nearby
Beachfront Vacation Rentals, P.O. Box 27, Pismo Beach, CA 93448, 805/773-4771 or 800/732-3766, website: www.gobeachfront.com.

9 WINE VALLEY INN & COTTAGES
off Highway 246 in Solvang

Luxury rating: ★ ★ ★ ★ ★   **Recreation rating:** ★ ★ ★ ☆ ☆

For the uninitiated, some background: Solvang is a popular tourist town northwest of Santa Barbara and south of Santa Maria. Its appeal is its Danish heritage; Danish architecture and culture preside throughout the town, including dozens of Danish bakeries. Although most visitors find Solvang charming and picturesque, its detractors accuse it of being a bit too Disneyland.

No matter how you view it, Solvang is perfectly situated for an outdoor vacation in the Santa Ynez Mountains. Within a few miles are

© ANN MARIE BROWN

several state and county parks, plus Los Padres National Forest. If you want to explore, a stay at Solvang's Wine Valley Inn & Cottages is the perfect base camp.

But a camp this is not. The Wine Valley Inn has six cottages, all beautifully appointed, plus a manicured garden with a tiny stream and footbridges. I stayed in Tuscany, a two-story cottage with a large bedroom upstairs and a living room, dining area, and small kitchen downstairs. It had two fireplaces—one in the bedroom and one in the living room—two bathrooms with unusual antique fixtures, and French doors that opened to a small patio and private hot tub. The place was so enchanting that I never wanted to go home.

All of the inn's cottages have king beds, fireplaces, and private patios, and most have spas. But these are just the bold strokes. The real beauty of this place lies in the details, such as the hand-painted tile work, wide-plank pine floors, and ambient lighting. What impressed me the most were the automatic drapes in the bedroom. With a push of a button placed strategically by the bed, the drapes would open and close at my command.

If you can bring yourself to leave this whimsical inn, go south on U.S. 101 to hike to the 80-foot waterfall at Nojoqui Falls County Park or the hot springs at Gaviota State Park. Or head west on Highway 246 to La Purisima Mission State Historic Park, where you can visit the historic mission and then hike around its lovely grounds. The 2.5-mile Las Zanjas and El Camino Loop is a good introductory walk. Take the short, steep side trail to Vista de la Cruz, where a cross on a hillside overlooks a sweeping view of the Pacific.

Facilities

There are six one- and two-bedroom cottages, plus 50 lodge rooms and suites. All cottages have fully equipped kitchens, fireplaces, and private patios; some have whirlpool tubs. Linens and towels are provided.

Reservations and Rates

Reservations are recommended. Fees are $195–299 per night for cottages, less for lodge rooms and suites. A continental breakfast is included. Pets are not permitted. Contact Wine Valley Inn & Cottages, 1564 Copenhagen Drive, Solvang, CA 93463, 805/688-2111 or 800/824-6444, website: www.winevalleyinn.com.

Directions

From Santa Barbara, drive north on U.S. 101 for 40 miles to the Buellton/Highway 246 exit. Drive east on Highway 246 for three miles to Solvang, then turn right on 5th Street. In one block, turn left on Copenhagen Drive and drive .2 mile to Wine Valley Inn & Cottages, on the right.

Other Cabins and Cottages Nearby

Solvang Inn & Cottages, 1518 Mission Drive, Solvang, CA 93463, 805/688-4702 or 800/848-8484, website: www.solvanginn.com.

10 THE ALISAL GUEST RANCH & RESORT
off Highway 246 near Solvang

Luxury rating: ★ ★ ★ ★ ★   **Recreation rating:** ★ ★ ★ ★ ☆

Rank: Best for Families

No one will complain that there's nothing to do when they visit the Alisal Guest Ranch & Resort. The main attraction is horseback riding, but if you tire of it (or if your butt gets too sore), you can go hiking, mountain biking, fishing, windsurfing, or swimming. Or you can play golf or tennis, visit the historic Santa Ynez Mission, or even take your kids to the Alisal's petting zoo.

The 10,000-acre ranch and resort is a family vacation center in the Santa Ynez Valley. This lovely, winery-filled valley, situated northwest of Santa Barbara near the Danish tourist town of Solvang, is home to a few wealthy folks, like Michael Jackson and Jane Fonda. As you might expect, the Alisal caters to a big-budget crowd.

However, there are ways to make it more affordable. First, rent a cottage at the resort and bring your family with you. The nightly fee is a bit hefty for two adults, but you can add on your children or an additional adult for very little. Plus, the resort offers a ton of kids' activities, from horseback riding and fishing to art and outdoor games.

Or second, show up on weekdays from mid-September to early June, or any day except holidays from November through March, and take advantage of the Alisal's off-season rate package. The fee is almost half of the summer rate, and it includes horseback riding, fishing, tennis, and golf for two people, plus all meals and accommodations.

© ANN MARIE BROWN

The Alisal's cottages look like ranch houses, with covered porches on the outside. Each has one or two large rooms, with high-beamed ceilings, a wood-burning fireplace, a refrigerator, and a coffeemaker. The cottages don't have kitchens; the resort operates on a Modified American Plan—breakfast and dinner are included in your room rate. Typical of a guest ranch, meals are a big deal here, with plentiful portions and a wide menu. And get this: Men wear jackets to dinner.

The Alisal runs a fly-fishing school at its spring-fed 100-acre lake, which is also used for windsurfing and canoeing. Both beginning and experienced fly-fishing enthusiasts are welcome; you'll learn fly techniques, knots, tackle, and fly-casting skills.

If you run out of things to do at the Alisal, you can always head for Lake Cachuma, a 20-minute drive away, where 150,000 rainbow trout are planted each year. Bass, catfish, crappie, and perch are also plentiful. From November through February, you can take a two-hour eagle cruise on the lake with a park naturalist. With any luck, you'll see an American bald eagle, but if not, you'll definitely see some of Lake Cachuma's more than 200 species of resident and migratory birds.

Facilities

There are 73 one- and two-bedroom cottages at the Alisal Guest Ranch & Resort; none have kitchen facilities. Breakfast and dinner are served at the ranch dining room and are included in the fee. Tennis courts and a golf course are on-site. Linens and towels are provided.

Reservations and Rates

Reservations are required. Fees are $425–525 per night for two people, which includes breakfast and dinner each day; each additional person is $80 per night ($50 for children under six). There is a two-night minimum. Reduced fees are available on the "round-up vacation package" from September through June. Pets are not permitted. Contact The Alisal Guest Ranch & Resort, 1054 Alisal Road, Solvang, CA 93463, 805/688-6411 or 800/425-4725, website: www.alisal.com.

Directions

From Santa Barbara, drive north on U.S. 101 for 40 miles to Buellton and take the Solvang/Highway 246 exit. Drive east on Highway 246 for four miles through Solvang, then turn right on Alisal Road. Drive 3.5 miles on Alisal Road, past the golf course, to the Alisal Guest Ranch & Resort, on the left.

Other Cabins and Cottages Nearby

Zaca Lake Resort, P.O. Box 187, Los Olivos, CA 93441, 805/688-5699, website: www.zacalakeretreat.com.

11 CIRCLE BAR B GUEST RANCH

off U.S. 101 near Santa Barbara

Luxury rating: ★ ★ ★ ★ ☆   **Recreation rating:** ★ ★ ★ ★ ☆

Rank: Best for Horseback Riding

Circle Bar B Guest Ranch is a study in contrasts—part horse ranch, part upscale hotel, part outdoor resort, and part dinner theater. Can any place be all those things and do them all well? Circle Bar B does.

The drive in tells you a lot about the place. As soon as you pull off Highway 101 onto Refugio Road, you know you're heading for something good. The road narrows and snakes its way through a lush canyon, crossing Refugio Creek a half dozen times on its 3.5-mile route to the ranch. In winter, the canyon is so lush and green you might think you're in the tropics.

As you near the ranch, you start seeing horses—lots of them—across the creek, grazing in the pasture, and hanging out in their stalls. At the ranch sign, you enter what looks like a small, Western village. Alongside an office and large swimming pool are several cottages, horse corrals, and even a brightly painted, false-front building with a sign reading Blacksmith Shop. Behind the ranch is a deeply carved, curving canyon, bordered by tall, chaparral-covered hillsides and crisscrossed by the ranch's horseback riding trails.

© ANN MARIE BROWN

The cabins at Circle Bar B Guest Ranch are modern and beautifully decorated in Western style. Two sizes are offered: large studios or two-bedroom suites, both with fireplaces and king or queen beds. Some have private decks or wet bars. None of the units come with kitchens, but the fee for a night's stay at Circle Bar B includes three hearty meals.

Most people ride horses while staying at the ranch; guided rides are offered every morning and afternoon. Each day's destination is a little different, but most likely you'll be treated to ridge-top views of the ocean and Channel Islands. If horses don't interest you, you can hike on the ranch's property or drive four miles to Refugio State Beach, where you can swim, surf, or fish from the shore.

Most surprising of the ranch's offerings is its comedy theater performances on Friday and Saturday evenings in summer. Guests come from all over Santa Barbara County to enjoy an outdoor tri-tip barbecue; then when the theater bell rings, they head to the barn to watch the evening's play.

Facilities

There are eight one- and two-bedroom cabins, plus six ranch rooms. None of the cabins have kitchens; meals are included in the price of your stay. Linens and towels are provided.

Reservations and Rates

Reservations are required. Fees are $225–285 per night for two people, including meals. Pets are not permitted. Contact Circle Bar B Guest Ranch, 1800 Refugio Road, Goleta, CA 93117, 805/968-1113, website: www.circle-barb.com.

Directions

From Santa Barbara, drive north on U.S. 101 for 18 miles and take the Refugio State Beach exit. Turn right (north) and drive 3.5 miles on Refugio Road to the Circle Bar B Ranch.

12 RANCHO OSO GUEST RANCH & STABLES
off Highway 154 near Santa Barbara

Luxury rating: ★ ★ ☆ ☆ ☆   **Recreation rating:** ★ ★ ★ ☆ ☆

Rank: Best for Families

© ANN MARIE BROWN

Did you ever want to spend the night the way the Western pioneers did, in a group of covered wagons drawn into a safe, tight circle? Well, call out "Westward ho!" because here's your chance.

At Rancho Oso Guest Ranch & Stables, in Santa Barbara's Santa Ynez Recreation Area, you can live out your pioneer fantasy in a rented covered wagon (minus the oxen), or stay in one of five Western-style bunkhouse cabins. Although Rancho Oso is one of the Thousand Trails chain of membership-style campgrounds, their cabins and covered wagons are open to nonmembers for rental.

The covered wagons look much like the real thing, except that their interiors contain only four simple cots, not an entire pioneer family's belongings. The five cute cabins are lined up in a row to look like the main street of an Old West town, complete with false fronts and clapboard siding. Each has a hitching post out front and a nameplate; guests vie for the one marked "Saloon."

As a rule, children tend to prefer camping in the covered wagons, whereas adults usually prefer the electric heat and privacy of the little cabins. Note that the cabins are very small; although they are supposed to accommodate five people, more than two will be a crowd. The cabins contain a full bed, plus a bunk bed with a twin upper bunk and a full lower bunk. Showers and restrooms are a few steps away.

Although all of the units have electricity, none have kitchens, so your cooking must be done on the outdoor barbecue grills. Meals are available at Rancho Oso's café on weekends and holidays only.

Rancho Oso is a private land holding in Los Padres National Forest. The Santa Ynez River runs along one side of the ranch and is accessible for fishing and swimming. Most people rent horses and go for guided rides when they visit Rancho Oso (or they bring their own horse and ride solo). You can also venture off on your own two feet, hiking the many trails of the Santa Ynez Recreation Area. A favorite is the hilly Aliso Canyon Loop Trail, which begins at nearby Sage Hill Campground. Check out the spring wildflowers from February to May.

One more option: If you like to fish or water ski, you'll want to spend at least one day on a boat at Lake Cachuma, only 12 miles away.

Facilities
There are five one-room cabins at Rancho Oso, plus 10 covered wagons. None have kitchen facilities. A general store and café are on-site. Linens and towels are not provided.

Reservations and Rates
Reservations are required. Fees are $54 per night for covered wagons and $79 per night for cabins. Covered wagons accommodate four people, and cabins accommodate five. Pets are permitted in the covered wagons, but not in the cabins. Contact Rancho Oso Guest Ranch & Stables, 3750 Paradise Road, Santa Barbara, CA 93105, 805/683-5686, website: www.rancho-oso.com.

Directions
From U.S. 101 in Santa Barbara, take Highway 154 north for 11 miles to the Paradise Road turnoff on the right. Turn right on Paradise Road and drive 5.5 miles to the sign for Rancho Oso on the right. Turn right and drive 1.5 miles to the entrance kiosk; the cabins and covered wagons are a quarter mile beyond the kiosk.

13 WHITE LOTUS FOUNDATION
off Highway 154 near Santa Barbara

Luxury rating: ★★☆☆☆   **Recreation rating:** ★★★☆☆

Rank: Most Unusual

White Lotus Foundation is a nonprofit, spiritual foundation in the mountains above Santa Barbara. It functions as a yoga retreat for teachers and students alike. If you are a yoga person or are even moderately curious about yoga, you'll enjoy a stay at White Lotus.

Although the foundation is often booked by large groups holding yoga classes or teacher workshops, White Lotus offers personal retreats for the general public. In their words: "Slip away from the city to our mountain oasis and enjoy a quiet, relaxing retreat."

Guests can sign up for a stay in one of White Lotus's six yurts—or domed tent structures—and then design their own restorative getaway. They can participate in hatha yoga classes if they wish, or hike and swim on their own. (Small waterfalls and swimming holes in San Jose Creek are on the property.) What a pleasant way to leave the everyday world behind.

White Lotus's yurts provide minimalist accommodations in a beautiful canyon setting. If you've stayed in a tent cabin, this is one step up on the luxury scale. Set in a grove of canyon oaks, the yurts have wood floors and canvas sides, with doors and windows of heavy plastic. Inside, each has pillows, futons, and mats, plus a reading lamp and water dispenser. You must walk to the restroom, but it's a winner: A beautiful bamboo building serves as the outhouse, and the outdoor sink is made of stone and wood and has a metal frog sculpture on the faucet. Showers are in a separate building. The yurts are a steep five-minute walk from where you leave your car.

For meals, you can cook in the communal kitchen, but don't think about grilling a juicy steak. Anything nonvegetarian would be a huge faux pas. If you don't want to cook, a dining room serves gourmet vegetarian meals.

It's so peaceful here that it may be difficult to drag yourself out of the lotus position, but if you get inspired, there is much to see in neighboring Los Padres National Forest. Start with the Painted Cave of the Chumash Indians, or the short hike to the ruins of Knapp's Castle, or the swimming holes along Oso Creek, accessible via the Santa Cruz Trail out of Upper Oso Campground.

Facilities

There are six yurts that can accommodate up to four people. A communal kitchen is available for vegetarian cooking only, and a dining room serves vegetarian meals. Restrooms are a short walk from the yurts. Linens and towels are not provided.

Reservations and Rates

Reservations are required. Fees are $75 per person per night. Pets are not permitted. Contact White Lotus Foundation, 2500 San Marcos Pass, Santa Barbara, CA 93105, 805/964-1944, website: www.whitelotus.org.

Directions

From U.S. 101 in Santa Barbara, take Highway 154 north for 5.8 miles. Shortly beyond Painted Cave Road, turn left into White Lotus Foundation's driveway.

14 EL ENCANTO HOTEL & GARDEN VILLAS
off U.S. 101 in Santa Barbara

Luxury rating: ★ ★ ★ ★ ☆   **Recreation rating:** ★ ★ ★ ☆ ☆

El Encanto Hotel is a historic and psychological landmark in Santa Barbara. Built in 1915, it's what the Ahwahnee Hotel is to Yosemite Valley—a statement of elegance and refinement; a place that stays the same while everything around it changes. From its hilltop location, the famous restaurant at El Encanto provides an unparalleled vista of Santa Barbara and the coast, and that view alone brings many guests back year after year.

The resort has only four free-standing cottages; the others are duplexes, triplexes, or suites. You can choose from two types of architecture: Spanish colonial (stucco and red-tile roofs) or Craftsman style (lots of wood). A few units, in the $500-and-up category, have kitchens or kitchenettes, but for that price you might as well hire a personal chef too.

The cottages are luxurious but not opulent; the decor is even a bit understated compared to other luxury resorts in Santa Barbara. However, this is scheduled to change in the winter of 2005-2006, when the hotel buildings will undergo a major renovation. As this book goes to press, the El Encanto expects to close for at least six months for a planned facelift. It will be exciting to see a new, updated look to the historic cottages. One thing will remain the same: at El Encanto,

© JULIE SHEER

the grounds have always been a major attraction. With 10 landscaped acres of tropical gardens surrounding the buildings, it's more fun to walk the brick pathways, cross the miniature bridges, and sit on the well-placed benches outside the cottages than it is being inside the cottages. The landscaping is a mix of sunny lawn areas and lush gardens of palm and magnolia trees and hibiscus and rose bushes. A swimming pool–sized lily pond lined with red bricks and bounded by a brick-and-wood arbor brings to mind the gardens of an English estate. Tennis courts and a lap pool are also found on the grounds.

El Encanto holds a prestigious spot on a hillside above the Santa Barbara Mission, which puts guests about a mile away from the trailhead for Tunnel and Jesusita trails, two of Santa Barbara's most popular local pathways. You can follow them three miles round-trip to Mission Creek's swimming holes and waterfalls, or five miles round-trip to 1,750-foot Inspiration Point, with its inspiring view of the coast. Beautiful Rattlesnake Canyon is also nearby and has more hiking options.

Facilities
There are three one-bedroom cottages, plus 12 cottage suites (duplex or triplex style). Some cottages have kitchens or kitchenettes. A restaurant, pool, and tennis courts are on-site. Linens and towels are provided.

Reservations and Rates
Reservations are required. Fees are $289–729 per night. Pets are not permitted. Contact El Encanto Hotel & Garden Villas, 1900 Lasuen Road, Santa Barbara, CA 93103, 805/687-5000 or 800/346-7039, website: www.elencantohotel.com.

Directions
From U.S. 101 in Santa Barbara, take the Mission Street exit and drive north for 1.2 miles. Turn left on Laguna Street and drive to the Santa Barbara Mission, then turn right on Los Olivos Street. Drive a short distance and turn right on Alameda Padre Serra, continue uphill to Lasuen Road, turn left on Alvarado Place, then turn right into the guest entrance for El Encanto.

15 SIMPSON HOUSE INN
off U.S. 101 in Santa Barbara

Luxury rating: ★ ★ ★ ★ ★   **Recreation rating:** ★ ★ ★ ☆ ☆

Rank: Most Luxurious

Downtown Santa Barbara is filled with bed-and-breakfast inns, including several with cottages, yet only one has been rated Five Diamond and proclaimed one of America's Ten Most Romantic Inns. In every respect, the Simpson House is a notch above other inns in its class.

Secluded among an acre of immaculate English gardens, Simpson House has four garden cottages in addition to its guest-room accommodations. Breakfast is served each morning in the main house, and tea, wine, and hors d'oeuvres are served each afternoon. (If you are staying in the cottages, you can have breakfast brought to your doorstep.) Although the main house is quite formal—filled with finely polished furniture, Victorian lamps, Oriental rugs, English antiques, and bustling servers in uniforms—the cottages have a more relaxed feel.

Pendle cottage has a full kitchen, skylights, a wood-burning fireplace, a lace coverlet on the brass king bed, and white wood-beamed ceilings. Plumstead cottage has a two-person whirlpool tub in the living room (it's the first thing you see as you walk in the door!), a wet bar, a wood-burning fireplace, and an upstairs bedroom. Greenwich and Abbeywood are duplex cottages and are mirror images of each other. They both have hot tubs and fireplaces. Each of the cottages is very cozy and beautifully furnished. Each has a small, secluded patio area with a table and chairs.

The inn rents bicycles and provides guests with handouts on suggested walks, things to do, and restaurants. Myriad recreation options exist in or near downtown Santa Barbara, from the beaches and harbor (for swimming, surfing, whale-watching, and sport fishing) to the forested canyons of Los Padres National Forest (for hiking and mountain biking). An excellent visitors center is near the Simpson House Inn, at the corner of Cabrillo Boulevard and Santa Barbara Street.

For people who want to stay in a nice neighborhood away

© SIMPSON HOUSE INN

from the bustle of downtown Santa Barbara yet still close enough to walk there, the Simpson House works. But keep in mind, this isn't the kind of place where you put your muddy boots up on the couch.

Facilities
There are four one-bedroom cottages, plus six guest rooms in the main house. One cottage has a fully equipped kitchen. Linens and towels are provided.

Reservations and Rates
Reservations are required. Fees are $565–575 per night for cottages, less for rooms. Pets are not permitted. Contact Simpson House Inn, 121 East Arrellaga Street, Santa Barbara, CA 93101, 805/963-7067 or 800/676-1280, website: www.simpsonhouseinn.com.

Directions
From U.S. 101 heading south in Santa Barbara, take the Mission Street exit and turn left. Drive east six blocks to Anacapa Street. Turn right on Anacapa Street, drive four blocks, then turn left on Arrellaga Street. Simpson House Inn is on the left.

Other Cabins and Cottages Nearby
Secret Garden Inn & Cottages, 1908 Bath Street, Santa Barbara, CA 93101, 805/687-2300, website: www.secretgarden.com.

Glenborough Inn Bed and Breakfast, 1327 Bath Street, Santa Barbara, CA 93101, 805/966-0589 or 888/966-0589, website: www.glenboroughinn.com.

The Upham Victorian Hotel and Garden Cottages, 1404 De la Vina Street, Santa Barbara, CA 93101, 805/962-0058 or 800/727-0876, website: www.uphamhotel.com.

16 CHESHIRE CAT INN & COTTAGES
off U.S. 101 in Santa Barbara

Luxury rating: ★ ★ ★ ★ ☆   **Recreation rating:** ★ ★ ☆ ☆ ☆

Cheshire Cat Inn & Cottages is a charming and creative bed-and-breakfast in downtown Santa Barbara. It is comprised of a collection of buildings: two stately Queen Anne Victorians filled with a dozen guest rooms, a carriage house, and three cottages across the street.

The one- and two-bedroom cottages have everything you need for a comfortable, extended stay: full kitchens, fireplaces, television, and a private deck or patio with outdoor hot tub, plus oak floors, "homey" pine furniture, and down comforters. You won't need to flip pancakes in your kitchen in the morning, because a gourmet breakfast is served on Wedgewood china in the main house. Wine and hors d'oeuvres are served in the afternoon.

© ANN MARIE BROWN

The set-up is ideal for families or two couples. The cottages are furnished in a comfortably elegant style; even small children couldn't get into too much trouble here. The maximum number of people in the cottages is four.

Once you're settled into your cottage, the inn's management basically leaves you alone to do your own thing, which is a bonus for people who enjoy privacy. And there is plenty to do in downtown Santa Barbara, from visits to the city's historic mission and Stearn's Wharf to shopping on State Street. The beach and all beach activities are the main draw on sunny summer days. If you seek some adventure, you can get on a dive boat, sport-fishing boat, or whale-watching cruise. You can rent bikes (or bring your own) and cycle Santa Barbara's lengthy paved bike path, or you could board a Channel Islands ferry for day hiking and exploring on Anacapa or Santa Cruz Islands.

Facilities
There are three one- and two-bedroom cottages that can accommodate up to four people. All have fully equipped kitchens. Linens and towels are provided.

Reservations and Rates
Reservations are required. Fees are $329–379 per night for cottages and $169–269 per night for rooms. Pets are not permitted. Contact Cheshire Cat Inn & Cottages, 36 West Valerio, Santa Barbara, CA 93101, 805/569-1610, website: www.cheshirecat.com.

Directions
From U.S. 101 in Santa Barbara, take the Arrellaga Street exit. Drive four blocks to Chapala Street and turn left. Drive one block to Valerio

Street. Cheshire Cat Inn & Cottages is at the corner of Valerio Street and Chapala Street.

Other Cabins and Cottages Nearby

Cabrillo Inn Spanish Vacation Cottages, 931 East Cabrillo Boulevard, Santa Barbara, CA 93101, 805/963-6774 or 800/648-6708, website: www.cabrillo-inn.com.

17 SAN YSIDRO RANCH
off U.S. 101 in Montecito

Luxury rating: ★ ★ ★ ★ ★   **Recreation rating:** ★ ★ ★ ☆ ☆

Rank: Most Luxurious

Lottery winnings burning a hole in your pocket? Lucky you, you can book a stay at San Ysidro Ranch.

A night at the ranch is prohibitively expensive (try $1,850 a night for the Kennedy Suite, where JFK and Jackie honeymooned), so most people save it for very special occasions. San Ysidro's management understands this. When guests check in, they are asked if they are celebrating an anniversary or birthday. If they say yes, the front desk sends a cake or strawberries and champagne to their room.

San Ysidro Ranch is all about this kind of service. Another example: If you bring your dog with you (yes, they're allowed in the cottages), a dog bed and bottled water will be delivered to your room. Of course, you pay $100 extra for pets, so you might want to reconsider how badly Fido needs a vacation.

Your favorite newspaper, tied in a red ribbon, is delivered to your cottage each day. Your name is branded in block letters on a wooden plaque outside your cottage, so you will feel like it's your very own home. Each cottage has a king bed, a private deck, and a fireplace or wood-burning stove, and firewood is delivered daily.

© JULIE SHEER

Except for these commonalities, each is unique in its room layout and furnishings, so there is nothing about staying here that reminds you of being in an impersonal hotel.

San Ysidro Ranch covers a whopping 500-plus acres, and only five of those are developed. Hiking trails crisscross the property, so you can wander as you wish. A horse stable, a pool, a fitness center, massage services, and two tennis courts are on-site. From the stable, you can access the San Ysidro Trail along San Ysidro Creek, a year-round stream with several lovely waterfalls. If you really want some exercise, hike to its terminus on East Camino Cielo; it's an eight-mile round-trip with a 2,800-foot elevation gain.

If you really want to stay here but are wondering if you can part with the money, know that San Ysidro Ranch is worth every penny. This is a place where every guest is treated like royalty. At the end of your stay, you'll feel like you've had a true taste of the good life.

Facilities
There are 12 cottages with a deck and a fireplace or wood-burning stove, plus 26 rooms and suites. None have kitchens. Two restaurants are on-site, as are a pool, a fitness center, and tennis courts. Linens and towels are provided.

Reservations and Rates
Reservations are required. Fees are $599–995 per night for one-bedroom cottages and $1,375–4,100 for larger cottages. Pets are permitted with a $100 fee. Contact San Ysidro Ranch, 900 San Ysidro Lane, Santa Barbara, CA 93108, 805/969-5046 or 800/368-6788, website: www.sanysidro-ranch.com.

Directions
From U.S. 101 in Montecito, take the San Ysidro Road exit and drive north for about one mile. Turn right on San Ysidro Lane and drive to the resort.

18 FOUR SEASONS BILTMORE
off U.S. 101 in Santa Barbara

Luxury rating: ★ ★ ★ ★ ★   **Recreation rating:** ★ ★ ★ ★ ☆

Rank: Most Luxurious, Best for Beach Activities

If I could afford it, I'd stay at the Biltmore every time I visited Santa Barbara. Heck, if I could afford it, I'd live there.

Even though it's a ritzy resort, the Biltmore is gracious and comfortable. Because it is situated on gorgeous Butterfly Beach, sandy feet and beachwear are typical attire around the property. And the Biltmore is one of the few luxury resorts in Southern California that allows dogs without any deposit or fee. You must not leave Fido

unattended, however, so plan on ordering room service for your meals.

For the sake of full disclosure, you should know that not one of the Biltmore's cottages is a stand-alone building; each of their 12 cottages is split into as many as five suites. Whereas that might disqualify another resort from this book, it doesn't rule out the Biltmore. Its ocean-side location is perfect for beach lovers, and its grand style and service are without reproach, so it's easy to forgive the multiplex cottages.

The cottages are not on the ocean side of the resort; they're located in the back of the main building in a beautiful garden, nestled among palm trees and trumpet vines. The lush landscaping keeps the individual cottage suites very secluded. For the $500-and-up price tag, you can expect a fireplace, refrigerator, private patio, and a lot of expensive upholstery.

The Biltmore is the kind of place where you will probably not leave the property once you arrive. It has pretty much everything you could need or want, including two restaurants, a spa, a beauty salon, tennis courts, a putting green, an art gallery, a gift shop, croquet, shuffleboard, a swimming pool, and a fitness center. The beach, of course, is the main draw, so make sure you bring a suitcase full of swimwear.

Facilities

There are 12 cottages that are divided into 58 suites. None have kitchens. Stores, tennis courts, a putting green, a swimming pool, and restaurants are on-site. Linens and towels are provided.

Reservations and Rates

Reservations are recommended. Fees are $495–2,200 per night (slightly less Sunday through Thursday). Pets are permitted in cottages. Contact Four Seasons Biltmore, 1260 Channel Drive, Santa Barbara, CA 93108, 805/969-2261 or 800/332-3442, website: www.fourseasons.com.

Directions

From U.S. 101 in Montecito, take the Olive Mill Road exit west. Turn right on Channel Drive and enter the resort.

19 EMERALD IGUANA COTTAGES
off Highway 33 in Ojai

Luxury rating: ★ ★ ★ ★ ☆   **Recreation rating:** ★ ★ ★ ☆ ☆

The Emerald Iguana Cottages are quintessential Ojai, which means they are artsy, eclectic, rustic, and even classy. Owned and operated by the same folks who run the nearby Blue Iguana Inn, Emerald Iguana's nine cottages are as individual as their whimsical names: Treehouse, Frog, Cricket, Lilypad, Toad, and so on.

Toad Cottage is the largest of the bunch. It's a lovely stone structure with three bedrooms, each with its own bath (one with a claw-foot tub and one with a whirlpool tub), plus a shady front porch. Two of the bedrooms have fireplaces. A particularly romantic unit is Treehouse Cottage, which has two levels. The upstairs bedroom is surrounded by uniquely shaped windows providing treetop views. The downstairs living room is decorated with exotic rugs and velvet drapes.

Each of the cottages is furnished with accessories from the owners' travels throughout the world. In Toad Cottage, these include an Indonesian headboard on the bed and Oriental rugs.

A pool and hot tub are located among the cottages, which are connected by stone walkways. Oaks, willows, and palms shade the grounds. A fountain made of green mosaic tiles, in the shape of an iguana, greets guests at the cottages' entrances. It is obvious—from the furnishing of the cottages to the landscaping of the grounds—that attention was paid to every detail. The entire resort is loaded with character; this, combined with its quiet location at the end of a side street, make Emerald Iguana a truly unique vacation spot.

© JULIE SHEER

While in Ojai, you have a long list of recreation options. The paved Ojai Valley bicycle trail runs alongside Highway 33. Lake Casitas, 15 minutes away, beckons swimmers, anglers, and boaters. And the hiking trails of Los Padres National Forest are within easy reach. The Ojai Ranger District Office is right in town on Ojai Avenue; it can provide maps and trail information.

Facilities
There are nine cottages ranging in size from one to three bedrooms, all with fully equipped kitchens. Linens and towels are provided.

Reservations and Rates
Reservations are recommended. Fees are $199–449 per night, less on weeknights. Weekly stays are discounted. Pets are not permitted in the cottages, but they are permitted at the nearby Blue Iguana Inn. Contact Emerald Iguana Cottages, 11794 North Ventura Avenue, Ojai, CA 93023, 805/646-5277, website: www.emeraldiguana.com.

Directions
From U.S. 101 in Ventura, take Highway 33 east to Ojai. When you pass the traffic light with a sign for Lake Casitas and Santa Barbara, continue on Highway 33 for a half mile more. Blue Iguana Inn is on the right, at the corner of Highway 33 and Loma Drive; check in there for Emerald Iguana Cottages.

Other Cabins and Cottages Nearby
Theodore Woolsey House, 1484 East Ojai Avenue, Ojai, CA 93023, 805/646-9779, website: www.theodorewoolseyhouse.com.

20 THE PIERPONT INN
off U.S. 101 in Ventura

Luxury rating: ★ ★ ★ ★ ☆   **Recreation rating:** ★ ★ ★ ★ ☆

The Pierpont Inn has two secluded garden cottages in addition to its 62 rooms, nine suites, award-winning restaurant, and tennis and fitness club. With all cottage and room rates less than $300 per night, it's Ventura's more affordable answer to the big resorts in nearby Montecito and Santa Barbara.

And like those resorts to the north, the Pierpont overlooks the magnificent Pacific coastline. Getting to the beach is easy, as is accessing the 13-mile-long bike path that winds along the coast from San Buenaventura Beach to Emma

© JULIE SHEER

Wood Beach. Perhaps best of all is the Pierpont's proximity to Channel Islands Harbor, where you can get on a boat for a day trip to Anacapa or Santa Cruz Islands then spend the day hiking or kayaking.

There's also plenty to do on the resort property. Tennis and racquetball courts are plentiful. A fitness club offers aerobics classes and exercise equipment. A spa provides facials, body scrubs, massages, and other treatments.

The resort's two Tudor-style cottages are Gardenia and Rose Garden. Gardenia is the smaller of the two and has a canopy bed, English cottage–type furnishings, a breakfast nook, a gas fireplace, and a patio garden area. Rose Garden has two rooms, a massive brick fireplace, and roses that surround the cottage and creep over its roof. Both cottages were built in the 1930s and have a charming, old-style feel. Because they are in the back of the resort, they have garden views and are much quieter than most of Pierpont's accommodations, which suffer from highway noise from U.S. 101.

Although there are many restaurants to choose from in Ventura, don't miss having a sunset dinner at Pierpont's restaurant, which offers lovely views of the Ventura coastline.

Facilities

There are two one-bedroom cottages without kitchens but with fireplaces. A restaurant, tennis and racquetball courts, a fitness club, and a spa are on-site. Linens and towels are provided.

Reservations and Rates

Reservations are recommended. Fees are $225–345 per night for the cottages, including breakfast. Rooms are $145–215 per night. Pets are not permitted. Contact The Pierpont Inn, 550 Sanjon Road, Ventura, CA 93001, 805/643-6144 or 800/285-4667, website: www.pierpontinn.com.

Directions

From U.S. 101 heading north in Ventura, take the Sanjon Road/Vista del Mar exit. Turn left to go under the overpass to Harbor Boulevard, then turn right on Harbor Boulevard and immediately right again on Sanjon Road. The Pierpont Inn is on the right. From Santa Barbara, drive south on U.S. 101, take the Seaward exit, turn right on Harbor Boulevard, and then right on Sanjon Road.

21 MOUNTAIN PROPERTIES VACATION RENTALS
Los Padres National Forest, off I-5 near Mount Pinos

Luxury rating: ★ ★ ★ ★ ☆   **Recreation rating:** ★ ★ ★ ★ ☆

Are there any surprises left in the Southern California great outdoors? Yes, there's seldom-visited Mount Pinos. Never heard of it, right? At 8,831 feet, Mount Pinos is the tallest mountain in Los Padres National Forest. It's a beautiful peak covered with pine forest and gets a fair share of snowfall every winter.

Mount Pinos is accessed from the unlikely town of Frazier Park on I-5, just south of Grapevine. Go 12 miles westward; a right turn on Mil Potrero Highway takes you through Los Padres National Forest to the small town of Pine Mountain Club, where numerous cabin rentals are available.

Each cabin is someone's private vacation home and comes with a fully equipped kitchen, linens, television, and all modern conveniences. The majority of homes have fireplaces or wood stoves, and firewood is often provided by the owner. Some cabins have views, some allow smoking, some have hot tubs, and so on, so make sure you request exactly what you want.

After you get settled in your cabin, head back to the main road to drive the remaining few miles to the top of Mount Pinos, where you'll find an awesome vista extending all the way to the San Joaquin Valley and the peaks of the Sierra Nevada. As you look around, watch for giant condors soaring in the sky; they are often seen here on the edge of the Chumash Wilderness.

If snow has fallen, many areas of the mountain will be open for cross-country skiing and snowshoeing (a National Forest Adventure Pass is required; see page 4). If the snow has vanished, numerous hiking trails are available, including the beautiful Vincent Tumamait Trail from Mount Pinos's summit. Or try Cedar Creek Trail, which leads from Thorn Meadows Campground in nearby Lake of the Woods. The drive to the trailhead will take a little less than an hour; get an early start so you have plenty of time to hike the nine-mile round-trip to the Fishbowls along Piru Creek. In summer, these

Little hiker on top of Mount Pinos

sandstone pools are popular swimming holes.

Several local hikes are possible right in Pine Mountain Club, including a short waterfall trail beginning on Woodland Drive. The nice folks at Mountain Properties Vacation Rentals can supply you with a street map and a list of trails and trailheads.

Facilities

There are 16 private vacation homes that can accommodate up to 12 people. All have fully equipped kitchens and modern conveniences, and some have fireplaces. Linens and towels are provided.

Reservations and Rates

Reservations are required. Fees are $100–250 per night. Weekly rentals are discounted. Pets are not permitted. Contact Mountain Properties Vacation Rentals, 16229 Pine Valley Lane, P.O. Box 6675, Pine Mountain Club, CA 93222, 661/242-2517, website: www.mtprop.com.

Directions

From Los Angeles, drive north on I-5 through the San Fernando Valley to Gorman. Just beyond Gorman, take the Frazier Park/Mount Pinos exit and turn west. Drive 12 miles on Frazier Mountain Park Road, which will become Cuddy Valley Road. At 12 miles, turn right on Mil Potrero Highway and drive six miles to Pine Mountain Club. Turn left at the gas station in town, across from the golf course, and enter the shopping center. Drive 50 yards on Pine Circle. Mountain Properties is in the shopping center at the intersection of Pine Circle and Pine Valley Lane.

Chapter 3

COURTESY OF LOS ANGELES VISITORS BUREAU

Los Angeles and Vicinity

Los Angeles and Vicinity

slands, mountains, beaches, lakes, snowfall, surfing, skiing . . . the Los Angeles region offers all this diversity and more. The region is so large and so varied that it's impossible to make a blanket statement about it without dividing it into smaller pieces.

Two large national forests hold most of the high-country land in the region—Angeles and San Bernardino. The 700,000-acre Angeles National Forest contains the San Gabriel Mountains, which form a high, impenetrable shield that prevents Los Angeles's smog from dissipating. The mountains, which geologists claim are the most fractured and unstable in California (rock slides are an everyday occurrence), feature a wonderful network of more than 500 miles of maintained trails for hiking and biking, plus two small ski resorts at Mount Baldy and Big Pines.

You'll find a number of authentic mountain lodges in the San Gabriels, with cabins for rent in the summer sun or winter snow—including Mount Baldy Lodge and Snowcrest Lodge on Mount Baldy, and the Mountain View Motel near Wrightwood.

A few miles to the east, the San Bernardino Mountains, in San Bernardino National Forest, form one of the highest mountain ranges in California, with peaks that rise to more than 11,000 feet in elevation. The San Bernardinos also contain Southern California's three major recreation lakes: Big Bear, Arrowhead, and Silverwood, plus smaller lakes Gregory and Green Valley. Whether you water ski, fish, windsurf, sail, canoe, or ride personal watercrafts, recreation opportunities abound on these lakes. In addition, Southern California's best skiing and snowboarding are found at two resorts at Big Bear (Snow Summit and Bear Mountain) and one at Running Springs (Snow Valley). With a base elevation of 6,800 feet and extensive snowmaking systems, these resorts provide consistent skiing typically from Thanksgiving through Easter.

Cabin resorts near the lakes and ski resorts in the San Bernardino

Mountains are too numerous to count; some of the best are featured in the pages that follow.

Yet another mountain range is found in San Bernardino National Forest: the San Jacintos, topped by 10,804-foot Mount San Jacinto, which towers over the low desert at Palm Springs. The San Jacinto Mountains rise abruptly from the desert floor and are completely separated from the other high-elevation ranges of Southern California by low passes and valleys. John Muir called the view from the summit of Mount San Jacinto "one of the most sublime spectacles seen anywhere on Earth."

To explore the dense cedar and pine forests of the San Jacinto Mountains, reserve a stay at one of the cabin resorts in the village of Idyllwild, a hiker-friendly town with easy access to numerous trailheads and mountain streams for fishing.

Combined, these three mountain ranges—San Gabriel, San Bernardino, and San Jacinto—contain Southern California's great triumvirate of hikeable peaks: Mount San Gorgonio, at 11,490 feet; Mount San Jacinto, at 10,804 feet; and Mount Baldy, at 10,064 feet. Every Los Angeles–area hiker worth his or her salt will bag all three summits at some point in his or her hiking career.

But if surf and sand appeal to you more than mountains and lakes, the Los Angeles region will not disappoint. In this chapter, you'll find cottage resorts within steps of the beaches at Malibu and Laguna, and one in the town of Avalon, on Catalina Island. If you want to sleep even closer to the water, this chapter includes two boat-and-breakfasts—one in Newport and one in Long Beach, where you can spend the night on a yacht in a calm harbor.

And last but not least, even glittering Hollywood has a cottage resort where you can sleep like a movie star: the venerable Chateau Marmont. Its cottages and bungalows have served as home to the likes of Greta Garbo and Bette Davis. Will you be next?

LOS ANGELES AND VICINITY

see
Death Valley and
the Deserts
page 318

see
San Diego
and Vicinity
page 132

see
Santa Barbara
and Vicinity
page 38

PACIFIC OCEAN

© AVALON TRAVEL PUBLISHING, INC.

Contents

1. Chateau Marmont 80

2. Mountain View Motel 81

3. Mount Baldy Lodge 83

4. Snowcrest Lodge 84

5. Sleepy Hollow Cabins 86

6. Arrowhead Pine Rose Cabins 88

7. Bracken Fern Manor 89

8. Saddleback Inn 91

9. Giant Oaks Lodge 92

10. Green Valley Lake Cozy Cabins 94

11. Quail Cove Lodge 95

12. Shore Acres Lodge 97

13. Wildwood Resort 99

14. Bear Manor Cabins and Lakeview Lodge 101

15. Castlewood Theme Cottages 102

16. Our Secret Garden Mountain Retreat 104

17. Seven Oaks Mountain Cabins 106

18. The Lodge at Angelus Oaks 107

19. Whispering Pines 109

20. Two Harbors Cabins 110

21. La Paloma Cottages 112

22. Dockside Boat and Bed 114

23. Boat and Breakfast Newport 116

24. Casa Laguna Inn 117

25. Manzanita Cottages 119

26. Zosa Ranch & Gardens 121

27. Knotty Pine Cabins 123

28. Fern Valley Inn 124

29. Wilder Cabins 126

1 CHATEAU MARMONT
off U.S. 101 in Hollywood

Luxury rating: ★ ★ ★ ★ ★   **Recreation rating:** ★ ★ ★ ☆ ☆

Rank: Most Luxurious

Chateau Marmont is legendary. Bette Davis and Greta Garbo slept here. Howard Hughes kept his harem here. Grace Kelly had affairs here. John Belushi died here. You get the picture.

Built like a Gothic citadel, a Mediterranean castle, or something with spare parts from both, Chateau Marmont has nine garden cottages, two hillside bungalows, and two poolside bungalows in addition to its 50 rooms. If you want to get a peek at a celebrity or just feel like one yourself, Chateau Marmont is the place.

Originally an apartment building, the Chateau was transformed into a hotel in the late 1920s and has been a movie-industry hangout ever since. Hotelier Andre Balazs purchased it in 1990 and completely renovated it in a mixed 1930s, '40s, and '50s style.

Each cottage, bungalow, and room has its own character. The bungalows are huge (1,500 to 2,500 square feet and two or three bedrooms) and offer the utmost in privacy. Each has its own kitchen, fireplace, and secluded patio or yard. They have the ambience of a very nice home, not a hotel—a factor that has appealed to celebrities for decades.

The garden cottages are smaller and more quaint (Arts and Crafts and Mission-style furnishings). Each has a bedroom, a living room, and a kitchen. They are grouped around a landscaped courtyard and accessed by a separate street entrance from the main hotel. The cottage and bungalow grounds are lush and manicured, with plenty of bougainvillea, trumpet vines, and palms. Brick walkways lead from the buildings to the inviting pool and lounge area.

In addition to hanging out by the pool, most guests take advantage of the proximity of the Sunset Strip. The Chateau is set just above Sunset Boulevard, with its multitude of nightclubs, restaurants, record stores, and the like.

But to complete your Hollywood experience, you must

© JULIE SHEER

head for Griffith Park and hike to the top of Mount Hollywood, elevation 1,625 feet. First-timers need to know that this is not the peak that bears the famous Hollywood sign (that's Mount Lee), although you can see that sign from this peak, which is the highest point in Hollywood. The round-trip is five miles from the trailhead near the Ferndell Nature Museum. Another option is to leave the hustle and bustle of Hollywood behind and explore the peaceful trails in nearby Franklin Canyon.

Facilities
There are nine garden cottages, two hillside bungalows, and two poolside bungalows, plus 50 rooms, suites, and penthouses. All cottages have fully equipped kitchens. Linens and towels are provided. Pets are not permitted.

Reservations and Rates
Reservations are required. Rates are $415–460 per night for garden cottages and $1,500 and up for hillside and poolside bungalows. Contact Chateau Marmont, 8221 Sunset Boulevard, Hollywood, CA 90046, 323/656-1010 or 800/242-8328, website: www.chateaumarmont.com.

Directions
From U.S. 101 in Hollywood, take the Sunset Boulevard exit west and drive approximately four miles. Watch for Crescent Heights Boulevard; two blocks beyond it, turn right on Marmont Lane (which is easy to miss). The hotel is on the right.

2 MOUNTAIN VIEW MOTEL
off Highway 2 in Wrightwood

Luxury rating: ★ ★ ★ ☆ ☆   **Recreation rating:** ★ ★ ★ ★ ☆

It's December in Los Angeles, and you just can't conjure up the feeling of Christmas amid the crowded malls, Santa Claus bikinis, and palm trees swaddled in twinkling lights. So book yourself a cabin at Mountain View Motel and take the one-hour drive to Wrightwood, a snowy mountain town that knows how to do winter right.

Mountain View Motel has cabins with and without whirlpool tubs, fireplaces, wood-burning stoves, and kitchens, so be sure to get one that is right for you. Make sure you've brought your warm clothes, because the elevation is 6,000 feet and it gets mighty chilly up here. After a good night's sleep, take your pick from the ski resorts in nearby Big Pines—Ski Sunrise or Mountain High—and make a few runs down the mountain.

If wintertime isn't your cup of tea, the other seasons are also fine at Mountain View Motel. In spring, summer, or fall, the big attraction around Wrightwood is hiking in the San Gabriel Mountains, with

Skiers at Ski Sunrise bunny hill

dozens of trailheads all within a 30-minute drive of your cabin. The elevation is high enough so that the temperature is rarely too hot, and the air is always fresh and clean—free of the valley smog. If you want an easy stroll, three nature trails are just five minutes away in Big Pines, near the Forest Service Visitor Center. If you seek more of an adventure, try the classic climb to the peak of Mount Baden-Powell, starting from either the Vincent Gap or Dawson Saddle trailheads on Highway 2.

You can even do some fishing in the Big Pines area, at little Jackson Lake along the Big Pines Highway (Road N4). The Department of Fish and Game keeps the lake stocked with trout all summer; just drive up to the picnic area and fish from shore. If you've always wanted to try your hand at gold prospecting, Big Rock Creek is the place, just a few miles down Highway 2.

Facilities
There are 10 duplex-style cabins ranging in size from one to three bedrooms. Some have fully equipped kitchens, fireplaces, and hot tubs. Linens and towels are provided.

Reservations and Rates
Reservations are recommended. Rates are $69–169 per night. Pets are not permitted. Contact Mountain View Motel, P.O. Box 458, 1054 State Highway 2, Wrightwood, CA 92397, 760/249-3553 or 888/383-5700, website: www.mountain-view-motel.com.

Directions
From I-10 at Ontario, drive east for seven miles and take I-15 north. Drive north on I-15 for 22 miles to Highway 138, then go west on Highway 138 for nine miles to the Highway 2 cutoff. Go west on Highway 2 for five

miles to Wrightwood; Mountain View Motel is on the right as you drive through town.

Other Cabins and Cottages Nearby

Oriole Lodge & Cottage, 663 Oriole Road, P.O. Box 1959, Wrightwood, CA 92397, 760/249-3873, website: www.oriolelodge.com.

3 MOUNT BALDY LODGE
off I-10 on Mount Baldy

Luxury rating: ★★★☆☆   **Recreation rating:** ★★★★☆

Twenty years ago, when I was a college student in Claremont, my class-mates and I would head to Mount Baldy at the first sign of snow in November. We'd stop our cars as soon as we drove into the white stuff for the sheer joy of throwing snowballs at each other. Other times, and in other seasons, we'd drive to our favorite trailhead at Ice House Canyon and hike in the conifers amid cool, clean mountain air. It was a sweet, revitalizing shock to our smog-ridden lungs.

Years later, I finally stayed overnight at Mount Baldy Lodge. I found myself wondering how I could have spent so much time on the mountain without staying at these wonderful cabins. I rented cabin No. 8, which has a huge stone fireplace. The bed was placed in a tiny alcove, separate from the main living area, which made it especially cozy.

All the cabins are old and rustic, with fine woodworking and details but also with modern conveniences like electric heaters. Although some are right next to the lodge restaurant and Mount Baldy Road, there is surpris-ingly little noise. The exception is when a band plays at the lodge; then you'll have to wait for them to quit before you can sleep. On the other hand, you could al-ways dance till you drop, then retire to your cozy cabin.

On the down side, there are no kitchens in the cabins, but you can get your meals at the lodge restaurant or at nearby Buckhorn Lodge. On the up side, you wake up in a mountain wonderland, just a half-hour from sprawling suburbs and smog, but so far away. In winter, you can drive up the hill to the Mount Baldy ski lift. If the mountain is snow-free, you can head for hiking adventures at nearby trailheads. An easy hike is the 1.7 miles (one-way) on Bear Canyon Trail from Mount Baldy Village to Bear Flats. A longer, more challenging trip is Icehouse Canyon Trail to Three T's Trail, where you can pay a visit to three peaks: Thunder, Timber, and Telegraph.

Facilities
There are six studio and one-bedroom cabins with a coffeemaker, a television, and a fireplace, but none have kitchen facilities. A restaurant is on-site. Linens and towels are provided.

Reservations and Rates
Reservations are recommended. Fees are $69–149 per night. Pets are not permitted. Contact Mount Baldy Lodge, P.O. Box 699, Mount Baldy, CA 91759, 909/982-1115, website: www.mtbaldylodge.com.

Directions
From I-10 at Ontario, exit on Mountain Avenue and drive north for six miles until Mountain Avenue joins Shinn Road. Bear left on Shinn Road and continue to Mount Baldy Road. Bear right and drive 5.5 miles north on Mount Baldy Road to Mount Baldy Village. Mount Baldy Lodge is on the right side of the road.

4 SNOWCREST LODGE
off I-10 on Mount Baldy

Luxury rating: ★ ★ ★ ☆ ☆   **Recreation rating:** ★ ★ ★ ★ ☆
Rank: Best for Winter Sports

Snowcrest Lodge is an authentic mountain lodge, with a café and bar that look exactly like a café and bar in the mountains should look. Various stuffed animal heads hang from the walls, including that of a very impressive moose. The stone fireplace is large enough to pitch a tent in. The dining room is immense and has an assortment of mismatched furniture. It's the kind of place where you would feel embarrassed wearing a suit and tie.

There are six cabins at Snowcrest, and the best ones are the larger cabins that come with kitchens. (Bring your own utensils, pots, and pans—none are provided.) If you're on a budget, the smaller cabins are cheaper, but you won't be able to cook. The large cabins are built of stone and are as cute as can be, while the small ones are duplexes and are a bit shabby. All of the cabins have big stone fireplaces, heaters, bathrooms, and comfortable beds.

The main reason people come to Snowcrest Lodge is because it's only a half mile from the Mount Baldy Ski Lift. You wake up in the morning, have some breakfast at the restaurant or make your own in your cabin, and then a few minutes later, you're on the chairlift. Sound easy? It is.

Another great activity for late winter and spring is hiking to San Antonio Falls, an 80-foot waterfall that drops in three tiers. The trailhead is only a quarter mile up the road from Snowcrest Lodge, so you can easily walk to it. The hike follows the ski lift–maintenance road gently uphill for three-quarters of a mile to a sharp curve in the road, where the big waterfall pours. The best time to see the fall is when the snow starts melting, usually in February or March.

Very fit hikers can continue past the waterfall for another six miles to the peak of Mount Baldy at 10,064 feet. This is one of the greatest hikes in all of Southern California, a 13-mile epic trip. If you go too early in the season, you'll need to carry ice axes and crampons; it's easier to wait until the snow is gone. Then the only requirements are full water bottles, some snacks, and plenty of energy. Views from the peak of Mount Baldy are extraordinary—a panorama of desert, city, ocean, and even the southern Sierra Nevada.

More tame activities abound on Mount Baldy. Kids love to visit the town's trout pools, where you pay a couple of bucks to toss a line in the water. No fishing license is required. Snowcrest Lodge has its own Olympic-sized swimming pool, great for lounging in the sun or playing in the water. In winter, some folks bring their trash-can lids or bodyboards up to the mountain and spend all day sledding down the hillsides.

Facilities

There are six cabins ranging in size from one to two bedrooms, some with kitchens and all with fireplaces, heat, and bathrooms. Cooking and eating utensils are not provided. A restaurant and pool are on-site. Linens and towels are provided.

Reservations and Rates

Reservations are recommended. Fees are $75–160 per night for two people, plus $10 for each additional person. A refundable cleaning deposit is required. Pets are not permitted. Contact Snowcrest Lodge, P.O. Box 383, Mount Baldy, CA 91759, 909/985-3012, website: www.snowcrest-lodge.com.

Directions

From I-10 at Ontario, exit on Mountain Avenue and drive north for six miles until Mountain Avenue joins Shinn Road. Bear left on Shinn Road and continue to Mount Baldy Road. Bear right and drive nine miles north on Mount Baldy Road, past Mount Baldy Village, to Snowcrest Lodge, on the left side of the road.

5 SLEEPY HOLLOW CABINS
off Highway 18 in Crestline

Luxury rating: ★ ★ ★ ☆ ☆   **Recreation rating: ★ ★ ★ ☆ ☆**

Sleepy Hollow Cabins are right in the middle of the main drag of Lake Gregory, next door to the bowling alley. Does this sound like a peaceful mountain retreat? Of course not. But Sleepy Hollow's affordable cabins are within a couple blocks of the lake's popular swimming beach, which makes it ideal for families who want to while away their days at Lake Gregory.

If you've never ridden a waterslide in your life, Lake Gregory is the place to do it. The lake is run by San Bernardino County and is much like a giant public pool. The waterslide is scarier than it looks—go feet-first the first time, not head-first. The lake's swimming beach has lifeguards, who make sure that everyone is out of the water at 5 P.M. each day. It seems too early in summer, but that's closing time at the lake.

© ANN MARIE BROWN

You can fish at Lake Gregory too. Rowboats are for rent, but most people fish from shore for brown trout in the winter and rainbow trout in the summer.

The cabins at Sleepy Hollow are basic but serviceable. All have full kitchens and microwaves; all except one have wood-burning fireplaces. They are clustered around the resort's heated, 20-foot by 40-foot pool. A communal picnic area with gas barbecues is also available. There isn't much about the cabins' concrete setting that seems like nature, but most guests don't seem to mind.

If you crave a little nature, it isn't hard to find. Take a drive west out to Highway 138, then head north to the small town of Valley of Enchantment. Just beyond it, turn left at the sign for Camp Seeley. A short and easy hike on the Seeley Creek Trail leads past giant conifers to beautiful Heart Rock Falls, where Mother Nature has carved a perfect heart-shaped bowl out of granite. The waterfall drops about 25 feet in springtime.

While you're in the neighborhood, you might want to drive up to Silverwood Lake, a huge waterskiing lake that makes Lake Gregory look like a tiny puddle. The lake covers more than 1,000 acres with 13 miles of shoreline, and it's popular with anglers as well as boaters.

Facilities
There are six one- and two-bedroom cabins that can accommodate up to six people, plus two suites and several motel rooms. All cabins have fully equipped kitchens. A pool and communal picnic area with gas barbecues are on-site. Linens and towels are provided.

Reservations and Rates
Reservations are recommended. Fees for cabins are $90–170 per night or $560–900 per week. Rooms and suites are less. Pets are not permitted. Contact Sleepy Hollow Cabins, P.O. Box 632, 24033 Lake Drive, Crestline, CA 92325, 909/338-2718 or 800/909-2718, website: www.theplacetorelax.com.

Directions
From I-10 near San Bernardino, take I-215 north five miles to Highway 30 east. Drive two miles east on Highway 30 and exit on Highway 18/Waterman Avenue. Drive north on Highway 18 for about 20 miles to the Lake Gregory/Twin Peaks turnoff (by the Cliffhanger Restaurant). Turn left on Lake Gregory Drive, then drive two miles to Lake Drive. Turn left; Sleepy Hollow Cabins is on the left.

6 ARROWHEAD PINE ROSE CABINS
off Highway 189 in Twin Peaks

Luxury rating: ★ ★ ★ ☆   **Recreation rating:** ★ ★ ★ ☆ ☆

© ANN MARIE BROWN

There are folks who are in the cabin business, and there are folks who are in the cabin business and know how to do it right. The folks who run Arrowhead Pine Rose Cabins fall into the latter category.

First, they have a great location: near Lakes Gregory, Silverwood, and Arrowhead, in the San Bernardino Mountains. Next, they do everything they can to make your stay extraordinary. Instead of just basic, cookie-cutter cabins and cottages, the owners have made Arrowhead Pine Rose Cabins into individual handcrafted masterpieces. Each one is different, although they all have kitchens and most have fireplaces.

I stayed in Rustic Romance, which has an open-beamed ceiling, a beautiful stone fireplace, and perfectly coordinated linens, rugs, lampshades, and hand-painted detailing on the walls. The centerpiece of the room is a whirlpool tub with a natural stone waterfall. If this sounds a bit too Las Vegas for you, let me emphasize that the overall effect is tasteful, subtle, and even rustic—not splashy.

On the porches outside the cabins are big willow chairs, where you can while away the hours watching the birds or reading a book. If you want more activity, you can swim in the heated outdoor pool or soak in the hot tub, which is shaped like an arrowhead!

If you can tear yourself away from Arrowhead Pine Rose Cabins, you'll want to take advantage of all the outdoor recreation in the area. In the winter, skiing at Snow Valley is a major draw. Ice-skating on the year-round rink in nearby Blue Jay (Ice Castle, 909/336-2111) is also popular.

Summer is the season for waterskiing, boating, and fishing on the area's lakes. Although many visitors are disappointed by the lack of public access to Lake Arrowhead, there are two good alternatives: big Lake Silverwood or little Lake Gregory. Silverwood is a huge reservoir that is popular for waterskiing, and Lake Gregory is a family-oriented place with swimming beaches, a waterslide, and rental boats. Trout fishing is good at both lakes.

Facilities
There are 17 cabins ranging in size from studios to seven-bedroom units. All have fully equipped kitchens, and most have a fireplace. A pool and hot tub are on-site. Linens and towels are provided.

Reservations and Rates
Reservations are recommended. Fees are $59–425 per night, with a two-night minimum on weekends. Pets are permitted in some cabins with prior approval. Contact Arrowhead Pine Rose Cabins, 25994 Highway 189, P.O. Box 31, Twin Peaks, CA 92391, 909/337-2341 or 800/429-7463, website: www.pinerose.com.

Directions
From I-10 near San Bernardino, take I-215 north five miles to Highway 30 east. Drive two miles east on Highway 30 and exit on Highway 18/Waterman Avenue. Drive north on Highway 18 for about 20 miles to the Lake Gregory/Twin Peaks turnoff (by the Cliffhanger Restaurant). Turn left, then turn right almost immediately on Highway 189. Take Highway 189 east for two miles to Twin Peaks. Arrowhead Pine Rose Cabins is on the left side of the road.

7 BRACKEN FERN MANOR
off Highway 18 near Lake Arrowhead

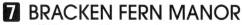

Luxury rating: ★ ★ ★ ★ ☆   **Recreation rating:** ★ ★ ★ ☆ ☆

Bracken Fern Manor was built in 1929 as a private gambling club for movie stars and mobsters in the Prohibition years. The boys who ran the place, including tough guy Bugsy Siegel, would lure aspiring movie actresses to staff the upstairs brothel, where the young women would have a chance to meet movie-industry heavies. No one is sure whether any of these women ever made it to the screen, but some of their letters were discovered when the inn was restored.

This fascinating historical landmark in Lake Arrowhead has one two-room cottage and 10 guest rooms. The cottage is alongside the manor but has its own separate parking and entrance. It has a fully equipped kitchen, a

fireplace, a whirlpool tub, a barbecue on the patio, and a television and VCR. If you stay in the
cottage, you won't be invited to
breakfast with the other manor
guests; be sure to bring groceries
so you can make your own.

The cottage and manor are
located only five minutes from
Lake Arrowhead Village and
all the services surrounding
the lake, including boat cruises and fishing tours. Hikers will want to explore the trails of San Bernardino National Forest; the Heaps Peak Arboretum Trail is only a few minutes from Bracken Fern Manor on
Highway 18. The .75-mile interpretive trail features 24 points of interest
about native plants and wildlife.

The best trail near Lake Arrowhead is the Pacific Crest Trail at Deep
Creek. Another popular option is the short but steep hike to Deep Creek
Hot Springs, where you can soak in one of several pools alongside the
creek. The Arrowhead Ranger District of San Bernardino National Forest
can provide you with maps and updated information.

Facilities

There is one two-room cottage that can accommodate up to four people,
plus 10 guest rooms. The cottage has a fully equipped kitchen, plus a fireplace, a hot tub, and a patio. Linens and towels are provided.

Reservations and Rates

Reservations are required. The fee for the cottage is $190 per night, with a
two-night minimum. Rooms are less. Pets are not permitted. Contact
Bracken Fern Manor, P.O. Box 1006, 815 Arrowhead Villas Road, Lake
Arrowhead, CA 92352, 909/337-8557 or 888/244-5612, website:
www.brackenfernmanor.com.

Directions

From I-10 near San Bernardino, take I-215 north five miles to Highway 30
east. Drive two miles east on Highway 30 and exit on Highway 18/Water-
man Avenue. Drive north on Highway 18 for about 25 miles to the Highway 173/Lake Arrowhead cutoff. Continue one mile beyond the Lake
Arrowhead cutoff to Arrowhead Villas Road on the left. Turn left and
drive two blocks to Bracken Fern Manor on the right.

8 SADDLEBACK INN
off Highway 173 in Lake Arrowhead

Luxury rating: ★ ★ ★ ★ ☆   **Recreation rating: ★ ★ ★ ★ ☆**

Lake Arrowhead is a tough nut to crack. The mile-high lake is undoubtedly one of Southern California's most beautiful bodies of water, yet gaining access to it is darn near impossible. Almost every inch of its shoreline is private property, neatly lined with the vacation homes of the ultrawealthy. Even though the lake is on public land in San Bernardino National Forest, the public has never felt welcome there.

That's why you should know about the cottages at Saddleback Inn. Located in the town of Lake Arrowhead, the Saddleback Inn's cottages are your chance to get close to Lake Arrowhead. Lakefront they are not, but around here, "lake-near" is as good as it gets.

When you drive up, Saddleback Inn looks like a nice, old-style hotel on a busy street. What isn't obvious is that behind the main building are nearly a dozen cottages tucked into the conifers. They are mostly one-bedrooms; many have luxuries like whirlpool tubs and gas fireplaces. My favorites are Nos. 24 and 36 (named Sooner and Maple Leaf); they are the most private. The Saddleback Inn also has two- and three-bedroom suites that sleep up to seven people.

How you spend your time at Lake Arrowhead depends on what season it is. In winter, the main attraction is downhill skiing and snowboarding at nearby Snow Valley Ski Resort, in Running Springs. If Snow Valley's runs aren't treacherous enough for you, you can drive a few miles farther east to Big Bear Lake's two ski areas. The neighboring town of Blue Jay has a year-round ice-skating rink where hopeful Olympians and wobbly-ankled skaters glide away the hours (Ice Castle, 909/336-2111).

In summer, most vacationers want to get out on Lake Arrowhead. The only way to do so is on a commercial tour, unless you know somebody who lives on the lake. (No public boat launching is permitted.) Fishing and waterskiing tours are available. Or you can take a cruise on the *Arrowhead Queen,* a

© ANN MARIE BROWN

60-seat paddle wheeler, out of the shopping area known as Lake Arrowhead Village.

Facilities
There are eight one-bedroom cottages, plus 26 rooms and suites. None of the cottages have kitchens; some have whirlpool tubs and fireplaces. A restaurant is on-site. Linens and towels are provided.

Reservations and Rates
Reservations are recommended. Fees are $115–199 per night on weekdays and $135–299 per night on weekends and holidays. Pets are not permitted. Contact Saddleback Inn, P.O. Box 1890, 300 South State Highway 173, Lake Arrowhead, CA 92352, 909/336-3571 or 800/858-3334, website: www.saddlebackinn.com.

Directions
From I-10 near San Bernardino, take I-215 north five miles to Highway 30 east. Drive two miles east on Highway 30 and exit on Highway 18/Waterman Avenue. Drive north on Highway 18 for about 25 miles to the Highway 173/Lake Arrowhead cutoff on the left. Drive two miles to Lake Arrowhead Village and Saddleback Inn on the right.

9 GIANT OAKS LODGE
off Highway 330 in Running Springs

Luxury rating: ★ ★ ★ ★ ☆   **Recreation rating:** ★ ★ ★ ☆ ☆
Rank: Best for Winter Sports

There is one primary reason that people come to stay at Giant Oaks Lodge, and that's to ski at Snow Valley Ski Resort. The ski area is a mere five miles from Giant Oaks, and Giant Oaks is a mere half-hour from San Bernardino. Add it up, and you have an easy trip to the mountains for a weekend of fun in the snow.

With a base elevation of 6,800 feet, Snow Valley provides consistent white stuff from Thanksgiving through Easter for skiers and snowboarders. The emphasis is on families and beginners, with plenty of learn-to-ski packages. In summer, Snow Valley leads another life—it transforms into a skateboard park with organized camps and classes for kids.

In any season, the cabins at Giant Oaks are a fine place to stay. All are beautifully decorated, and many have mountain views. Surrounded by oaks, cedars, and pines, the cabins are mostly protected from road noise on nearby Highway 18. One "family-friendly cabin" has a full kitchen and stone fireplace; it's large enough for six people. Cabin No. 4 is the most romantic; it has a spa tub

© ANN MARIE BROWN

for two in a rock setting with a fireplace, plus a shower for two. Giant Oaks' smaller cabins do not have kitchens, but they do have fireplaces and spas. Each unit has a television (with HBO) and a telephone. An indoor heated pool and spa are available, and they are a welcome sight after a day on the slopes.

Facilities
There are three cabins that can accommodate up to six people, plus 10 rooms and suites. One cabin has a fully equipped kitchen; the rest have microwaves, refrigerators, and coffeemakers. Some have fireplaces and hot tubs. A pool and spa are on-site. Linens and towels are provided.

Reservations and Rates
Reservations are recommended. Fees are $129–239 per night for cabins and $59–109 for rooms. Pets are not permitted in the cabins, but they are permitted in some rooms for a $25 fee per night. Contact Giant Oaks Lodge, 32180 Highway 18, Running Springs, CA 92382, 909/867-2231 or 800/786-1689, website: www.runningsprings.com.

Directions
From I-10 at Redlands, drive north on Highway 30 for five miles to the Highway 330 exit. Drive north on Highway 330 for 13 miles to Running Springs, at the junction with Highway 18. Giant Oaks Lodge is on the left.

Other Cabins and Cottages Nearby
Rainbow View Lodge, 2726 View Drive, P.O. Box 1084, Running Springs, CA 92382, 909/867-1810, website: www.rainbowviewlodge.com.

10 GREEN VALLEY LAKE COZY CABINS

off Highway 18 near Green Valley Lake

Luxury rating: ★ ★ ★ ★ ☆   **Recreation rating:** ★ ★ ★ ★ ☆

Rank: Best Value

One of the best reasons to spend a cabin vacation at Green Valley Lake is that most other people will be somewhere else. Sure, the scenery is pretty, the lake has good fishing, and there are miles of trails to explore in San Bernardino National Forest. But that's true of many places in the nearby area, most notably Big Bear Lake and Arrowhead Lake. The difference is that the masses are assembled at those places; it's just you and a few others at Green Valley Lake.

The lake and the town are at 7,200 feet, midway between Big Bear and Arrowhead in the San Bernardino Mountains. The important elements are in place: cool mountain air; big conifers; a pretty lake for fishing, swimming, and kayaking; and more than 50 rental cabins to choose from. The cabins are privately owned, and Green Valley Lake Cozy Cabins manages them. Because they are private homes, they have many amenities: fully equipped kitchens, fireplaces or wood-burning stoves, televisions, stereos, microwaves, coffeemakers, and so on. Blankets and pillows are provided in each cabin, but bring your own sheets, pillowcases, and towels, as well as paper products like toilet paper and paper towels.

The cabins vary from one-bedroom bungalows in the forest to five-bedroom minimansions on the small lake. Most people stay for a week; the fee for seven nights is a real bargain, at less than $500 for a cabin that sleeps four to six people.

After you arrive at Green Valley Lake, take your pick from a huge selection of outdoor activities. In winter, the Green Valley Cross Country Ski

Area is open down the road by Green Valley Campground. The most advanced trail leads 10 miles one-way to Fawnskin at Big Bear Lake. Also available is a small, family-run ski and snow-play area just up the road from the lake.

In summer, anglers rent rowboats and row around the edges of Green Valley Lake, or fish with bait from the shoreline. Trout are planted regularly in spring and summer. No motorized boats are allowed on the small lake, so it is always quiet and serene. Plenty of swimmers access the lake as well.

Hikers can find a few short trails near Green Valley Campground, or they can drive down Camp Road and Meadow Lane to the Little Green Valley YMCA Camp. From there, hike the Little Green Valley Trail into Snow Valley. The trail is four miles one-way and nearly flat, and it passes some large and glorious stands of big pines and cedars.

Facilities
There are 55 vacation rental cabins ranging in size from one to five bedrooms, all with fully equipped kitchens. All feature modern amenities. Linens and towels are not provided.

Reservations and Rates
Reservations are required. Fees are $150–395 per night; a two-night minimum is required. Weekly rates are discounted. A $200 refundable cleaning deposit is required. Pets are permitted in some cabins with prior approval. Contact Green Valley Lake Cozy Cabins, 33231 Green Valley Lake Road, Green Valley Lake, CA 92341, 909/867-5335, website: www.mountaininfo.com/cozy.

Directions
From I-10 at Redlands, drive north on Highway 30 for five miles to the Highway 330 exit. Drive north on Highway 330 for 13 miles to Running Springs. Turn east on Highway 18 and drive four miles to Green Valley Lake Road. Turn north on Green Valley Lake Road and drive three miles. The rental office is located at 33231 Green Valley Lake Road; check in there to get keys and directions to your cabin.

11 QUAIL COVE LODGE
off Highway 38 in Big Bear

Luxury rating: ★ ★ ★ ☆ ☆   **Recreation rating:** ★ ★ ★ ★ ☆

Quail Cove Lodge has a lot going for it, but probably the best thing is its location: on the far edge of Big Bear Lake, in the small town of Fawnskin, not the big town of Big Bear Lake. On weekends, it can be difficult to find a quiet spot in Big Bear Lake, but Fawnskin is always quiet. From your

© ANN MARIE BROWN

Quail Cove cabin, the only sound you'll hear is the lake lapping near your doorstep.

Two of the lodge's cabins are so close to the lake that you could cast a line out your bedroom window. If you really want a lakeside vacation, reserve cabin No. 1 or 2. Both are studios that sleep only two people and have a full kitchen, a fireplace, and a queen bed. Cabin No. 2 has the prettiest view, both of the lake and the ski slopes. If you have a larger party, reserve cabin No. 6, which has three bedrooms, a fireplace, a big dining room table, and a dishwasher. You can do all your own cooking in your fully equipped kitchen, or you can head for the multitude of restaurants in Big Bear.

Luckily for mountain bikers, Quail Cove is right across the highway from the Grout Bay trailhead. The dirt roads leading to Butler Peak Lookout make a great 14-mile round-trip bike ride, with terrific views from the 8,400-foot peak. For hikers, Castle Rock Trail is close by, as is the uphill romp to Bertha Peak on the Cougar Crest Trail.

Anglers can fish right from the cabin property by casting or bait-dunking in the lake or the creek, or they can rent a motorboat at Gray's Landing, only a half mile away. In addition to fishing boats, you can also rent personal watercrafts, waterskiing boats, and the like.

Facilities

There are six cabins ranging in size from studios to three bedrooms, all with fully equipped kitchens. Linens and towels are provided.

Reservations and Rates

Reservations are recommended. Fees are $99–289 per night. Pets are permitted with a $20 fee per night. Contact Quail Cove Lodge, P.O. Box 117, 39117 North Shore Drive, Fawnskin, CA 92333, 800/595-2683, website: www.quailcove.com.

Directions

From I-10 at Redlands, drive north on Highway 30 for five miles to the Highway 330 exit. Drive north on Highway 330 for 13 miles to Running Springs. Turn east on Highway 18 and drive 14 miles to the Highway 38 fork at Big Bear Lake. Bear left on Highway 38 (Northshore Drive) and drive three miles to Quail Cove Lodge on the right side of the road.

Other Cabins and Cottages Nearby

Creek Runner's Lodge, 374 Georgia Street, P.O. Box 58, Big Bear Lake, CA 92315, 909/866-7473, website: www.pineknot.com/creekrunner.

Timberline Lodge, 39921 Big Bear Boulevard, P.O. Box 1955, Big Bear Lake, CA 92315, 909/866-4141 or 800/803-4111, website: www.thetimber-linelodge.com.

Cienaga Creek Ranch, 43630 Rainbow Lane, Big Bear Lake, CA 92315, 888/336-2891, website: www.allbigbear.com.

12 SHORE ACRES LODGE
off Highway 18 in Big Bear

Luxury rating: ★ ★ ★ ☆ ☆   **Recreation rating:** ★ ★ ★ ★ ☆

Rank: Best for Boating & Water Sports

There are so many lodging options at Big Bear Lake, including hundreds of cabins, that it's hard to know which is the best place to stay. One place I endorse wholeheartedly is Shore Acres Lodge, particularly for families visiting Big Bear Lake.

Shore Acres Lodge rents 11 cabins on its premises, but it also manages a huge list of private vacation homes in the nearby area. If you rent one of the latter, you still get full use of the resort's facilities, but you're away from the hubbub of the lodge. At Shore Acres, you get to choose the kind of vacation experience you want.

The 11 cabins on-site are cozy and comfortable. Although they are nestled in tall pine trees, many have lake views. A few are literally steps from the lake. All have fully equipped kitchens and barbecues on their decks, and most have fireplaces. A pool and spa are available, as are a children's playground and a private boat dock.

Fishing is excellent at Lagunita Point and Gibraltar Point, a few hundred yards from the lodge. Many people simply drop in a line from shore, but the best success is to be had by trolling. You can rent boats at nearby Holloway's Marina. A full list of water-recreation activities are possible at Big Bear Lake, from sailing to personal watercraft riding to swimming.

If you can leave your beach chair at the lake's edge for an afternoon, several excellent hiking trails are nearby. On the north shore, one of the best trails starts .5 mile west of the Big Bear Discovery Center on Highway 38. Cougar Crest Trail climbs two miles to a junction with the Pacific Crest Trail. Head east (right) for .5 mile to the summit of Bertha Peak, elevation 8,502 feet. The peak is covered with transmitter towers, but these don't take away from the glorious view of Bear Valley, Holcomb Valley, and the Mojave Desert.

In the same neighborhood, the paved Alpine Pedal Path starts at the Big Bear Discovery Center, heads through a tunnel under Highway 38, and then follows the sparkling lakeshore for nearly three miles. This makes a perfect easy bike ride or hike for families.

Facilities
There are 11 cabins and dozens of private vacation rentals ranging in size from one to five bedrooms. All have fully equipped kitchens. The cabins have a deck with a barbecue, and most have a fireplace. A pool, a spa, a children's playground, and a private boat dock are available. Linens and towels are provided.

Reservations and Rates
Reservations are recommended. Fees are $110–250 per night. Pets are permitted with a $10 fee per night. Contact Shore Acres Lodge, 41693 Big Bear Boulevard, P.O. Box 110410, Big Bear, CA 92315, 909/866-1580 or 800/524-6600, website: www.shoreacreslodge.com.

Directions
From I-10 at Redlands, drive north on Highway 30 for five miles to the Highway 330 exit. Drive north on Highway 330 for 13 miles to Running Springs. Turn east on Highway 18 and drive 14 miles to the Highway 38 fork at Big Bear Lake. Stay right on Highway 18 and continue 3.5 miles. Turn left on Lakeview Drive and drive .75 mile to Shore Acres Lodge.

Other Cabins and Cottages Nearby
Pine Knot Guest Ranch, 908 Pine Knot Avenue, P.O. Box 3446, Big Bear Lake, CA 92315, 909/866-6500 or 800/866-3446, website: www.pine-knotguestranch.com.

Big Bear Frontier Lodge, 40472 Big Bear Boulevard, Big Bear Lake, CA 92315, 800/457-6401, website: www.bigbearfrontier.com.

🔟🔢 WILDWOOD RESORT
off Highway 18 in Big Bear

Luxury rating: ★ ★ ★ ☆ ☆   **Recreation rating:** ★ ★ ★ ★ ☆

The cabins at Wildwood Resort have something you rarely get in a rental cabin—space. I rented a studio cabin but found it had more square footage than most one-bedrooms. The full kitchen had a large dining table, the bed was king-size, and the big fireplace made the whole place warm and cozy. I was also surprised to find a coffeemaker, a microwave, and a toaster in addition to the usual pots, pans, and dishes in the kitchen.

The owners of Wildwood Resort run a tight and tidy ship. The outdoor pool and whirlpool tub are well cared for, and flowers are planted around the cabins in summer. Most people never see the blossoms, however, because most people come to Big Bear in the middle of winter. Skiing and snowboarding top the recreation list, with two large resorts just outside of town: Bear Mountain and Snow Summit. More atypical snow activities include the Alpine Slide at Magic Mountain, where you can go inner tubing down a ski hill or try out the bobsled track. Cross-country skiing and snowshoeing are also popular.

Summer rates are much lower than winter rates at Wildwood, so don't neglect a warm-weather visit. In summer, Snow Summit ski resort turns into a mountain bike park. (You ride the ski lift uphill, then fly downhill like a maniac; it's fun.) Bike rentals are available. If you want to get out on the water, you can take a dinner or brunch cruise on Big Bear Lake

aboard the *Big Bear Queen,* or you can rent your own boat at one of the lake's marinas. Fishing is excellent in Big Bear Lake; the best results come from trolling.

Miles of hiking trails exist in San Bernardino National Forest, some beginning right at the lake's edge. Waterskiing, personal watercraft riding, and windsurfing are all possible on the lake, and several marinas rent equipment and even provide lessons. Then there are the tamer pursuits, like golf and tennis, but who has time for the tamer pursuits?

Facilities
There are 32 cabins ranging in size from studios to two bedrooms, all with fully equipped kitchens. An outdoor pool and a hot tub are on-site. Linens and towels are provided.

Reservations and Rates
Reservations are recommended. Fees are $100–270 per night. Summer rates and weekdays are discounted. Pets are not permitted. Contact Wildwood Resort, 40210 Big Bear Boulevard, P.O. Box 2885, Big Bear Lake, CA 92315, 909/878-2178 or 888/294-5396, website: www.wildwood-resort.com.

Directions
From I-10 at Redlands, drive north on Highway 30 for five miles to the Highway 330 exit. Drive north on Highway 330 for 13 miles to Running Springs. Turn east on Highway 18 and drive 14 miles to the Highway 38 fork at Big Bear Lake. Stay right on Highway 18/Big Bear Boulevard and continue three miles to the village of Big Bear Lake. Wildwood Resort is on the left side of the road.

Other Cabins and Cottages Nearby
Big Bear Mountain Resort Rentals, 40729 Village Drive, Big Bear Lake, CA 92315, 909/878-2233.

Boulder Creek Resort, P.O. Box 92, Big Bear Lake, CA 92315, 909/866-2665 or 800/966-9971, website: www.bigbearmountainrentals.com.

Grey Squirrel Resort, 39372 Big Bear Boulevard, P.O. Box 1711, Big Bear Lake, CA 92315, 909/866-4335 or 800/381-5569, website: www.greysquirrel.com.

14 BEAR MANOR CABINS AND LAKEVIEW LODGE
off Highway 18 in Big Bear

Luxury rating: ★ ★ ★ ★ ☆   **Recreation rating: ★ ★ ★ ☆ ☆**

If you are new to Big Bear, you might feel a little put off when you see that almost everything in the town has the word "bear" worked into its title. The cabins at Bear Manor are no exception, but you'll quickly get over the annoying cuteness of their moniker when you see how nice your accommodations are, and how much fun awaits in Big Bear.

Boulder Bay at Big Bear Lake

© ANN MARIE BROWN

Bear Manor Cabins and Lakeview Lodge are run by the same folks. Both have one major element in common: hot tubs in every unit. Otherwise, they're different. Bear Manor Cabins are made for two people and are older in style, with knotty-pine interiors, fireplaces, and small kitchenettes (some have gas cook tops and convection ovens; all have microwaves, refrigerators, toasters, and coffeemakers). If you're a larger group, you'll stay at Lakeview Lodge's cabins or townhouses, which can sleep 4 to 10 people. In addition to the ubiquitous hot tubs, Lakeview Lodge's units have full kitchens, fireplaces, and two or three bedrooms.

Big Bear is best known for skiing in winter and for water sports in summer, but don't miss out on the excellent hiking trails that start at or near the lake. Off Mill Creek Road on the south shore, an easy half-mile trail leads to the Champion Lodgepole Pine, a 400-year-old tree with a circumference of 20 feet. It stands 112 feet tall, and because it's a lodgepole, it's the straightest 112 feet of lumber you'll ever see. If you show up in early summer, check out the wildflowers in the adjacent meadow.

From the same trailhead, the Siberia Creek Trail parallels trickling Siberia Creek for 1.5 miles until it reaches The Gunsight, a granite rock formation that looks like its name. A more challenging trail leads to Castle Rock from a turn in the highway near the lake's Boulder Bay. A short but steep climb through granite boulders and ponderosa pines brings you to increasingly larger boulders, the largest of which is Castle

Rock. As you climb, keep turning around to check out the views of Big Bear Lake. The view from the top is breathtaking.

Facilities
There are six cabins that can accommodate two people, plus eight larger cabins and townhouses that can accommodate up to 10 people. The two-person cabins have kitchenettes; the larger cabins have full kitchens. Linens and towels are provided.

Reservations and Rates
Reservations are recommended. Fees are $89–269 per night; weekdays are discounted. Pets are not permitted. Contact Bear Manor Cabins and Lakeview Lodge, 40393 Big Bear Boulevard, P.O. Box 3874, Big Bear Lake, CA 92315, 909/866-6800 or 800/472-2327, website: www.bigbearlakecabins.com.

Directions
From I-10 at Redlands, drive north on Highway 30 for five miles to the Highway 330 exit. Drive north on Highway 330 for 13 miles to Running Springs. Turn east on Highway 18 and drive 14 miles to the Highway 38 fork at Big Bear Lake. Stay right on Highway 18/Big Bear Boulevard and continue three miles to Bear Manor Cabins on the right.

Other Cabins and Cottages Nearby
Cal-Pine Chalets, 41545 Big Bear Boulevard, Big Bear Lake, CA 92315, 909/866-2574 or 800/965-7463, website: www.cal-pine.com.

🔢15 CASTLEWOOD THEME COTTAGES
off Highway 18 in Big Bear

Luxury rating: ★ ★ ★ ☆   **Recreation rating:** ★ ★ ★ ☆
Rank: Most Unusual

Castlewood is far and away the most unique and creative place to stay in Big Bear. If you're the kind of person who enjoys a little whimsy and who wants to stay somewhere that is the antithesis of an ordinary motel room or plain cabin, Castlewood will tickle your fancy.

Each of Castlewood's 11 cabins is elaborately decorated around a theme. What theme, you ask? Well, the King Arthur cabin looks like a chamber in a medieval castle, with fake stone, velvet drapes, stained glass, and a coat of arms over the fireplace. King Arthur and Guinevere costumes hang on the wall. The Gone with the Wind cabin is a miniature two-story Southern mansion, with Vivian Leigh's portrait over the mantle and two of Scarlet's dresses and Rhett's hat and cane hanging in the closet. The cabin has a massive television

© ANN MARIE BROWN

set with surround sound and a video of . . . well, you know.

The Captain's Quarters cabin features a treasure chest spilling out gold and jewels. A hatch in the floor opens to display the skeleton of a pirate. You'll hear his voice calling "Yo ho ho!" The Enchanted Forest cabin is one of the most elaborate: It's three levels, with a canopy of trees and a grotto in the lower level with a waterfall hot tub. Forest sounds play from hidden speakers.

Then there are the Crystal Cave and Antony and Cleopatra cabins. And yet another, my favorite, The Castle Garden, which includes a talking suit of armor (he tells dragon stories).

Perhaps the best thing about this quirky resort is that the exteriors of the small cabins belie their interiors. From the outside, they look like typical Big Bear Bavarian-style cabins, perhaps a little tidier and better painted than most. So a wonderful surprise awaits when you step inside the door.

Whatever their theme, all of the cottages have whirlpool tubs and fireplaces, televisions and VCRs, coffeemakers, microwaves, and small refrigerators. And because they are a few blocks off Big Bear Boulevard, Big Bear's full array of recreation options are within easy reach. But then again, it's quite possible that these cottages will keep you so entertained that you'll never step outside your door.

Facilities

There are 11 one-bedroom cottages that can accommodate two people. None of the cottages have kitchens, but they do have whirlpool tubs, fireplaces, televisions and VCRs, coffeemakers, microwaves, and small refrigerators. Linens and towels are provided.

Reservations and Rates

Reservations are recommended. Fees are $69–209 per night; holiday rates are higher. A two-night minimum is required on weekends. Pets are not permitted. Contact Castlewood Theme Cottages, 547 Main Street, P.O.

Box 1756, Big Bear Lake, CA 92315, 909/866-2720, website: www.castle-woodcottages.com.

Directions

From I-10 at Redlands, drive north on Highway 30 for five miles to the Highway 330 exit. Drive north on Highway 330 for 13 miles to Running Springs. Turn east on Highway 18 and drive 14 miles to the Highway 38 fork at Big Bear Lake. Stay right on Highway 18/Big Bear Boulevard and continue five miles, past the village of Big Bear Lake, to Main Street. Turn right and drive .25 mile; Castlewood is on the left.

Other Cabins and Cottages Nearby

Black Forest Lodge, 41121 Big Bear Boulevard, Big Bear Lake, CA 92315, 909/866-2166, website: www.blackforestlodge.com.

Goldmine Lodge, 42268 Moonridge Road, P.O. Box 198, Big Bear Lake, CA 92315, 800/641-2327, website: www.bigbear-goldmine-lodge.com.

Log Cabin Resort Rentals, 39976 Big Bear Boulevard, Big Bear Lake, CA 92315, 909/866-8708 or 800/767-0205, website: www.logcabinresorts.com.

16 OUR SECRET GARDEN MOUNTAIN RETREAT
off Highway 18 in Big Bear

Luxury rating: ★ ★ ★ ★ ☆   **Recreation rating:** ★ ★ ★ ★ ☆

Rank: Best for Winter Sports

Our Secret Garden is unlike any of the other cabin resorts in Big Bear. It's outside of town and away from the lake by about a mile. It's situated in a peaceful residential neighborhood, far from the weekend hustle and bustle of Big Bear. And its adorable white cabins are clustered around colorful summer gardens. Even their interiors reflect a garden theme—each one is focused around a different flower: roses, sunflowers, tulips, and lilacs.

The four cabins at Our Secret Garden are sized for two, with all of the standard amenities for romance: fireplaces, hot tubs, and comfortable robes. One cottage, Sunflower, has a fully equipped kitchen; the rest have refrigerators and microwaves.

Ski enthusiasts will enjoy the fact that Our Secret Garden is only min-

utes from the slopes of Snow
Summit and Bear Mountain.
With more than 120 inches of
annual snowfall and extensive
snowmaking systems, both ski
resorts provide a multitude of
skiing and snowboarding options. Combined, their two
areas offer more than 20 chairlifts and 500 groomed acres.
The owners of Our Secret Gar-

den will show you their secret back way to get to the lifts.

Even though you are outside of town at Our Secret Garden, you are
still close enough to walk to restaurants, shopping, and the lake. Pine
Knot Landing is less than .5 mile away, where you can rent boats and
stock up on fishing supplies in summer. Big Bear is filled with trout, bass,
and catfish, and anglers share the waters with sailboats, personal watercrafts, and water-skiers.

Facilities
There are four one-bedroom cabins that can accommodate two people. All
have a fireplace and hot tub. One cabin has a fully equipped kitchen.
Linens and towels are provided.

Reservations and Rates
Reservations are recommended. Fees are $119–179 per night. Pets are not
permitted. Contact Our Secret Garden Mountain Retreat, 784 Berkley
Lane, Big Bear Lake, CA 92315, 909/866-0966, website: www.bigbear-
secretgarden.com.

Directions
From I-10 at Redlands, drive north on Highway 30 for five miles to the
Highway 330 exit. Drive north on Highway 330 for 13 miles to Running
Springs. Turn east on Highway 18 and drive 14 miles to the Highway 38
fork at Big Bear Lake. Stay right on Highway 18/Big Bear Boulevard and
continue three miles to the village of Big Bear Lake. Bear right on Village
Drive, then stay on Village Drive as it curves around and turns into Penn-
sylvania Drive. Turn right on Marin Drive then left on Berkley Lane.

Other Cabins and Cottages Nearby
Golden Bear Cottages, 39367 Big Bear Boulevard, Big Bear Lake, CA
   92315, 909/866-2010 or 800/461-1023, website: www.goldenbear.net.

Lakeview Forest Resort, 40715 Lakeview Drive, P.O. Box 1976, Big Bear Lake, CA 92315, 909/866-8686 or 800/211-1085, website: www.bigbearparadise.com.

17 SEVEN OAKS MOUNTAIN CABINS
off Highway 38 near Angelus Oaks

Luxury rating: ★ ★ ☆ ☆ ☆   **Recreation rating:** ★ ★ ★ ★ ☆

Rank: Most Secluded

© ANN MARIE BROWN

Everybody in Southern California knows about Big Bear Lake, and almost everybody in Southern California knows about the nearby Falls Recreation Area, where Big Falls tumbles down the mountainside. But in between those two stellar destinations is a place that almost nobody knows about—Seven Oaks Mountain Cabins.

Seven Oaks Mountain Cabins are hidden three miles off the main highway. You don't find them by accident. The resort has only six small, rustic cabins (you could barely squeeze in a family of five). They have fully equipped kitchens, but otherwise they are bare bones: no phones or television sets, no fancy decor. There's nothing else on the stretch of road surrounding Seven Oaks, so if you want nightlife, you're going to have to make your own. Pack along the Yahtzee game.

Of course, who cares about nightlife when you have a complete array of national forest adventures to look forward to? The Santa Ana River runs right through Seven Oaks' grounds and provides excellent stream fishing prospects. The river is typically about 10 to 15 feet across and a foot deep—a perfect fishing creek. It is stocked with rainbow trout every other week in spring and summer. A few of the cabins overlook the river; make sure you request one of them.

Those who love to fish can also head for little Jenks Lake, which is pretty year-round but is especially scenic in early spring, when the surrounding mountains are snow-covered. The biggest peak you see is

Mount San Gorgonio, which at 11,490 feet is the tallest mountain in Southern California. Jenks Lake isn't stocked until May each year, but it's worth visiting any time.

Be sure to check out the numerous hiking and mountain biking trails in the area. If you aren't up for the 14-mile round-trip to the top of Mount San Gorgonio on the Vivian Creek Trail, you can find plenty of shorter options nearby. Don't miss the Ponderosa Vista Nature Trail and the Whispering Pines Trail, which are conveniently located right across the highway from each other. You can walk both of them in just over an hour while getting a good lesson in the natural and human history of the area.

If you're not feeling ambitious, you can always just hang out at the lodge at Seven Oaks. It's not the slightest bit fancy, but it's the kind of place where you can play pool or table tennis and exchange a few stories with the lodge owners, who are really nice people.

Facilities
There are six one-bedroom cabins, all with fully equipped kitchens. Linens and towels are provided.

Reservations and Rates
Reservations are recommended. The fee is $70–75 per night for two people, plus $5 for each additional person (up to five). Pets are permitted with a $5 fee per night. Contact Seven Oaks Mountain Cabins, 40700 Seven Oaks Road, Angelus Oaks, CA 92305, 909/794-1277.

Directions
From I-10 just west of Redlands, take the Highway 38 exit. Drive 25 miles on Highway 38 to Angelus Oaks, then continue six more miles to Glass Road. Turn left and drive three miles (keep to the left at all junctions). Seven Oaks is on the right side of the road.

18 THE LODGE AT ANGELUS OAKS
off Highway 38 in Angelus Oaks

Luxury rating: ★ ★ ☆ ☆ ☆   **Recreation rating:** ★ ★ ★ ★ ☆

The cabins at The Lodge at Angelus Oaks are the embodiment of rustic and cozy. This is the kind of vacation place that makes you want to say good-bye to civilized life forever. For starters, they have a first-rate location on the Rim of the World Highway, halfway between Big Bear Lake and the Falls Recreation Area. Two of San Bernardino National Forest's premier recreation spots are within a few minutes' drive of your cabin, but you're not stuck in the middle of town with a whole bunch of tourists.

The possibilities for outdoor adventures are endless and change with each passing season. In winter, the snow usually falls thick and fast for at least a few weeks, which opens up possibilities for snow play. In spring, summer, and fall, hiking is spectacular in the national forest and San Gorgonio Wilderness. Trails range from very easy ones for families—like the half-mile walk to Big Falls, Southern California's largest year-round waterfall—to very difficult ones, like the 14-mile round-trip ascent of 11,490-foot Mount San Gorgonio, Southern California's tallest peak.

Families can enjoy a fishing trip to nearby Jenks Lake, where they can stand on the shoreline and cast for stocked trout. Experienced anglers can drive down the Middle Control Road from Angelus Oaks to Forest Service Road 1N09. From there, they can access Bear Creek, a wild-trout area on a tributary stream to the Santa Ana River. The limit is two fish, with a minimum length of eight inches. Only artificial lures or flies with barbless hooks can be used in Bear Creek.

However you decide to spend your days, you'll end each one by returning home to your Angelus Oaks cabin. The cabins are minimalist, and the paint's peeling, but hey, this is the mountains. You can make dinner in your cabin's kitchen, barbecue outside, or just head for the restaurant a mile down the road. Evenings can be spent in the main lodge, playing pool, listening to somebody play the lodge's organ, or looking through the telescope at the stars. I found the main lodge to be so cozy—like an old Canadian hunting lodge right out of a movie set—that I spent almost every evening there, playing board games in front of the fire.

Facilities

There are eight cabins that can accommodate up to six people. All cabins have fully equipped kitchens. The lodge has a fireplace and a pool table. Linens and towels are provided.

Reservations and Rates

Reservations are recommended. Fees are $70–90 per night. Pets are permitted with prior approval and with a $10 fee per night. Contact The Lodge at Angelus Oaks, 37825 Highway 38, Angelus Oaks, CA 92305, 909/794-9523, website: www.angelusoakslodge.com.

Directions

From I-10 just west of Redlands, take the Highway 38 exit. Drive 25 miles on Highway 38 to Angelus Oaks. The Lodge at Angelus Oaks is on the right side of the road.

19 WHISPERING PINES
off Highway 38 in Angelus Oaks

Luxury rating: ★ ★ ★ ☆ ☆   **Recreation rating:** ★ ★ ★ ★ ☆

Whispering Pines is a set of cheerful red cabins right off Highway 38, the Rim of the World Scenic Byway. It's in the town of Angelus Oaks at 6,000 feet in elevation—the first town you reach when driving into the mountains from the Los Angeles basin.

The five cabins at Whispering Pines can be configured according to how large your party is. Four of them are duplexes with interior doors that open to become single units; the fifth unit is a single unit. If you are traveling with your family, you'll be all set here, and you'll be able to close the doors when your kids stay up giggling all night.

New owners took over at Whispering Pines in 2002, and they are doing their best to keep the place in the same good condition it has always been. A couple things haven't changed one bit: The wonderful pine trees surrounding the cabins, and the marauding bears who patrol the area at night searching for untethered garbage cans. Another element that hasn't changed is Whispering Pines' wonderful location, a few miles from the Big Falls Recreation Area and San Gor-

© ANN MARIE BROWN

gonio Wilderness. Hikers have their pick of trails; first on my list is a visit to Big Falls, Southern California's largest year-round waterfall at more than 500 feet. It's most impressive in springtime, shortly after snowmelt.

In winter, you can bring your sleds and snowman-making supplies to the snow-play areas around Angelus Oaks or Big Falls, then let loose. In mid-summer, the Big Falls area is excellent for blackberry picking. Fill up your berry baskets and then go bake a pie in your Whispering Pines kitchen.

Right off Highway 38, the South Fork, Forsee Creek, and Aspen Grove trailheads (all near Jenks Lake) head into the San Gorgonio Wilderness. In summer or autumn, be sure to walk at least the first section of the Aspen Grove Trail, which leads to one of a very few aspen groves found this far south in California. The drive to the trailhead alone is worth the trip; it provides fabulous views of the surrounding mountains and valleys.

Facilities

There are five cabins that can accommodate up to six people. Some cabins have fully equipped kitchens. Linens and towels are provided.

Reservations and Rates

Reservations are recommended. Fees are $60–110 per night. Pets are not permitted. Contact Whispering Pines, P.O. Box 237, 5850 Manzanita Avenue, Highway 38, Angelus Oaks, CA 92305, 909/794-9644.

Directions

From I-10 just west of Redlands, take the Highway 38 exit. Drive 25 miles on Highway 38 to Angelus Oaks. Turn right at the fire station sign; Whispering Pines is a few yards off Highway 38. If you reach the Lodge at Angelus Oaks, you've passed it.

20 TWO HARBORS CABINS
Two Harbors, Catalina Island

Luxury rating: ★ ★ ☆ ☆ ☆   **Recreation rating:** ★ ★ ★ ★ ☆
Rank: Best Value

If you study the ways of Southern California vacationers, you find that in the winter months, most people head to the mountains to ski. The rest stay home. This is a puzzling phenomenon, since the finest days at the Southern California coast often occur in winter, creating perfect vacation conditions. Nonetheless, from October to March, long stretches of Southern California sand do not have a single human footprint set upon them.

If the beaches seem empty along the mainland in winter, you should see what it's like at Two Harbors on Catalina Island. Although Catalina's big city of Avalon still attracts win-

ter visitors, Two Harbors becomes ghostly quiet. It's so quiet that the mobile home–style cottages in town, which serve as summer housing for Two Harbors employees, are left vacant for the winter. The cottages are then made available for rent to anybody who wants an inexpensive vacation.

Inexpensive? How about 40 bucks per night for two people during the week, and 50 bucks per night on the weekends? Sounds good, yes? But don't come with high expectations. The "cottages" are trailer homes stuck in the middle of town next to the tennis courts and children's playground. Each cottage is just large enough for two people; you have your choice of bunk beds or a double bed. Communal restrooms, showers, and laundry facilities are nearby. Outside the cottages is a communal kitchen area with picnic tables, barbecues, gas burners, and even a microwave. Inside the cottages are a heater and refrigerator. You bring your own cooking and eating utensils, as well as bedding and towels. You will also want to pack in groceries from the mainland, then supplement your stock with supplies from the Two Harbors General Store, a short walk away.

But since the cottages are available only from November to April, what do you do if you want to stay at Two Harbors the rest of the year? Easy: You rent a tent cabin at Two Harbors Campground. Set on a bluff overlooking the Pacific, the tent cabins are only a quarter-mile away from all the amenities at Two Harbors. They sleep four to six people in a relatively luxurious manner (considering that they are, after all, canvas cabins), complete with cots, a camp stove, a lantern, a picnic table, a barbecue, a fire ring, and a sun shade. You can even buy propane for your stove right at the campground so you don't have to schlep it in from the mainland.

If you stay at the cottages at Two Harbors in the summer, you can take advantage of numerous outdoor gear rental operators, who rent bikes, kayaks, and scuba equipment. In the winter, these concessionaires depart for busier locales, so you'll have to bring your own toys from home.

Of course, many visitors will be satisfied packing only their hiking boots, because excellent trails lead from Two Harbors. A terrific easy walk (only .5 mile) heads across the narrowest part of the island to Catalina Harbor. At the harbor's southwest edge, on a hillside knoll, you'll spot a single bench perfectly placed for sunset watching.

Longer hikes are possible along the island's dirt roads to Cherry Cove and Parson's Landing. If you are lucky enough to time your trip for late winter or early spring, you'll see Cherry Cove's native Catalina cherry trees blooming bright white, as well as acres of prickly pear cactus flowering across the island.

Facilities
There are 18 mobile home–style housekeeping cabins; each accommodates two people (available from November to April only). Communal kitchen facilities are outside the cabins; refrigerators are provided inside the cabins. Restrooms and showers are nearby. From May to October, there are six tent cabins at Two Harbors Campground; each accommodates four to six people. Linens and towels are not provided.

Reservations and Rates
Reservations are required. Fees are $40 per night on weekdays and $50 per night on weekends for the cottages. Tent cabins at Two Harbors Campground are $40 per night. Pets are not permitted. Contact Santa Catalina Island Company, P.O. Box 737, Avalon, CA 90704, 310/510-0303 or 310/510-2000, website: www.scico.com.

Directions
Catalina Express provides year-round ferry transportation to Two Harbors from San Pedro. For a schedule and reservations, call 310/519-1212 or 800/481-3470, or visit the website: www.catalinaexpress.com.

21 LA PALOMA COTTAGES
Avalon, Catalina Island

Luxury rating: ★ ★ ★ ☆ ☆   **Recreation rating:** ★ ★ ★ ★ ★

Rank: Best for Beach Activities

The island of Catalina has two faces: the subdued, rustic profile of Two Harbors on the north side of the island, and the bustling metropolitan profile of Avalon on the south side. If outdoor adventure is your thing, you'll find it in both places. But if you want your adventure combined with a few good restaurants and some nightlife, Avalon is the place to go.

Avalon is the city on Catalina that never sleeps. While Two Harbors has a busy season (summer) and a dead season (winter), Avalon stays busy year-round. Even on weekdays, it's surprising how many people are touring the streets, shops, and businesses in Avalon's downtown and signing up for a

The oceanfront Casino Ballroom at Avalon Harbor

whole variety of commercial tours and outdoor adventures. At Avalon, everything is for rent or for sale; you don't even need to bring gear with you. The long list of recreation possibilities includes snorkeling, scuba diving, sport fishing, kayaking, horseback riding, swimming, hiking, and ocean rafting. All you have to do is get on a ferry in Los Angeles and show up at the Avalon pier.

La Paloma Cottages is one of the few establishments in Avalon that offers cottage-style accommodations. La Paloma is on Sunny Lane, a side street a few blocks from the busy downtown area. Although it has lovely outdoor flower-box gardens, iron balconies, and brick walkways, the interiors of the cottages are unremarkable. But hey, they're clean and affordable, so who's complaining?

This is Avalon, so your accommodations are urban in style and ambience. The cottages are packed in, one right next to the other, much like motel rooms. They do not have ocean views, although some of La Paloma's apartment units do have views. All the basic necessities are provided in the cottages, and some have fully equipped kitchens. Best of all, La Paloma prides itself on being diver-friendly. Translation: They don't mind if you leave a trail of sand in your cottage.

Facilities

There are eight cottages and seven apartment-style units that can accommodate two to six people. Some have fully equipped kitchens. Linens and towels are provided.

Reservations and Rates

Reservations are recommended. Fees are $69–149 per night. Pets are not permitted. Contact La Paloma Cottages, P.O. Box 1505, Avalon, CA 90704, 310/510-1505 or 800/310-1505, website: www.catalina.com/lapaloma.html.

Directions
Several companies provide ferry transportation to Avalon from San Pedro, Long Beach, Redondo Beach, and Newport Beach. For reservations, call Catalina Express at 310/519-1212 or 800/481-3470 or visit the website: www.catalinaexpress.com. Another ferry company is Catalina Passenger Service, 949/673-5245. Transportation is also possible by plane or helicopter; call Island Express, 310/510-2525.

Other Cabins and Cottages Nearby
Catalina Cottages and Hermosa Hotel, P.O. Box 646, 131 Metropole Street, Avalon, CA 90704, 310/510-1010 or 877/453-1313, website: www.hermosahotel.com.

22 DOCKSIDE BOAT AND BED
off I-710 in Long Beach

Luxury rating: ★ ★ ★ ☆ ☆   **Recreation rating:** ★ ★ ★ ☆ ☆

You've stayed at bed-and-breakfasts; well, this is a boat-and-breakfast. For people who want to indulge in the fantasy of owning their own yacht, it doesn't get any better than this.

Dockside Boat and Bed offers six boats for nightly rentals in Long Beach's Rainbow Harbor. Take your pick from a 53-foot authentic Chinese junk, a 44-foot Pacemaker motor yacht, or a 54-foot racing sailboat. Now don't get carried away: You don't get to sail any of them, you just get to sleep on them.

Mei Wen Ti, the Chinese junk, is Dockside's showpiece accommodations. It is the roomiest of the boats and is loaded with character. Built in China in 1990 and displaying a hand-painted exterior, it is purported to be the only authentic Chinese junk on the West Coast. There's enough room on deck for eight people to hang around and eat egg rolls, or to have drinks and watch the sun set. Down below is a cozy master stateroom (that's a bedroom for you landlubbers) with a queen bed. (Although the deck provides enough room for up to eight people, a maximum of four are permitted overnight.) The galley (right, that's the kitchen) seats four and has a refrigerator, a microwave, a coffeemaker, and a toaster. The boat features Asian touches throughout.

Whimsy, the motor yacht, features crisp navy and white lines and elegant wood detailing in its cabin. The first stateroom has two twin bunks,

and the master stateroom has a
queen-size bed.

© JULIE SHEER

If neither *Mei Wen Ti* nor
Whimsy floats your boat, you
have four more boats to choose
from. All of them are moored
at Rainbow Harbor, which is
next to the Aquarium of the Pacific and the shops of Shoreline
Village. The *Queen Mary* is directly across the water. The
most coveted rental nights at
Dockside are summer Satur-
days, when boat-and-bed guests
have the best seat in the house
for the weekly fireworks display alongside the *Queen Mary*. The Fourth of
July show is out of this world.

After smelling the salt air, listening to the gentle lapping of the waves,
and being lulled to sleep by the rocking of your boat, what else do you do
at Dockside Boat and Bed? There's always personal watercraft riding, sea
kayaking, whale-watching trips, sport fishing, tours of the *Queen Mary* and
the Aquarium of the Pacific, and miles of beachfront boardwalks and
trails for walking, running, in-line skating, and bicycling (bikes are available for rent). Pretty much anything you want to do is possible at Rainbow
Harbor; take your pick.

Facilities
There are six rental yachts that can accommodate up to four people. All
have small galleys with a microwave, a refrigerator, a toaster, and a coffeemaker. Linens and towels are provided.

Reservations and Rates
Reservations are required. Fees are $190–250 per night for two people (in-
cluding taxes). A continental breakfast is included. Pets are not permitted.
Contact Dockside Boat and Bed, Rainbow Harbor, Gate 5 (send mail to
316 East Shoreline Drive), Long Beach, CA 90802, 562/436-3111, website:
www.boatandbed.com.

Directions
From Los Angeles, take I-710 south to where it ends at Shoreline Drive in
Long Beach. Keep heading south on Shoreline Drive, then turn west
(right) on Pine Avenue. Park at the turnaround parking circle by the pier

(temporary parking) and walk to Dock 5, the first dock on the right. Dockside's office is on a houseboat.

Other Cabins and Cottages Nearby

Seal Beach Inn and Gardens, 212 5th Street, Seal Beach, CA 90740-6115, 562/493-2416 or 800/HIDEAWAY (800/443-3292), website: www.sealbeachinn.com.

Lord Mayor's B&B Inn, 435 Cedar Avenue, Long Beach, CA 90802, 562/436-0324, website: www.lordmayors.com.

23 BOAT AND BREAKFAST NEWPORT
off Highway 55 in Newport Beach

Luxury rating: ★ ★ ★ ☆ ☆   **Recreation rating: ★ ★ ★ ☆ ☆**

If you've ever dreamed of living on a boat and going to sleep to the music of tinkling halyards on metal masts, your ship just came in. Boat and Breakfast Newport can make your dreams come true.

Boat and Breakfast Newport rents out private boats—yachts, actually—for overnight stays. Each yacht comes equipped with a private bath, a television and VCR, and all linens and towels. The yachts run the gamut, from small vessels that sleep two (the kind of toy a millionaire would own) to colossal ones that sleep up to seven (a toy more appropriate for a billionaire). A few of the large yachts are Coast Guard–certified for cruising the water with large groups of people on board. They are often rented for an afternoon or evening wedding; after a two-hour cruise around the bay, the bride and groom spend the night on the boat.

Each rental yacht offers excellent water views, but some are moored clos-

er to the shops and restaurants, while others are farther out in the harbor. Make sure you ask about the location of the boat you rent; you want to be in a first-rate spot for sunsets.

You're allowed to cook on board on only some of the yachts—the ones with electric ranges. For safety reasons, renters aren't permitted to use propane-fueled stoves. No matter; a continental breakfast is brought to your boat each morning. In addition, a restaurant in the marina will bring you dinner, room-service style, for a fee. Many people just pack along their own take-out dinner, plus a bag of groceries for snacks. Evening cocktails on the aft deck usually hold an important place in the itinerary, so don't forget your supplies.

There isn't much incentive to leave your yacht and head for dry land, but after your stay is over, you might take a stroll on the lovely sands of Newport Beach.

Facilities

There are eight rental yachts that can accommodate up to seven people. Some have fully equipped galleys. Linens and towels are provided.

Reservations and Rates

Reservations are required. Fees are $300–650 per night. A continental breakfast is included. Pets are not permitted. Contact Boat and Breakfast Newport, 3400 Via Oporto, Suite 103, Newport Beach, CA 92663, 949/723-5552 or 800/262-8233, website: www.boatbed.com.

Directions

From I-5 at Santa Ana, take Highway 55 south to Costa Mesa. Highway 55 becomes Newport Boulevard; follow it for two miles until it crosses the Pacific Coast Highway. Just beyond the Pacific Coast Highway, turn left on Via Lido. Drive about 100 yards, then turn left on Via Oporto. Boat and Breakfast Newport is in Lido Marina Village.

24 CASA LAGUNA INN
off Highway 1 in Laguna Beach

Luxury rating: ★ ★ ★ ★ ★   **Recreation rating:** ★ ★ ★ ☆ ☆

Casa Laguna Inn offers a classic Southern California experience: red-tile roofs and Spanish-style architecture, towering palm trees punctuating views of the Pacific, and lush flower-filled gardens with trickling musical fountains. It is truly a getaway spot in one of Orange County's most vacation-minded cities, Laguna Beach.

If you're unfamiliar with the area, there's much to do. The main part of town, about a mile from Casa Laguna, is filled with myriad art galleries, upscale clothing stores, surf shops, antique stores, and restaurants. Hikers and bikers head for Crystal Cove State Park, where 2,000 acres of wooded canyons and coastal hills wait to be explored. Park rangers conduct guided nature hikes in the winter, but it's easy enough to wander on your own.

If you want to go stick your toes in the sand, two beautiful beaches are a short walk from the inn: Victoria Beach (soft white sand) and Moss Point (good tidepools and rock formations). Mid-December to April is primetime for whale-watching; you might get lucky from the coast, or you can increase your chances by taking a whale-watching tour out of Dana Point.

Casa Laguna has 19 rooms and suites, plus a spectacular cottage that is set on the hillside overlooking the swimming pool. It's a one-bedroom bungalow with a full kitchen, a sitting room with fireplace, and a large living/dining room with ocean views. Unusual features include a piano, stained-glass windows throughout, and beautiful Catalina tiles. The cottage's wraparound deck is its showpiece, offering expansive blue-water Pacific views. Not surprisingly, the cottage is often rented for honeymoons.

Casa Laguna's suites offer an alternative for families or groups of four, although they are not freestanding units, so they aren't quite as private as the cottage. They come with separate bedrooms and a sofa-sleeper in the living room. Some have kitchens, fireplaces, and ocean views.

It's hard to guess how many gardeners must be employed at Casa Laguna. The grounds are a wealth of bougainvillea, queen palms, banana trees, ferns, and impatiens. Many nooks and crannies on the property provide spots to find your own private sanctuary, including four blossom-filled patios, a gazebo and potting shed behind the cottage, and a classic California bell tower, with its staircase leading to an observation deck. Framing wide ocean views, the bell tower has *sunset* written all over it.

Guests at Casa Laguna enjoy a buffet breakfast served in the main house each morning (juice, coffee, bagels, eggs, fruit), plus wine, cheese, and hors d'oeuvres each evening. The food is ample and elegantly served.

Only one downside is apparent at Casa Laguna, and that's the steady hum of traffic from the Pacific Coast Highway. But with all the visual stimulation at this lovely inn, you'll soon tune it out and focus on your scenic surroundings.

Facilities
There is one one-bedroom cottage, plus 19 rooms and two suites. The cottage and two suites (unit Nos. 1 and 2) have fully equipped kitchens. Linens and towels are provided.

Reservations and Rates
Reservations are required. The cottage fee is $300–450 per night for two people, including breakfast. The rooms and suites are $160–425 per night, including breakfast. There is a two-night minimum on weekends. Pets are permitted with prior approval and with a $5 fee per night. Contact Casa Laguna Inn, 2510 South Coast Highway, Laguna Beach, CA 92651, 949/494-2996 or 800/233-0449, website: www.casalaguna.com.

Directions
From I-405 in Irvine, take the Highway 133/Laguna Canyon Road exit. Turn west and drive eight miles to Pacific Coast Highway. Turn south and drive 1.5 miles to the resort, on the left (east) side.

25 MANZANITA COTTAGES
off Highway 1 in Laguna Beach

Luxury rating: ★ ★ ★ ★ ☆   **Recreation rating:** ★ ★ ★ ☆ ☆

Rank: Best for Beach Activities

Manzanita Cottages is the place to indulge your *Hansel and Gretel* fantasies, if you have any. It's also the place to get away from the hustle and bustle of downtown Laguna Beach—which can be quite overwhelming on summer weekends—while still having access to all the town offerings.

Tucked away in a secluded garden compound in a residential neighborhood of Laguna Beach, Manzanita Cottages features four small cottages and one studio apartment. All have been quaintly restored with tons of Old World charm. Think Solvang, and you've got the picture: shingled roofs, brightly painted front doors, open-beamed ceilings, fireplaces, hardwood floors, and hand-painted tiles.

The cottages have weathered a few lives before their present incarnation. They were built in 1927 by Harry Greene, a film producer, who wanted a

© JULIE SHEER

secluded compound where he could invite his Hollywood friends for overnight getaways. Legend has it that Joan Crawford was a frequent guest.

Owners came and went over the years, and by the time present owners Debbie and Todd Herzer bought the property, the place was in disrepair. With a desire to create the ambience of a 1930s vacation retreat, but with the added benefits of modern amenities, the Herzers went to work on renovations and opened Manzanita Cottages to the public in late 1999.

Although only about 500 square feet in size, each of the cottages is completely self-contained and fully stocked for housekeeping. They are decorated with tasteful furnishings and artwork, but their best feature is that each has a private patio accessed by French doors in the bedroom. The surrounding grounds are beautifully landscaped with fragrant flowers and vines.

If you can bring yourself to leave your adorable cottage, it's only a 10-minute walk to the Laguna village area, with its many shops, restaurants, and diversions. It's a 10-minute drive to the Festival Center on Laguna Canyon Road, where two hugely popular festivals take place each summer: the Sawdust Art Festival and Pageant of the Masters. Crystal Cove State Park is a few miles to the north (on Highway 1) for hiking and biking activities. For something really special, check out Laguna Coast Wilderness Park, a 5,000-acre wildlife sanctuary, where naturalists conduct guided hikes and mountain bike rides. Entry to the park is by reservation only, except for certain days and times; call ahead at 949/494-9352.

And of course, Laguna is renowned for its miles of sandy beaches. Main Beach, considered to be the center of beach life in Laguna, is a brief walk from the cottages.

Facilities

There are four cottages that can accommodate up to four people, plus a studio apartment that can accommodate two people. Each has a fully equipped kitchen. Linens and towels are provided.

Reservations and Rates

Reservations are required. Fees are $195–250 per night, depending on the season and length of stay. Rates are discounted for weekly and monthly stays. There is a one-week minimum in summer and two-night minimum in spring and fall. Pets are not permitted. Contact Manzanita Cottages, 732 to 738 Manzanita Drive, Laguna Beach, CA 92651, 949/661-2533, website: www.manzanitacottages.com.

Directions

From I-405 in Irvine, take the Highway 133/Laguna Canyon Road exit. Turn west and drive eight miles to Pacific Coast Highway. Turn south and drive to Legion Street (the fourth traffic light). Turn left and drive to where Legion Street ends at Park Avenue. Turn right and drive one short block to Manzanita Drive; turn left on Manzanita. The cottages are the third property on the left.

26 ZOSA RANCH & GARDENS
off I-15 in Temecula

Luxury rating: ★ ★ ★ ☆ ☆   **Recreation rating:** ★ ★ ★ ☆ ☆

Zosa Ranch & Gardens is an avocado ranch transformed. Set in the warm, dry hills between Temecula and Escondido, this 22-acre Spanish hacienda is a place where a couple or family can go for a secluded weekend or where a larger group can hold a small wedding or family reunion.

The grounds and gardens are the star of the show. Citrus and exotic fruit trees, palms, and 150 avocado trees dot the property. Oleander and bougainvillea bloom with profusion amid an elegant gazebo, a koi pond, courtyard fountains, tennis courts, and a swimming pool.

There are two main units on the property: a two-bedroom cottage and one guest house with four suites. The guest house is often rented as one unit for a large group. A highlight is the bathroom in the master suite, which has

a black, two-person whirlpool tub and a window overlooking the surrounding hills. The house has a huge patio with a whirlpool tub and a fire pit.

The two-bedroom cottage is a charming little blue house with white shutters and fronted by a trickling fountain surrounded by flowers. The interior decor is country floral, with lots of

© JULIE SHEER

wicker and bamboo. It is large enough for a small family or two couples to be comfortable. It too has its own whirlpool tub on the patio.

You can do your own cooking in the cottage or guest house, but you won't need to bother with breakfast. A generous meal is served each morning in the main ranch house—fruit, omelets, eggs Benedict, freshly squeezed orange juice from the ranch's trees, and the like.

Zosa Ranch & Gardens is set in a rural area, so if you're someone who needs something to do right outside your door, you won't be happy here. However, if you're willing to drive a few minutes, you can head for Temecula, which is loaded with wineries and has an Old West–style main street featuring antique shops and restaurants. Or, in a half hour, you can be at the coast at Oceanside, where sport fishing, boating, surfing, and pier fishing are available. The San Diego Wild Animal Park is also a half-hour drive away.

Cycling is possible on many of the rural roads surrounding Zosa Ranch & Gardens. Hikers shouldn't miss the chance to explore nearby Palomar Mountain State Park. In the state park, try the Lower Doane Valley and Weir Trail Loop (big conifers and grassy meadows) or the trail to the 1880s Scott's Cabin. Or, in neighboring Cleveland National Forest, take the trail from Observatory Campground to Palomar Observatory, home of the 200-inch Hale telescope.

Facilities

There is one two-bedroom cottage that can accommodate four people and a guest house with four suites that can accommodate eight people, all with fully equipped kitchens. Linens and towels are provided.

Reservations and Rates

Reservations are required. Fees are $250 per night for the cottage, and $190–250 for each individual suite or $700 per night for the entire guest house. Rates include breakfast. Pets are not permitted. Contact Zosa Ranch & Gardens, 9381 West Lilac Road, Valley Center, CA 92026, 760/723-9093 or 800/711-8361, website: www.zosagardens.com.

Directions

From I-15 in Temecula, drive south for 12 miles to Route 76 (Pala Road). Turn right (west) and drive a short distance to old Highway 395. Turn left (south) and drive to West Lilac Road. Turn left and drive 1.5 miles to Lilac Walk. Turn right; Zosa Ranch & Gardens is on the left.

27 KNOTTY PINE CABINS
off Highway 243 in Idyllwild

Luxury rating: ★ ★ ★ ☆ ☆   **Recreation rating: ★ ★ ★ ☆ ☆**

The derivation of the name Idyllwild is simple: First, *idyll,* as in *idyllic,* suggests peace or contentment in a picturesque or rustic setting. Then *wild,* as in, you can still find some wilderness there. Hooray for that.

© ANN MARIE BROWN

Idyllwild is 5,500 feet in elevation, roughly west of Palm Springs and south of Banning, on the border of the San Jacinto Wilderness. The town is in the midst of San Bernardino National Forest, near 10,160-foot Newton B. Drury Peak and 10,804-foot San Jacinto Peak. It has plenty of splendid scenery, particularly big conifers and granite walls.

Because the Idyllwild area was never developed for downhill skiing, it doesn't get anywhere near the amount of winter traffic as Big Bear to the north, but it does good business with summer hikers. In fact, on summer holiday weekends it can be difficult to get a wilderness permit for some of the best trails in the area, including the spectacular Devils Slide Trail to the top of 8,828-foot Tahquitz Peak (a wilderness permit is required).

Make your trip easier by visiting during nonholiday periods and by reserving a stay at Knotty Pine Cabins. Tucked among tall pines and oaks, Knotty Pine is close enough to downtown Idyllwild that you can walk to shops and restaurants if you like. All cabins have fireplaces and porches; all except one have a kitchen. Barbecue grills are available.

While you're in Idyllwild, be sure to hike the Devils Slide Trail. The route is 8.4 miles round-trip and offers incredible views from the fire lookout tower on top of Tahquitz Peak. A slightly easier hike is possible on Deer Springs Trail to the overlook at Suicide Rock, providing good views of Tahquitz Peak and Idyllwild. Easiest of all is the Ernie Maxwell Scenic Trail, a good family walk through the pines and cedars. All of these trailheads are within a 15-minute drive of Knotty Pine Cabins.

For picnicking or fishing, take a drive over to pretty little Lake Fulmor on Highway 243, where you and your kids can cast a line in the water from shore. Or stop at the picnic area across the highway from Lake Fulmor at Fuller Mill Creek, where you can fish for stocked trout in springtime. Another option is to seek out the pretty waterfall on Fuller Mill Creek, just a few hundred feet from the highway on the east side.

Facilities
There are eight cabins ranging in size from studios to three bedrooms. All except one have fully equipped kitchens. Linens and towels are provided.

Reservations and Rates
Reservations are recommended. Fees are $59–135 per night on weekends with a two-night minimum; weekday stays cost less. Pets are permitted in some cabins for a $20 fee. Contact Knotty Pine Cabins, 54340 Pine Crest, P.O. Box 477, Idyllwild, CA 92549, 909/659-2933, website: www.idyllwild .com/knotty.

Directions
From I-10 at Banning, take Highway 243 south and drive 27 winding miles to Idyllwild. Just before you reach the village, look for a sign on the left for Knotty Pine Cabins. Turn left and drive up the driveway.

Other Cabins and Cottages Nearby
Woodland Park Manor, 55350 South Circle Drive, P.O. Box 86, Idyllwild, CA 92549, 909/659-2657, website: www.woodlandparkmanor.com.

28 FERN VALLEY INN
off Highway 243 in Idyllwild

Luxury rating: ★ ★ ★ ★ ☆   **Recreation rating: ★ ★ ★ ★ ☆**

It's so quiet at Fern Valley Inn, in Idyllwild, that you can hear the squirrels chewing on pine cones. No kidding. The inn is away from the downtown area of Idyllwild, only a half mile from Humber Park and its trailheads. Quite simply, it couldn't be better situated for people who like quiet and for people who like to hike.

The 11 cabins at Fern Valley are on the small side, but the management accommodates larger groups in one of their many rental vacation homes. If the most you need is a two-bedroom cabin, you can stay right at Fern Valley. The cabins are grouped around a heated outdoor swimming pool.

All have fireplaces and queen-size beds; some have full kitchens. They are decorated with antiques and handmade quilts, and each has a patio or deck where you can sit outside and listen to the birds (or the squirrels chewing on pine cones). Some cabins are duplexes, so make sure you request a single unit if you want one.

© ANN MARIE BROWN

While you're vacationing at this 5,300-foot mountain paradise, you might want to do some exploring. Fishing enthusiasts can head to tiny Lake Fulmor for shoreline fishing or to Fuller Mill Creek for creek fishing. Horseback riding is possible at stables nearby. And best of all is the proximity of trailheads at Humber Park, including the spectacular Devils Slide Trail to Tahquitz Peak (8.4 miles round-trip, wilderness permit required) and the easy but scenic Ernie Maxwell Trail (5.2 miles round-trip). The former leads to an operating fire lookout with a panoramic view of the San Jacinto and Santa Rosa Mountains. The latter offers some good views of Tahquitz Peak, especially on the way back.

If you want to hike someplace where you're more likely to be alone, drive out to Idyllwild's Dark Canyon Campground and try the Seven Pines Trail, which meets up with the north fork of the San Jacinto River. Hike out and back as far as you like; any distance on this trail is satisfying.

Facilities

There are 11 single and duplex cabins ranging in size from studios to two bedrooms. All have decks or patios. Some cabins have fully equipped kitchens. There is a heated pool on-site. A wide range of vacation homes are also for rent. Linens and towels are provided.

Reservations and Rates

Reservations are recommended. Fees are $85–135 per night for two people, plus $10 for each additional person. Pets are not permitted. Contact Fern Valley Inn, 25240 Fern Valley Road, P.O. Box 116, Idyllwild, CA 92549, 909/659-2205 or 800/659-7775, website: www.fernvalleyinn.com.

Directions

From I-10 at Banning, take Highway 243 south and drive 27 winding miles to Idyllwild. Drive through town, following Village Center to its end. Turn left on South Circle Drive. Drive a half mile and turn right on Fern Valley Road. Fern Valley Inn is on the right.

Other Cabins and Cottages Nearby

Strawberry Creek Inn, 26370 Highway 243, Idyllwild, CA 92549, 909/659-3202 or 800/262-8969, website: www.strawberrycreekinn.com.

29 WILDER CABINS
off Highway 243 in Idyllwild

Luxury rating: ★ ★ ★ ☆ ☆   **Recreation rating:** ★ ★ ★ ☆ ☆

© ANN MARIE BROWN

If you like your mountain cabins with a little history attached, you'll like Wilder Cabins. In 1932, Ida and Sylvester Wilder built a summer home in Idyllwild. Since then, four generations of Wilders and their friends have vacationed at their homestead, and you can too.

Wilder Cabins offers three one-room cabins for rent, and each one is tucked into the forest alongside Strawberry Creek. Squirrel's Inn has a view of the creek and a queen-size bed. Cozy Rest is the largest cabin, with one queen- and one twin-size bed; it can sleep three. Journey's End is the most enchanting cabin. To reach it, you cross a wooden bridge and walkway over the creek. It has one queen-size bed and a private porch. All of the cabins have kitchen facilities; buy your groceries in downtown Idyllwild a quarter mile away, and you're all set.

Historically, the cabins have only been used as summer cabins, and even today they are for rent only from May through September. The property surrounding them consists of a secluded cedar and pine grove with picnicking and reading areas. Even though there is so much hiking and fishing to do in the Idyllwild area, it's tempting to spend your days just hanging out on the Wilder property, pondering what life was like in Ida and Sylvester's time.

Facilities

There are three one-room cabins that can accommodate up to three people. All cabins have fully equipped kitchens. Linens and towels are provided.

Reservations and Rates

Reservations are recommended. Fees are $75–80 per night for two people. The resort is open from May through September. Pets are permitted for an $8 fee per day. Contact Wilder Cabins, 54550 South Circle Drive, P.O. Box 31, Idyllwild, CA 92549, 909/659-2926, website: www.wildercabins.com.

Directions

From I-10 at Banning, take Highway 243 south and drive 27 winding miles to Idyllwild. Drive through town, following Village Center to its end. Turn left on South Circle Drive; Wilder Cabins is the second driveway on the left.

Other Cabins and Cottages Nearby

The Quiet Creek Inn, 26345 Delano Drive, P.O. Box 240, Idyllwild, CA 92549, 909/659-6110 or 800/450-6110, website: www.quietcreek.com.

Chapter 4

© ANN MARIE BROWN

San Diego and Vicinity

San Diego and Vicinity

San Diego is a sun-drenched region with 76 miles of beaches, two distinct mountain ranges (the Palomar and Laguna-Cuyamaca Mountains) and one giant-sized desert, Anza-Borrego. Blessed with a nearly perfect year-round climate and stunning natural beauty, San Diego has long been a favorite destination of vacationers from California and worldwide.

The huge county's landscape is so varied that it is best described by splitting it into parts. In few other places of the world can you swim in the ocean, hike to a 6,500-foot mountain peak, and admire the stillness of a desert palm grove—all in the same day.

Let's begin with the desert. Anza-Borrego Desert State Park encompasses 600,000 acres of palm groves, year-round creeks, slot canyons, and badlands. It is California's largest state park and is more than three times the size of Zion National Park. Desert flora runs the gamut, from the expected, like barrel cactus and mesquite, to the rare: stands of jumping cholla cactus and aptly named elephant trees. Majestic and endangered bighorn sheep are commonly seen from park roads and trails. Two accommodations in this chapter, La Casa del Zorro Desert Resort and Stagecoach Trails Resort, provide you with the opportunity to stay within a few miles of the park's borders.

Just to the west of this giant desert lie the Laguna and Cuyamaca Mountains. The Cuyamacas are mostly contained within Cuyamaca Rancho State Park, which was badly burned in the major wildfires of 2003. Man and nature have joined forces to rebuild this popular park, which before the great fires hosted extensive mixed forests of ponderosa and Jeffrey pine, fir, incense cedar, and live and black oak. With elevations ranging from 4,000 to 6,500 feet, the landscape of the Cuyamaca Mountains is a world vastly different from neighboring Anza-Borrego Desert. In a few years, the scars of the fires will heal, and the park will once again be lush with greenery. Several rustic cabins are for rent at Cuyamaca Rancho State Park, and also at neighboring William Heise County Park.

Alongside the Cuyamacas are the Lagunas, which are managed as part of Cleveland National Forest. With a dramatic setting that overlooks the desert thousands of feet below, the Lagunas are easily explored on foot, bike, or horseback. Several times each winter, they are covered in snow. Two mountain resorts, Blue Jay Lodge and Laguna Mountain Lodge, offer cabin rentals near the summit of Mount Laguna.

Near the Laguna-Cuyamaca Mountains lies one of San Diego County's most interesting country towns—Julian, the apple capital of Southern California. Each year in autumn, the town comes alive with apple festivals and events. Several local bakeries make pies and as other apple delicacies year-round. In addition to its gastronomic delights, the town of Julian is centrally located for exploring surrounding parklands, including William Heise County Park and Cleveland National Forest, whether by bike or on foot. A number of cabin accommodations are in or near Julian.

The Palomar Mountains' most notable feature is the Palomar Observatory, home of the 200-inch Hale telescope, which for many years was the world's largest. The entire mountain range extends only 25 miles along the northern border of San Diego County, but what it lacks in size, it makes up for in beauty. Its 6,000-foot elevation gives rise to dense stands of fir, cedar, spruce, and black oak. Most of the land in the Palomar Mountains is part of Palomar Mountain State Park or Cleveland National Forest. The easiest way to explore this area is to stay at Lake Henshaw Resort; in addition to its proximity to Palomar Mountain, the resort is right across the road from great fishing at Lake Henshaw.

Two excellent city parks are in San Diego: Balboa Park, with its museums, galleries, theaters, restaurants, and the world-famous San Diego Zoo; and 5,000-acre Mission Bay Park, with its labyrinth of bikeways, swimming beaches, lawns, and boating and fishing charters. Sailing, waterskiing, and windsurfing are popular, as is Sea World, one of the world's largest oceanariums. Several cottage resorts are in or near downtown San Diego.

Last but never least are the 76 miles of San Diego beaches. They require no introduction, only a reminder to pack along your sunscreen and a few extra towels. The pages that follow contain several lodgings from which you can gaze at (or walk to) the ocean.

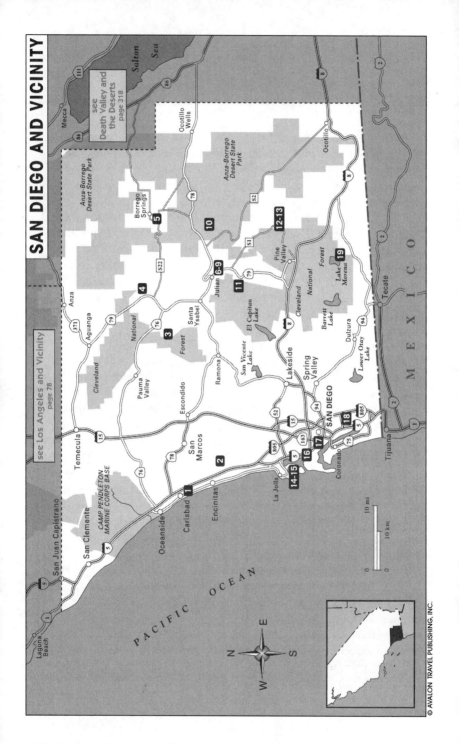

Contents

1. Adventure in Camping Travel Trailers 134

2. The Inn at Rancho Santa Fe 135

3. Lake Henshaw Resort 137

4. Warner Springs Ranch 138

5. La Casa del Zorro Desert Resort 140

6. Julian Bed and Breakfast Guild 141

7. Shadow Mountain Ranch 143

8. Pine Hills Lodge 145

9. William Heise County Park Cabins 146

10. Stagecoach Trails Resort 148

11. Cuyamaca Rancho State Park Cabins 149

12. Blue Jay Lodge 151

13. Laguna Mountain Lodge 153

14. Crystal Pier Hotel 154

15. The Beach Cottages 155

16. San Diego Vacation Cottages 157

17. Harbor Vacations Club 158

18. San Diego Metro KOA 160

19. Lake Morena County Park Cabins 161

1 ADVENTURE IN CAMPING TRAVEL TRAILERS

off I-5 at San Diego Coast State Beaches

Luxury rating: ★ ★ ☆ ☆ ☆   **Recreation rating:** ★ ★ ★ ★ ☆

Have you ever camped in a tent on a cold, rainy night? You put up your rain fly, adjust your ground tarp, snuggle in with your mate, and hope it doesn't last long. Sleepless hours crawl by while you are possessed by the nagging fear that water is seeping in through the tent seams.

When the sun comes out in the morning, do you ever wonder if those people in RVs and travel trailers are just a hair smarter than you? Parked next door in the campground, they cheerfully cook breakfast over a hot fire while you yawn and dry out your socks.

Purchasing a travel trailer may seem too far-fetched or high-priced, but renting one for your next vacation isn't. A company called Adventure in Camping takes care of the details; you reserve your choice of trailer models, then decide where you want to camp along the San Diego coastline.

Your options include the following state beaches: South Carlsbad, Mission Bay, San Elijo, and San Onofre. Of these, South Carlsbad and San Elijo are the most popular. At both bluff-top campgrounds, the beach is easily accessed by a series of wooden stairways. In addition to the usual activities—like surf fishing, swimming, beach walking, and surfing—campers can go snorkeling or diving at an offshore reef.

Because the campgrounds are set on a bluff about 50 feet above the ocean, you won't have much trouble finding a good place to watch the sun set. Half the campsites overlook the water; don't even consider the rest, which face the road or train tracks.

Adventure in Camping delivers your trailer to your chosen campsite, levels the trailer, and sets it up for use. When you arrive, the kitchen appliances work, the water runs, and the toilets flush. At the end of your stay, you drive off in your own car, and Adventure in Camping picks up the trailer.

If you want serious luxury, you can rent a trailer with all the options, like a television and VCR, microwave oven, and generator. But even the basic model comes with a full bath and kitchen (including all cooking and eating utensils), plus battery-run lights, hot and cold running water, and forced-air heat. The only thing that isn't provided is linens; bring your own towels and sleeping bags.

Facilities
The rental trailers range from 18 to 27 feet long and come in a variety of floor plans that sleep three to seven people. Linens and towels are not provided.

Reservations and Rates
Reservations are required. Fees are $190–227 for two nights. A $100 cleaning and damage deposit is required. Pets are permitted with a $10 fee.

Directions
For San Elijo State Beach: From San Diego, drive north on I-5 for 25 miles and take the Lomas Santa Fe exit. Turn west and follow Lomas Santa Fe until you reach the Pacific Coast Highway. Turn north on Pacific Coast Highway and drive 2.5 miles to San Elijo State Beach, near Chesterfield Drive.

For South Carlsbad State Beach: From San Diego, drive north on I-5 for 30 miles and take the Poinsettia exit. Turn west and follow Poinsettia to the park entrance. Contact Adventure in Camping, P.O. Box 100, PMB 311, Mammoth Lakes, CA 93546, 858/452-6594 or 800/417-7771, website: www.adventureincamping.com.

2 THE INN AT RANCHO SANTA FE
off Highway S-6 in Rancho Santa Fe

Luxury rating: ★ ★ ★ ★ ☆   **Recreation rating:** ★ ★ ★ ☆ ☆

Built in 1923, The Inn at Rancho Santa Fe has been run by the same family for three generations. Although all of its low-slung, Spanish-style accommodations edged by wide green lawns are appealing, its freestanding adobe cottages are something special. Each is beautifully decorated in a traditional, understated style and is ideally suited for a relaxing getaway.

The inn is in one of San Diego's wealthiest neighborhoods, and it attracts a fairly upscale crowd. Because the cottages are separate from the main inn, you can choose to socialize or not, depending on what you want out of your vacation. While many guests come here to play tennis or golf on the premises, others simply use Rancho Santa Fe as a base for exploring the area's attractions, including San Diego's marvelous Wild Animal Park, which is 20 miles east. Cyclists can take to the country roads around Rancho Santa Fe, and hikers and joggers will find more than 20 miles of trails strung throughout the area. Mountain bikers and hikers can also head for Los Penasquitos Canyon Preserve, 12 miles to the south.

© ANN MARIE BROWN

If you want to spend some time at the ocean, the inn has a lovely beach cottage eight miles away in Del Mar. Day use of the cottage is included in your stay; it has easy access to the sand and surf, plus dressing rooms, showers, and a private patio.

The intimate one-, two-, and three-bedroom cottages at The Inn at Rancho Santa Fe all have two baths, a living room with fireplace, a patio, and a full kitchen. The three-bedroom cottages have the same features, plus three full baths. If you don't want to cook on your vacation, the inn has two restaurants: The Library and The Garden Room.

Facilities

There are eight cottages ranging in size from one to three bedrooms. All have fully equipped kitchens. Guest rooms and suites are also available. Two restaurants, tennis courts, and a golf course are on-site. Linens and towels are provided.

Reservations and Rates

Reservations are required. Fees are $420–695 per night for cottages; rooms and suites are less. Pets are not permitted. Contact The Inn at Rancho Santa Fe, P.O. Box 869, Rancho Santa Fe, CA 92067, 858/756-1131 or 800/843-4661, website: www.theinnatrsf.com.

Directions

From San Diego, take I-5 north for 20 miles to the Lomas Santa Fe Drive (Highway S-8) exit. Turn east and drive 4.5 miles to the inn, on the right.

❸ LAKE HENSHAW RESORT
off Highway 76 near Santa Ysabel

Luxury rating: ★ ★ ★ ☆ ☆   **Recreation rating:** ★ ★ ★ ★ ☆

"Take a boy fishing. Take a girl fishing too." That's what the sign says at
Lake Henshaw Resort, and it sums up the spirit of the place. Lake Henshaw is no Lake Tahoe in terms of natural beauty, but it's a great place
to catch catfish or bass, then cook them up for dinner in a comfortable
hillside cabin.

Lake Henshaw is near the charming country hamlet of Santa Ysabel,
just a few miles from the border of Cleveland National Forest and Palomar Mountain State Park. At 2,727 feet in elevation, the lake looks much
like a wide, shallow, flooded meadow, complete with cows lining the edges.
It boasts nearly 25 miles of shoreline.

The cabins at Lake Henshaw Resort are across the road from the lake.
They come in a variety of sizes and configurations and are spaced far
enough apart to prevent you from breathing down your neighbor's neck.
Be sure to ask for one of the upper hillside cabins, which are farthest from
the road. Each cabin has a full kitchen, complete with cooking and eating
utensils. A sign inside states: "Please do not clean fish or game in the cottage. Facilities for this are provided in the campground." Fair enough.

Because Henshaw is a private lake, a $5 per person lake-use fee is
charged, whether you bring your own boat or rent one from the resort.
(Children under 13 are free.) A five-mile-per-hour speed limit is enforced
on the water, and no canoes, rafts, or boats less than 10 feet long are allowed. (Swimming in Lake Henshaw is not permitted.)

The resort's small store can keep you supplied with all the fishing advice
and tackle you want, plus snacks and drinks. A café offers basic fare; a frequent dinner special is All You
Can Eat Catfish. For more
elaborate shopping or restaurants, the town of Santa Ysabel
is a mere 10 miles away, and
the larger town of Julian is another seven miles beyond that.

If the fish aren't biting, many
other activities are possible
near Lake Henshaw, including
hiking on 6,140-foot Palomar

© ANN MARIE BROWN

Mountain. The conifers on the mountain are big and beautiful, reminiscent of the southern Sierra. Go see the famous Palomar Observatory and its Hale telescope, or the Santa Ysabel Mission. On warm days, pay a visit to the San Luis Rey River day-use area, a couple of miles down Highway 76, for swimming, inner-tubing, and picnicking.

Facilities
There are 18 cabins ranging in size from studios to two bedrooms. All have fully equipped kitchens. A private campground with RV and tent sites is also available. A small grocery store and café are on-site. Linens and towels are provided.

Reservations and Rates
Reservations are recommended. Fees are $55–80 per night. Pets are permitted with prior approval. Contact Lake Henshaw Resort, 26439 Highway 76, Santa Ysabel, CA 92070, 760/782-3487 or 760/782-3501, website: www.lake-henshawca.com.

Directions
From Escondido on I-15, take Highway 78 east for 32 miles to Santa Ysabel. Turn left (north) on Highway 79 and drive seven miles, then turn left on Highway 76 and drive four miles to Lake Henshaw Resort, on the left.

4 WARNER SPRINGS RANCH
off Highway 79 in Warner Springs

Luxury rating: ★ ★ ★ ★ ☆   **Recreation rating:** ★ ★ ★ ★ ☆

Most San Diegans know Warner Springs Ranch as a private golf and tennis resort in the far north region of the county. The ranch is immense (2,500 acres) and filled with history: It was founded as a trading post in 1844 by John Warner, who recognized the healing benefits of its natural hot springs.

If you aren't a member of the private resort, the easiest way to take part in a vacation here is to sign up for a spa package. The package provides lodging in one of the ranch's bungalows, three meals a day, and a spa treatment, such as a one-hour massage. The rest of the ranch's amenities are then yours for the taking, although you must pay extra to play golf or to go for a horseback ride. If you're not a spa kind of person, you can sign up for a golf or horseback-riding package instead. But then, if you get a sudden urge for a mud wrap or aromatherapy, you'll have to pay extra for it.

No matter what your chosen activity, your home base will be one of resort's lovely bungalows, which are classic, old California–style structures with rustic pine interiors and red-tile roofs. Many cottages have fireplaces; about half are air-conditioned. All are blissfully free of telephones and televisions.

Regardless of which package they signed up for, many guests simply hang around Warner Springs' three huge pools, which offer both hot mineral water and ordinary pool water. For guests with children, the list of activities is long: arts and crafts, pony rides, beginner horseback riding, junior tennis clinic, and so on. Adults can choose from plenty of structured activities too, like guided horseback rides, tennis lessons, and so forth.

If you want to ignore all the organized activities and go for a solitary hike, you're in the perfect spot for bagging the summit of Hot Springs Mountain (elevation 6,533 feet), the highest peak in San Diego County. For a much easier hike, the trail into Love Valley, in Cleveland National Forest, is a short drive away (three miles up Highway S-7 on the west side of Lake Henshaw). Additionally, the Pacific Crest Trail crosses through Warner Springs, and Anza-Borrego Desert State Park is only a half hour away.

Facilities

There are 240 cottages ranging in size from one to three bedrooms; none have kitchens. A general store and restaurant are on-site. Linens and towels are provided.

Reservations and Rates

Reservations are recommended. Fees are $150–300 per night for two people. Package rates include three meals a day and a chosen activity: golf, horseback riding, or spa treatment. Pets are not permitted. Contact Warner Springs Ranch, 31652 Highway 79, P.O. Box 399, Warner Springs, CA 92086, 760/782-4200 or 760/782-4255, website: www.warnersprings.com.

Directions

From San Diego, drive north on I-15 for 15 miles and take the Scripps Poway Parkway exit. Turn east and drive 10 miles to Highway 67, then turn north (left). Follow Highway 67 through Ramona to Santa Ysabel, then turn north (left) on Highway 79. Drive 15 miles to Warner Springs Ranch.

5 LA CASA DEL ZORRO DESERT RESORT
off Highway S-3 near Borrego Springs

Luxury rating: ★ ★ ★ ★ ★   **Recreation rating:** ★ ★ ★ ☆ ☆

Rank: Best in the Desert

La Casa del Zorro is the most luxurious place in or near Anza-Borrego Desert. It may seem extravagant to rent a cottage with terry bathrobes, two TV sets, a morning newspaper at the front door, and bath towels folded into fancy shapes like dinner napkins. But if you're going to spend some time adventuring in the desert, you might as well have a comfortable home base. Why rough it 24 hours a day?

The cottages at La Casa del Zorro are the antithesis of roughing it. Each detached one- to four-bedroom casita comes with a long list of luxuries. Even the one-bedroom casita is generously oversized, with a large separate bedroom, a bathroom and dressing area, a combination living/dining room, and a kitchenette tucked into a corner. The four-bedroom casitas have a sizable amount of property around them, plus their own swimming pools. All have kitchenettes (microwave oven, small refrigerator, coffeemaker, and a basic set of dishes and silverware). Some casitas have an outdoor spa, others have fireplaces for those chilly desert nights. The casitas are ideal for families with young children, since parents can keep an

eye on their kids but everybody has their own space.

If the kitchenettes don't match up to your culinary needs, you can rent a barbecue grill from the front desk and cook on your casita's patio, or you can have your meals in one of La Casa del Zorro's restaurants. The main restaurant is formal (jackets required), but the next-door lounge and pub serves a full menu of food in a casual atmosphere. (They didn't even blink at my dirty hiking boots and sweatshirt.) At both locations, the food (best described as California cuisine) is first-rate. Try the kit fox salad with dates and butter lettuce, or the lobster medallions.

Many guests at La Casa del Zorro never leave the resort grounds. After all, La Casa has three swimming pools and hot tubs, six lighted tennis courts, a fitness room, aerobics classes . . . you get the idea. But if "civilized" recreation doesn't interest you, head for nearby Anza-Borrego Desert State Park. Within a 20-minute drive, you can access several trailheads, including the one for Borrego Palm Canyon near the park's excellent visitors center. The trail leads to a grove of more than 800 native palm trees and a boulder-lined waterfall. Bighorn sheep are often spotted on the high canyon walls.

Facilities
There are 19 casitas ranging in size from one to four bedrooms, all with kitchenettes. Some include an outdoor pool or spa and fireplace. Resort rooms are also available. A restaurant, three swimming pools, hot tubs, tennis courts, and a fitness center are on-site. Linens and towels are provided.

Reservations and Rates
Reservations are recommended. Fees are $255–1,525 per night, depending on season and size of accommodations. Pets are not permitted. Contact La Casa del Zorro Desert Resort, 3845 Yaqui Pass Road, Borrego Springs, CA 92004-5000, 760/767-5323 or 800/824-1884, website: www.lacasadelzorro.com.

Directions
From Julian, drive east on Highway 78 for 19 miles to Highway S-3/Yaqui Pass Road. Turn left (north) on Highway S-3 and drive six miles to La Casa del Zorro Desert Resort, on the right side of the road.

6 JULIAN BED AND BREAKFAST GUILD
off Highway 79 in Julian

Luxury rating: ★ ★ ★ ★ ☆   **Recreation rating:** ★ ★ ★ ★ ☆

The biggest event in the charming mountain town of Julian is apple season (from September to November), when the primary activity of locals and tourists alike is visiting bakeries and taste-testing apple pies. But if

mountain biking, horseback
riding, fishing, and hiking interest you as much as baked
goods, you're in luck. Julian is
the place for all these things.

Plan your trip with a phone
call to the Julian Bed and
Breakfast Guild, a group of individuals who are the keepers
of 20 different cabins and
country lodgings. (Make sure
you state specifically that you
want a cabin; other accommodations are also available.) The
colorful names of the cabin offerings tell you how special they
are: Lutz Castle, Little Nest, the

© ANN MARIE BROWN

The summit of Stonewall Peak at Cuyamaca
Rancho State Park

Artist's Loft, Rocking Horse, Mountain High, and so on. All the cabins
are different, but most are in a wooded or country setting and include a
fireplace, fully equipped kitchen, television, and VCR. Many have
whirlpool tubs or spas.

I stayed at Lutz Castle, a 50-year-old adobe cottage a few miles outside
of town. The innkeepers were a lovely couple who did everything possible to make me feel at home and to provide me with information on outdoor recreation around Julian. The choice of nearby parks is wider here
than almost anywhere in Southern California—there's William Heise
County Park, Cuyamaca Rancho State Park, Cleveland National Forest,
and Anza-Borrego Desert State Park—and all are within a 30-minute
drive. You can hike, mountain bike, or ride your horse on hundreds of
miles of trails.

For tamer excursions, visit the area's wineries or the Santa Ysabel
Mission. Or take an interesting tour of Eagle and High Peak Mines, Julian's hard rock gold mines that date back to 1870. Each of Julian's four
seasons has its own charm: In spring, the plentiful lilac bushes and daf-
fodils bloom; in summer, the mountain breezes keep the temperature
comfortable; in fall, the area's black oaks do their color-changing trick
and the apple harvest occurs; and in winter, you might even get caught
in a sudden snowstorm.

Facilities

There are 20 lodgings ranging in size from one to two bedrooms. Some have fully equipped kitchens and a whirlpool tub or spa. Linens and towels are provided.

Reservations and Rates
Reservations are recommended. Fees are $79–250 per night, depending on season and type of accommodations. Pets are permitted in some lodgings. Contact Julian Bed and Breakfast Guild, P.O. Box 1711, Julian, CA 92036, 760/765-1555, website: www.julianbnbguild.com; Lutz Castle, P.O. Box 1285, Julian, CA 92036, 760/765-0208, website: www.lutzcastle.com.

Directions
From San Diego, drive east on I-8 for 40 miles to the Highway 79 exit. Drive north on Highway 79 for 25 miles to Julian.

7 SHADOW MOUNTAIN RANCH
off Highway 79 in Julian

Luxury rating: ★ ★ ★ ☆   **Recreation rating:** ★ ★ ★ ☆

Shadow Mountain Ranch is a unique bed-and-breakfast in the Pine Hills area outside of Julian, San Diego's famous apple town. Situated on eight forested acres, the ranch has four theme cottages that are filled with whimsy and fantasy.

The Gnome Home is not only packed with gnome carvings, books, and figurines, it also resembles a gnome's home. The ranch owners describe the exterior as looking like a tree stump; I'd call it something closer to a mushroom. Regardless, the cabin has hand-carved doors and furniture, as well as a rock waterfall shower and sink.

The Tree House is nestled high in the branches of an ancient oak tree. A stairway leads up to it from the deck below. The Enchanted Cottage sits on a grassy knoll overlooking the pine trees. It has a cozy window seat, a woodstove, and a Bavarian-style exterior with an arched wooden doorway. Manzanita Cottage is a two-bedroom unit

© ANN MARIE BROWN

that sits alongside a meadow. It is the only cottage with a kitchen, and it is large enough for two couples.

There is much to do on the ranch property, including swimming in the lap pool, soaking in the whirlpool tub, feeding the ranch animals, and participating in archery, badminton, croquet, and horseshoes. A hearty country breakfast is served each morning, plus tea in the afternoon and a glass of sherry or warm vanilla milk in the evening. Shadow Mountain Ranch has no facilities for children; this is primarily an adult bed-and-breakfast.

The ranch is perfectly situated for a visit to William Heise County Park, just two miles down the road. First-timers should hike the Desert View and Canyon Oak Loop to check out the high vista at Glen's View. Although this region was burned in the wildfires of 2003, the foliage is rapidly making a comeback, and in a few short years, the landscape will be completely green once again. It will be fascinating to watch as the changes occur.

Facilities
There are four one- and two-bedroom cottages that can accommodate two to four people. One cottage has a fully equipped kitchen. Linens and towels are provided.

Reservations and Rates
Reservations are recommended. Fees are $130–260 per night, including breakfast. Pets are not permitted. Contact Shadow Mountain Ranch, P.O. Box 791, 2771 Frisius Road, Julian, CA 92036, 760/765-0323, website: www.bnbcity.com/inns/20002.

Directions
From San Diego, drive east on I-8 for 40 miles to the Highway 79 exit. Drive north on Highway 79 for 25 miles to Julian. Turn left on Highway 78, drive one mile past town, then turn left on Pine Hills Road. Drive three miles and turn left on Frisius Road; Shadow Mountain Ranch is on the right.

8 PINE HILLS LODGE
off Highway 79 in Julian

Luxury rating: ★ ★ ★ ☆ ☆   Recreation rating: ★ ★ ★ ☆ ☆

The Pine Hills Lodge in Julian is part cabin resort, part historic lodge and Western pub, and part dinner theater. Built in 1912, the lobby has an open-beamed log ceiling, a huge native-stone fireplace, and inviting willow chairs. The adjacent Pine Hills Pub is popular with Julian locals and visitors alike; it's the kind of place that fills up whenever a big football game is on television.

The lodge's cabins look quite ordinary on the outside but have been completely remodeled on the inside. They feature wrought-iron and wood furniture, down comforters, and fireplaces or wood-burning stoves. The best of the lot are North Star, a one-bedroom cabin with a screened porch, a king bed, and a sitting room with a wood-burning stove; and Blue Bird One, a two-bedroom cabin with a stone fireplace and an antique claw-foot tub.

None of the cabins have kitchens; a continental breakfast is served in the dining room each day, and the lodge restaurant is open most nights for dinner. The town of Julian is only five minutes away and has several casual but good restaurants. Try breakfast at the Julian Cafe (out-of-this-world apple oatmeal pancakes) or any meal at the Julian Grille or Rongbranch Cafe. In addition to good food, you'll find a warm Western ambience at all of Julian's establishments—a tribute to its rich history as a 19th-century gold mining town.

One of Pine Hills Lodge's highlights is its weekend dinner theater, with musicals and comedies performed following a country barbecue of baby-back ribs, baked chicken, and all the trimmings. Combined cabin-and-the-ater packages are offered for Friday nights.

The surrounding area is filled with recreation opportunities, from hiking the trails of nearby William Heise County Park to exploring the more remote areas of Cleveland National Forest. Although much of this land was badly burned in the wildfires of 2003, a surprising

© ANN MARIE BROWN

amount was spared, and even the burned areas are quickly recovering. Call the local Forest Service office at 760/788-0250 to find out the status of local trails at the time of your visit. For cyclists, the pedaling opportunities are endless on the hilly country roads around Julian.

Facilities
There are 12 cabins ranging in size from one to two bedrooms. Some cabins are duplexes; none have kitchens. Lodge rooms are also available. A restaurant is on-site. Linens and towels are provided.

Reservations and Rates
Reservations are recommended. Fees are $96–178 per night and include the continental breakfast. Pets are not permitted. Contact Pine Hills Lodge, 2960 La Posada Way, P.O. Box 2260, Julian, CA 92036, 760/765-1100, website: www.pinehillslodge.com.

Directions
From San Diego, drive east on I-8 for 40 miles to the Highway 79 exit. Drive north on Highway 79 for 25 miles to Julian. Turn left (west) on Highway 78, drive one mile past town, then turn left (south) on Pine Hills Road. Drive 2.5 miles and turn right at the sign for Pine Hills Lodge.

9 WILLIAM HEISE COUNTY PARK CABINS
off Highway 79 in Julian

Luxury rating: ★ ★ ☆ ☆ ☆   **Recreation rating:** ★ ★ ★ ☆ ☆

Rank: Best Value

William Heise County Park was hit hard by the Cedar Fire of October 2003, but it is undergoing a rapid recovery and will soon be lush and green again. The park has always been a favorite of San Diego hikers and campers—even more so in recent years, since four wooden cabins were added to the campground. The cabins are designed for year-round use, which at this 4,000-foot elevation means they come equipped with a fireplace heater and insulation.

More deluxe than you might expect, the cabins also have electric lights, a table and chairs, a food pantry, and wooden bunks that can accommodate up to four people. You bring your own sleeping pad or mattress for the bunks, as well as your own bedding or sleeping bag. If there are more than four people in your party, you are allowed to set up a tent or two out-side your cabin.

Even though the cabins are nice and modern, this is still camping, so you will have to walk to the public bathrooms when nature calls. Hot showers are available, but you'll have to wait your turn at the camp shower facility. And if you want to cook a meal, you must do it outside your cabin, either over a campfire or on a camp stove. You could argue that an overnight stay in one of these cabins is only one step up from regular tent camping, but in the winter months, when the temperature hits freezing, it's a big step.

What you'll see at William Heise County Park is a dense woodland re-covering from a major wildfire. Many of the park's oak trees were burned in the fire but still stand tall and have started producing new leaves. As this book goes to press, only four miles of park trails have been reopened for public use, including the campground's nature trail: Desert View and Canyon Oak Loop. The three-mile loop provides visitors with a great op-portunity to view the process of fire ecology close up, as new shoots pop up from the ground and the land greens up. The trail tops out at a high overlook known as Glen's View. Since the fire, the vista here is better than it has been for years. You'll spy the Anza-Borrego Desert, the Salton Sea, and even the Pacific Ocean.

Facilities
There are four cabins that can accommodate up to four people. None of the accommodations have kitchens or bathrooms. Linens and towels are not provided.

Reservations and Rates
Reservations are recommended. The fee is $35 per night. Pets are not per-mitted. Contact William Heise County Park, 760/765-0650; San Diego County Parks and Recreation Department, 2454 Heritage Park Row, San Diego, CA 92110, 858/694-3049, website: www.sdparks.org.

Directions
From San Diego, drive east on I-8 for 40 miles to the Highway 79 exit. Drive north on Highway 79 for 25 miles to Julian. Turn left (west) on Highway 78, drive one mile past town, then turn left (south) on Pine Hills Road. Drive two miles, turn left on Frisius Drive, and drive two more miles. Frisius Drive turns into Heise Park Road and enters the park.

Other Cabins and Cottages Nearby
Julian Gold Rush Hotel, 2032 Main Street, P.O. Box 1856, Julian, CA 92036, website: www.julianhotel.com.

10 STAGECOACH TRAILS RESORT

off Highway S-2 near Agua Caliente Hot Springs

Luxury rating: ★ ★ ☆ ☆ ☆   **Recreation rating:** ★ ★ ★ ☆ ☆

You won't rent a cabin or cottage at Stagecoach Trails Resort; instead, it will be a mobile home. But you can't be too picky when you're in the middle of 600,000-acre Anza-Borrego Desert State Park. In this southern stretch of the huge desert, your only other options are tent camping or sleeping in the shade of a mesquite tree. Suddenly, a trailer starts to look really good.

Palm Bowl Grove at Anza-Borrego Desert State Park

Stagecoach Trails Resort is in the desolate but beautiful Shelter Valley area of Anza-Borrego. The resort is very popular with the horsey set; more than 70 corrals are here for folks who travel with their horses. There are more horseback trails around this area of the desert than you could cover in a month of galloping.

For those who prefer to get around on their own two feet, the resort's proximity to the park's trailheads at Blair Valley allow you to hike to see Native American pictographs and the remains of a 1930s desert homestead. It's also near Agua Caliente County Park, where you can soak away your cares in hot spring pools; the water temperature is 96°F year-round. Another few miles to the south is Mountain Palm Springs Campground at Anza-Borrego, where hiking trails lead to five different palm groves, including Pygmy Grove's 50 short palms, and spectacular Palm Bowl, ringed by more than 100 palms.

The trailer rentals have everything you need for your stay, including kitchen utensils and linens. If you don't want to cook inside your trailer, a fire ring and charcoal barbecue are outside. Two of the trailers have large decks where you can sit out and watch the desert days turn to desert nights.

The best season to visit Anza-Borrego is unquestionably early spring, when you can witness the spectacle of blooming desert wildflowers. Call the park's wildflower hotline (760/767-4684) in season to find out the exact status of the bloom; it usually occurs between mid-February and mid-March. If you can't make it then, plan your trip for any time from November until May, when the desert has comfortable temperatures for hiking and exploring almost every day. Summer is too hot for anything but stargazing and sitting still.

Facilities

There are five rental trailers that can accommodate up to four people. A general store is on-site. Linens and towels are provided.

Reservations and Rates

Reservations are recommended. Fees are $50–150 per night, with a two-night minimum. Pets upon request. Contact Stagecoach Trails Resort, 7878 Great Southern Overland Stage Route of 1849, Julian, CA 92036, 760/765-2197 or 877/896-2267, website: www.stagecoachtrails.com.

Directions

From Julian, drive east on Highway 78 for 11 miles to Highway S-2. Turn right and drive four miles to the resort on the right.

11 CUYAMACA RANCHO STATE PARK CABINS
off Highway 79 near Julian

Luxury rating: ★★☆☆☆   **Recreation rating:** ★★★★☆

Most people assume that the cute little cabins at Cuyamaca Rancho State Park burned to the ground in the Cedar Fire of October 2003, which destroyed an estimated 90 percent of the park's acreage. In fact, three of the six cabins at Paso Picacho Campground were reduced to ashes, but the rebuilding process has already begun. Park officials expect that all six cabins will be available for rent once again beginning in May of 2005.

Before the fire, Cuyamaca Rancho State Park was known as one of San Diego's biggest and loveliest parks, with elevations ranging from 4,000 to 6,500 feet and a whopping 25,000 acres of deciduous forest, conifers, chaparral, meadows, and rocky peaks. Although the fire seemed like a great tragedy to many San Diego hikers, fire is a normal and necessary part of the ecosystem here, and the landscape recovers remarkably quickly. Although it will be decades until the dense forests of Cuyamaca Rancho return to their previous splendor, many of the lower growing plants and shrubs are already green and growing. Hikers can look forward to spectacular wildflower displays in the next several spring seasons. Progress is being made daily as park employees and volunteers work to reopen many of the park's original 100 miles of hiking trails. (For current details on the rebuilding and reopenings of trails and structures at Cuyamaca Rancho State Park, see the websites: www.cuyamaca.us or www.cuyamaca.statepark.org.)

Assuming that the cabins will reopen on schedule, visitors will once again be able to choose from five modern pine cabins and the Nature Den, a charming old stone-and-wood building built in 1933 by the Civilian Conservation Corps (the Nature Den lost its roof in the fire, but its stone walls withstood the inferno). The pine cabins are 12-foot by 12-foot one-room structures, with bunk beds that sleep four (there are no mattresses, so bring a sleeping bag and pad), a deck, a picnic table, a fire ring, and a barbecue. As many as eight people are allowed per cabin, but if your group is more than four, bring along a tent for the extras, because there is no way they will fit inside. The Nature Den offers a few luxuries, including cots with mattresses, electricity, a coffeemaker, a microwave oven, and a fireplace. As at the other cabins, you must take a short walk to use the campground restroom and shower facilities.

In the past, the cabins at Cuyamaca Rancho were so popular that you had to reserve your stay as much as six months in advance for the summer months. The same is likely to be true for the future. Although it is hard to believe in the immediate aftermath of the fire, nature heals, and heals quickly. Cuyamaca Rancho State Park will be reborn and made beautiful once again.

Facilities

There are six cabins at Paso Picacho Campground and one at Los Caballos Horse Camp. Each cabin can accommodate four people. Water and restrooms are nearby. One cabin (the Nature Den) has electricity, a microwave, and a coffeemaker. Linens and towels are not provided.

Reservations and Rates

Reservations are required; call Reserve America at 800/444-7275 or visit their website: www.reserveamerica.com. Fees are $25–40 per night. Pets are permitted. Contact Cuyamaca Rancho State Park, 12551 Highway 79, Descanso, CA 91916, 760/765-0755 (see above for reservations phone number), website: www.cuyamaca.org.

Directions

From San Diego, drive east on I-8 for 40 miles to the Highway 79 exit. Drive north on Highway 79 for 11 miles, then turn left (west) into Paso Picacho Campground.

12 BLUE JAY LODGE
off Highway S-1 on Mount Laguna

Luxury rating: ★ ★ ★ ☆ ☆   **Recreation rating:** ★ ★ ★ ★ ☆

The Laguna Mountain Recreation Area is a fun-filled land of outdoor adventure within an hour's drive of downtown San Diego. Favorite activities include hiking, horseback riding, mountain biking, and—as unlikely as it sounds—frolicking in the snow. At just shy of 6,000 feet in elevation, the Laguna Mountains are San Diego's backyard snow-play area, at least during the few weeks each year when the white stuff sticks to the ground.

In any season, there is so much fun outdoor recreation in the Lagunas that you should plan to stay for a few days. If you like your cabin vacation a little on the eccentric side, Blue Jay Lodge might be your place. Although it looks normal enough from the outside, inside the Blue Jay's restaurant and saloon is some funky decor: The barstools are bright red tractor seats; wagon wheels and antique farming tools hang from the ceiling and walls, interspersed with a few dozen trophy fish; the dining tables and benches are carved from giant Northwest pine trees; and two stuffed bears stand on their back paws, with teeth bared and tongues wagging.

The Blue Jay Lodge does not

© ANN MARIE BROWN

allow children or pets; each of the cabins is for one or two adults only. All the log cabins have cozy fireplaces, but bring your own firewood. Also, make sure you pack along dishes, utensils, and cooking supplies, because the cabins have full kitchens but not so much as a plastic spoon.

Although they are quaint one-room structures built in the 1920s, the cabins are surprisingly large, with a separate sleeping area, a kitchen/dining area, and a living area. The cabin I visited had some rather whimsical furniture, including a bed made of logs. After a good night's rest on it, I sat outside on the deck in the morning and watched the acorn woodpeckers flitting in the oak trees. The cabins are spaced far enough apart for privacy and quiet.

Not-to-be-missed activities in the Laguna Mountain Recreation Area include a four-mile round-trip hike to Garnet Peak for spectacular views of the Anza-Borrego Desert. Shorter walks can be taken on the Lightning Ridge Trail, Desert View Nature Trail, and the Wooded Hill Nature Trail. Hiking, mountain biking, and equestrian trails are also in Cuyamaca Rancho State Park, a short drive away.

Facilities
There are four cabins that can accommodate two people each. All have kitchens, but none have cooking or eating utensils. An on-site restaurant is open Friday through Sunday only. Linens and towels are provided.

Reservations and Rates
Reservations are recommended. Fees are $85–100 per night. Pets and children are not permitted.

Directions
From San Diego, drive east on I-8 for 47 miles to the Highway S-1/Sunrise Scenic Byway turnoff. Drive north on Highway S-1 for 10 miles to the town of Mount Laguna. Blue Jay Lodge is on the east side of the road.

From Julian, drive south on Highway 79 for six miles, then turn left and continue south on Highway S-1 for 15 miles to the town of Mount Laguna. Blue Jay Lodge is on the east side of the road. Contact Blue Jay Lodge, P.O. Box 150, Mount Laguna, CA 91948, 619/473-8844.

13 LAGUNA MOUNTAIN LODGE
off Highway S-1 on Mount Laguna

Luxury rating: ★ ★ ★ ☆ ☆   **Recreation rating:** ★ ★ ★ ★ ☆

© ANN MARIE BROWN

Blue Jay Lodge (see the previous listing) and Laguna Mountain Lodge are across the road from each other, near the summit of Mount Laguna, in the Laguna Mountain Recreation Area. Both offer an authentic mountain cabin experience in all four seasons of the year, but Blue Jay Lodge's cabins are only large enough for two adults, and pets and children are not permitted. If you are traveling with kids or Fido, plan a stay at Laguna Mountain Lodge, which has cabins ranging in size from one to three bedrooms. Some have fireplaces and kitchens, so be sure to ask for exactly what you want.

Just like at Blue Jay Lodge, Laguna Mountain Lodge's cabin kitchens are not equipped with utensils, dishes, pots, or pans. If you plan to cook, come prepared. If you plan to eat out, understand that there are few services in the Lagunas. Unless you're willing to drive, you're confined to the restaurant at Blue Jay Lodge (open from Friday to Sunday only) and the small grocery store at Laguna Mountain Lodge.

Trails for hikers, mountain bikers, and equestrians are plentiful in the area, and road cyclists can ride the spectacular scenic byway. Laguna Mountain Lodge is next to the Forest Service's Laguna Mountain Visitor Information Station, where you can pick up maps and get all the information you need. If you're lucky enough to time your visit for when snow is on the ground, you won't need any instructions. Just get out there and make some snow angels, or, for the more sophisticated, try sledding or cross-country skiing.

Facilities
There are 15 cabins ranging in size from one to three bedrooms, plus motel units. Most cabins have kitchens; none have cooking or eating utensils. A general store is on-site. Linens and towels are provided.

Reservations and Rates

Reservations are recommended. Fees are $60–135 per night. Pets are permitted in some cabins for a $10 fee.

Directions

From San Diego, drive east on I-8 for 47 miles to the Highway S-1/Sunrise Scenic Byway turnoff. Drive north on Highway S-1 for 10 miles to the town of Mount Laguna. Laguna Mountain Lodge is on the west side of the road.

From Julian, drive south on Highway 79 for six miles, then turn left and continue south on Highway S-1 for 15 miles to the town of Mount Laguna. Laguna Mountain Lodge is on the west side of the road. Contact Laguna Mountain Lodge, P.O. Box 146, 10678 Sunrise Highway, Mount Laguna, CA 91948, 619/445-2342 or 619/473-8533, website: www.lagunamountain.com.

14 CRYSTAL PIER HOTEL
off I-5 in Pacific Beach

Luxury rating: ★ ★ ★ ★ ☆   **Recreation rating:** ★ ★ ★ ★ ☆

Rank: Best for Beach Activities

The Crystal Pier Hotel is not a hotel at all but a series of side-by-side cottages perched on top of weather-beaten Crystal Pier, in Pacific Beach. From your cottage, you overlook a large expanse of wide blue ocean, and simultaneously, you sit on top of it. The surf rumbles beneath you day and night; it's much like being on a boat at sea but without needing the Dramamine.

In the 1930s, 20 cottages were built on the pier. Six more were added in the 1990s, near the pier's end. The end units are more modern, with nicer amenities and a slightly higher price tag. These are by far the best choice; their views are exquisite, and they offer the most privacy.

All 26 cottages are charming blue and white buildings, each with a design carved into its wooden shutters: starfish, dolphins, sailboats, even Mickey Mouse. Each has a full kitchen, allowing you to prepare your meals then carry your food to your deck for an ocean-side picnic. And each cottage comes with a precious privilege: one parking space on the pier and a key code for the driveway gate.

Although the Crystal Pier Hotel is wildly popular in summer, the best time to visit is in fall or winter. Not only do the hotel's rates drop after October 1, but also the beach crowds dissipate and the carnival atmosphere

© ANN MARIE BROWN

of Pacific Beach quiets down. If you surf, swim, beachcomb, or just like to walk on the sand and gaze at the waves, you'll be in heaven.

There's one more perquisite worth mentioning: because you're situated on a pier just above the ocean, you can go fishing right outside your door. The hotel rents equipment if you didn't bring your own.

Facilities
There are 26 one- and two-bedroom cottages, all with kitchenettes. Linens and towels are provided.

Reservations and Rates
Reservations are recommended. Fees are $180–280 per night. Pets are not permitted. Contact Crystal Pier Hotel, 4500 Ocean Boulevard, San Diego, CA 92109, 858/483-6983 or 800/748-5894, website: www.crystalpier.com.

Directions
From I-5 in Pacific Beach, exit at Garnet Avenue and drive west to the ocean. Crystal Pier is at the end of Garnet Avenue.

15 THE BEACH COTTAGES
off I-5 in Pacific Beach

Luxury rating: ★ ★ ★ ☆ ☆   **Recreation rating:** ★ ★ ★ ★ ☆
Rank: Best for Beach Activities

If you have a family or a group of friends who want to play at the beach for a few days or a week, The Beach Cottages are the ideal vacation home base. Located inches from the sand in Pacific Beach, the cottages come fully equipped with towels, linens, dishes, and silverware, so all you need to pack are your bathing suits and surfboards.

Keep in mind that this won't be a peaceful, solitary getaway. Pacific Beach (or "PB," as the locals say) is a hopping party town, with a wide and varied

© ANN MARIE BROWN

selection of bars and late-night eateries. Its oceanfront biking/jogging/in-line skating trail runs between The Beach Cottages and the sand, and upon its level pavement, a perpetual chain of beach people ride, stride, and roll. Basically, you'll be living in a fishbowl. Also, the cottages are placed about a foot apart, so you'll certainly get to know your vacationing neighbors.

Nonetheless, you won't find a Southern California beach experience more authentic than this one. Volleyball, bikinis, ice cream, perfect San Diego weather . . . they have it all here. Pacific Beach is especially popular with surfers, so if you are one or enjoy watching them, you'll be happy here.

Kids will find much to amuse themselves: The beach is an obvious magnet, but when parents insist that it's time to get out of the water, they can play shuffleboard or ping-pong in the common area between the cottages. Those with bikes or in-line skates can join the throngs on the paved beach trail; it runs nearly two miles south to the Mission Bay breakwater.

If you decide you're ready for some peace and quiet, drive a few miles north to Torrey Pines State Reserve and walk a few of its short but sweet coastal trails. Be sure to check out the views of the dramatic coastal badlands from Razor Point Trail.

Facilities

There are 17 one- and two-bedroom cottages that can accommodate up to six people; all have fully equipped kitchens. Apartments and motel rooms are also available. Linens and towels are provided.

Reservations and Rates

Reservations are recommended. Fees are $160–260 per night. Pets are not permitted. Contact The Beach Cottages, 4255 Ocean Boulevard, San Diego, CA 92109, 858/483-7440, website: www.beachcottages.com.

Directions

From I-5 in Pacific Beach, exit at Garnet Avenue and drive west to Mission Boulevard. Turn left, drive four blocks, and turn right on Reed Avenue. The Beach Cottages are at Reed Avenue and Ocean Boulevard.

16 SAN DIEGO VACATION COTTAGES
off I-5 in Old Town and Ocean Beach

Luxury rating: ★ ★ ★ ☆ ☆   **Recreation rating:** ★ ★ ★ ☆ ☆

San Diego Vacation Cottages is a company run by a couple of transplanted Australians who have the right idea about how to structure a fun, economical vacation. Their formula is simple: offer cottages and apartments for rent in appealing neighborhoods, where people can stay for a few days, a week, or longer and be surrounded by the comforts of home, not the impersonal amenities of a hotel.

The company offers cottages in two locations within a short distance of each other: Old Town and Ocean Beach. The Old Town cottages are small garden bungalows that were completely remodeled in 2000. Despite their small size, they are bright and cheerful inside, with Mexican-style decor (Saltillo tile and colorful fabrics) and brand-new kitchens. Although the cottages share common walls, they are surprisingly quiet and private, both inside and out. Each unit includes a flower-lined patio and barbecue. All of Old Town's shops and restaurants, plus Old Town State Historic Park, are within walking distance.

The Ocean Beach cottages were remodeled in 1999 and also feature new kitchens and furnishings. They are similar to the Old Town cottages but have brightly colored beach decor instead of Mexican styling and a choice of one, two, or three bedrooms. The beach is a one-block walk from the cottages. Because they are right next door to Mission Bay, guests can take advantage of personal watercraft riding, sailing, biking, and windsurfing at Mission Bay Park.

Both locations are only minutes from San Diego's popular attractions: Sea World, the Historic Gas Lamp District, and San Diego Zoo, as well as many natural attractions, including the rare trees at Torrey Pines State Reserve and the tidepools at Cabrillo National Monument.

Facilities

There are 12 one-bedroom cottages in Old Town and 10 one-, two-, and three-bedroom cottages in Ocean Beach. All cottages have fully equipped kitchens. Linens and towels are provided.

Reservations and Rates

Reservations are recommended. Fees are $89–269 per night. Pets are not permitted. Contact San Diego Vacation Cottages, Booking Office, 2422 San Diego Avenue, San Diego, CA 92110, 619/291-9091 or 888/271-5496, website: www.sandiegovacationapts.com.

Directions

From I-5 in downtown San Diego, drive north for five miles to the Old Town exit. Turn east and drive two blocks to Congress Street; follow Congress Street until it becomes San Diego Avenue. The reservations office is at 2422 San Diego Avenue.

17 HARBOR VACATIONS CLUB
off I-5 on Harbor Island

Luxury rating: ★ ★ ★ ☆ ☆   **Recreation rating:** ★ ★ ★ ☆ ☆

They don't call them cottages at Harbor Vacations Club, they call them "floating dockside villas." And if spending the night in a floating villa doesn't float your boat, you can choose between a few luxury yachts.

Harbor Vacations Club, on Harbor Island, bills itself as the world's only floating resort. What makes it unique from other boat-and-breakfast companies is that it is a full-service property with a heated pool, bicycle rentals, and on-site catering. You don't just have access to your rented boat or villa, you also have access to amenities that are usually associated with a hotel or motel.

The floating villas look a lot like tall, square mobile homes set in the shallow harbor water. Three are 700 square feet in size and are fully equipped with washer and dryer, microwave, television, and VCR. They sleep four comfortably. One villa, the *Capistrano,* is a whopping 1,250 square feet spread out over two stories. It has three bedrooms and a great view of the marina from the upper level. If you want a more traditional boat to spend the night in, Harbor Vacations Club has a 41-foot luxury yacht with a mahogany-and-teak interior and two state-rooms, plus three 55-foot Bluewater yachts.

You can prepare your own meals in all of the yachts and villas, but you won't need to worry about breakfast: Each guest receives a coupon for a full breakfast at a harbor café. No matter which accommodations you choose, understand that Harbor Vacations Club's location, on Harbor Island, is within a couple miles of San Diego airport. Although you won't hear much plane traffic at night, you will hear it during the day.

Harbor Vacations Club also offers charter services on its yachts and sailboats. For an extra fee, you can hire a captain (since you're not allowed to drive the yacht yourself) and go for a cruise around the bay before retiring for the night.

Facilities
There are four floating villas and four yachts for nightly rentals. They can accommodate four to six people. All boats have fully equipped galleys. Linens and towels are provided.

Reservations and Rates
Reservations are recommended. Fees are $150–325 per night. Pets are not permitted. Contact Harbor Vacations Club, 1880 Harbor Island Drive, G-Dock, San Diego, CA 92101, 619/297-9484 or 800/922-4836, website: www.harborvacationsclub.com.

Directions
From I-5 heading south in San Diego, take the Highway 209/Rosecrans Street exit. Drive south about three miles, then turn left on Nimitz Boulevard and drive to its end. Turn left on North Harbor Drive, drive two miles, then turn right on Harbor Island Drive. Turn right for Marina Cortez G-Dock.

18 SAN DIEGO METRO KOA
off I-805 in Chula Vista

Luxury rating: ★ ★ ☆ ☆ ☆   **Recreation rating:** ★ ★ ★ ☆ ☆

The San Diego Metro KOA is one of the largest and busiest KOA campgrounds in California. It's no surprise, considering the popularity of San Diego as a vacation destination and the low cost of staying in a KOA cabin.

© ANN MARIE BROWN

The KOA has 24 cabins—both the old-style one-room log cabins that sleep four and the newer two-room cabins that sleep six. The one-room cabins have twin bunk beds and a double bed (all with mattresses, but you must bring your own bedding). The two-room cabins have two sets of bunk beds in one room and a double bed in the second room.

Additionally, a KOA Kamper Kitchen is placed among the cluster of cabins. This is a gazebo-style kitchen (roof but no walls) that consists of sinks, stove tops, and a propane barbecue. It is shared among everyone in the campground but is mostly used by cabin guests.

The campground is loaded with extra amenities, including a year-round heated pool, a playground, a convenience store, and children's bike rentals. Everything is packed tightly into a fairly small space, but nobody seems to mind.

Most people use the KOA as a base for exploring San Diego and going to the beach. The campground is within minutes of Silver Strand State Beach and the attractions of Coronado Island. Sea World, Mission Bay Park, Balboa Park, and Birch Aquarium are a 20-minute drive to the north. Lovers of tidepools and history should head for Cabrillo National Monument, where they can visit the historic Point Loma Lighthouse, walk the Bayside Trail, and study the invertebrate life at Cabrillo's tidepools.

Facilities
There are 18 one-room cabins and six two-room cabins. A shared outdoor

kitchen is available. A heated pool, a playground, and a small general store are on-site. Linens and towels are not provided.

Reservations and Rates
Reservations are recommended. Fees are $45–65 per night. Pets are not permitted. Contact San Diego Metro KOA, 111 North Second Avenue, Chula Vista, CA 91910, 800/562-9877, website: www.sandiegokoa.com.

Directions
From I-5 in Chula Vista, take the Bonita Road exit. Drive west for one mile to Second Avenue. Turn right and drive one mile to the KOA, on the right.

19 LAKE MORENA COUNTY PARK CABINS
off I-8 near Campo

Luxury rating: ★ ★ ☆ ☆ ☆   **Recreation rating:** ★ ★ ★ ☆ ☆

Morena Reservoir is so far south, it is practically in Mexico, but not quite. At 3,200 feet in elevation, the lake is the highest and most remote of San Diego County's reservoirs. But it is well known and well loved by people who like to fish. The reservoir, which everyone calls Lake Morena, is known for high catch rates and big fish; the lake-record bass weighed near-ly 20 pounds, and the lake-record trout weighed nearly 10 pounds. Bass fishing is best in spring, of course; trout fishing is best in winter.

Camping is another popular activity at Lake Morena, and it's gotten even more popular now that the county of San Diego installed 10 wooden cabins amid the numerous tent and RV sites. Suddenly, "camping" has gone deluxe, and groups of up to eight people can enjoy having a roof over their head. It's still not too deluxe though—the cabins don't have elec-tricity or running water. You bring your own flashlights or lanterns to light your cabin, you walk to the camp restrooms when the need strikes you in the middle of the night, and you sleep in bunk-style beds in your own sleeping bag.

Nobody complains though, because these little cabins are cozy and warm, and best of all, each one has a great view of Lake Morena. Even if you don't fish, you'll enjoy sitting outside on the porch of your cabin, admiring the ancient oaks that dot the campground and watching small boats cruise around the lake. Rowboats can be rented at the nearby ma-rina. If you get inspired, you can lace up your boots and set off on the

Pacific Crest Trail, which runs right through the park. If you would prefer a less vigorous excursion, you can drive over to the nearby town of Campo and take a ride on a historic Pacific Southwest Railway train, or spend an hour or two in the railroad museum.

The only possible downer to a trip to Lake Morena is that you never know what you'll get until you show up: the lake's water level fluctuates constantly, and when the level is low, it ain't pretty.

Facilities

There are 10 cabins that can accommodate up to eight people. None of the accommodations have kitchens or bathrooms. Linens and towels are not provided.

Reservations and Rates

Reservations are recommended. Fees are $25 per night. Pets are not permitted. Contact San Diego County Parks and Recreation Department, 2454 Heritage Park Row, San Diego, CA 92110, 858/694-3049, website: www.sdparks.org.

Directions

From San Diego, drive approximately 50 miles east on I-8. Take the Buckman Springs Road/County Road S1 exit and drive 5.5 miles south. Turn right on Oak Drive and follow signs to the park at 2330 Lake Morena Drive.

Chapter 5

© ANN MARIE BROWN

Yosemite and Mammoth Lakes

Yosemite and Mammoth Lakes

lunging waterfalls, stark granite, alpine lakes, pristine meadows, giant trees, snowbound slopes, and raging rivers—you'll find them all in this region, which encompasses not only world-famous Yosemite National Park but also the popular recreation areas of Mammoth Lakes and the eastern Sierra, as well as the central Sierra foothills and recreation lakes.

One of the most plentiful areas for outdoor recreation, the Yosemite region offers something for everybody—hikers, anglers, boaters, skiers, rock climbers, bikers, equestrians, and those who simply want to breathe the mountain air. Along with limitless recreation opportunities come an abundance of interesting places to stay—ski chalets, cozy bed-and-breakfast cottages, fishing camp–style rustic cabins, and hike-in tent cabins.

The centerpiece of this region, of course, is Yosemite National Park, a must-see on every traveler's itinerary. Because it receives more than four million visitors each year, you'd expect the park to be constantly overrun. But vacation-wise visitors understand that the best way to see the famous park is to show up in the off-season (October to April) or to keep to weekday trips in summer.

The off-season happens to be primetime in Yosemite anyway. Spring is the optimal season to view Yosemite Valley's famous waterfalls, three of which are among the tallest in the world. Autumn is the best time to admire the towering granite of El Capitan, Half Dome, and Sentinel Rock as the valley's many deciduous trees turn colors then drop their leaves. Winter brings the chance to downhill ski and snowboard at Badger Pass or to cross-country ski or snowshoe on Glacier Point and among the Giant Sequoias.

Whereas the park accommodations described in this chapter may be difficult or impossible to obtain on Memorial Day or Fourth of July weekends, many lodgings are hungry for guests in the off-season or even on Tuesday nights in summer. Your chances for a roof over your head in the busy season are greater if you consider staying at one of several lodgings just outside the park boundary. Most are still within a 45-minute drive of Yosemite Valley, and many are even closer to Yosemite's high country on Tioga Road and Glacier Point Road. Keep in mind there are many ways to make a Yosemite vacation work—even in the peak months, and even without having reservations months in advance.

Nearly as popular as the national park itself are the resort towns just to the east, particularly Mammoth Lakes and June Lake, on the U.S. 395 corridor. With easy access from Los Angeles and San Diego (a straight shot up U.S. 395), the eastern Sierra has long been a favorite destination for Southern Californians.

Heavily visited for skiing and snowboarding in winter, the eastern Sierra is also ideal for fishing, hiking, and biking in the warmer seasons. Expect a more rugged, dramatic landscape than what you'll find in the western Sierra; the east side boasts higher peaks and a steeper escarpment than the gentler west side. This means a longer and more deeply snowbound winter. It also means strenuous hiking and biking in summer (most trails include a steep climb!) and sometimes highly technical fishing (bring your float tube and fly fishing gear).

Resorts in the eastern Sierra are frequently full-service enterprises, and may include cabins, a marina with rental boats and fishing gear, a pack station with horse rentals, a restaurant, and a store. These resorts range from very rustic to very luxurious, and everything in between. Many have a loyal string of customers who come back year after year.

Last but not least in this chapter are the towns and resorts just north, west, and south of Yosemite National Park, where the Sierra foothills mark the transition zone between the low-elevation Central Valley and the high peaks of the Sierra crest. In this area, elevations range from 3,000 to 7,000 feet. Snow falls in the higher areas in winter but doesn't hang around until June. Forests are a dense mix of pines, cedars, and firs. Streams and rivers are filled with fishing spots and swimming holes, and recreation lakes like Pinecrest Lake and Beardsley Reservoir beckon boaters, water-skiers, swimmers, and anglers.

Renting a cabin or cottage in these areas usually means your vacation will be centered on the water: You wear your bathing suit or fishing clothes all day, hang your beach towels to dry on your cabin's front porch, and sit outside on warm nights bragging about the day's feats on the lake.

Clearly, there's something for everybody in Yosemite and Mammoth Lakes. Check out the pages that follow to locate the perfect cabin or cottage for your getaway to this world-class setting.

YOSEMITE AND MAMMOTH LAKES

© AVALON TRAVEL PUBLISHING, INC.

Contents

1. The Rivers Resort 169

2. The Cabins at Strawberry 170

3. Pinecrest Lake Resort 172

4. Pinecrest Chalet 173

5. Annett's Mono Village Resort 175

6. Twin Lakes Resort 176

7. Doc & Al's Resort 178

8. Hunewill Guest Ranch 179

9. Virginia Creek Settlement 181

10. Virginia Lakes Resort 183

11. Lundy Lake Resort 185

12. Tioga Pass Resort 186

13. Tioga Lodge 188

14. Yosemite Lakes 190

15. Evergreen Lodge 191

16. White Wolf Lodge 193

17. Yosemite High Sierra Camps 195

18. Tuolumne Lodge 197

19. Curry Village Cabins 198

20. Glacier Point Ski Hut 200

21. Silver Lake Resort 201

22. Reverse Creek Lodge 203

23. Fern Creek Lodge 204

24. The Four Seasons 206

25. Double Eagle Resort 207

26. Big Rock Resort 209

27. Alpers Owens River Ranch 211

28. KOA Yosemite-Mariposa 213

29. Yosemite West 215

30. Ostrander Ski Hut 216

31. The Redwoods Cabins 218

32. Owl's Nest Cabins 219

33. Apple Tree Inn 221

34. Mammoth Mountain Chalets 222

35. Red's Meadow Resort 224

36. Tamarack Lodge Resort 226

37. Crystal Crag Lodge 228

38. Woods Lodge 229

39. Wildyrie Resort 231

40. Hot Creek Ranch 232

41. Convict Lake Resort 234

42. Tom's Place Resort 236

43. Rock Creek Lakes Resort 238

44. Rock Creek Lodge 239

45. Paradise Resort 241

1 THE RIVERS RESORT
off Highway 108 in Strawberry

Luxury rating: ★ ★ ★ ☆ ☆   **Recreation rating:** ★ ★ ★ ☆ ☆

If you're not sure where Strawberry is, think small mountain town at 5,300 feet in elevation on the South Fork Stanislaus River. Think fishing in the river, swimming and boating at Pinecrest Lake, hiking in Stanislaus National Forest, and skiing at Dodge Ridge Ski Area.

Then think about The Rivers Resort, or as they say in their brochure, The Rivers Condominium Resort. Why condominium? It's a mystery, since their accommodations consist of 10 cabins ranging in size from one to four bedrooms and bearing no resemblance to condos except for their fully equipped kitchens and cable television. Although the cabins were built in the 1950s and are older in style, many have remodeled kitchens and bathrooms.

Cabin No. 3, a large four-bedroom unit for up to eight people, is right on the river. It's the preferred choice for those who want to sit on their deck and watch the water roll by. The rest are clustered nearby amid the conifers, only a stone's throw from the river. Not one of them is a bad choice.

It can get quite warm here in summer, so the resort has a 25- by 50-foot swimming pool on the grounds. Plenty of visitors cool off in the river too. (The pool, unlike the river, is heated.) A grocery store is right next door, so you can purchase anything you need. Across the road is a restaurant and bar at the historic Strawberry Inn.

The Rivers Resort makes a great base camp for day hikers. Among the many hikes possible in Stanislaus National Forest, one of the most fascinating is the Trail of the Gargoyles, off nearby Herring Creek Road. It's a short walk that passes by bizarre-looking geological formations perched on a high canyon rim. Another popular day hike is the short but strenuous climb to Burst Rock and Powell Lake in the Emigrant Wilderness.

If you want to let somebody else do the walking for you, there are horse rentals at two stables within a few miles of the resort.

Facilities

There are 10 cabins ranging in size from one to four bedrooms. All cabins have fully equipped kitchens. A store and restaurant are on-site. Linens and towels are provided.

Reservations and Rates

Reservations are recommended. Fees are $650–1,025 per week or $95–200 per night in the summer high season; during the rest of the year, rates are discounted. There is a two-night minimum. Pets are permitted in some cabins with a $150 deposit. Contact The Rivers Resort, P.O. Box 81, Strawberry, CA 95375, 209/965-3278 or 800/514-6777, website: www.gorrr.com.

Directions

From Fresno, take Highway 99 north to Modesto. Turn east on Highway 108 and drive 52 miles to Sonora. Continue east on Highway 108 for 32 miles to Strawberry (past the Pinecrest turnoff). Rivers Resort is on the right, across from Strawberry Inn.

2 THE CABINS AT STRAWBERRY
off Highway 108 in Strawberry

Luxury rating: ★ ★ ★ ★ ☆   **Recreation rating:** ★ ★ ★ ☆ ☆

The Cabins at Strawberry are right next door to the historic Strawberry Inn and are owned by the same folks. But the two accommodations have distinctly different characters. The inn, built in 1939, provides standard motel rooms and a restaurant on the river. The adjacent Cabins at Strawberry are large, modern structures that were built in the 1990s. They are perfectly suited for family vacations and group ski trips.

It's not uncommon for a wedding to be held at the inn and for the guests to stay at the cabins. The cabins are two-story, three-bedroom, two-bath units that can comfortably contain eight people. They are set on the south fork of the Stanislaus River, and some have river views (be sure to pay the additional 20 bucks to get one). The sound of the river greatly diminishes the sound of nearby Highway 108, which runs by the resort.

All cabins have fully furnished kitchens, gas fireplaces, cable television, and VCRs. These are clean, modern homes, not funky riverside cabins. The only downside is that they were built too close together, with only enough space around them to park a car or two.

The restaurant at Strawberry Inn is well known for its American and California cuisine. You might not expect the food to be that great way out here in the little town of Strawberry, but this place will surprise you.

Since The Cabins at Strawberry require a three-night minimum, you're going to need something to do with your time.

In winter, everybody heads to Dodge Ridge for skiing and snowboarding, or to Leland Meadows Sno-Park for sledding and snow play. If you're a budding Kristi Yamaguchi, drive to nearby Long Barn to ice skate. All these options are just a few miles away. In summer, the focus is on the south fork of the Stanislaus River for fishing; nearby Pinecrest Lake for boating, fishing, and swimming; and Stanislaus National Forest and the Emigrant Wilderness for hiking.

Facilities

There are eight three-bedroom cabins that can accommodate up to eight people. All cabins have fully equipped kitchens and gas fireplaces. A store and restaurant are on-site. Linens and towels are provided.

Reservations and Rates

Reservations are recommended. Fees are $149–189 per night. There is a three-night minimum. A $100 refundable cleaning deposit is charged. Pets are permitted in some cabins with a $100 deposit. Contact The Cabins at Strawberry, P.O. Box 109, 31888 Highway 108, Strawberry, CA 95375, 209/965-0885 or 888/965-0885, website: www.strawberrycabins.com.

Directions

From Fresno, take Highway 99 north to Modesto. Turn east on Highway 108 and drive 52 miles to Sonora. Continue east on Highway 108 for 32 miles to Strawberry (past the Pinecrest turnoff). Check in at the Strawberry Inn, on the left side of the road.

Other Cabins and Cottages Nearby

Darlene's Vacation Cabins, P.O. Box 35, Long Barn, CA 95335, 800/273-0740, website: darlenesvacationcabins.com.

3 PINECREST LAKE RESORT
off Highway 108 near Sonora

Luxury rating: ★ ★ ★ ☆ ☆

Recreation rating: ★ ★ ★ ★ ★

Rank: Best for Families

Got kids? Then Pinecrest Lake Resort is your ticket to vacationland. Located in Stanislaus National Forest on the edge of granite-rimmed Pinecrest Lake, the resort caters to families with its two- and three-bedroom housekeeping cabins nestled among the sugar pines.

From the door of your cabin, walk to the lake's sandy beach for swimming and sunning. Walk to the marina to rent a boat and go fishing. Walk to the store to buy the stuff you forgot to pack. Walk to the post office to mail your postcards. Walk to the restaurant and order dinner when you can't stand grilling one more hamburger.

Pinecrest Lake Resort, as well as the lake itself, is a social place where families make friends with other families. Organized activities are plentiful: there are nightly movies in the outdoor amphitheater, sailboat and paddleboat rentals, bike rentals, guided nature hikes, and video games at the resort center. Even teenagers will be happy here; they'll meet all the other teenagers and talk about how boring their parents are.

In case you haven't gotten the picture yet, don't expect a tranquil, private mountain escape. A four-mile recreation trail circles Pinecrest Lake; on a July Saturday morning, it was overflowing with joggers. If you want peace and quiet, you'll have to drive down the road to the trailheads for the Emigrant Wilderness.

Or just show up in the off-season. The resort is open year-round, and it's only five minutes from Dodge Ridge Ski Area, which is usually snowbound by December 1. Discounted lift tickets are sold to resort guests.

Autumn is by far the quietest time. On one October trip, I was the only customer in the resort's Steam Donkey Restaurant. Built of weathered timbers from an old bridge over the Tuolumne River, the Steam Donkey's food is excellent (sandwiches and salads for lunch; a variety of entrées for dinner) and reasonably priced to boot.

The only downer at Pinecrest Lake Resort? The cabins are right next to the resort's tennis courts, so the annoying *thwack* of tennis balls punctuates the sound of the wind in the pines.

Facilities
There are seven two- and three-bedroom housekeeping cabins, plus two- and three-bedroom townhouses and numerous motel rooms. The cabins and townhouses have fully equipped kitchens. A store and restaurant are on-site. Linens and towels are provided.

Reservations and Rates
Reservations are recommended. Fees are $120–195 for cabins; motel rooms cost less. Sunday through Thursday nights are discounted. There is a one-week minimum in July and August. Pets are not permitted. Contact Pinecrest Lake Resort, P.O. Box 1216, Pinecrest, CA 95364, 209/965-3411, website: www.pinecrestlakeresort.com.

Directions
From Fresno, take Highway 99 north to Modesto. Turn east on Highway 108 and drive 52 miles to Sonora. Continue east on Highway 108 for 31 miles to the Pinecrest turnoff. Turn right and drive one mile to Pinecrest Lake Resort.

4 PINECREST CHALET
off Highway 108 in Strawberry

Luxury rating: ★ ★ ★ ☆ ☆   **Recreation rating:** ★ ★ ★ ★ ★

Rank: Best for Winter Sports

Pinecrest Chalet is the closest lodging to the Dodge Ridge Ski Area, and for an easy winter vacation, that could be all you need to know. Winter recreation at Dodge Ridge includes family-oriented downhill and cross-country skiing, plus snowboarding, snowmobiling, ice skating, and sledding. If you want to teach your kids how to ski, or if you want to take the love of your life somewhere where you can snowshoe far from the madding crowd, a reservation for Pinecrest Chalet fits the bill.

Snowboarding at Dodge Ridge Ski Area

The resort offers a variety of cabin and townhouse accommodations, including minichalets (one-room cabins with fully stocked kitchens and fireplaces), economy cabins (one-room housekeeping bungalows with kitchenettes), and larger deluxe cabins (with two to four bedrooms, so you can bring the whole clan). The honeymoon chalet has a king bed and a whirlpool tub.

Pinecrest Chalet gets its share of summer visitors too. The resort is only a couple of minutes from popular Pinecrest Lake, where fishing, boating, and swimming are the main activities. Numerous hiking trails begin within a few miles of Pinecrest Chalet, at the Gianelli Cabin trailhead for the Emigrant Wilderness. If you want to ride your mountain bike, drive west on Highway 108 to the turnoff for Lyons Reservoir. From the parking area by the lake, advanced riders should head east to Fraser Flat Bridge (10 miles one-way). Those who are less ambitious should head west on an old railroad grade to Confidence Road (only five miles, and level all the way).

Some visitors are happy just to hang around their chalet or cabin. The north fork of the Tuolumne River flows through Pinecrest's property. A swimming pool, volleyball court, basketball court, and jungle gym can keep the kids occupied.

Facilities

There are 23 cabins and townhouses that can accommodate up to 14 people, plus an RV park. All cabins have kitchen facilities; some are fully equipped. There is a swimming pool on-site. Linens and towels are provided.

Reservations and Rates

Reservations are recommended. Fees are $150–315 per night in winter and summer, and $115–240 per night in spring and fall. Discounted weeklong rentals are available. Pets are permitted only with prior approval. Contact Pinecrest Chalet, 500 Dodge Ridge Road, P.O. Box 1279, Pinecrest, CA 95364, 209/965-3276, website: www.pinecrestchalet.com.

Directions

From Fresno, take Highway 99 north to Modesto. Turn east on Highway 108 and drive 52 miles to Sonora. Continue east on Highway 108 for 31 miles to the Pinecrest turnoff. Turn right, then right again for Dodge Ridge Ski Area.

5 ANNETT'S MONO VILLAGE RESORT
off U.S. 395 near Bridgeport

Luxury rating: ★ ★ ★ ☆ ☆   **Recreation rating:** ★ ★ ★ ★ ☆

Don't expect peace and quiet when you come to Annett's Mono Village Resort. The place is a miniature city, with cabins, motel rooms, rental trailers, a grocery store, a gift shop, a restaurant, a cocktail lounge, a marina, and a 300-site campground. It's one of the busiest places on the east side of the Sierra.

Why? Well, in addition to excellent fishing, Upper Twin Lake is one of the few lakes around that allows waterskiing, a sport that always attracts

Tumbling cascades on Horse Creek

a crowd. Waterskiing is limited to the hours of 10 A.M. to 3 P.M., and during those five hours, the fast boats fly. The rest of the time, anglers can have some peace. And the fishing doesn't disappoint. The lake is regularly stocked by the Department of Fish and Game, but Mono Village supplements the plants with larger, two- to four-pound trout. Sometimes they grow really big: a 26-pound, 8-ounce brown trout was caught here in 1987.

It goes without saying that Mono Village is a full-service resort. They operate under a "something for everyone" philosophy; in addition to waterskiing and fishing, opportunities abound for swimming, hiking, road biking, deer hunting in autumn, and just plain relaxing. Two Hoover Wilderness trailheads are right at Mono Village's campground. Many people just hike the trail uphill for a mile or two to see the cascades on Horse Creek. More ambitious hikers take the eight-mile round-trip to Barney Lake. There are also hot springs nearby.

For the best experience, rent one of the resort's newer, updated log cabins. Older, rustic models are also available, but they are on the dilapidated side. Definitely ask for a cabin with a lake view, or even better, for one on the lakeshore. Some of the cabins are in a busy parking lot between the bar and the store—not exactly a fantasy vacation spot.

One more tip: Smart vacationers show up in September or October, after the summer crowds have dispersed. The fishing is often best at this time, and the autumn colors are outstanding.

Facilities
There are 18 cabins ranging in size and accommodating up to six people, plus rental trailers, motel rooms, a campground, and an RV resort. All cabins have fully equipped kitchens. A general store, a restaurant, a bar, and a marina are on-site. Linens and towels are provided.

Reservations and Rates
Reservations are recommended. Fees are $65–70 per night for rustic cabins and $100–150 per night for newer and lakeshore cabins. Pets are not permitted. Contact Annett's Mono Village Resort, P.O. Box 455, Bridgeport, CA 93517, 760/932-7071, website: www.monovillage.com.

Directions
From the junction of U.S. 395 and Highway 120 in Lee Vining, drive north on U.S. 395 for 25 miles to Bridgeport. Turn left (west) on Twin Lakes Road and drive 14 miles to Annett's Mono Village (on Upper Twin Lake). Take the right fork signed for motel and cabin reservations.

6 TWIN LAKES RESORT
off U.S. 395 near Bridgeport

Luxury rating: ★ ★ ★ ☆ ☆   **Recreation rating:** ★ ★ ★ ★ ☆

Twin Lakes Resort, on Lower Twin Lake, is a fine place to toss your line in the water, gaze up at the jagged peaks of the Sawtooth Range, and forget your troubles for a while. Located west of Bridgeport in the Twin Lakes Recreation Area of Toiyabe National Forest, Twin Lakes Resort is the quieter of the two large resorts on Twin Lakes. (Annett's Mono Village, the other resort, is .5 mile up the road on Upper Twin Lake; see the previous listing.) Twin Lakes Resort's housekeeping cottages are set across the road from the lower lake, spread out amid a large, grassy lawn. Some have partial views of the water.

From your cabin, you can walk 50 yards to the marina and rent a boat for the day. If you brought your own boat, you can launch it from there. If you don't like boats, you can fish from shore. If you don't like fishing, you can sit on the shore and admire the scenery. If you get bored, you can jump off the rope swing and swim in the lake. Choices, choices.

Everything about your vacation here is simple. The resort has a general store, serves three meals a day, and provides bike rentals. If you catch a big fish, they have a taxidermy service. If you forgot your fishing license, they'll sell you one.

Lower Twin Lake, like its neighbor Upper Twin Lake, is famous for large and plentiful fish: rainbow and brown trout and kokanee salmon. The general rule is to fish deep. If you don't catch anything, the eye-popping Sierra scenery will more than compensate. The best views are had in late spring and early summer, when the Sawtooth Range is crowned in thick snow.

Hikers should head to the Hoover Wilderness trailhead at Upper Twin Lake. From there, they can hike the Robinson Creek Trail steeply uphill to Barney Lake, four miles out. If you'd rather relax, there are hot springs nearby on Buckeye Creek.

Facilities

There are seven one-, two-, and three-bedroom cabins that can accommodate two to six people; all cabins have fully equipped kitchens. A small general store and restaurant are on-site. Linens and towels are provided.

Reservations and Rates

Reservations are recommended. Fees are $110–168 per night for two people, plus $20 for each additional person. The resort is open year-round. Pets are permitted with a $25 fee. Contact Twin Lakes Resort, P.O. Box 248, Bridgeport, CA 93517, 760/932-7751 or 877/932-7751, website: www.lowertwinlakesresort.com.

Directions

From the junction of U.S. 395 and Highway 120 in Lee Vining, drive north on U.S. 395 for 25 miles to Bridgeport. Turn left (west) on Twin

Lakes Road and drive 10 miles to Twin Lakes Resort, on the right (by Lower Twin Lake).

7 DOC & AL'S RESORT
off U.S. 395 near Bridgeport

Luxury rating: ★ ★ ★ ☆ ☆   **Recreation rating:** ★ ★ ★ ☆ ☆

There's nothing fancy about Doc & Al's Resort, but ask yourself: Did I come here to admire the furniture, or did I come here to fish?

Right answer. Doc & Al's Resort is on Robinson Creek, in the Twin Lakes Recreation Area of Toiyabe National Forest. Just up the road are a half dozen campgrounds, and everybody at those has come here to fish, too.

Doc & Al's one-room rustic cabins are a small step up from camping. You get a roof over your head, a wall heater, beds and bedding, and outdoor cooking facilities. Bathrooms are a short walk away. The tiny cabins are squeezed in tightly, each one only a few feet from the next.

If you're smart, you'll spring for the much larger housekeeping cabins on the creek. They are more appealing in every way: they're spaced farther apart, they have large decks that overlook Robinson Creek, and, best of all, they have kitchens and bathrooms. Forest and Ranger are the newest cabins and are the best of the lot.

The resort also has a busy RV and tent camping area, as well as a communal lodge with a fireplace and an old piano. Anglers gather here to play chess and cards while telling lies about fish.

The surrounding terrain is a mix of aspens, Jeffrey pines, and sage at this 7,000-foot elevation. Those who can't wait to fish take their pick from fly, lure, and bait fishing for rainbows, browns, brooks, and even cutthroat

trout and kokanee salmon. Robinson Creek is the main draw, since it runs right alongside the resort, but Buckeye and Eagle Creeks are also nearby. Fish are planted in Robinson Creek at the bridge by Doc & Al's Resort.

If the fish aren't biting, you can go explore a few nearby ghost towns: Masonic, Aurora,

Boulder Flat, and most famous of them all, Bodie State Historic Park. Hot-springs lovers will want to check out Buckeye Hot Springs, a short distance from the resort, or Travertine Hot Springs, on the east side of Bridgeport.

Facilities
There are 10 one-room cabins without bathrooms that can accommodate up to four people, and 12 housekeeping cabins with bathrooms that can accommodate up to 10 people. The housekeeping cabins have fully equipped kitchens. A campground for RVs and tents is also available. A small general store is on-site. Linens and towels are provided.

Reservations and Rates
Reservations are recommended. The fee for rustic one-room cabins is $45 per night for two people; the fee for housekeeping cabins is $86–101 per night for two people. Pets are permitted with a $3 fee per night. Contact Doc & Al's Resort, 85 Twin Lakes Road, P.O. Box 266, Bridgeport, CA 93517, 760/932-7051.

Directions
From the junction of U.S. 395 and Highway 120 in Lee Vining, drive north on U.S. 395 for 25 miles to Bridgeport. Turn left (west) on Twin Lakes Road and drive seven miles, then turn right on Buckeye Road to enter Doc & Al's Resort.

8 HUNEWILL GUEST RANCH
off U.S. 395 near Bridgeport

Luxury rating: ★ ★ ★ ☆ ☆   **Recreation rating:** ★ ★ ★ ★ ☆

Rank: Best for Horseback Riding

Hunewill Guest Ranch is for horse lovers. If you've seen *Black Beauty* or *The Horse Whisperer* more times than you can remember, you will be among friends here. As you drive in to the ranch, you are greeted by miles of open pasture and dozens, sometimes hundreds, of horses and cows. That scene sums up your entire vacation.

So pack up your cowboy boots and a big sack of apples and carrots, and head for Bridgeport. Hunewill Guest Ranch comprises 26,000 acres of meadows and sagebrush, backed by the rugged mountains of the high Sierra. The original ranch was founded by Napoleon Bonaparte Hunewill (no kidding) in 1861. The guest ranch was opened by his descendants in the 1930s. The Hunewill family has been handling horses, cattle, and visitors around here long enough to know what they're doing.

The ranch caters to families, couples, singles, and people who travel with their own horses—in short, just about everybody. They try to provide a complete ranch experience, which means a wide mix of activities: evening cookouts and square dances, home-style meals in the Victorian ranch house, trout fishing in the East Walker River, cowboy-skills lessons at the 1,200-head cattle ranch, and all the horseback riding you could want. (They have 120 horses on the ranch, so if you didn't bring your own, they'll assign you one.)

The cabins, which are cozy and clean, are near the horse pasture, so you can stand on your front porch and watch the horses to your heart's content. Some of the cabins are newer than others, but all are in excellent shape. Not surprisingly, they're decorated in Western style.

Most people sign up for a seven-day package deal, which includes housing in cabins with private baths, plus all meals and activities. This costs about $1,000 for adults and half that for children. Not bad for a week's vacation, considering you won't spend another dime once you're there—although tips for the wrangler and ranch hands are appreciated—unless you plan to use the trophy trout pond. If you have a serious fly fisher in your family, he or she can pack along a float tube, pay an hourly fee, and catch a few two- to seven-pound rainbow trout.

If you're an equestrian but your spouse is not, Hunewill Ranch offers reduced rates for nonriding guests. If you bring your own horse, you can subtract $117 per week. Five- and three-day packages are also available. The ranch is open from late May to October 1, and the best time to visit may be the last week of the season, when the fall colors are on display and the air is cooler.

If for some reason you have the urge to leave the property, Buckeye Hot Springs and Travertine Hot Springs are nearby.

Facilities
There are 24 cabins, each with two rooms and two bathrooms. The cabins do not have kitchens; meals are included in your stay. A small general store and restaurant are on-site. Linens and towels are provided.

Reservations and Rates
Reservations are required. Rates are $1,119–1,288 per week for adults, including all meals and activities. Rates for children are $275–966 per week, depending on their ages. Five- and three-day packages are also available. The resort is open from late May to October 1. Pets are not permitted. Contact In summer: Hunewill Guest Ranch, P.O. Box 368, Bridgeport, CA 93517, 760/932-7710, website: www.hunewillranch.com.

Directions
From the junction of U.S. 395 and Highway 120 in Lee Vining, drive north on U.S. 395 for 25 miles to Bridgeport. Turn left (west) on Twin Lakes Road and drive four miles to Hunewill Guest Ranch, on the left.

In winter: Hunewill Guest Ranch, 200 Hunewill Lane, Wellington, NV 89444, 775/465-2201, website: www.hunewillranch.com.

9 VIRGINIA CREEK SETTLEMENT
off U.S. 395 near Lee Vining

Luxury rating: ★ ★ ☆ ☆ ☆　　　　**Recreation rating:** ★ ★ ★ ☆ ☆
Rank: Best for Families, Best for Value

If you want to visit the ghost town at Bodie, there's no better place to stay than Virginia Creek Settlement. This is especially true if you're traveling with kids—or kids-at-heart. Not only is Virginia Creek Settlement the closest lodging to Bodie State Historic Park, it's also designed to get you into the spirit of the Old West.

The place looks like a movie set. The cabins, or camptown units as they are called, are large converted sheds with clever false fronts crafted to look like the buildings of an Old West town. Each represents a different enterprise, including Cooper's Freight and Mercantile Company, Assay and Land Office, and Anthony Agony, MD. Three covered wagons (also for rent) complete the scene. Not surprisingly, kids love the look of this place. If you want something more conventional, the resort has motel rooms,

© ANN MARIE BROWN

larger and more traditional cabins, and tent sites—but why spoil the ghost town mood?

Here's the unbelievable part: The camptown units and covered wagons cost a mere $22 a night for two people, plus $2.50 for each additional person. What a deal. So you don't have your own bathroom . . . who's complaining?

Inside, the camptown units and covered wagons are one single room with beds. A communal restroom and shower area is a few feet away. Meals are served at the settlement's historic dining room; the menu is a mix of Italian and American and includes pizza and wine. Order something Italian and pretend you're in a spaghetti Western.

Most people who stay at Virginia Creek Settlement have Bodie State Historic Park on their itinerary. Bodie was a gold mining town that saw its heyday in the 1870s, when it boasted more than 30 operating mines, 65 saloons, and a population of more than 10,000 people. Like most mining towns, it eventually suffered a complete decline, and all its residents moved elsewhere. Still, Bodie's buildings have withstood the test of time. You can walk around the old town, peek in windows, and imagine what life was like in another era. A museum is open daily, but there are no other facilities or food services in the park.

To get to Bodie, drive one mile south on U.S. 395 and turn east on Highway 270. It's 13 miles to the ghost town (the last couple miles are gravel). For advice on other recreation in the area, the Toiyabe National Forest Ranger Station is just five miles north of Virginia Creek Settlement, on U.S. 395.

Facilities

There are six camptown units and three covered wagons that can accommodate two to four people, plus four larger cabins, motel rooms, and tent sites. There is a communal bathroom and showers. A restaurant is on-site. Linens and towels are provided for a $7.50 fee, or you can bring your own.

Reservations and Rates

Reservations are recommended. Fees for the camptown units and covered wagons are $22 per night for two people, plus $2.50 for each additional person. Fees for the larger cabins are $112–122 per night. Pets are permitted with a $5 per night fee. Contact Virginia Creek Settlement, HCR 62

Box 1050, Bridgeport, CA 93517, 760/932-7780, website: www.virginiacrk-settlement.com.

Directions
From the junction of U.S. 395 and Highway 120 in Lee Vining, drive north on U.S. 395 for 20 miles to Virginia Creek Settlement, on the left (it's one mile north of the Bodie turnoff).

🔟 VIRGINIA LAKES RESORT
off U.S. 395 near Lee Vining

Luxury rating: ★ ★ ★ ☆ ☆   **Recreation rating:** ★ ★ ★ ★ ★

"Watch your step; sea level is 9,770 feet down," notes the sign above the door at Virginia Lakes Resort. It should warn you to check your footing because of the scenery: The neighboring peaks are so spectacular, you could trip over something while gazing upward.

The resort is set on Little Virginia Lake, which is right next to Big Virginia Lake and within a half-mile drive of Trumbull Lake. Behind the lakes rise a few magnificent Sierra summits: Dunderberg Peak, Mount Olsen, Virginia Peak, and Black Mountain. In addition to its cabins, Virginia Lake Resort has a store, the small but good Summit Cafe (breakfast and lunch only), and rowboat rentals. No gas motors are permitted on any of the nearby lakes.

Unlike the resorts to the north at Bridgeport and Lundy Lake Resort to the south, Virginia Lakes Re-sort caters to a somewhat more upscale crowd, with tidier cabins and newer furnishings. We're not talking Ritz-Carlton quality here—it's more like Best Western—but the place is clean, attractive, and appealing.

© ANN MARIE BROWN

Nine of the cabins have lake views; the other 10 are on Virginia Creek. For the best experience, make sure you request a cabin with a fireplace and a deck overlooking the lake. Not surprisingly, the resort is wildly popular, so its cabins are rented only by the week from June 15 to Labor Day. The rest of the season, there is a three-night minimum.

And get this—in a world of instant ATMs, automatic deposits, and plastic everything, Virginia Lakes Resort does not take credit cards. Hooray for them.

The main activity at the resort is fishing. Little Virginia, Big Virginia, and Trumbull Lakes are planted weekly with rainbow trout. If you want to catch only big ones, trophy fish are stocked on a monthly basis. The three lakes, plus seven others in the basin, also contain populations of native trout—eastern brook and German brown. It's a regular fish-o-rama.

Don't like to fish? There's plenty for hikers to do around Virginia Lake. From the trailhead at the end of the road, you can hike to several high alpine lakes, including Blue Lake, Cooney Lake, and Frog Lakes, all in the first 1.5 miles. If you can ignore the siren call of these pretty lakes, keep climbing up to 11,110-foot Summit Pass, where the views will knock your socks off. More lakes await on the other side.

Facilities
There are 19 cabins ranging in size and accommodating 2 to 12 people. All cabins have fully equipped kitchens. Some have fireplaces. A small general store and restaurant are on-site. Linens and towels are provided.

Reservations and Rates
Reservations are required; deposits must be mailed by check (the resort does not take credit cards). From June 15 to Labor Day, fees are $485–1,645 per week, depending on the number of people and cabin size. The rest of the season, nightly rentals are available; the fee is $81–273 per night. The resort is usually open from late May to mid-October, depending on weather. Pets are permitted with a $20 fee. Contact Virginia Lakes Resort, HCR 1 Box 1065, Bridgeport, CA 93517, 760/647-6484, website: www.virginialakesresort.com.

Directions
From the junction of U.S. 395 and Highway 120 in Lee Vining, drive north on U.S. 395 for 12 miles to the left turnoff for Virginia Lakes (at Conway Summit). Turn left and drive six miles to the resort.

11 LUNDY LAKE RESORT

off U.S. 395 near Lee Vining

Luxury rating: ★ ★ ☆ ☆ ☆   **Recreation rating:** ★ ★ ★ ★ ☆

Lundy Lake Resort is the opposite of fancy or showy. If you
spend much time thinking
about what clothes to wear or
what kind of car you drive, you
won't like it here.

© ANN MARIE BROWN

To illustrate my point, the
owner told me he has owned
the resort for 10 years and has
never done a thing to the
cabins. They are barebones and
rustic, although they do come
furnished with linens, bedding, and cooking utensils. Electricity comes
from a generator, so forget about bringing along your hair dryer or espresso maker. They aren't going to function well here, or if they do, somebody
else will be groping around in the dark.

All that is irrelevant to the people who stay at Lundy Lake Resort, because they are here for one reason: to fish Lundy Lake and the neighboring streams in Lundy Canyon. At an elevation of 7,800 feet, Lundy Lake is
one mile in length and has 100 surface acres, with a Southern California
Edison dam at one end. The lake is set among pines, quaking aspens, and
breathtaking granite mountains. In the 1880s, it was the site of a historic
sawmill and mining town.

Brown and rainbow trout are regularly planted by the Department of
Fish and Game. The resort rents boats with or without motors, and plenty
of folks fish from shore too. Mill Creek, the stream that feeds Lundy
Lake, is also stocked. Brook and rainbow trout can be caught by anglers
who hike into Lundy Canyon.

Speaking of hiking, a trailhead is two miles west of the resort. It's the
access point for Lundy Canyon, from which you can hike into the spectacular 20 Lakes basin in 5.4 miles, or cut your trip short and enjoy the
waterfalls and wildflowers in the first two miles. Another trailhead is at
the dam at the east end of Lundy Lake; this will take you to Crystal and
Oneida Lakes and a historic gold mine in 3.5 miles. Mountain bikers
also use this trail.

Two natural events shouldn't be missed at Lundy Lake Resort: the riotous wildflower bloom in Lundy Canyon, which usually occurs around July, and the colorful autumn aspen show in October.

Facilities
There are six cabins that can accommodate up to five people, plus four mobile-home rentals. All have fully equipped kitchens. A small general store is on-site. Linens and towels are provided.

Reservations and Rates
Reservations are recommended. Fees are $60–100 per night for two people, plus $5 for each additional person. There is a three-night minimum from June 15 to September 15. The resort is open from late April to November 1. Pets are permitted. Contact Lundy Lake Resort, P.O. Box 550, Lee Vining, CA 93541, 626/309-0415.

Directions
From the junction of U.S. 395 and Highway 120 in Lee Vining, drive north on U.S. 395 for seven miles to the left turnoff for Lundy Lake. Turn left and drive five miles to the resort.

12 TIOGA PASS RESORT
off Highway 120 near Tioga Pass

Luxury rating: ★ ★ ★ ☆ ☆   **Recreation rating:** ★ ★ ★ ★ ★
Rank: Best for Winter Sports

You can forget about staying at Tioga Pass Resort in the summer unless you're one of those people who can plan way in advance. A year in advance, to be exact. Tioga Pass Resort is heavily booked for several reasons: It's perfectly situated next to Yosemite's high country, it's very well managed, and it has a loyal clientele of folks who come back year after year.

If you've driven to Yosemite National Park from the east via U.S. 395, you've passed right by the resort. It's on Highway 120, just two miles from Yosemite's eastern entrance, at the mighty elevation of 9,600 feet. In summer, the resort's store, café, and outdoor espresso cart are popular stops for folks driving in and out of the park.

But only a lucky few stay in the cabins. In summer, they are for rent with a five-night minimum. To get a reservation during June, July, or August, you should call or email the summer before. In September or October, you might be able to get a reservation just by phoning a week or two before.

From the outside, the cabins don't bowl you over. They are quaint and rustic-looking, built of logs and painted brown with yellow and green trim. They are set quite close to the road and the resort parking lot, but luckily, a stream runs between them, keeping noise to a minimum.

In addition to all the wonderful hikes in neighboring Yosemite (try the short but steep tromp to Gaylor Lakes, right by the park entrance station), resort guests can take advantage of their proximity to hiking and fishing opportunities at Saddlebag Lake and the 20 Lakes basin. Mountain bikers will want to try out the Moraines and Meadows Trail, near the junction of Tioga Pass Road and U.S. 395. Folks looking for an easy stroll should walk the trail to Bennettville, the site of an ill-fated 1882 silver mining operation that led to the construction of the original Tioga Road.

You can cook in your cabin if you wish, but it's hard to justify when Tioga Pass Resort's café makes such great food. Their Tioga Burgers are legendary. Breakfasts are just what you want in the mountains—big fluffy pancakes and huge omelets. Pie is served all day.

In winter, Tioga Pass Resort transforms into a cozy ski lodge. Most years, both deep powder and spring corn snow are in plentiful supply. The road to the resort isn't plowed in winter; you have to ski in six miles, which makes reservations a lot easier to come by. Guests sleep in the comfortable heated cabins, ski all day, then get together in the main lodge for meals, which are included in the price.

Facilities

There are 10 one- and two-bedroom cabins, plus four motel rooms. All cabins have fully equipped kitchens. A small general store and restaurant are on-site. Linens and towels are provided in summer only; in winter, ski in with your own.

Reservations and Rates

Reservations are required. Fees are $700–900 per five-night stay in summer and $150 per person per night in winter (meals included in winter rates only). A reduced rate is offered midweek in winter. Pets are not permitted.

Directions

From U.S. 395 at Mammoth Lakes, drive north 26 miles on U.S. 395 to Highway 120. Turn west on Highway 120 and drive 12 miles to Tioga Pass Resort, on the right.

Coming from the west in Yosemite National Park, take Highway 120 east. Pass the Tioga Pass entrance station, then continue two more miles to Tioga Pass Resort, on the left. Contact Tioga Pass Resort, P.O. Box 7, Lee Vining, CA 93541, 209/372-4471, website: www.tiogapassresort.com.

13 TIOGA LODGE
off U.S. 395 near Lee Vining

Luxury rating: ★ ★ ★ ☆ ☆   **Recreation rating:** ★ ★ ★ ★ ☆

© ANN MARIE BROWN

Considering how wonderful it is, it's a pity that Tioga Lodge suffers from an identity crisis: People keep confusing it with similarly named Tioga Pass Resort. That's partly because Tioga Lodge is the relatively new kid in town, having opened in 2000, whereas Tioga Pass Resort has been around forever. And it's partly because the two resorts are only 15 miles apart, and both have cabins for rent.

The lodge is right smack on U.S. 395, which could deter from its desirability because of incessant road noise, except that its roadside setting allows open views of Mono Lake. No other cabin resort overlooks this spectacular 60,000-acre saltwater oddity, with its corallike tufa spires and strange-looking volcanic islands. If you want to see or visit Mono Lake, Tioga Lodge is your ticket.

The lodge may have opened relatively recently, but it isn't new at all. Several of its buildings were transported here in the 1880s; they came from the nearby gold mining town of Bodie (now a state historic park). One hundred years later, the long-closed buildings had become an eyesore. But along came current owners, Walter and Lou Vint, who restored the original buildings and added new ones to Tioga Lodge. They have done a remarkable job.

The cabins are furnished with late-19th-century antiques and pine log furniture. No two cabins are alike; each has its own personality that reflects the Mono basin area's history. None of the cabins have kitchens, so you'll eat at the lodge's excellent restaurant or at the highly acclaimed Mono Inn, just up the road. For something more casual, you can always drive south into Lee Vining and get a hamburger at the Mono Cone or a barbecue dinner at Bodie Mike's.

Tioga Lodge is friendly to anglers; in fact, as long as you clean your catch, they will cook and/or smoke your fish for you. They open up in April each year (as long as the snow isn't too deep) so that the trout fishers will have a place to stay for the season opener. The lodge remains open until late October, catering mostly to travelers heading up or down U.S. 395.

The most obvious attraction, of course, is Mono Lake. Tioga Lodge is just two miles north of the Mono Basin National Forest Scenic Area Visitor Center, perched high on a hill above Mono Lake. At the center, you can learn everything about the 700,000-year-old body of water. The lodge is across the highway from Mono Lake County Park, where you can get a close look at some of the lake's tufa spires, put in your kayak or canoe, or go swimming (the saltwater makes you extremely buoyant!). At the lodge, you can sign up for a boat tour of the lake, or drive south a few miles to Mono Lake Tufa State Reserve, where the most impressive group of tufas is located.

Facilities
There are 12 one- and two-bedroom cabins, plus four motel rooms. Some cabins are duplexes; none have kitchens. A small general store and restaurant are on-site. Linens and towels are provided.

Reservations and Rates
Reservations are recommended. Fees are $55–107 per night. Seasonal discounts are available. The resort is open from April to October. Pets are not permitted. Contact Tioga Lodge, P.O. Box 580, Lee Vining, CA 93541, 760/647-6423 or 888/647-6423, website: www.tiogalodge.com.

Directions
From the junction of U.S. 395 and Highway 120 in Lee Vining, drive north on U.S. 395 for 2.5 miles to Tioga Lodge, on the left.

14 YOSEMITE LAKES
off Highway 120 in Groveland

Luxury rating: ★ ★ ★ ☆ ☆   **Recreation rating:** ★ ★ ★ ☆ ☆

Rank: Best for Families

© ANN MARIE BROWN

Most people who stay at Yosemite Lakes make the five-mile drive into Yosemite National Park at least once during their stay, but a surprising amount are happy to hang around on the resort's grounds and just sink into vacation mode. You know vacation mode: the operating procedure in which you get up every morning, put on your bathing suit and flip-flops, and then wear them right up until bedtime. In between, you read a few chapters of a book, sip cool drinks and eat chips, and maybe debate the merits of catch-and-release fishing with your cohorts. The hours pass quite pleasantly this way.

Yosemite Lakes is off Highway 120, midway between Groveland and Yosemite National Park, on the south fork of the Tuolumne River. It's just hot enough in summer that you'll probably want to hang around the river all day, but just shady enough that you'll never be too hot.

Members of the Thousand Trails/NACO camping organization have a sweet deal here; they can rent Yosemite Lakes' cabins and yurts for a 20 percent discount over the regular prices. The cabins are typical rustic wood-frame units—nice but not especially noteworthy and without bathrooms. But the yurts are unique: They're circular, tentlike structures with a skylight and windows, and they are equipped with full kitchens and baths. They even have satellite TV, for whatever that's worth. Ten yurts are clustered together in Yurt Village, but each one has an abundance of space around it. Barbecues and picnic tables are outside each yurt if you don't feel like cooking inside.

Recreation opportunities abound. The South Fork Tuolumne River runs through Yosemite Lakes' property and monopolizes a good portion of guests' itineraries. Kayaks, inner tubes, fishing poles, and gold pans are for rent. Horseback riding is popular from mid-May to mid-September; stables are on the grounds. Most visitors don't do anything more ambitious than an hour-long ride through the pines, but it's great fun for families.

Facilities
There are 10 cabins and 10 yurts that can accommodate up to four people, plus hostel and inn accommodations, an RV park, and tent sites. The yurts have full kitchens and baths; the cabins do not. A store is on-site. Linens and towels are provided.

Reservations and Rates
Reservations are recommended. Fees are $70–140 per night from May to October and $50–105 per night from November to April, except holidays. Thousand Trails/NACO members receive a 20 percent discount. Pets are permitted. Contact Yosemite Lakes, 31191 Hardin Flat Road, Groveland, CA 95321, 209/962-0121 or 800/533-1001, website: www.1000trails.com.

Directions
From Fresno, take Highway 99 north to Manteca. Turn east on Highway 120 and drive 65 miles to Groveland. From Groveland, continue east on Highway 120 for 16 miles to the sign for Yosemite Lakes, on the right, at Hardin Flat Road.

Other Cabins and Cottages Nearby
Sunset Inn Yosemite Guest Cabins, 33569 Hardin Flat Road, Groveland, CA 95321, 209/962-4360, website: www.sunsetinnusa.com.
Yosemite Pines RV Resort, 20450 Old Highway 120, Groveland, CA 95321, 209/962-7690 or 877/962-7690, website: www.yosemitepinesrv.com.

15 EVERGREEN LODGE
off Highway 120 in Yosemite

Luxury rating: ★ ★ ★ ☆ ☆   **Recreation rating:** ★ ★ ★ ☆ ☆

Most everybody in California has visited Yosemite Valley at one time or another, but not everybody has visited Hetch Hetchy Valley, Yosemite's twin, in the northern section of the park. Of the five park entrance stations, Hetch Hetchy gets the fewest number of cars passing through, day after day.

Hetch Hetchy Valley was flooded in 1906 to create a water supply for the city of San Francisco. It was the tragic end of a long fight for naturalist

© ANN MARIE BROWN

John Muir, who tried in vain to save Hetch Hetchy from the big-city politicians. Remarkably, Hetch Hetchy is still beautiful today, even though it's covered with 400 feet of water.

When it's your time to visit Hetch Hetchy, book a stay at the cabins at Evergreen Lodge. If you think you know the place, this isn't the same Evergreen Lodge that had been on this spot since the 1920s and never changed a hair. This is the new, improved Evergreen Lodge that was taken over in 2004 by a group of ambitious owners and given a major facelift. How major? Let's just say that instead of the 12 rickety old cabins that used to be here, now there are 64 cabins, and the word *rickety* no longer applies. In addition to the cabins, there is a first-class restaurant serving three meals a day and a ton of organized activities—nature hikes, campfire talks, full-moon hikes and the like—most of which are free to guests. This is a great place for a family vacation during which you want your kids to be kept active.

Located nine miles up the Hetch Hetchy Road from Highway 120, Evergreen Lodge is only a half-hour drive from Hetch Hetchy's spectacular water-filled valley. You can spend a comfortable night in your cabin, then get up early and head to the trailhead at Hetch Hetchy's impressive dam. In a single day, you can hike out and back along the length of the reservoir, passing spectacular waterfalls, granite cliffs, and a prolific variety of trees, plants, and wildflowers. The entire round-trip is 13 miles; plenty of people just hike a portion of it. Wapama Falls, at two miles out, is a highlight. (Remember that the waterfalls flow only in springtime though and are mostly dry by late June.)

Other recreation options include a visit to pretty Carlon Falls, on the South Fork Tuolumne River (a 1.5-mile hike from the trailhead at Carlon Day-Use Area), and fishing in the Tuolumne. Additionally, Yosemite Valley, with all of its splendors, is only an hour from Evergreen Lodge. One thing is for sure: you won't run out of things to do here.

Facilities
There are 64 one- and two-bedroom cabins. A restaurant, deli, bar, and store are on-site. Linens and towels are provided.

Reservations and Rates
Reservations are recommended. Fees are $99–189 per night. The lodge is

open year-round. Pets are not permitted. Contact Evergreen Lodge, 33160 Evergreen Road, Groveland, CA 95321, 209/379-2606 or 800/935-6343, website: www.evergreenlodge.com.

Directions

From Fresno, take Highway 99 north to Manteca. Turn east on Highway 120 and drive 65 miles to Groveland. From Groveland, continue east on Highway 120 for 22 miles to the left turnoff for Evergreen Road and Hetch Hetchy. Turn left and drive nine miles to Evergreen Lodge, on the left.

Other Cabins and Cottages Nearby

Yosemite Riverside Inn, 11399 Cherry Lake Road, Groveland, CA 95321, 209/962-7408 or 800/626-7408, website: www.yosemiteriversideinn.com.

16 WHITE WOLF LODGE

off Highway 120 in Yosemite

Luxury rating: ★ ★ ☆ ☆ ☆   **Recreation rating:** ★ ★ ★ ★ ☆

The first time you glimpse the cabins at White Wolf, you sense the realization of your Yosemite lodging dreams. Set at the sweet high-country elevation of 8,000 feet, the white wooden cabins are trimmed in hunter green, with Adirondack chairs lined up on the porches to face a wildflower-filled meadow. If you think that it doesn't get any better than this, you're exactly right.

Except that you might be wrong. The trick is that not every White Wolf cabin is one of those quaint *Sunset* magazine–style jobs; only the ones visible from the parking lot fit that bill. Right behind them are dozens of typical Yosemite tent cabins— large, dirty-white tents on raised wooden platforms, almost bare inside except for a wood-burning stove, candles for lighting, and a couple of beds.

There are four white wooden cabins, and they have their own bathrooms, propane heat, daily

© ANN MARIE BROWN

maid service, and electricity (generated only during certain hours of the day). There are 24 tent cabins, and they have none of the above. Guess which ones are harder to come by?

Regardless of which type of cabin you reserve, everything about a stay at White Wolf is easy. An excellent restaurant on the premises serves breakfast and dinner and makes box lunches to go. Dinners include steak, fish, chicken, a vegetarian entrée, and hamburgers. Prices are reasonable ($10–16 for entrées). A small store sells snacks, drinks, and a few minimal supplies.

Hikers can set out right from their cabins. The best options are the 2.5-mile trail to Lukens Lake and the three-mile trail to Harden Lake. The Harden Lake Trail is great for wildflowers, but the lake itself practically dries up by the end of summer. Go see it in June or July. Lukens Lake is ideal for swimming throughout the summer; the shallow water warms up to a comfortable temperature.

The big question is this: How do you get one of those white-and-green cabins at White Wolf? Plan on calling at least a year in advance. Rub your rabbit's foot, then pick up the phone.

Facilities
There are four wooden cabins with a private bathroom, propane heat, and electricity that can accommodate up to four people. There are 24 tent cabins that can accommodate up to four people. A restaurant and small store are on-site. Linens and towels are provided.

Reservations and Rates
Reservations are required. Fees are $71 per night for tent cabins and $105 per night for wooden cabins. The lodge is open from mid-June to early September. Pets are not permitted.

Directions
From Fresno, take Highway 99 north to Manteca. Turn east on Highway 120 and drive 65 miles to Groveland. From Groveland, continue east on Highway 120 for 23 miles to the Big Oak Flat entrance at Yosemite. Continue east on Highway 120 for nine miles to Crane Flat, then turn left and drive 15 miles to the White Wolf turnoff, on the left.

If you're coming from U.S. 395, White Wolf is 32 miles west of the Tioga Pass entrance station to Yosemite. Contact Yosemite Reservations, 6771 North Palm Avenue, Fresno, CA 93704, 559/252-4848 or 559/253-5635, website: www.yosemitepark.com.

YOSEMITE HIGH SIERRA CAMPS

off Highway 120 in Yosemite

Luxury rating: ★ ★ ☆ ☆ ☆   **Recreation rating:** ★ ★ ★ ★ ☆

Rank: Best for Hiking

© ANN MARIE BROWN

Among people who love to hike but hate to carry a heavy backpack, the Yosemite High Sierra Camps are legendary. The five camps are spaced 5.7–10 miles apart along a loop trail that begins at Tuolumne Meadows. With nothing on your back but a light daypack filled with water, a change of clothes, sheets, and a towel, you hike through the high country for nearly a week. Along the way, you eat first-rate meals, enjoy hot showers, and sleep in a comfortable bed in a tent cabin each night.

Not everybody does the whole loop and stays at all five camps. In fact, unless you plan a year in advance, it's virtually impossible to do so. Reservations for the High Sierra Camps are taken on a lottery basis each autumn, and only a lucky few win the lottery.

Still, many people manage to get reservations for an out-and-back trip to one or more of the camps. Even those who wait until the last minute have a fair chance, because each summer, there are cancellations. The key is to call the High Sierra Camp desk on a regular basis; availability changes minute by minute. Another option is to sign up for organized four- and seven-day trips led by National Park Service rangers; these cost more, but you get the benefit of having a naturalist guide along on your trip. Organized horseback trips are also available.

If you aren't traveling the entire loop, the one-way hikes to the camps are as follows: Glen Aulin, at 7,800 feet, is five miles from the Lembert Dome trailhead. May Lake, at 9,300 feet, is one mile from the May Lake trailhead. Sunrise Camp, at 9,400 feet, is five miles from the Sunrise trailhead. Vogelsang Camp, at 10,300 feet, is seven miles from the Tuolumne Meadows trailhead. Merced Lake Camp, at 7,200 feet, is the only one that's a bit far to reach if you're not traveling from another camp on the loop; it's 15 miles from Tuolumne Meadows or 13 miles from Yosemite Valley.

The set-up is basically the same at all five camps, although each has a varying number of tent cabins, so the size of the crowd will differ. (Merced Lake Camp is the largest, with a 60-person occupancy; the others fit 30 to 40 guests at a time.) Dinner and breakfast are served in a main dining tent; box lunches can be purchased to go. Generally, the camps are very social: Meals are served family-style, and the tent cabins are spaced within a few feet of each other, so you'll get to know your neighbors. Hope they don't snore.

Speaking of snoring, one critical rule at the High Sierra Camps is that overnight accommodations are dormitory style, which means that men and women are usually housed in separate tents, four people to a tent. If your significant other is of the opposite sex, you may have to wave good-bye at night. However, if space allows (some camps have two-person tents in addition to four-person tents), the camp hosts will do their best to keep couples together.

Facilities
Glen Aulin and May Lake have eight tent cabins each, Sunrise has nine tent cabins, Merced Lake has 19 tent cabins, and Vogelsang has 12 tent cabins. The cabins can accommodate up to four people. Meals are provided. Pillows and blankets are provided, but not linens and towels; guests may purchase sleep-sacks and trek towels by mail order from the High Sierra Camp desk, or they can bring their own sheets and towels.

Reservations and Rates
Reservations are required and are taken on a lottery basis. Applications for the lottery are available from September 1 to November 20; completed applications are accepted from October 15 to November 30. The lottery is usually held in the first week of December. Limited reservations are available after the lottery is completed; call 559/253-5674. Fees are $120 per night and include meals. Pets are not permitted.

Directions
From Fresno, take Highway 99 north to Manteca. Turn east on Highway 120 and drive 65 miles to Groveland. From Groveland, continue east on Highway 120 for 23 miles to the Big Oak Flat entrance at Yosemite. Continue east on Highway 120 for nine miles to Crane Flat, then turn left and drive to the appropriate trailhead for your High Sierra Camp.

If you're coming from U.S. 395, drive west on Highway 120 to Crane Flat, then turn right and drive to the appropriate trailhead for your High Sierra Camp. Contact Yosemite High Sierra Camps, 6771 North Palm Avenue, Fresno, CA 93704, 559/253-5674, website: www.yosemitepark.com.

18 TUOLUMNE LODGE

off Highway 120 in Yosemite

Luxury rating: ★ ★ ☆ ☆ ☆   **Recreation rating:** ★ ★ ★ ★ ★

Rank: Best for Hiking

Tuolumne Lodge has the same upsides as other tent-cabin resorts in Yosemite's high country: a chance to stay in convenient lodging right in the midst of Yosemite's best day-hiking, fishing, and scenery-watching country, with easy access to hearty meals and necessary supplies.

It also has the same downsides as the other resorts: the cabins are a bit dark and dreary (canvas-covered tents on raised wooden platforms with nothing but beds, candles, and a wood-burning stove). Also, they are packed in so tightly that you can hear your neighbors talking, coughing, and snoring at night. At Tuolumne Lodge, it's slightly worse than at nearby White Wolf, because Tuolumne has a whopping 59 tent cabins. That's enough for a small tent-cabin city.

Of course, few people who stay here ever complain. The upsides simply far outweigh the downsides. Guests come to be within a stone's throw of Tuolumne Meadows, and not for any other reason. The cabins are across the road from Lembert Dome and the Soda Springs trailhead and are within 100 yards of the John Muir and Pacific Crest Trails. Hiking options are virtually unlimited. Short, long, easy, hard—whatever kind of trails you like, you can access them without needing to drive anywhere.

If hiking isn't your bag, you can always rock climb, fish, ride horses from the Tuolumne Meadows stables, or take the free shuttle bus to other points along Tioga Road. After exploring the high country all day, you'll sit down to a hearty dinner at the Tuolumne Meadows Lodge dining tent, alongside the Tuolumne River. The food is excellent, and prices are reasonable, especially considering the spectacular setting.

If you prefer something more casual, the Tuolumne Meadows Grill is a half mile down the road by the Tuolumne Meadows campground and store. They make great buckwheat pancakes, plus the usual burgers and fries.

Facilities
There are 59 tent cabins that can accommodate up to four people. A restaurant and small store are on-site. Linens and towels are provided.

Reservations and Rates
Reservations are required. Fees are $75 per night. The lodge is open from mid-June to mid-September. Pets are not permitted.

Directions
From Fresno, take Highway 99 north to Manteca. Turn east on Highway 120 and drive 65 miles to Groveland. From Groveland, continue east on Highway 120 for 23 miles to the Big Oak Flat entrance at Yosemite. Continue east on Highway 120 for nine miles to Crane Flat, then turn left and drive 39 miles to the Tuolumne Meadows Lodge turnoff, on the right, just past Lembert Dome.

If you're coming from U.S. 395, Tuolumne Meadows Lodge is 6.5 miles west of the Tioga Pass entrance station to Yosemite. Contact Yosemite Reservations, 6771 North Palm Avenue, Fresno, CA 93704, 559/252-4848 or 559/253-5635, website: www.yosemitepark.com.

19 CURRY VILLAGE CABINS
off Highway 140 in Yosemite Valley

Luxury rating: ★ ★ ★ ☆ ☆   **Recreation rating:** ★ ★ ★ ★ ★

Rank: Best for Families

Many visitors have a love/hate relationship with Curry Village in Yosemite Valley. On the one hand, they love Curry Village, because it's centrally located in the valley and it comes with all the amenities: lodging, food, parking, bus shuttles, stores, etc. On the other hand, they hate Curry Village, because it embodies the worst of Yosemite Valley on its most hectic summer days: too many people and too noisy.

That said, make sure you know what you are signing up for when you book a stay at Curry Village. In the off-season (or even in summer, if you plan way in advance), you could be fortunate enough to rent one of Curry Village's private, cozy, wooden cabins. If you were born under a lucky star, you might even get one of the cabins with a private bath, which will save you from a hike to the restroom in the middle of the night.

Nevada Fall in Yosemite Valley

But most of the time, and for the vast majority of visitors, the only cabins available at Curry Village are the 400-plus tent cabins. The two facts you need to know about these cabins are that they are made of canvas, and they are placed about nine inches apart. This is convenient if you want to stay up late and learn a new language from the bevy of international visitors. Of course, it's inconvenient if you enjoy sleeping. The tent cabins have electric lights, and some of them are heated. Other than that, don't expect much other than a couple of beds with linens.

Regardless of how much sleep you get, you are situated in the most glorious national park in California, so you can't complain all that much. Every imaginable form of outdoor recreation is right outside your door—hiking, biking, fishing, rock climbing, waterfall watching, horseback riding, you name it. Curry Village is ideally situated near the Happy Isles trailhead, where the spectacular hikes to Vernal and Nevada Falls, and the arduous trek to the summit of Half Dome, begin.

In winter, Curry Village's ice-skating rink is open daily. In summer, naturalist programs are held every evening, and bicycle and raft rentals are available. One of the greatest ways to see Yosemite Valley in early summer is to take a lazy float down the Merced River in an inflatable raft.

Facilities
There are 102 wooden cabins with private bath, 80 wooden cabins without a private bath, and 427 canvas tent cabins, plus 19 standard motel rooms. None of the cabins have kitchens. A restaurant, café, store, swimming pool, and equipment rentals are on-site. Linens and towels are provided.

Reservations and Rates
Reservations are recommended. Fees are $69–79 per night for tent cabins and $85–195 per night for wooden cabins. Pets are not permitted. Contact Yosemite Reservations, 6771 North Palm Avenue, Fresno, CA 93704, 559/252-4848 or 559/253-5635, website: www.yosemitepark.com.

Directions

From Merced, take Highway 140 east for 75 miles to the Arch Rock entrance station at Yosemite. Continue east into Yosemite Valley for 11.5 miles to Curry Village, on the right.

20 GLACIER POINT SKI HUT

off Glacier Point Road in Yosemite

Luxury rating: ★ ★ ☆ ☆ ☆   **Recreation rating: ★ ★ ★ ☆ ☆**

If you like the sound of an overnight stay at a cross-country ski hut but think that getting there may be beyond your abilities, the Glacier Point Ski Hut will ease your fears about your snow skills. Although the distance to be covered on skis or snowshoes is a substantial 10 miles from where you leave your car, the going is easy, and you have almost nothing to carry.

If you've driven to Glacier Point in summer, you've seen the Glacier Point Ski Hut. But in summer, it's not a ski hut, it's an impressive log building that houses a snack shop a few yards from one of the West's most spectacular viewpoints. While savoring the incomparable view of Half Dome and the valley floor 3,000 feet below, you can buy a snow cone here in August or make a snowman here in February—take your pick. Completely renovated in 1997, the ski-hut building is a lovely structure in any season, with its massive timber beams and huge stone fireplace. In winter, Yosemite Concession Services (YCS) removes the store shelves and cash registers and puts in bunk beds, then leads guided ski trips with an overnight stay at the hut.

The fact that the trip requires a guide makes it suitable even for beginners. Although YCS requests that you are at least an intermediate-level cross-country skier, plenty of beginners make the trip. It's doable

because the 10-mile route from Badger Pass is on a well-groomed track that follows Glacier Point Road all the way. With one guide in front of your group and one in back, everybody skis at their own pace, and nobody gets left behind.

It's also doable for beginners because you carry almost

nothing on your back. YCS issues each skier his or her own lightweight liner to stuff inside the hut's sleeping bags. You carry that and some water and snacks for the trip; the guides take care of the rest, including all meals and wine.

The minimum number of people for a night at Glacier Point Ski Hut is 5; the maximum is 20. On weeknights, you and your family or friends can have the place to yourselves (plus your guides, of course). On weekends, you're likely to share the place with company, unless you managed to convince 19 people to go with you.

Facilities
There is one ski hut that can accommodate 5 to 20 people. Meals are provided. There are no showers or bathrooms. Sleeping bags and liners are provided.

Reservations and Rates
Reservations are required. For a one-night ski trip, the fee is $160–192 per person per night, including meals. For a two-night ski trip, the fee is $240–288 per person, including meals. Pets are not permitted. Contact Yosemite Reservations, 6771 North Palm Avenue, Fresno, CA 93704, 559/252-4848 or 559/253-5635, website: www.yosemitepark.com.

Directions
From Fresno, take Highway 41 north for 65 miles to Wawona/southern entrance station at Yosemite National Park. Continue north on Highway 41 for 17 miles to the right turnoff for Glacier Point Road. Turn right and drive six miles to Badger Pass Ski Area.

21 SILVER LAKE RESORT
off Highway 158 in June Lake

Luxury rating: ★ ★ ★ ☆ ☆   **Recreation rating:** ★ ★ ★ ★ ☆

Of all the real estate for sale in the June Lake area, the toughest properties to buy are those on the shore of Silver Lake. They almost never come up for sale. Why? Because most people agree that 110-acre Silver Lake is the prettiest of the four lakes on the June Lake Loop, and having a piece of it is too good to give up.

Luckily, there's Silver Lake Resort, where anybody can get a little piece

© ANN MARIE BROWN

of Silver Lake—at least for a few days or a week. Silver Lake Resort is a full-service operation with a general store, cabins, a café, an RV park, and boat rentals. It was established in 1916, which makes it the oldest resort in the eastern Sierra.

The resort has plain, brown, log-style cabins that are rustic-looking on the outside but clean and well cared for on the inside. Many have remodeled interiors, including new curtains and bedding. None have telephones, and only a few have televisions. The cabins are set amid a grove of aspens, giving the illusion of seclusion, even though they are close together. All cabins are only a stone's throw from the lake; a few have lake views.

Most resort guests take advantage of fishing on Silver Lake; motorboats and canoes are for rent by the hour or the day. If you want to hike, the Rush Creek trailhead is about 100 yards away, from which a spectacular day hike can be taken to Agnew and Gem Lakes. If you have the urge to ride Old Paint, a pack station is next door to the resort.

Facilities
There are 17 cabins ranging in size and accommodating two to eight people. All cabins have fully equipped kitchens. A general store, a café, and an RV park are on-site. Linens and towels are provided.

Reservations and Rates
Reservations are recommended. Fees are $90–225 per night, depending on cabin size. For the eight-person cabins, a five-night minimum is required. The resort is open from June to October, weather permitting. Pets are not permitted. Contact Silver Lake Resort, P.O. Box 116, June Lake, CA 93529, 760/648-7525, website: silverlakeresort.net.

Directions
From U.S. 395 at the Highway 203/Mammoth Lakes turnoff, drive 15 miles north on U.S. 395 to Highway 158, the southern turnoff for the June Lake Loop. Turn west on Highway 158 and drive 7.5 miles to Silver Lake Resort, on the left.

22 REVERSE CREEK LODGE
off Highway 158 in June Lake

Luxury rating: ★★★☆☆   **Recreation rating:** ★★★★☆

"Our family welcomes yours" is the motto at Reverse Creek Lodge. The Reverse Creek Lodge (similarly—but not quite literally—named after Reversed Creek) family is David and Denise Naaden and their 12 children, whom they call their "cleaning crew." With that many kids, the place ought to be clean as a whistle, and sure enough, it is.

The Naadens took over the lodge and its cabins and A-frame chalets in 1995. The rustic cabins are set in the pines along Reversed Creek, but the modern A-frame chalets are the more popular rentals. Located down the street about 100 yards from the rest of the resort, the chalets are perched above Reversed Creek in a cluster of pines. Some have a fair view of 10,909-foot Carson Peak, a mammoth granite landmark in June Lake.

The only disadvantage is that the five chalets are a bit cramped, each one only a few feet from the next. Like the cabins, the A-frames have fully stocked kitchens, cable TV, VCRs, gas fireplaces, gas barbecues, and all the other amenities of home. For big groups, the resort has a private residence cabin with four bedrooms and two full baths.

At Reverse Creek Lodge, all the recreation opportunities of the June Lake area are at your disposal. The ski resort is only a half mile away, fishing is possible in four lakes (June, Silver, Gull, and Grant) and several streams, horses and bicycles can be rented, and so on. Hikers can head for the Yost Creek Trail, next door to the resort. Featuring a hearty climb, the trail leads to Yost and Fern Lakes. The last mile to Fern Lake is the steepest; if you want something a little easier, take the left fork to Yost Lake. Both are scenic, high-alpine lakes.

Facilities

There are eight cabins with one or two bedrooms, five A-frame chalets that can accommodate up to six people, and one large four-bedroom house. All have fully equipped kitchens. A store and restaurant are nearby. Linens and towels are provided.

Reservations and Rates
Reservations are recommended. Fees are $75-120 per night for the cabins, $140 per night for the chalets, and $285 per night for the four-bedroom house. The resort is open year-round. Pets are not permitted. Contact Reverse Creek Lodge, P.O. Box 605, June Lake, CA 93529, 760/648-7535 or 800/762-6440, website: www.reversecreeklodge.com.

Directions
From U.S. 395 at the Highway 203/Mammoth Lakes turnoff, drive 15 miles north on U.S. 395 to Highway 158, the southern turnoff for the June Lake Loop. Turn west on Highway 158 and drive 4.5 miles to Reverse Creek Lodge, on the left.

23 FERN CREEK LODGE
off Highway 158 in June Lake

Luxury rating: ★ ★ ★ ☆ ☆   **Recreation rating:** ★ ★ ★ ★ ☆

All of the cabin resorts in June Lake are clean, serviceable, and well situated for recreation enthusiasts. But some simply have more character than others, and Fern Creek Lodge is in that category. Maybe it's because the lodge has been around since 1927 (it's the oldest year-round lodge on the June Lake Loop), or maybe it's that each of its cabins is completely different in style and appearance. There's just something about this resort that makes it cozy and appealing.

The cutest cabin is the green-and-white Old Schoolhouse, a tiny little house for two people only. It's at the back of the property, farthest from the road. Dutch Lady and Heart Tree are the largest cabins; they're both two-story units with four bedrooms, two bathrooms, and a sundeck around the front.

A modern hot tub is set in the middle of the cabins; guests take turns using it. The main lodge area has a selection of games and—get this—Internet access. A common barbecue area and fish-cleaning facilities are available. If you don't feel like cooking, you can always drive down the road a half mile to the Carson Peak Inn, a popular dinner spot in June Lake.

© ANN MARIE BROWN

For recreation, take your pick from all that June Lake has to offer: trout fishing in four good-sized lakes, water sports, and swimming in summer; downhill skiing, cross-country skiing, snowboarding, and snowmobiling in winter; and watching the aspens turn bright gold in autumn. Hiking and biking in the area are excellent any time the ground is snow-free. The lodge is a half mile from June Mountain Ski Area and midway between Gull and Silver Lakes. Basically, nothing you might want to do is more than five miles away.

Facilities

There are 10 cabins ranging in size from one to four bedrooms, plus four apartment units. All cabins have fully equipped kitchens. A hot tub and a small store are on-site; a restaurant is nearby. Linens and towels are provided.

Reservations and Rates

Reservations are recommended. Fees are $70 per night for the one-bedroom cabins, $125–150 per night for the two-bedroom cabins, and $235 per night for the four-bedroom cabins, which can accommodate up to 14 people (the rate is based on eight people; add $10 per night for each additional person). The resort is open year-round. Pets are permitted with a $10 fee per night. Contact Fern Creek Lodge, 4628 Highway 158, June Lake, CA 93529, 760/648-7722 or 800/621-9146, website: www.ferncreeklodge.com.

Directions

From U.S. 395 at the Highway 203/Mammoth Lakes turnoff, drive 15 miles north on U.S. 395 to Highway 158, the southern turnoff for the June Lake Loop. Turn west on Highway 158 and drive five miles to Fern Creek Lodge, on the right.

24 THE FOUR SEASONS
off Highway 158 in June Lake

Luxury rating: ★ ★ ★ ☆ ☆   **Recreation rating:** ★ ★ ★ ★ ☆

© ANN MARIE BROWN

If the idea of looking out your cabin's floor-to-ceiling windows at 10,909-foot Carson Peak appeals to you, you'll enjoy staying at the Four Seasons. The resort's A-frame chalets are just off the road at the base of Carson Peak, across the street from the popular restaurant at Carson Peak Inn.

From the front, they don't look like much. The six chalets are packed in like sardines (they're almost touching each other). But once you're inside, you remember why you came here: The view of Carson Peak's snow-covered granite is truly stunning.

Each chalet is identical: 800 square feet in size and with an enclosed master bedroom, plus a loft bedroom that overlooks the living room. The living room has the giant windows with the view. If you want an even better view, go sit outside on your chalet's sundeck. In summer, you can flip hamburgers while you gaze at the scenery; the chalets have gas barbecues. If you prefer to cook indoors, the kitchens are fully stocked with everything you need except food.

Just about every kind of recreation imaginable is possible from your Four Seasons chalet. Within a 10-minute drive are the four lakes of the June Lake Loop (including five marinas and a swimming beach). A horse stable is just down the road, as are several hiking trailheads. Cyclists enjoy riding the 21-mile June Lake Loop (it's wise to get an early morning start, especially on weekends, before the traffic gets going). In winter, June Mountain Ski Area provides the fun. Or, if you strap on a pair of snowshoes or cross-country skis, you can explore the closed-in-winter section of the June Lake Loop.

As this book goes to press, the Four Seasons is for sale. Expect some changes to happen here in the next few years; this is one gorgeous piece of property and may well end up being developed into something much larger and more extensive than its current six chalets. Stay tuned.

Facilities

There are six chalets that can accommodate up to seven people. All cabins have fully equipped kitchens. A store and restaurant are nearby. Linens and towels are provided.

Reservations and Rates

Reservations are recommended. Fees are $119 for two people, plus $20 for each additional person. Rates are slightly higher in August and during summer and winter holidays. A three-night minimum is required. The resort is open year-round. Pets are not permitted. Contact The Four Seasons, Star Route 3, Box 8-B, June Lake, CA 93529, 760/648-7476, website: www.junelake.com/lodging/foursns.

Directions

From U.S. 395 at the Highway 203/Mammoth Lakes turnoff, drive 15 miles north on U.S. 395 to Highway 158, the southern turnoff for the June Lake Loop. Turn west on Highway 158 and drive five miles to the Four Seasons, on the left.

Other Cabins and Cottages Nearby

Gull Lake Lodge, P.O. Box 25, June Lake, CA 93529, 760/648-7516 or 800/631-9081.

June Lake Pines Cottages, P.O. Box 97, June Lake, CA 93529, 760/648-7522 or 800/481-3637.

June Lake Motel and Cabins, P.O. Box 98, June Lake, CA 93529, 760/648-7547 or 800/648-6835, website: www.junelake.com/jlmotel.

Lake Front Cabins, P.O. Box 696, June Lake, CA 93529, 760/648-7527, website: www.lake-front-cabins.com.

Whispering Pines Motel and Cabins, Route 3, Box 14-B, June Lake, CA 93529, 760/648-7762 or 800/648-7762, website: www.junelake.com/wpines.

25 DOUBLE EAGLE RESORT
off Highway 158 in June Lake

Luxury rating: ★ ★ ★ ★ ★   **Recreation rating:** ★ ★ ★ ★ ☆

Rank: Most Luxurious

When the Double Eagle Resort opened in 1999, most June Lake regulars weren't sure what to think of it. It was (and is) far more upscale than other local resorts, or even those in nearby Mammoth Lakes. Would people want to stay there? Would all that money spent on a fancy restaurant, health spa, picture-perfect cabins, and trophy trout ponds go to waste? And what would it mean for the future of June Lake? Would it change the character of the place?

Well, a few years have gone by, and after all the hubbub, it seems that little is different in June Lake, except now the town has a really plush cabin resort and a great restaurant, and the locals can join the resort's health club for a discounted fee. The Double Eagle owners are well respected for bringing in more business to the June Lake Loop.

No doubt about it, the Double Eagle is the most luxurious place to stay in June Lake. It features brand-new two-bedroom cabins with fully equipped kitchens and fireplaces. They are tastefully decorated and large enough to fit four to six people. All the extra amenities are provided: microwave oven, barbecue, TV and VCR, and the like. They even have telephones, a rarity in the cabin world.

Additionally, the resort features the Creekside Spa and Fitness Center, which includes a gorgeous 60-foot indoor pool and hot tub, as well as all kinds of fitness equipment and classes. There is even a full-service salon for guests who want to get their nails or hair done or to have a facial treatment or massage. Honestly, that's about the last thing I would do on vacation in June Lake, but whatever floats your boat.

Then there's the Eagle's Landing Restaurant, which serves the best food in town and offers a scenic view besides. Every table has a look at Carson Peak and Reversed Creek. In addition to the regular menu, the restaurant offers a spa menu, just in case you're taking this fitness thing seriously.

So when you've finally finished your pedicure, aromatherapy massage, tai chi class, and gourmet lunch, what's next? You can head outside and try out the resort's trophy trout pond, which is stocked with trout up to 18 pounds. What, you don't know how to fly-fish? No matter, they offer lessons daily. There's even a fly-fishing pond just for kids. Full guide service is available, as is a fly-fishing shop.

There's so much to do at Double Eagle Resort, not to mention in the surrounding June Lake area, that you should probably stay at least a week.

Otherwise, you won't have time for one of the best activities: sitting on your cabin's deck and staring at the view of Carson Peak and Carson Falls. In case you haven't guessed, this resort was built on some spectacular property.

Facilities
There are 13 two-bedroom cabins that can accommodate up to six people, plus one group cabin that can accommodate up to 12 people. All cabins have fully equipped kitchens and fireplaces. A restaurant, spa, and fitness center are on-site. Linens and towels are provided.

Reservations and Rates
Reservations are recommended. Fees are $258–319 per night. Some weekday and five-night discounts are available. The resort is open year-round. Pets are permitted in a limited number of cabins. Contact Double Eagle Resort, 5587 Highway 158, P.O. Box 736, June Lake, CA 93529, 760/648-7004, website: www.doubleeagleresort.com.

Directions
From U.S. 395 at the Highway 203/Mammoth Lakes turnoff, drive 15 miles north on U.S. 395 to Highway 158, the southern turnoff for the June Lake Loop. Turn west on Highway 158 and drive six miles to Double Eagle Resort, on the left.

26 BIG ROCK RESORT
off Highway 158 in June Lake

Luxury rating: ★ ★ ★ ☆ ☆   **Recreation rating:** ★ ★ ★ ★ ★

When Southern Californians think of taking a serious skiing or snowboarding trip, they bypass all their local ski areas and load up their SUVs for the long drive to Mammoth. There's nothing wrong with the ski resorts in the nearby San Gabriel and San Bernardino Mountains; they just aren't the eastern Sierra.

The majority of those SUVs head for the glamour runs on Mammoth Mountain and the town of Mammoth Lake's popular hotels, restaurants, and nightlife. But there's a less-visited ski mountain just 30 miles to the north, in the town of June Lake. If you want to have a skiing vacation in a place that doesn't feel like a transplanted Los Angeles, give June Lake a try.

At June Mountain Ski Area, you'll find less crowds and cheaper lift tickets. You'll have snowmobiling, sledding, snow-shoeing, and cross-country ski-ing options. And best of all, you'll be sharing a quiet winter wonderland vacation with your loved ones in a lakeside cabin at Big Rock Resort.

The cabins at Big Rock are a perfect destination in any season. Because they're perched next to large June Lake, they allow summer visitors easy access to excellent trout fishing, sailing, and boating. The resort provides motorboat and paddleboat rentals, or cabin guests can bring their own boat and launch it for free.

Cyclists can saddle up at their cabin and ride the spectacular June Lake Loop. For hikers, a trailhead is across the street from Big Rock Resort, by the June Lake Firehouse. From there, you can hike five miles through flower-filled Yost Meadows and the June Mountain Ski Area to Yost Lake.

In winter, 2,500 vertical feet of skiing are on June Mountain, just 1.5 miles from Big Rock Resort. Many snowboarders insist that the boarding is better here than at neighboring Mammoth Mountain. One thing is certain: The lines at the chair lifts are shorter.

The one- to three-bedroom cabins at Big Rock Resort have everything you need for either a winter or summer vacation. Some of the cabins are duplexes, however, so make sure you request a single unit if you don't want to share exterior walls.

Facilities

There are eight cabins ranging in size from one to three bedrooms, all with fully equipped kitchens. A small store and restaurant are on-site. Linens and towels are provided.

Reservations and Rates

Reservations are recommended. Fees are $125–225 per night, depending on cabin size. Reduced rates are available in September, October, and May, excluding holidays. The resort is open year-round. Pets are permitted with advance permission, a $50 deposit, and a $10 fee per night. Contact

Big Rock Resort, P.O. Box 126, 1 Big Rock Road, June Lake, CA 93529, 760/648-7717 or 800/769-9831, website: www.bigrockresort.net.

Directions
From U.S. 395 at the Highway 203/Mammoth Lakes turnoff, drive 15 miles north on U.S. 395 to Highway 158, the southern turnoff for the June Lake Loop. Turn west on Highway 158 and drive 2.5 miles to Big Rock Road, on the right. Turn right and drive to the resort.

27 ALPERS OWENS RIVER RANCH
off U.S. 395 near Mammoth Lakes

Luxury rating: ★ ★ ★ ☆ ☆   **Recreation rating:** ★ ★ ★ ☆ ☆

Rank: Best for Fishing

If you don't know what Alpers means, you won't know why a stay at Alpers Owens River Ranch is so special. Tim Alpers is the name of a man who raises world-class trophy trout. Alpers trout, known for their size, beauty, and feisty nature, are planted in many waters of the eastern Sierra, including the trophy ponds of several resorts.

That same man owns Alpers Owens River Ranch, where nine cabins, a lodge, and a general store surround two miles of the Owens River. Quite simply, guests come here because they are passionate about fly-fishing for trout.

When you enter the main lodge, the first thing you notice is an enormous stuffed beaver on the coffeetable, accompanied by a sign that reads: "Don't pet the dam beaver." As your eyes adjust to the dim light, you discover lots more: old black-and-white photographs, taxidermied trout, and assorted bric-a-brac and antiques from earlier days. There is much dust and even some rust. But it's infinitely charming.

Alpers Owens River Ranch is a throwback to the old days— let's say the 1920s. It doesn't try to be anything else. Take cabin No. 6, for example. It's the most luxurious cabin on the ranch, which means it has a propane

© ANN MARIE BROWN

refrigerator and stove. All of the furniture looks like it's been sat on by a herd of elephants. Sound like a fishing camp? Yes, this is a fishing camp.

Cabin No. 6 is the preferred rental choice because it's six feet from the Owens River. You can practically fly-fish off your porch. Of course, that's after you've had your try at the trophy pond or the headwaters of the Owens River (barbless fly-fishing for native trout). River access and access to artificially constructed Alpers Creek (bait fishing and fly-fishing for stocked one- to two-pound rainbows) is included in your stay. To access the four-acre trophy pond, you pay $35 for three hours. Make a reservation for a three-hour slot, then inflate your float tube while you're waiting.

Two other cabins are also right on the river. If any of the riverfront cabins are available, don't even think of renting the others, which are clustered near the main lodge and parking lot.

What do nonanglers do at Alpers Owens River Ranch? Not much except sit on the porch with a good book or seek out nearby hot springs. But around here, a nonangler is a rare species.

Facilities
There are nine cabins ranging in size and accommodating 2 to 10 people. All cabins have kitchens. Linens and towels are provided.

Reservations and Rates
Reservations are required. Fees are $100 per night for two people, plus $40 for each additional person. The resort is open from April to October. Pets are not permitted. Contact Alpers Owens River Ranch, Route 1, Box 232, Mammoth Lakes, CA 93546, 760/648-7334 (summer) or 760/647-6652 (winter).

Directions
From U.S. 395 at the Highway 203/Mammoth Lakes turnoff, drive seven miles north on U.S. 395 to Owens River Road on the right. Turn right (east) and drive three miles to Alpers Owens River Ranch on the left.

28 KOA YOSEMITE-MARIPOSA

off Highway 140 near Mariposa

Luxury rating: ★ ★ ☆ ☆ ☆   **Recreation rating:** ★ ★ ☆ ☆ ☆

Rank: Best Value

© ANN MARIE BROWN

You can say what you want about a place that spells cabins with a K, but the KOA Yosemite-Mariposa is a godsend for Yosemite travelers. Located in the town of Midpines, 10 minutes from Mariposa and 45 minutes from Yosemite Valley, this unit of the national KOA campground chain has 12 Kamping Kabins that serve as a home away from home for about 60 bucks a night. That's right, 60 smackers for a one-room cabin accommodating a family of four.

The Kamping Kabins are the same as what you'll find at most KOAs across America. They are one-room log buildings, with two working windows and a locking front door. Inside are a log-frame double bed and log-frame twin bunk beds (complete with mattresses but not bedding), plus a tiny table/shelf to set your stuff on. Amazingly, there is still enough room left so you can walk around (but not enough room to do the hustle).

Each cabin (or Kabin, if you must) has electric lights and a small heater, plus a front porch with a swing wide enough for two. With a barbecue grill and picnic table right outside your door, you can cook your dinner at your cabin if you wish.

Probably the only downer to a KOA Kabin is the lack of a private bathroom, resulting in occasional hikes to the restroom in the middle of the night. But hey, what do you expect for 60 bucks? At the KOA Mariposa, the central restrooms are bright and clean and have plenty of hot water in the showers.

So what do you do if your family or group consists of more than four people? You rent a KOA Lodge (not called a Klodge, as you might expect). The two KOA Lodges on the property are larger and plusher versions of the Kabins; they sleep up to six people and have private bathrooms and full kitchens. Even the posh-by-comparison Lodges are a relative bargain; they rent for about $150 per night.

The KOA also has a swimming pool, a fish pond, a real train caboose with video games inside, a TV lounge with Yosemite videos, and a small store. The owners make a real effort to keep the place clean, safe, and friendly. They're nice folks who will gladly help you plan a visit to nearby Yosemite.

One last bonus at the KOA: In spring and summer, when everything in or near Yosemite is booked, you have a decent chance of finding lodging here. I've called several times on a Thursday or Friday and been lucky enough to get a cabin for the weekend.

Facilities

There are 12 cabins that can accommodate up to four people, two lodges that can accommodate up to six people, and RV and tent sites. Each cabin has a barbecue but no kitchen; the lodges have kitchens and bathrooms. A small store and a swimming pool are on-site. Linens, towels, sleeping bags, blankets, and pillows are not provided.

Reservations and Rates

Reservations are recommended. Fees for the cabins are $55 per night for two people, plus $5 for each additional person; fees for the lodges are $138–155 per night. Children under eight years old are free. Pets are not permitted in the cabins or lodges, but they are permitted in the campground. Contact KOA Yosemite-Mariposa, P.O. Box 545, 6323 Highway 140, Midpines, CA 95345, 209/966-2201 or 800/562-9391, website: www.yosemitekoa.com.

Directions

From Fresno, take Highway 99 north to Merced. Turn east on Highway 140 and drive 37 miles to Mariposa, then continue for six more miles to Midpines. The KOA is on the left.

Other Cabins and Cottages Nearby

Meadow Creek Ranch, 2669 Triangle Road, Mariposa, CA 95338, 209/966-3843 or 800/853-2037, website: www.meadowcreekranchbnb.com.

Little Valley Inn, 3483 Brooks Road, Mariposa, CA 95338, 209/742-6204 or 800/889-5444, website: www.littlevalley.com.

29 YOSEMITE WEST
off Highway 41 in Yosemite

Luxury rating: ★ ★ ★ ★ ☆   **Recreation rating: ★ ★ ★ ★ ★**

Yosemite National Park is packed with people every day all summer long, but over at Yosemite West you can hear a pin drop on your cabin's deck. Oh, you haven't heard of Yosemite West? Chances are you drove right by its turnoff on your last trip to the park. Yosemite West is an inholding—a privately owned property within the federal park boundary. It's a collection of private homes, most of which are for rent, located on a hillside right across from the junction of Highway 41 and Glacier Point Road.

You couldn't have a better location for exploring the Glacier Point area of Yosemite, which features the best easy day hiking in the park. The short, mostly level trails leading to spectacular valley overlooks at Dewey Point, Taft Point, and Sentinel Dome are less than a 30-minute drive from your Yosemite West cabin. If you choose to drive into the valley, it's less than an hour away.

A cabin at Yosemite West is also the best choice for a winter Yosemite vacation, because it's the closest lodging to the downhill runs at Badger Pass Ski Area (a 20-minute drive). Badger Pass serves as the starting point for snowshoeing and cross-country skiing trails, too, including the spectacular day trip to Dewey Point for a view of the valley below. Rentals and skiing lessons are available.

The rental homes at Yosemite West are on the upscale, modern side. They vary in size and shape, and most come with one or more extras, like a hot tub, barbecue, pool table, or home entertainment center. Most have fireplaces, and free firewood is provided. The homes' lot sizes are fairly large, so you probably won't hear or see much of your neighbors. This place is for those who want peace, quiet, and seclusion.

Several companies, as well as private individuals, offer homes for rent in Yosemite West (see the list below). This is a bonus for vacationers; if you strike out for reservations with one company, call another.

Facilities

There are more than 140 vacation home rentals, ranging in size from two to six bedrooms. All have fully equipped kitchens. Most have fireplaces. Linens and towels are provided.

Reservations and Rates

Reservations are recommended. Fees are $140–465 per night, depending on the size of the accommodations. Off-season rates are available midweek from October to April, excluding holidays. Pets are not permitted. Contact Several companies handle rentals in Yosemite West, including Yosemite West Cottages, 559/642-2211, website: www.yosemitewestreservations.com; Yosemite's Scenic Wonders, 800/296-7364 or 888/967-3648, website: www.scenicwonders.com; Yosemite's Four Seasons, 209/372-9000 or 800/669-9300, website: www.yosemitelodging.com.

Directions

From Fresno, take Highway 41 north for 65 miles to the Wawona/southern entrance station at Yosemite National Park. Continue north on Highway 41 for 16.5 miles to the left turnoff for Yosemite West, just south of Glacier Point Road. Turn left and drive approximately one mile to your Yosemite West rental office.

---

30 OSTRANDER SKI HUT

off Glacier Point Road in Yosemite

Luxury rating: ★ ☆ ☆ ☆ ☆   **Recreation rating:** ★ ★ ★ ☆ ☆

You have to earn your stay at the Ostrander Ski Hut. It's not for everybody; it's only for those who are strong and skilled enough to ski or snowshoe 10 miles on mostly ungroomed track. But for those who make the snowy journey, the reward is a warm night in a two-story stone cabin perched on the edge of Ostrander Lake, at 8,500 feet in elevation.

Still reading? Good. The Ostrander Ski Hut is operated by the Yosemite Association, a nonprofit educational organization. It's open each year from mid-December to mid-April, depending on snow conditions. The hut sleeps 25 people and has bunks, mattresses, a wood stove, solar lights, a kitchen with a gas stove, and assorted cooking and eating utensils. For drinking water, you walk 100 feet down to Ostrander Lake, fill up a bucket, then bring it back and filter it.

You're on your own for your trek to Ostrander Ski Hut, so you must possess some winter backcountry skills. Skiers should be at least intermediate level and in good physical shape. You'll need to carry quite a few items with you: sleeping bag, sleeping pad, head lamp, water filter, water bottle, snow emergency gear, food, and so on.

© ANN MARIE BROWN

Even with all these prerequisites, reservations for Ostrander Ski Hut can be tough to come by. The Yosemite Association starts taking reservations in the fall. If you don't get the dates you want at that time, try calling later on to see if there are cancellations. Of course, your chances are much better midweek than on weekends.

Facilities
There is one ski hut that can accommodate up to 25 people. It has a minimally equipped kitchen. Drinking water must be filtered. Linens and towels are not provided.

Reservations and Rates
Reservations are required and are made by lottery in early November; some reservations are possible by phone after December 1. The fee is $30 per person per night. Pets are not permitted. Contact Yosemite Association, Ostrander Reservations, P.O. Box 545, Yosemite, CA 95389, 209/372-0740 or 209/379-2648, website: www.yosemite.org.

Directions
From Fresno, take Highway 41 north for 65 miles to the Wawona/southern entrance station at Yosemite National Park. Continue north on Highway 41 for 17 miles to the right turnoff for Glacier Point Road. Turn right and drive six miles to Badger Pass Ski Area. Ski trails lead from there.

31 THE REDWOODS CABINS
off Highway 41 in Yosemite

Luxury rating: ★ ★ ★ ☆ ☆　　　　　**Recreation rating:** ★ ★ ★ ★ ★

The Wawona area of Yosemite is like the poor cousin of Yosemite West up the road. Like Yosemite West, it's an inholding within the national park, where anyone can own (or rent) a home. But unlike at Yosemite West, the homes in the Wawona area are clustered tightly together on small lots. Many of the houses are truly cabins—meaning they're a bit on the rustic side.

However, being the poor cousin isn't necessarily a bad thing. The Wawona cabins, collectively known as The Redwoods Vacation Home Rentals, are beautifully situated at the southern entrance to the park. This is perfect for Southern Californians making the long drive north to Yosemite. Within moments of passing through the park gates, you pull up to your rental cabin. After a good night's sleep, you're perfectly situated to hike the eight-mile round-trip to Chilnualna Falls (the trailhead is five minutes from your cabin) or to take a shorter walk around the spectacular Giant Sequoias of the Mariposa Grove.

In addition, the many trailheads and attractions of Glacier Point Road are only 30 minutes away; Yosemite Valley is an hour away. On hot summer days, Flat Rocks and Swinging Bridge swimming holes in the nearby south fork of the Merced River offer a chance to cool off. Sometime during your stay, be sure to visit the Pioneer History Center in Wawona to gain a glimpse at different periods of Yosemite's history.

Another advantage to being the poor cousin is that The Redwoods Cabins are a real bargain. For as little as $82 per night in winter, two people can rent a small cabin, complete with linens, cookware, dishes, barbecue, and firewood. (Rates go up by about 20 percent in summer.) Larger houses that

can accommodate a whole family or large group are also available. Every home is privately owned and reflects the owner's personal tastes and requirements, so there should be one that suits you too.

To make it easy, The Redwoods Cabins arranged its 130 vacation rentals into categories. Category C includes the

© ANN MARIE BROWN

smallest, least expensive cabins with the least amenities (no fireplace, for example). Category U contains the priciest cabins; these may have as many as six bedrooms, plus amenities like satellite TV, a dishwasher, or a gas grill. Every kind of cabin in between falls into one of four other categories.

Facilities
There are 125 cabins and vacation homes, sized from one bedroom to six bedrooms, all with fully equipped kitchens. A store and restaurant are nearby. Linens and towels are provided.

Reservations and Rates
Reservations are recommended. Fees are $121–600 per night, depending on the size and luxury level of the rental. There is a three-night minimum in summer and on holidays, and a two-night minimum in the off-season. Pets are permitted in some cabins. Contact The Redwoods Cabins, P.O. Box 2085, 8038 Chilnualna Falls Road, Wawona Station, Yosemite, CA 95389, 209/375-6666, website: www.redwoodsinyosemite.com.

Directions
From Fresno, take Highway 41 north for 65 miles to the Wawona/southern entrance station at Yosemite National Park. Continue north on Highway 41 for seven miles to Chilnualna Falls Road, in Wawona. Turn right and drive one mile on Chilnualna Falls Road to The Redwoods Cabins rental office, on the right.

32 OWL'S NEST CABINS
off Highway 41 in Fish Camp

Luxury rating: ★ ★ ★ ☆ ☆   **Recreation rating:** ★ ★ ★ ☆ ☆

Some people are well suited for the jobs they do, and that's certainly true for Bob and Barbara Taylor. The couple runs Owl's Nest Cabins, in Fish Camp, just south of the southern entrance to Yosemite National Park. When I first met them, they had just returned from a day's exploration in the wilds of Sierra National Forest. Barbara was very excited about the huge marmot she'd seen, and Robert wanted to talk about the old mining cabins they'd discovered.

   The Taylors love living in Fish Camp, and they enjoy having visitors come stay at their three cabins, just across the street from their house. The

© ANN MARIE BROWN

cabins are all completely different; one is a small upstairs unit above a utility room, another is a large chalet for a family, and the third is a rounded A-frame, sized just right for two people. All three have fully furnished kitchens, plus a barbecue grill outside. Each includes a TV and VCR, but since it's too mind-numbing to sit around and watch game shows and reruns, the Taylors have provided a stock of videotapes about Yosemite.

The Taylors will happily supply guests with information about what to do and see in Yosemite (two miles north) and Sierra National Forest (all around to the south and east). A stream runs behind the Taylors' main house, and visitors can fish in it or just enjoy its coursing flow.

Because Fish Camp is so close the southern entrance to Yosemite, you might think it's logical to spend all your vacation time there, visiting the Wawona and Mariposa Grove areas and hiking the many trails on Glacier Point Road. But don't neglect the many attractions to the south, including the Nelder Grove of Giant Sequoias and Fresno Dome in Sierra National Forest. Another must is a hike along the Lewis Creek National Recreation Trail, three miles south of Fish Camp. The trail follows the historic Madera Sugar Pine Lumber flume route, passing Corlieu Falls, Red Rock Falls, and a wide variety of wildflowers in early summer.

Facilities

There are three cabins that can accommodate up to six people. All have fully equipped kitchens. A store and restaurant are nearby. Linens and towels are provided.

Reservations and Rates

Reservations are recommended. Fees are $90–150 per night for two people, plus $20 for each additional person (up to six). Pets are not permitted. Contact Owl's Nest Cabins, 1237 Highway 41, P.O. Box 33, Fish Camp, CA 93623, 559/683-3484, website: www.owlsnestlodging.com.

Directions

From Fresno, take Highway 41 north for 63 miles to Fish Camp (two miles south of the Wawona entrance to Yosemite). Owl's Nest Cabins are on the left side of the road, in the center of town (look for the owl statues).

Other Cabins and Cottages Nearby

Chalet for Two, 1191 Highway 41, P.O. Box 130, Fish Camp, CA 93623, 559/683-7962.

33 APPLE TREE INN
off Highway 41 in Fish Camp

Luxury rating: ★ ★ ★ ★ ☆   **Recreation rating:** ★ ★ ★ ☆ ☆

The Apple Tree Inn is one of the nicest places to stay in the town of Fish Camp, but because it's only a few years old, surprisingly few people know of it. Set on seven pine-covered acres, the inn is a peaceful spot right off Highway 41, just two miles from Yosemite's southern gate.

Fish Camp, elevation 5,000 feet, is the home of the Yosemite Mountain Sugar Pine Railroad, an attraction that brings to life memories of long-gone logging camps. On the same route where sturdy flumes once transported lumber from Fish Camp to Madera, visitors today can ride an authentic narrow-gauge steam train *(The Logger)* through scenic woodlands. The Apple Tree Inn is only a half mile from the railroad, which also features special moonlight rides, a museum, gift shop, and evening barbecues.

The other obvious draw for guests at the Apple Tree Inn is southern Yosemite National Park. After only a 10-minute drive, visitors can be gazing upward at the Giant Sequoias in the Mariposa Grove, or they can head farther into the park to explore the sights and trails of Glacier Point Road or Yosemite Valley.

Those who choose to hang around the resort's 11 acres will find an indoor swimming pool, a hot tub, and a racquetball court. The cottages are new-looking and prettily decorated in Laura Ashley fabrics; each comes with convenient amenities like hair dryers and coffeemakers. Each unit also has a gas fireplace.

Most guests don't attempt to make dinner in their very limited kitchenette (small refrigerator and microwave). Instead, they walk the short

© ANN MARIE BROWN

footpath to the restaurant at neighboring Tenaya Lodge. A complimentary continental breakfast is served each morning in the Apple Tree Inn's dining room.

Facilities
There is one freestanding cottage at Apple Tree Inn, plus 53 duplex- and triplex-style cottages. The cottages have refrigerators and microwaves, plus fireplaces. An indoor pool and a hot tub are on-site. A store and restaurant are nearby. Linens and towels are provided.

Reservations and Rates
Reservations are recommended. Fees are $125–180 per night midweek from September through mid-May, and $160–229 per night the rest of the year, and on weekends and holidays. A continental breakfast is included. Pets are permitted in some cottages with a $50 fee. Contact Apple Tree Inn, 1110 Highway 41, Fish Camp, CA 93623, 559/683-5111 or 888/683-5111, website: www.appletreeinn-yosemite.com.

Directions
From Fresno, take Highway 41 north for 63 miles to Fish Camp (two miles south of the Wawona entrance to Yosemite). Apple Tree Inn is on the right side of the road, a half mile north of the Yosemite Mountain Sugar Pine Railroad.

34 MAMMOTH MOUNTAIN CHALETS
off Highway 203 in Mammoth Lakes

Luxury rating: ★ ★ ★ ★ ☆   **Recreation rating:** ★ ★ ★ ★ ★

Rank: Best for Winter Sports

For people who love to ski or snowboard but don't like to drive to the lifts, Mammoth Mountain Chalets are ideal. They're right across the street from Chairs 1 and 11 at Mammoth Mountain Ski Area, so you can literally ski to the lifts. The 11,053-foot summit of Mammoth Mountain is easily accessible via a glass-paneled gondola.

By the same token, for people who love to mountain bike but don't like a long drive to the trailhead, Mammoth Mountain Chalets are ideal. They're right across the street from Mammoth Mountain Bike Park, the summer persona of the ski resort. The park is famous for its occasional

pro races, when all the big-
name mountain bikers show
up. Most of the time, however,
it's just regular vacationers
cruising around the trails,
which run the full spectrum
from easy to extremely difficult.
Bike rentals are available if you
don't bring your own.

Mammoth Mountain's A-
frame chalets are big enough for
a whole group. Most have two or three bedrooms, plus assorted extra beds
to accommodate up to 10 people. They're modern in style and include
amenities like dishwashers, phones, televisions, and fireplaces. In winter, you
can't drive right up to your chalet; instead, you park at the main lodge and a
snowmobile carries you and your gear to your front door.

Everything, absolutely everything, can be purchased in the town of
Mammoth Lakes, so don't worry if you forgot all your belongings except
the clothes on your back. Next door to the chalets are a huge lodge and
restaurant complex, where you'll find many shops and places to eat.

Other area highlights include a summer day trip to Devils Postpile National Monument. During daylight hours, you can't drive your own car
into the park; you must pay a fee and ride a shuttle bus. (Traffic is restrict-
ed in the park because of its narrow, winding access road.) Once there,
you can hike to the columnar basalt formation known as the Devils Postpile, plus view spectacular Rainbow Falls and Lower Falls.

Another must is enjoying a sunset at Minaret Vista, a Forest Service
overlook that is within walking distance of your cabin. The vista takes in
the entire sawtooth range of the Minarets, including 12,936-foot Banner
Peak and 13,143-foot Mount Ritter. It's a popular spot at any time, but especially at the close of the day.

Last but not least, try bathing in the nearby springs at Hot Creek.

Facilities

There are 20 chalets that can accommodate 4 to 10 people. All have fully
equipped kitchens and fireplaces. Stores and restaurants are nearby.
Linens and towels are provided.

Reservations and Rates

Reservations are recommended. Fees are $150–220 per night in summer
(higher during bike race events) and $250–380 per night in winter (higher
on holidays). There is a two-night minimum; three nights on holidays.

The resort is open year-round. Pets are not permitted. Contact Mammoth Mountain Chalets, P.O. Box 513, Mammoth Lakes, CA 93546, 760/934-8518 or 800/327-3681, website: www.mammothmtnchalets.com.

Directions
From U.S. 395 at Mammoth Lakes, take the Highway 203 turnoff and drive west for four miles, through the town of Mammoth Lakes, to the intersection of Highway 203 and Lake Mary Road. Turn right on Highway 203 (Minaret Road) and drive five miles to Mammoth Mountain Chalets, across from the ski area.

Other Cabins and Cottages Nearby
Zwart House, P.O. Box 174, Mammoth Lakes, CA 93546, 760/934-2217.
Pine Cliff Resort, P.O. Box 2, Mammoth Lakes, CA 93546, 760/934-2447, website: www.pinecliff.net.
Edelweiss Lodge, P.O. Box 658, Mammoth Lakes, CA 93546, 760/934-2445 or 877/233-3593, website: www.edelweiss-lodge.com.

35 RED'S MEADOW RESORT
in Devils Postpile National Monument

Luxury rating: ★ ★ ☆ ☆ ☆   **Recreation rating:** ★ ★ ★ ★ ☆

Rank: Best for Horseback Riding

With all the people who pour into Devils Postpile National Monument during the few short months it's open each year, it's surprising how few know about the cabins at Red's Meadow Resort. Red's is the only commercial service in the park; they run a pack station, small store, and café, plus they rent out eight cabins and 10 motel rooms. Technically, the resort is just outside the park in Inyo National Forest, but nobody ever notices the difference.

The cabins are A-frames, older in style but clean and serviceable inside. They have small kitchens with a stovetop but no oven (don't plan on basting a turkey). Meals are also served at the resort's Mule House Cafe.

Chances are you won't spend much time at your cabin because there's much to do in surrounding Devils Postpile and Inyo National Forest. Fishing enthusiasts head for Starkweather Lake, Sotcher Lake, and the middle fork of the San Joaquin River (good for fly-fishing). Hikers can walk the short and easy Rainbow Falls Trail from the trailhead right next to the resort; the 1.5-mile pathway leads to a spectacular 101-foot waterfall on the

San Joaquin River. And yes, Rainbow Falls does have a rainbow, but to see it clearly you must show up in the late morning, when sunlight hits the fall's spray just right.

From Rainbow Falls, you can hike downstream to Lower Falls or upstream to Devils Postpile, a spectacular display of columnar basalt left from an ancient lava flow. First-time visitors always walk away from it shaking their heads; it's like nothing you've seen anywhere else. For a more ambitious trek, start hiking at Agnew Meadows and head past Olaine Lake to large and beautiful Shadow Lake at 8,737 feet. The round-trip is about seven miles, with some unforgettable Sierra scenery.

Red's Meadow Resort's big business is its pack station; in addition to two-hour, half-day, and full-day horseback rides, they run a dizzying array of multiday trips into the wilderness. Many are oriented toward fishing, often with an experienced guide. Where do the pack trips go? Just about everywhere in the surrounding John Muir and Ansel Adams Wilderness Areas, where more than 100 lakes and many miles of streams are within a day's ride. Some trips allow riders as young as five years old, making them an ideal outing for families.

Facilities

There are eight cabins ranging in size and accommodating two to eight people, plus 10 motel rooms. All cabins have kitchenettes (stovetop but no oven). A small general store and restaurant are on-site. Linens and towels are provided.

Reservations and Rates

Reservations are recommended. Rates are $125 per night for two people, plus $30 for each additional person. Motel rooms are $79 per night for two people. The resort is open from mid-June to early October, weather permitting. Pets are permitted. Contact Red's Meadow Resort, P.O. Box 395, Mammoth Lakes, CA 93546, 760/934-2345 or 800/292-7758, website: www.redsmeadow.com.

Directions

From U.S. 395 at Mammoth Lakes, take the Highway 203 turnoff and drive west for four miles, through the town of Mammoth Lakes, to the intersection of Highway 203 and Lake Mary Road. Turn right on Highway 203 (Minaret Road) and drive five miles to the Mammoth Mountain ski area, then continue beyond it for 10 miles to the resort. (Because you are staying at Red's Meadow, you do not have to ride the shuttle bus into the monument.)

36 TAMARACK LODGE RESORT
off Highway 203 in Mammoth Lakes

Luxury rating: ★ ★ ★ ☆ ☆ .   **Recreation rating:** ★ ★ ★ ★ ★

Rank: Best for Winter Sports

Twin Lakes, in the town of Mammoth Lakes, was once two separate lakes, but they are now adjoined by a marshy area. Set in a granite-lined bowl, the large, hourglass-shaped body of water is continually replenished by the rushing cascade of 250-foot Twin Falls. The lake is also continually replenished by the Department of Fish and Game, which keeps it filled with rainbow trout all summer long. This makes Twin Lakes a favorite spot of both fishing enthusiasts and scenery-lovers.

If you want to hang around the lake for a few days, book a stay at Tamarack Lodge Resort, which has 29 cabins spaced on six acres along the shore of Twin Lakes. The only resort on Lake Mary Road that is open year-round, Tamarack is a classic 1924 mountain lodge with a big stone fireplace and log-lined walls. Only some of its cabins have views of Twin Lakes, but if you don't stay in one of them, your disappointment will disappear when you see that with a few footsteps, you're standing on its shoreline.

The list of outdoor activities at Tamarack Lodge is long enough to fill an entire book. The winter list includes skiing and snowboarding at Mammoth Mountain Ski Resort, as well as cross-country skiing and snowshoeing right from your cabin door on more than 45 kilometers of groomed track. Equipment rentals and instructions are available. The summer list includes trout fishing in Twin Lakes and neighboring lakes, swimming in

Horseshoe Lake, mountain biking at Mammoth Ski Area's summer bike park, and discovering nearby hot springs.

Plus hiking, hiking, hiking. The best trails near Tamarack Lodge are the short hike to Panorama Dome and the strenuous hike to Mammoth Mountain Summit. Panorama Dome Trail begins off Lake Mary Road, just past the turnoff to Twin Lakes. It's an easy half-mile hike to the top of a rocky dome with stunning summit views. The Mammoth Mountain Summit Trail starts in the west loop of Twin Lakes Campground, then climbs 2,500 feet over four miles to the 11,053-foot summit. If you tire out, Seven Lakes Point is a spectacular overlook and a potential turnaround at 1.3 miles out.

One final highlight of Tamarack Lodge is its restaurant. It's easy to imagine that an old fishing and skiing lodge would serve little besides steak and potatoes or burgers and fries, but not so at Tamarack's dining room, The Lakefront. Its French-California cuisine has a reputation that has spread far beyond Mammoth Lakes; it's been written up in *Sunset* and *Bon Appétit* magazines. For something different, try the elk or wild-boar medallions.

Facilities
There are 29 cabins ranging in size from studios to three bedrooms, all with fully equipped kitchens. Lodge rooms are also available. A restaurant and general store are on-site. Linens and towels are provided.

Reservations and Rates
Reservations are recommended. Fees are $125–350 per night ($195–425 on holidays), depending on cabin size. The resort is open year-round. Pets are not permitted. Contact Tamarack Lodge Resort, P.O. Box 69, Mammoth Lakes, CA 93546, 760/934-2442, website: www.tamaracklodge.com.

Directions
From U.S. 395 at Mammoth Lakes, take the Highway 203 turnoff and drive west for four miles, through the town of Mammoth Lakes, to the intersection of Highway 203 and Lake Mary Road. Continue straight on Lake Mary Road for 2.2 miles, then bear right on Twin Lakes Road and follow it for a quarter mile to Tamarack Lodge Resort.

37 CRYSTAL CRAG LODGE
off Highway 203 in Mammoth Lakes

Luxury rating: ★ ★ ★ ☆ ☆   **Recreation rating:** ★ ★ ★ ★ ☆

It's confusing, but let's try to get this straight: Crystal Crag Lodge doesn't have a view of 10,377-foot Crystal Crag; Woods Lodge (see the next listing) does. Crystal Crag Lodge faces Mammoth Mountain and Red Mountain. It's geographically below Crystal Crag but not within sight of it.

Despite its misleading name, Crystal Crag Lodge is just right for many visitors. The lodge is across the road from 140-acre Lake Mary, the largest of the lakes in Mammoth Lakes basin, where you can fish from shore or by boat for brown, rainbow, and brook trout. A bonus is that the lodge rents 14-foot aluminum boats.

Hikers can easily access the Sky Meadows Trail, which begins at neighboring Coldwater Campground. The path is short and easy to tiny Emerald Lake, then it continues to Sky Meadows, where the summer wildflowers bloom with enthusiasm. Many other trails for hikers and bikers are throughout the Mammoth Lakes basin. There are also several hot springs nearby, which can make for a nice side trip.

The cabins are surprisingly modern and updated inside, considering their bland exteriors. I rented the resort's smallest and least expensive cabin, Twin, which was quite spacious: two main rooms (bedroom and combined kitchen/living/dining area with a big fireplace) and a large bathroom. Like the resort's other cabins, it has a very workable kitchen, complete with a microwave, toaster, and coffeemaker.

Some cabins are directly across from the lake, so be sure to request one. Twin is at the back of the resort, farthest from the lake, but this wasn't a minus: On a busy Memorial Day weekend, it was quiet and peaceful.

Noisy neighbors could potentially be a problem at Crystal Crag Lodge, because the resort packs 20 large A-frame cabins into a small space. But nobody cares about the crowds. Most visitors are just so darn happy to be staying here in the basin, right across from Lake Mary, that they aren't about to complain about anything.

© ANN MARIE BROWN

Facilities

There are 20 cabins ranging in size from one to four bedrooms. All have fully equipped kitchens. A general store is on-site. Linens and towels are provided.

Reservations and Rates

Reservations are recommended. A seven-night minimum is required for advance reservations for the larger cabins. Fees are $130–265 per night, depending on cabin size. The resort is open from late May to early October. Pets are permitted with a $9 fee per night. Contact Crystal Crag Lodge, P.O. Box 88, Mammoth Lakes, CA 93546, 760/934-2436, website: www. crystalcraglodge.com.

Directions

From U.S. 395 at Mammoth Lakes, take the Highway 203 turnoff and drive west for four miles, through the town of Mammoth Lakes, to the intersection of Highway 203 and Lake Mary Road. Continue straight on Lake Mary Road for 3.5 miles to Crystal Crag Lodge, on the left.

38 WOODS LODGE
off Highway 203 in Mammoth Lakes

Luxury rating: ★ ★ ★ ☆   **Recreation rating:** ★ ★ ★ ☆

Woods Lodge qualifies as one of my fantasy cabin vacations. It's the kind of getaway spot your mind drifts to again and again when you're immersed in the pedestrian details of everyday life.

Woods Lodge is in Mammoth Lakes basin at George Lake, one of four lakes at the end of Lake Mary Road. All four lakes are breathtaking, but few would disagree that Lake George is the most breathtaking of them all. At 9,200 feet in elevation, it is deep blue and lined with granite, but what sets it off is Crystal Crag, a spectacular chunk of rock in the lake's background. You see it for the first time and you say, "Wow."

Woods Lodge is also one of the classier cabin resorts in the Mammoth area. It is owned and managed by the Schotz family, the same folks who run Wildyrie Resort (see the next listing) on Lake Mamie. They've owned Woods Lodge since 1950. Their longevity is easy to understand; who would give up this place?

The cabins are one- to three-bedroom models, with full kitchens and outside barbecues. Their furnishings are clean and simple. Because they

© ANN MARIE BROWN

are set on a hill overlooking Lake George, each one has a view from its deck of the lake and Crystal Crag.

Unlike at many resorts, the cabins at Woods Lodge are spaced a good distance apart. The ambience is more like a nice neighborhood of private homes than a pack-'em-in cabin resort. The cabins are on a separate driveway from the main access road and parking area for Lake George, so you won't have a lot of anglers and hikers driving past your cabin. There's no traffic at all, except from the cars belonging to the two dozen other cabins.

What's there to do at Woods Lodge? Fishing is a big draw, both at Lake George and at the neighboring Mammoth lakes. Equally convenient are the two hiking trails that start almost at your Woods Lodge cabin door. You can hike to Barrett and T.J. Lakes in an easy half mile, or to Crystal Lake and the Mammoth Crest in a much steeper three miles. Crystal Lake is hidden at the base of magnificent Crystal Crag (1.75 miles out); Mammoth Crest provides 360-degree views of the surrounding countryside. If you're up to driving a bit, there are hot springs nearby at Hat Creek.

Facilities
There are 25 cabins ranging in size from one to three bedrooms. All have fully equipped kitchens. Linens and towels are provided.

Reservations and Rates
Reservations are recommended. A seven-night minimum is required on advance reservations. Fees are $595–1,792 per week, depending on cabin size. One-night rentals are $92–281 per night. The resort is open from late May to early October. Pets are permitted in some cabins with an $8 fee per night. Contact Woods Lodge, P.O. Box 108, Mammoth Lakes, CA 93546, 760/934-2261, website: www.mammothweb.com/lodging/woodslodge.

Directions
From U.S. 395 at Mammoth Lakes, take the Highway 203 turnoff and drive west for four miles, through the town of Mammoth Lakes, to the intersection of Highway 203 and Lake Mary Road. Continue straight on Lake Mary Road four miles to the Lake George turnoff. Turn left and drive a half mile to Woods Lodge.

39 WILDYRIE RESORT
off Highway 203 in Mammoth Lakes

Luxury rating: ★ ★ ★ ★ ☆   **Recreation rating:** ★ ★ ★ ★ ☆

The same smart folks who run Woods Lodge (see the previous listing) on Lake George also run Wildyrie Resort on Lake Mamie, about two miles away. Like Woods Lodge, Wildyrie Resort has a genteel, but not stuffy, air to it. It feels like an older, established vacation resort.

© ANN MARIE BROWN

The high points about Woods Lodge also apply here at Wildyrie: The cabins are perched on a hillside overlooking a lake—this one being deep blue Lake Mamie, which is apt, considering that *wildyrie* is an old Scottish word for eagle's nest. The cabins are spaced far enough apart for privacy and quiet, and because they are behind the main lodge and off the road, they are safe from road noise. Each cabin has a front deck and most have a lake view, although it is somewhat obscured by trees. The best views are from cabin Nos. 5, 6, and 7, which are all two-bedrooms.

Wildyrie Resort rents rowboats on Lake Mamie (a 100-foot walk to the dock from your cabin). No motorboats are permitted on the lake, which is filled with rainbow, brown, and brook trout.

If you don't want to fish, there's plenty to do within walking distance of your cabin. Bike rentals are available at Pokonobe Country Store on Lake Mary. Mammoth Lakes Pack Outfit is nearby; guided horseback rides are available. Twin Falls picnic ground is across the street from Wildyrie, and Horseshoe Lake is a quarter mile away. A trailhead at Horseshoe Lake leads to McLeod Lake in a half mile. More ambitious hikers can walk four miles downhill to Red's Meadow at Devils Postpile National Monument, then turn around and hike back up (a moderate 1,700-foot gain). While at Red's Meadow, you can ride the free shuttle bus to other points in the monument.

If you're up to venturing farther from the resort, hot springs are nearby at Hat Creek.

Facilities

There are 11 cabins ranging in size from one to four bedrooms, plus lodge rooms and apartments. All cabins have fully equipped kitchens. Linens and towels are provided.

Reservations and Rates

Reservations are recommended. A seven-night minimum is required on advance reservations. Fees are $784–1,694 per week, depending on cabin size. One-night cabins rentals are $125–258 per night. Lodge rooms and apartments are $90–95 per night. The resort is open from late May to early October. Pets are not permitted. Contact Wildyrie Resort, P.O. Box 109, Mammoth Lakes, CA 93546, 760/934-2444, website: www.mammoth-web.com/lodging/wildyrieresort.

Directions

From U.S. 395 at Mammoth Lakes, take the Highway 203 turnoff and drive west for four miles, through the town of Mammoth Lakes, to the intersection of Highway 203 and Lake Mary Road. Continue straight on Lake Mary Road for three miles, then turn right, and quickly right again, at the sign for Lake Mamie and Horseshoe Lake. Wildyrie Resort is on the left.

40 HOT CREEK RANCH
off U.S. 395 near Mammoth Lakes

Luxury rating: ★ ★ ★ ★ ★   **Recreation rating:** ★ ★ ★ ★ ☆

Rank: Best for Fishing

Hot Creek Ranch is where fly fishers should go when their spouses don't like to fly-fish. For one thing, the nonfishing spouse can sit around and admire the modern cabin they're inhabiting, which is nicer and has a much better view than the average suburban home. For another, a wealth of recreation alternatives abound.

Let's start with the fly-fishing, since that is the big draw at Hot Creek Ranch. The ranch is along Hot Creek in the Owens River Valley, which is well known for two things: trout and hot springs. The trout in Hot Creek are not easy to catch; this is for experienced fly fishers only. When you catch them, you don't keep them: this is barbless fly–only, catch-and-release fishing with a zero limit. On the private stretch of stream owned by

© ANN MARIE BROWN

the ranch, an additional restriction is in effect: dry flies only.

Hot Creek originates as an underground creek, formed from a combination of 11 different springs. It bubbles forth from a fissure in volcanic rock then runs down a narrow gorge, creating excellent habitat for wildlife, including wild rainbow and brown trout. How big are the fish? The standard trout is at least 12 inches; fish in excess of 20 inches are not unusual.

So what are non–fly fishing partners to do? When they get tired of admiring the view of Mammoth Mountain and the Minarets beyond, they can scan the sky for bald eagles and osprey (both are fairly common). They can drive down the road 1.5 miles (or hike on the trail beside Hot Creek) to the Hot Creek Geologic Area, a public hot springs run by the Forest Service. The springs bubble up from the middle of the river, so bathers alternate between hot and cold water with just one swimming stroke. Hot Creek is a popular, family-oriented spot that is usually filled with swimmers from sunup to sundown.

Nonanglers can also head into Mammoth Lakes, just six miles away, and take advantage of myriad hiking, biking, swimming, and boating opportunities. Some years, the Mammoth Mountain ski area is open until the beginning of July—well into fly-fishing season.

The cabins at Hot Creek Ranch aren't really cabins at all, more like small private homes. With only nine cabins total at the ranch, guests aren't saddled with a passel of neighbors. And because the ranch has a gated driveway, nobody drives in unless they have a reservation. Each cabin has electric heat and appliances, an enclosed carport, a spectacular view, and an outdoor barbecue. Even better is what they don't have: televisions and phones.

Facilities
There are nine cabins that can accommodate four people and one apartment for one person. All cabins have fully equipped kitchens. Linens and towels are provided.

Reservations and Rates
Reservations are required. Fees are $182 per night for two people on weekdays with a minimum two-night stay. The weekend rate is $545 for

two people, Friday to Monday. The weekly rate is $1070. Each additional person is $80 per night (but only three fly fishers are permitted per cabin). The one-person apartment is $110 per night. The resort is open from the end of April to the end of October. Pets are not permitted. Contact Hot Creek Ranch, Route 1, Box 206, Mammoth Lakes, CA 93546, 760/924-5637 or 888/695-0774, website: www.hotcreekranch.com.

Directions
From U.S. 395 at Bishop, drive north for 36 miles to Hot Creek Hatchery Road (it's 2.7 miles south of the Mammoth Lakes turnoff). Turn right (east) and drive 1.7 miles to the ranch on the left.

41 CONVICT LAKE RESORT
off U.S. 395 near Mammoth Lakes

Luxury rating: ★ ★ ★ ☆ ☆   **Recreation rating:** ★ ★ ★ ★ ★

Rank: Best for Fishing

The first question that rises to mind as you drive up the road to Convict Lake Resort is something like, "What is that incredible peak looming in the background?"

It's 12,277-foot Mount Morrison.

Next question: How did Convict Lake get its name?

A group of convicts escaped from a Nevada prison in 1871. They were sighted camping at Monte Diablo Lake, which quickly became known as Convict Lake. The convicts shot it out with a posse on the shores of the lake; one member of the posse, Robert Morrison, was killed. Mount Morrison (see the first question) was named in his honor.

Final question: How can I live at Convict Lake Resort for the rest of my life?

You'll have to figure that one out for yourself.

Convict Lake Resort is set at 7,600 feet in elevation, just south of the town of Mammoth Lakes in the eastern Sierra. It's about 150 yards from Convict Lake, a 168-acre, half-mile wide, one-mile-long lake. The lake's water is remarkably clear blue and stunning, partly because much of the lake is more than 100 feet deep. Its deepest point is 140 feet.

Nestled in a grove of aspens, many of the resort's cabins bear fishing-related names, like Steelhead, Cutthroat, Golden, and Rainbow. If you get to choose among them, pick Golden. It's the most private and also the most scenic, with a wide-open view of Mount Morrison and surrounding peaks. Unfortunately, none of the cabins have lake views, but the mountain views are fair compensation.

Fishing is the main task of vacationers here. The lake is stocked weekly with rainbow trout, and they share the waters with some trophy-size brown trout. Convict Creek, which runs by the resort, is also stocked. The resort rents motorboats, pontoon boats, rowboats, and canoes, and its store sells bait and tackle, as well as basic groceries.

Perhaps more notable than even the fishing is the restaurant at Convict Lake Resort. Open for dinner year-round, it's the only four-diamond restaurant in Mono or Inyo Counties. The "country French" menu includes entrées and appetizers such as quail, salmon, rack of lamb, mussels, escargot, scallops, and other gourmet items. The food isn't cheap (entrées are $22–32), but if you want to save money you can select from an alternate café menu. The restaurant's martini bar brags of having the stiffest cocktail in the Sierra.

If you tire of fishing and eating, you can rent horses at Convict Lake pack station and take a guided horseback ride along the lakeshore, or a longer ride into the John Muir Wilderness. Or you can do your own walking: An easy and level trail travels the lakeshore for a mile, then starts to ascend with a vengeance to Mildred Lake and Lake Dorothy (five and six miles out). Or, if you want water that's naturally hot and perfect for soaking in, hot springs are nearby, at Hat Creek.

Since Convict Lake is primarily a fishing resort, it's surprising that it stays open year-round, but it does. Winter visitors use the resort as their base for cross-country skiing at local snow parks, plus downhill skiing at Mammoth Mountain (it's a 25-minute drive to the lifts). After a rigorous day on the slopes, it's nice to have a four-diamond dinner to look forward to.

Facilities

There are 25 cabins ranging in size and accommodating up to 10 people, plus large group houses for 13 to 30 people. All have fully equipped kitchens. A store and restaurant are on-site. Linens and towels are provided.

Reservations and Rates

Reservations are recommended. Fees are $90–310 per night for cabins, depending on cabin size. Weekly discounts are available. Group houses for 13 to 30 people are $495–695 per night. There is a two-night minimum on weekends. The resort is open year-round. Pets are permitted with a $10 fee. Contact Convict Lake Resort, Route 1, Box 204, Mammoth Lakes, CA 93546, 760/934-3800 or 800/992-2260, website: www.convictlake.com.

Directions

From U.S. 395 at Bishop, drive north for 35 miles to the Convict Lake turnoff (it's 3.7 miles south of the Mammoth Lakes turnoff). Turn left (west) and drive two miles to the resort.

42 TOM'S PLACE RESORT
off U.S. 395 in Tom's Place

Luxury rating: ★ ★ ☆ ☆ ☆   **Recreation rating:** ★ ★ ★ ☆ ☆

Crowley Lake is the huge, shallow-looking lake on the east side of U.S. 395 midway between Bishop and Mammoth Lakes. The largest lake in the eastern Sierra at 5,183 acres, Crowley is essentially a flooded valley that's loaded with fish. Anglers share the waters with sailboaters, windsurfers, personal watercraft riders, and water-skiers, and it all adds up to a big party on the lake on summer days.

Tom's Place Resort is 3.5 miles south of Crowley Lake, and that is the primary reason why anyone would stay there. Unlike most lakes in the eastern Sierra, Crowley Lake doesn't have a resort nestled on its shoreline, so unless you're camping, Tom's Place is the closest possible lodging.

Tom's Place Resort has a lodge, store, café, and bar. The bar is a historic watering hole that brags of its "world-famous Bloody Marys." The café serves three meals a day—basic food like ham and eggs for breakfast, patty melts for lunch, and pork chops for dinner. The cabins are scattered around the property; some are in sight of U.S. 395, so steer clear of those. All are fairly rustic, but there is one luxury: some are surrounded by lilac bushes that deliver an intoxicating scent in early summer.

The resort has been open since 1917, long before U.S. 395 was a paved road. It has an interesting history as a stopover for Southern Californians traveling to Yosemite, but otherwise, it is unremarkable—except that it provides bargain-priced access to the outdoors, particularly Crowley Lake and Lower Rock Creek. Quite simply, it's a cheap place to stay if you want to fish, boat, or windsurf. How cheap? Try 55 bucks a night for a cabin for two, or 90 bucks a night for a cabin for six.

© ANN MARIE BROWN

The money you'll save will be spent at Crowley Lake. Operated by the Los Angeles Department of Water and Power (the largest reservoir in its aqueduct system), Crowley Lake's fees are $6 per day to park, or $15 per day to park and launch a boat. Boat rentals and a tackle shop are available.

Fishing rules are a bit complicated: Trout season runs the usual end-of-April to end-of-October schedule, but starting August 1, no bait fishing is allowed—only barbless lures or flies. The planted trout run the gamut, from Kamloop rainbows, Eagle Lake rainbows, and Coleman rainbows to browns and cutthroats. Perch fishing follows the same schedule (no bait fishing after August 1) and a big Perch Derby is held each August. The largest perch ever caught in California was hauled out of Crowley Lake—a 3-pound, 10-ouncer.

If you get too hot hanging out in the boat all day, you're out of luck. No swimming or diving is ever permitted at the lake.

Facilities
There are 12 cabins ranging in size from one to three bedrooms, plus seven lodge rooms. All cabins have fully equipped kitchens. A store, café, and bar are on-site. Linens and towels are provided.

Reservations and Rates
Reservations are recommended. Fees are $55–100 per night, depending on the size of the cabin and the number of people. Lodge rooms are $45–55 per night. The resort is open year-round. Pets are permitted in some cabins with an $8 fee per night. Contact Tom's Place Resort, HCR 79 Box 22-A, Crowley Lake, CA 93546, 760/935-4239, website: www.tomsplaceresort.com.

Directions
From Bishop, drive 25 miles north on U.S. 395 to Tom's Place, at the junction with Rock Creek Drive (on the left).

43 ROCK CREEK LAKES RESORT

off U.S. 395 near Tom's Place

Luxury rating: ★ ★ ★ ☆ ☆   **Recreation rating:** ★ ★ ★ ★ ☆

Rank: Best for Hiking

If you can get a cabin at Rock Creek Lakes Resort, you must have been born under a lucky star. The resort is right across the road from Rock Creek Lake in gorgeous Rock Creek Canyon, and with all that scenery, its cabins are booked up most all the time.

Still, if you can live spontaneously, you have a chance. The resort keeps a waiting list for cancellations, and if you are willing to pack up and go on short notice, you'll get your cabin. I tried the waiting-list technique one summer and was offered two different weeks. Another option is to visit on weekdays, especially before or after the main summer season.

Why is Rock Creek Lakes Resort so popular? Two reasons: fishing and hiking. For starters, you can walk from your cabin to the boat dock at Rock Creek Lake and fish your heart out all week long. Rock Creek Lake is stocked all summer with rainbow trout. Small boats are for rent (trolling motors only), but many anglers float around in rubber rafts and kayaks or fish from the shore. If you want to fish other waters, the Owens River, Crowley Lake, McGee Creek, and Hot Creek are a short drive away.

If hiking appeals to you, Rock Creek Lakes Resort is ideally located for accessing the John Muir Wilderness, a dramatic landscape of 13,000-foot peaks, permanent snow fields, and gemlike lakes. The Hilton and Davis Lakes trailhead is a quarter mile from the cabin turnoff; you could walk to the trailhead and then hike four miles to the Hilton Lakes or five miles to Davis Lake. Or drive one mile to the Mosquito Flat trailhead, at the end of Rock Creek Road. At 10,300 feet, it's one of the highest trailhead elevations

in California. Set off on the easy, level trail through Little Lakes Valley and you'll see dozens of small lakes, one after another about every half mile. For something more ambitious, follow the Mono Pass Trail to Ruby Lake and beyond, heading steeply uphill to 12,400-foot Mono Pass.

If you have a choice when you make your reservation at

© ANN MARIE BROWN

Rock Creek Lakes Resort, ask for one of the higher numbered cabins. All cabins are secluded and in the trees, but cabin Nos. 1, 2, and 3 are the closest together. The cabins are on the modern side, painted a cheerful red and fully furnished, with kitchens, bathrooms, linens, and everything you need for your stay except food.

The resort has a small lunch counter that is renowned for its homemade pies and soups. (The list of pies is longer than the list of main courses.) Their soups are outrageously good, as are their breakfasts, but you're on your own for dinner.

Facilities
There are 10 cabins ranging in size from one to three bedrooms. All have fully equipped kitchens. A lunch counter and general store are on-site. Linens and towels are provided.

Reservations and Rates
Reservations are required. A four-night minimum is required in July and August. Fees are $115–275 per night, depending on cabin size. The resort is open from mid-May to mid-October. Pets are not permitted. Contact Rock Creek Lakes Resort, P.O. Box 727, Bishop, CA 93515, 760/935-4311, website: www.rockcreeklake.com.

Directions
From Bishop, drive 24 miles north on U.S. 395 to the Rock Creek turnoff near Tom's Place. Turn west on Rock Creek Road and drive nine miles to Rock Creek Lakes Resort, on the right.

44 ROCK CREEK LODGE
off U.S. 395 near Tom's Place

Luxury rating: ★★★☆☆   **Recreation rating:** ★★★★☆
Rank: Best for Winter Sports

From November to May, Rock Creek Lodge is the only resort in spectacular Rock Creek Canyon that is open for business. Cross-country skiers are grateful for those extra winter months, because at 9,373 feet in elevation, midway between Bishop and Mammoth Lakes, Rock Creek Canyon is snow heaven.

Rock Creek Lodge was founded in the 1920s as one of the first ski resorts in America. Although summer is busy at Rock Creek Lodge, with hordes of visitors showing up for the plentiful fishing and hiking opportunities, the winter season has always been Rock Creek Lodge's special niche.

Here's how a winter visit works: First, you confirm your cabin reservation, then drive to the town of Tom's Place. At a prearranged time, you leave your car at the East Fork Sno-Park, and a snowmobile shuttles you the last two miles to your cabin. (Rock Creek Road is not plowed beyond East Fork in winter.) From the moment you arrive, you strap on your skis and glide wherever you wish.

Even if you've never cross-country skied before, you won't be left out in the cold; equipment rentals and lessons are available. Experienced skiers can go off on their own and even stay overnight at a backcountry hut.

Since you can't drive anywhere once the snowmobile has dropped you off, the resort is fully equipped. A beautiful log cabin serves as the restaurant. Inside are long wooden tables where you eat hearty meals and meet all your neighbors. You don't choose from a menu; instead, you eat whatever they are serving that night. During our visit, it was lasagna on Saturday, teriyaki chicken on Sunday, enchiladas on Monday, and so on.

The lodge has both modern and rustic cabins. Modern means they have their own showers; rustic means you walk to a separate building for showers. The cabins are spaced well, with plenty of breathing room between them. You must bring your own sleeping bag and towels (pillows and pillowcases are provided).

It's hard to pin down the best part of a winter trip to Rock Creek Lodge, but after debating it a while, I settled on this: The road is closed, so there are no cars visible anywhere in this snowy wonderland. Civilization? You'll quickly forget all about it.

Facilities

There are 14 cabins that can accommodate two to eight people. Eight cabins have full bathrooms and showers. All cabins have kitchenettes. A restaurant and general store are on-site. Pillows and pillowcases are provided; bring your own sleeping bag and towels.

Reservations and Rates

Reservations are required. Winter fees are $100–125 per night per person, including breakfast and dinner; children under 12 stay for reduced rates.

Summer fees are $100–160 per night for two people. Pets are permitted in summer only; $10 fee per night. Contact Rock Creek Lodge, Route 1, Box 12, Mammoth Lakes, CA 93546, 760/935-4170 or 877/935-4170, website: www.rockcreeklodge.com.

Directions
From Bishop, drive 24 miles north on U.S. 395 to the Rock Creek turnoff near Tom's Place. Turn west on Rock Creek Road and drive eight miles to Rock Creek Lodge on the left. In winter, drive six miles on Rock Creek Road and park at the East Fork lot. A snowmobile will meet you and take you the final two miles to the lodge.

45 PARADISE RESORT
off U.S. 395 near Bishop

Luxury rating: ★ ★ ★ ☆ ☆   **Recreation rating:** ★ ★ ★ ☆ ☆

A stay at Paradise Resort is a different kind of vacation experience than others in the eastern Sierra. The resort is set along Lower Rock Creek in the arid, desertlike Owens Valley, quite a few miles from the nearest set of high mountain peaks. If you're looking for sawtooth ridges or an alpine lake right outside your cabin door, this isn't the place.

On the other hand, if fishing is your bag, this *is* the place. Right outside your cabin is what the resort calls "family-style fishing," which means you drop a line in Lower Rock Creek and hope that something with fins swims past. Lower Rock Creek is regularly stocked with trout, so your chances are pretty good, especially early in the year. Experienced anglers head for the myriad lakes and streams in the area, including Lake Sabrina, North Lake, South Lake, Rock Creek Lake, Crowley Lake, and the Owens River.

Hikers can drive to the nearby John Muir Wilderness trailheads in Rock Creek Canyon or try out the Lower Rock Creek Trail. A section of it runs right by Paradise Resort. The trail is popular with both hikers and mountain bikers, especially in the early summer when wildflowers are blooming. (Bikers, take note: This isn't a trail for amateurs.) Other great side trips include a drive east out of Bishop to visit the White Mountains and the Ancient Bristlecone Pine Forest. Here, you'll find the oldest living trees on earth.

Paradise Resort's cabins are set close together along the river, with a few RVs sprinkled among them. They're nothing fancy, to say the least: one or two bedrooms, a serviceable kitchen and bathroom, and a small front porch where you can sit outside and listen to the creek gurgle. They have no views, except of the other cabins and of something that appears like a mirage in the dry Owens Valley—a large expanse of green lawn, with Lower Rock Creek coursing through the middle of it. At first, I mistook it for a golf course, but Paradise Resort's owners call it a "picnic-and-play meadow."

If you don't catch any fish, you can pay a visit to Paradise Resort's restaurant, which serves far more than typical lodge fare. The menu includes Alaskan snow crab (reportedly flown in fresh), various gourmet cuts of beef, and a good selection of wine. If a more rustic meal appeals to you, you can always use the barbecue outside your Paradise cabin to prepare some blackened hot dogs and roasted marshmallows.

Facilities
There are 17 cabins ranging in size from one to two bedrooms. All have fully equipped kitchens. RV sites are also available. A restaurant is on-site. Linens and towels are provided.

Reservations and Rates
Reservations are recommended. Fees are $84–134 per night with a two-night minimum. The resort is open year-round; rates are discounted in winter. Pets are permitted with a $10 fee. Contact Paradise Resort, Route 2, Bishop, CA 93514, 760/387-2370, website: www.theparadiseresort.com.

Directions
From Bishop, drive north on U.S. 395 for 12 miles to the turnoff for Paradise/Lower Rock Creek Road/Gorge Road. Turn left (west), then turn right immediately and drive two miles north on Lower Rock Creek Road to the resort.

Chapter 6

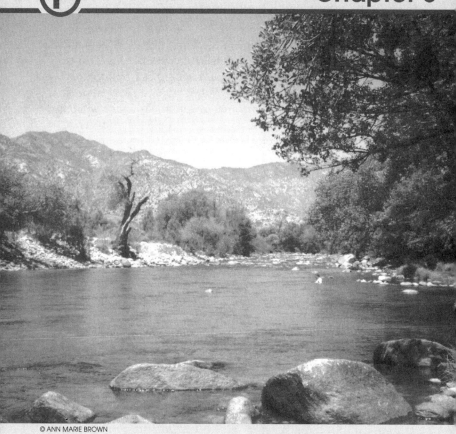

© ANN MARIE BROWN

Sequoia and Kings Canyon

Sequoia and Kings Canyon

Located on the western slope of the Sierra Nevada Mountains, Sequoia and Kings Canyon National Parks are famous for their Giant Sequoia groves, tall mountains, deep canyons, roaring rivers, and spectacular hiking trails with views of the jagged peaks of the Great Western Divide. Often referred to as "Yosemite without the masses," these two side-by-side national parks offer classic Sierra scenery without the infamous overcrowding that plagues that great park to the north. Kings Canyon and Sequoia have been managed jointly by the National Park Service since 1943.

The parks abound with superlatives. The highest peak in the contiguous United States—Mount Whitney, at 14,494 feet—is found in Sequoia National Park. Several other park summits top out at more than 14,000 feet. The largest living tree in the world, the Sherman Tree, is found in Giant Forest in Sequoia. At 275 feet tall and with a 103-foot circumference at the ground, the massive tree is still growing; every year, it adds enough wood to make another 60-foot-tall tree. The Sherman Tree is estimated to be 2,300 to 2,700 years old.

The second- and third-largest trees in the world, named Washington and General Grant, respectively, are also found in Sequoia and Kings Canyon. The easiest way to visit these record-holders is to reserve a stay at Grant Grove Lodge, situated less than a mile from the General Grant Tree, or at Montecito Sequoia Lodge, near Giant Forest.

Three powerful rivers course through the boundaries of Sequoia and Kings Canyon: the Kings, Kern, and Kaweah. The steep and barren canyons through which these rivers flow are as awe-inspiring as the raging waters themselves. The canyon of the Kings River is carved to a depth of 8,000 feet below the summit of neighboring Spanish Mountain. This makes Kings Canyon deeper than the Grand Canyon or any other canyon in North America. One cabin resort, Kings Canyon Lodge, is found along the Kings River canyon. Several more are along the Kaweah in the town of Three Rivers, just outside the parks.

Less visited areas in the parks include the South Fork and Mineral King Valley areas of Sequoia. Mineral King is a glacier-carved bowl surrounded by massive peaks, topped by the distinct pointed pinnacle known as Sawtooth Peak. Reaching the 7,800-foot valley requires a circuitous 25-mile drive from the foothills of Three Rivers, the same route that was taken by miners seeking their fortune in the 1880s. The easiest way to visit Mineral King is to reserve a stay at the cabins at Silver City Resort or Paradise Canyon Cabins.

In December 2000, a new national park joined the borders of Sequoia and Kings Canyon: Giant Sequoia National Monument. Administered by the Forest Service, not the National Park Service, the new national monument contains two noncontiguous land areas, both designed to increase protection for the last remaining Giant Sequoia groves in the world. (Although Sequoias once ranged across the planet, today they are found only in a narrow strip of land, approximately 40 miles wide and 150 miles long, in the Sierra Nevada.) Several cabins can be rented in both parts of the new national monument, including four historic fire stations belonging to the United States Forest Service.

The recreation options don't stop at the national park and monument borders. Boaters and anglers head to Bass, Shaver, and Huntington Lakes in Sierra National Forest for warm summer days on the water. Skiers and snowboarders enjoy uncrowded lift lines at Sierra Summit, near Huntington Lake, and Shirley Meadows, near Kernville. White-water rafters flock to the Kern and Kaweah Rivers. Fly fishers head for the Kern River north of Kernville. And hikers can walk through magnificent and much less visited Giant Sequoia groves in national forest and state-forest lands near Dinkey Creek (McKinley Grove), Oakhurst (Nelder Grove), and Springville (Mountain Home State Forest).

In each of these places, you can look forward to choosing from a variety of interesting places to spend the night, including the cabins and cottages listed in the pages that follow.

SEQUOIA AND KINGS CANYON

see Yosemite and
Mammoth Lakes
page 166

see
Death Valley and
the Deserts
page 318

Contents

1. The Homestead 249

2. Hounds Tooth Inn 250

3. The Forks Resort 252

4. Miller's Landing 254

5. Bonnie B Ranch 255

6. Shaver Lake Lodge 257

7. Dinkey Creek Inn 259

8. Cedar Crest Resort 260

9. Huntington Lake Resort 262

10. Lakeview Cottages 263

11. Lakeshore Resort 265

12. Mono Hot Springs Resort 266

13. Vermilion Valley Resort 268

14. Muir Trail Ranch 270

15. Cardinal Village Resort 272

16. Bishop Creek Lodge 274

17. Parcher's Resort 275

18. Glacier Lodge 277

19. Sequoia View Vineyard 278

20. Grant Grove Lodge 280

21. Kings Canyon Lodge 282

22. Big Meadows Guard Station 284

23. Montecito Sequoia Lodge 285

24. Pear Lake Ski Hut 287

25. Bearpaw High Sierra Camp 289

26. Wicky-Up Ranch 291

27. Sequoia Motel 292

28. Sequoia Village Inn 294

29. Lake Elowin Resort 296

30. Paradise Canyon Cabins 297

31. Silver City Resort 299

32. Mountain Home Guard Station 301
33. Camp Nelson Cabins 302
34. Golden Trout Wilderness Pack Trains Cabins 304
35. Mountain Top Bed and Breakfast 305
36. Whispering Pines Lodge 307
37. Sierra Gateway Cottages 309
38. Oak Flat Lookout Tower 310
39. Rankin Ranch 312

1 THE HOMESTEAD
off Highway 49 in Ahwahnee

Luxury rating: ★ ★ ★ ★ ☆   Recreation rating: ★ ★ ★ ★ ☆

© ANN MARIE BROWN

Cindy Brooks and Larry Ends are the perfect kind of people to run a resort for outdoor enthusiasts, because they are outdoor lovers themselves. In 1992, they left their desk jobs and big-city life in Los Angeles and moved to Ahwahnee to open The Homestead, an oak-dotted resort on 160 acres.

The Homestead's six cottages are all modern in style and beautifully appointed. (Cindy and Larry did much of the construction themselves.) The interiors are lined with Saltillo tiles, warm pinewood, and simple but tasteful furnishings. Each cottage, including an above-the-barn, star-gazing loft, has a fully equipped kitchen and a fireplace. They also have air-conditioning, a real bonus in the summer at this 2,000-foot elevation. Those traveling with a family or small group will appreciate the ranch-house rental that opened in 2004.

The Homestead is far and away the nicest cabin or cottage resort in the southern Yosemite region. The owners have thought of every detail: kitchens are stocked with coffees, teas, milk, juice, muffins, and so on. One of the cottages has an oversized soaking tub and a waterfall shower-head. All of them have satellite TV, robes, hairdryers, daily maid service, and beautiful quilts and comforters on the beds. Quite simply, The Homestead has been done right by owners who really care about the quality of their guests' vacation.

If horses are your thing, and you like to travel with yours, you'll be all set at The Homestead. In addition to its cottages, The Homestead has a corral where your horse can go on vacation. Cindy and Larry will provide you with information on all of the local horseback riding trails.

If you are traveling sans horse, a great place to start your exploration of the area is on the Sierra Vista National Scenic Byway, a driving loop that begins near Bass Lake. The road ascends as high as 7,300 feet to a land of big conifers, imposing granite domes, and wide-angle vistas of the Sierra Crest and surrounding wilderness areas.

Another option is to head a few miles north on Highway 41 to Sky Ranch Road, from which you can access the Nelder Grove of Giant Sequoias and the lovely Shadow of the Giants National Recreation Trail, or the short and scenic trail to the top of Fresno Dome (wow, what a view!). Heading north on Highway 41, you'll find a trailhead for Lewis Creek Trail (great wildflowers and two small, pretty waterfalls). Or head farther north to Fish Camp and the Yosemite Mountain Sugar Pine Historical Railroad, where you can relive history with a ride on its narrow-gauge steam trains. A few miles beyond Fish Camp is the southern entrance to Yosemite National Park.

Needless to say, there's much to do. Let Larry and Cindy at The Homestead provide you with maps and brochures, then get out there and get busy.

Facilities
There are five one-bedroom cottages and one two-bedroom ranch house; all have fully equipped kitchens, fireplaces, and air-conditioning. Linens and towels are provided.

Reservations and Rates
Reservations are recommended. Fees are $134–295 per night for two adults. There is a two-night minimum on weekends. The resort is open year-round. Pets are not permitted. Contact The Homestead, 41110 Road 600, Ahwahnee, CA 93601, 559/683-0495 or 800/483-0495, website: www.homesteadcottages.com.

Directions
From Fresno, drive north on Highway 41 for 45 miles to Oakhurst. Turn left (northwest) on Highway 49 and drive 4.5 miles. Turn left on Road 600 and drive 2.5 miles to The Homestead on the right side of the road.

2 HOUNDS TOOTH INN
off Highway 41 in Oakhurst

Luxury rating: ★ ★ ★ ☆   **Recreation rating:** ★ ★ ★ ☆

Hounds Tooth Inn's location might discourage potential guests: It's set within a few yards of busy Highway 41 in Oakhurst. But in actuality, its placement is one of its assets: From the door of your Hounds Tooth Inn cottage, all the recreation opportunities of the Bass Lake and southern Yosemite area await. It's not so much *what* Hounds Tooth Inn is, but *where* it is that makes it work.

That said, Hounds Tooth Inn is a lovely new lodging with one separate 850-square-foot cottage and 12 guest rooms. It looks like a country inn that was moved out of the country. The Hounds Tooth does a fair job of concealing its roadside location: It's set below the highway and out of its sight line, and its three-acre grounds are beautifully landscaped with walkways, trees, and foliage.

The cottage features a large suite with a king bed, spa, fireplace, and small kitchenette, plus its own private patio with a garden and small waterfall. It is frequently used for honeymoons but can also fit a small family. The kitchenette is a bit of a disappointment for people who like to cook, but because the town of Oakhurst is a mere two minutes away, you probably won't starve. Also, a complimentary breakfast and afternoon tea are served each day at the main building.

For recreation, Bass Lake is a mere 10 minutes away, and the southern entrance to Yosemite is 20 minutes away. Horseback riding in the area is popular, as are mountain biking, hiking (maps are at the inn), fishing, all water sports, and all winter sports.

Facilities
There is one one-bedroom cottage with a kitchenette (microwave and refrigerator), fireplace, and patio, plus 12 guest rooms. Linens and towels are provided.

Reservations and Rates
Reservations are recommended. Fees for the cottage are $225 per night on weekends or $185 per night on weekdays, including breakfast. Guest rooms are $95–175. Pets are not permitted. Contact Hounds Tooth Inn, 42071 Highway 41, Oakhurst, CA 93644, 559/642-6600 or 888/642-6610, website: www.houndstoothinn.com.

Directions
From Fresno, drive north on Highway 41 for 45 miles to Oakhurst. From

the main part of town, continue north for two more miles to Hounds Tooth Inn on the right.

Other Cabins and Cottages Nearby

Pine Rose Inn, P.O. Box 2341, Oakhurst, CA 93644, 559/642-2800.

🄳 THE FORKS RESORT
off Highway 41 on Bass Lake

Luxury rating: ★ ★ ★ ☆ ☆   **Recreation rating:** ★ ★ ★ ★ ☆

Rank: Best for Boating & Water Sports

Bass Lake fits the bill for anybody who likes boating or fishing. The lake is at 3,500 feet in elevation in Sierra National Forest, and if that makes you think of warm summer days and waterskiing, you're thinking clearly.

Bass Lake is only 14 miles from the southern entrance to Yosemite National Park, but the folks who come here usually don't head for Yosemite. Instead, they while away their days on the big, pretty lake, which covers more than 1,000 acres when full. Although waterskiing is the main attraction, personal watercraft riders, anglers, and swimmers also share the waters.

The Forks Resort is one of the old-style resorts on the lake; it's been owned and operated by the same family for three generations. It has cabins of varying sizes, a good general store, its own dock with boat rentals (patio boats, motorboats, rowboats, and canoes), and a café that looks like the kind of place where the waitresses are all named Thelma. Seriously, "the home of the world-famous Forks Burger" is right out of the 1950s. Order a milkshake or a root beer float while you're there.

The cabins at The Forks Resort are unremarkable, but they make the

perfect base camp for a Bass Lake vacation. Only a handful of them have lake views, but all are right across the road from the water's edge, about a two-minute walk. Each cabin has a fully equipped kitchen, plus a porch with a barbecue grill so you can cook up all the fish you catch. The one-bedroom cabins have two double beds; you can squeeze in four people. The one-bedroom suite cabins have an extra room. The two-bedroom cabins can accommodate as many as six people. In addition to the extra space, you also get a fireplace and a microwave.

The Forks Resort is a family-oriented place, and it's reinforced by a "no party" policy. That keeps the ambience quiet and peaceful, even though this is a very busy and popular resort. You won't be woken up at 2 A.M. by a bunch of drunkards next door.

Facilities
There are 20 cabins ranging in size from one to two bedrooms; they can accommodate up to six people. All cabins have fully equipped kitchens and a porch with barbecue. A general store and café are on-site. Linens and towels are provided.

Reservations and Rates
Reservations are recommended. Fees are $95–180 per night. The resort is open year-round. Pets are permitted with a $50 fee. Contact The Forks Resort, 39150 Road 222, Bass Lake, CA 93604, 559/642-3737, website: www.theforksresort.com.

Directions
From Fresno, drive north on Highway 41 for 45 miles to Oakhurst, then turn east (right) on Road 426 (Crane Valley Road). Drive seven miles on Road 426, then turn left at the sign for Bass Lake. Drive one mile; The Forks Resort will be on your left, at the junction with Road 222.

Other Cabins and Cottages Nearby
The Pines Resort, P.O. Box 109, Bass Lake, CA 93604, 800/350-7463, website: www.basslake.com.

Bass Lake Vacation Rentals, P.O. Box 507, Bass Lake, CA 93604, 559/642-2211.

Bass Lake Realty, P.O. Box 349, Bass Lake, CA 93604, 559/642-3600, website: www.basslakerealty.com.

4 MILLER'S LANDING
off Highway 41 on Bass Lake

Luxury rating: ★ ★ ★ ☆ ☆   **Recreation rating:** ★ ★ ★ ★ ☆

Rank: Best for Boating & Water Sports

© ANN MARIE BROWN

Bass Lake has so much development around its edges that it can seem like a small city. With several campgrounds, restaurants, and resorts, plus numerous places to rent boats or buy fishing equipment, the lakeshore is more like a vacation town than a peaceful mountain retreat.

That's why a stay at Miller's Landing is so refreshing. Located at the southern edge of the lake, Miller's Landing has easy access to the lake's commercial services but is far from the hubbub of the busy Pines Village area. The resort is self-contained—it features cabins, a restaurant, and its own marina with boat rentals (patio boats, ski boats, personal watercrafts, fishing boats, kayaks, and canoes)—so you don't need to go anywhere else if you don't feel like it.

The cabins at Miller's Landing run the gamut, from barebones to more elaborate. The most deluxe cabins sleep eight; they have two bedrooms, two baths, satellite television, and a full kitchen with all the accoutrements. My personal favorites are cabin Nos. 3 through 6, which are two-bedroom rustic cabins with a full kitchen. You must use restroom and shower facilities located a short walk away, and you have to bring your own linens, bedding, dishes, pots, and pans, but you get a roof over your head and a fair amount of space for 50 bucks a night. A picnic table and a fire ring are right outside your door. Cabin No. 2 is of the same minimalist ilk, but even smaller and a few bucks cheaper.

A nice day hike is possible from the trailhead at neighboring Spring Cove Campground. Follow Spring Cove Trail uphill to join Goat Mountain Trail, which connects with Goat Mountain Road and leads to an operating fire lookout tower perched at 4,675 feet. The entire round-trip is 8.4 miles; views of the lake and surrounding forest are exceptional.

Fishing is good at Bass Lake—but not necessarily for bass, as the lake's name leads you to believe. Instead, trout fishing is popular in winter and spring; the Department of Fish and Game drops in heavy plants of rainbows. In summer, people catch a little bit of everything: catfish, bluegill, bass, crappie, and trout.

Facilities
There are 13 cabins ranging in size and accommodating two to eight people. Some cabins have fully equipped kitchens; rustic cabins have refrigerators and stoves only, and there are no cooking or eating utensils or private restrooms. A general store and café are on-site. Linens and towels are provided in some cabins; for cabin Nos. 2 through 6, you must bring your own.

Reservations and Rates
Reservations are recommended. Fees are $40–50 per night for rustic cabins without bathrooms (but with kitchens) and $175–250 per night for cabins with bathrooms and full kitchens. The resort is open year-round. Pets are permitted with a $25 fee. Contact Miller's Landing, 37976 Road 222, Wishon, CA 93669, 559/642-3633, website: www.millerslanding.com.

Directions
From Fresno, drive north on Highway 41 for 45 miles to Oakhurst, then turn east (right) on Road 426 (Crane Valley Road). Drive seven miles on Road 426, then turn left at the sign for Bass Lake. Drive one mile to Road 222, then turn right and drive three miles to Miller's Landing Resort, on the right.

5 BONNIE B RANCH
off Highway 41 near North Fork

Luxury rating: ★ ★ ★ ★ ☆   **Recreation rating:** ★ ★ ★ ★ ☆

Rank: Best for Horseback Riding

A lot of people have a private fantasy about owning their own ranch . . . the kind of place with horses grazing on the grounds, a big house with extra bedrooms for your friends, and maybe even a few fishing ponds sprinkled around the property.

You can dream about having a place like this, or you can rent Bonnie B Ranch and make it real. Here's how to do it: Gather up a group of five to

© ANN MARIE BROWN

eight people—invite your family, your friends, or what the heck, even your boss; tell them to pack up their fishing gear, outdoor clothes, and a week's worth of groceries; then head to the town of North Fork, just southeast of Oakhurst and Bass Lake, and begin your private ranch vacation.

You need your friends because you're paying to rent an entire ranch house and the 440 acres surrounding it. This doesn't come cheap; current rates are $350 per night or $2,300 per week. At the weekly rate, a group of six people will pay about $55 each per night. For that price, they get lodging in a beautiful 3,000-square-foot ranch house, plus all the catch-and-release fishing they can stand. The ranch has five small lakes that are loaded with hand-raised bass, bluegill, and crappie. The largest lake can be fished by float tube or pram (bring your own); the rest are for shore fishing. Hikers and equestrians can choose from 16 miles of trails on the property. Horses are for hire for the nominal fee of $15 per person per hour.

If you're wondering if you'll be staying in a rundown barn, here are some details on the house: It's a three-bedroom, three-bath home perched on a hill, with a fully equipped country kitchen and wraparound deck, plus a large living area with a fireplace and giant picture windows. From the living room, you can gaze at the ranch's largest pond, or the horses grazing in the pasture, or the high mountains of the Sierra. It's so scenic that the property has been used as a location for countless movies, including *Mousetrap* and *The Giant of Thunder Mountain.* Spring wildflowers are breathtaking, maple and oak trees bring autumn colors, and winter snow turns the ranch into a white wonderland.

The ranch dates back to 1891. On the property, you will find a covered bridge, historic gristmill, stonework, and split-rail cedar fences. A staff person lives in a separate building on the premises to help with the horses and make sure everything runs smoothly during your stay.

Facilities

There is one three-bedroom, three-bath ranch house with a fully equipped kitchen, fireplace, and deck. It can accommodate up to eight people. There is access to 440 acres, including hiking and horseback riding trails and five private fishing ponds. Linens and towels are provided.

Reservations and Rates

Reservations are required. Fees are $350 per night or $2,300 per week. A $150 cleaning fee is charged (nonrefundable), and a refundable $400 security deposit is required. Weeklong stays are required from June to August; there is a two-night minimum the rest of the year. Pets are not permitted. Contact Kerry Bryant, Bryant Farms/Bonnie B Ranch, 323 26th Street, Manhattan Beach, CA 90266, 805/636-6733, website: www.bonnieb.com.

Directions

From Fresno, drive north on Highway 41 for 25 miles to Road 200 (North Fork Road) and turn right. Drive northeast on Road 200 for 17 miles, past the turnoff for Road 221, to the left turnoff at Bonnie B Road. (If you reach the town of North Fork, you've gone too far.) Turn left on Bonnie B Road and enter the ranch.

6 SHAVER LAKE LODGE
off Highway 168 on Shaver Lake

Luxury rating: ★ ★ ★ ☆ ☆   **Recreation rating:** ★ ★ ★ ★ ☆

Rank: Best for Boating & Water Sports

People who have never been to Shaver and Huntington Lakes usually think of them as a package deal. They're both big reservoirs, both are owned by Southern California Edison, and both are popular for fishing and boating. They're just 20 miles apart, on Highway 168 in the southern Sierra.

But those who vacation at Shaver Lake and those who vacation at Huntington Lake are unlikely to belong to the same club, because Shaver Lake is known for fast boats and waterskiing, and Huntington Lake is known for sailing.

Other differences? Shaver is smaller than Huntington, but the fishing is more reliable, especially in its sheltered coves. Shaver is set at 5,500 feet in elevation, while Huntington is nearly 2,000 feet higher, so Shaver is a bit warmer for swimming and water sports. And Shaver Lake has much less

© ANN MARIE BROWN

development along its edges. In fact, other than two Forest Service campgrounds, the only place you can spend the night at Shaver Lake is in the cabins at Shaver Lake Lodge.

When you call to make your reservation, be sure to ask for a cabin numbered between 7 and 14. These are the cabins with the best lake views. Some of the higher-numbered cabins are clustered too close together on the hillside and have views of the other cabins. Cabin No. 9 is the best of the lot.

If you plan on setting up housekeeping, be forewarned that the cabins do not have full kitchens. They have a small refrigerator and a microwave, but that's all; it's just enough to make your oatmeal and coffee in the morning. Dishes and utensils are not provided; bring your own from home.

The Shaver Lake Lodge Marina rents all kinds of boats: kayaks, canoes, sailboats, fishing boats, personal watercrafts, pontoon boats, and so on. If everything is rented out, Sierra Marina at Shaver Lake is up the road a mile.

Shaver Lake's cabins sit right next to the lodge restaurant, which features an extensive menu for lunch and dinner. The food is well prepared, priced fairly, and served in mountain-sized portions. Dinner entrées include prime rib, pork chops, halibut, and chicken breast, as well as more casual food like hamburgers and salads. In summer, you can sit outside on the deck overlooking the lake and linger over long meals.

The lodge is also open in winter. Downhill skiers stay in the cabins and drive 15 miles up Highway 168 to Sierra Summit Ski Area. Cross-country skiers and snowmobilers head for Tamarack Winter Sports Area, where there are miles of snow-covered trails.

Facilities
There are 20 single and duplex cabins ranging in size from studios to two bedrooms. Most have microwaves and small refrigerators; none have full kitchens. A restaurant, small store, and marina are on-site. Linens and towels are provided.

Reservations and Rates
Reservations are recommended. Fees are $65–125 per night. The lodge is open year-round. Pets are not permitted. Contact Shaver Lake Lodge, 44185 Highway 168, Shaver Lake, CA 93664, 559/841-3326.

Directions
From Fresno, drive north on Highway 41 for six miles to the Highway 168/Clovis turnoff. Turn east on Highway 168 and drive 47 miles to the town of Shaver Lake. Continue two miles past the town; the resort is on the right side of the road.

Other Cabins and Cottages Nearby

Shaver Lake Vacation Rentals, P.O. Box 349, Shaver Lake, CA 93664, 800/422-4102, website: www.shaverlakevacationrentals.com.

7 DINKEY CREEK INN
off Highway 168 near Shaver Lake

Luxury rating: ★ ★ ★ ☆ ☆   **Recreation rating:** ★ ★ ★ ★ ☆

If you've heard about the Dinkey Lakes Wilderness your whole life but somehow never managed to make the trip, here's the perfect way to do it without joining the hordes of backpackers who infiltrate the area. Book a stay at the Dinkey Creek Inn, then spend a few days hiking, fishing, swimming, and exploring the territory.

The inn's chalets were built in 1992, so they are modern in style, with fully equipped kitchens and baths, wood-burning stoves, and satellite TV. Each one is nestled in the conifers, with a redwood deck out front that is perfect for barbecuing and dining al fresco. You don't need to worry about packing everything for your vacation; a small store is on the premises, and almost anything you can think of can be purchased in the town of Shaver Lake, 13 miles away.

The chalets are within a few hundred feet of Dinkey Creek and its historic trestle bridge, the only free-span redwood bridge in California. The McKinley Grove of Giant Sequoias is only six miles from the chalets. Closer to home is Honeymoon Pool, a granite-lined, 20-foot-deep swimming and fishing hole in Dinkey Creek, located at the upper end of the neighboring Forest Service campground.

The beauty continues as you head for the Dinkey Lakes Wilderness, a short drive away via Rock Creek Road and Forest Service Road 9S10. (Be prepared for two miles of rough road at the end.) A perfect day hike is the seven-mile loop to First Dinkey Lake, which also passes Mystery, Swede, and South Lakes. From First Dinkey Lake, you can loop back to the parking lot, or backtrack a short distance toward

© ANN MARIE BROWN

South Lake and continue on to Second Dinkey Lake, Island Lake, Rock Lake, and so on. The trail is remarkably level; you cover a surprising amount of ground in little time.

In winter, cross-country skiing, snowmobiling, and snowshoeing are all possible right outside the door of your chalet. Downhill skiers can drive up the highway to Sierra Summit Ski Area, about 40 minutes away.

Facilities
There are five chalets that can accommodate up to six people. All have fully equipped kitchens. Three rustic hiker's cabins are also available and come without kitchens, baths, or linens. A store and lunch counter are on-site. Linens and towels are provided.

Reservations and Rates
Reservations are recommended. Fees are $85–140 per night; weekly rates are discounted. The chalets are open year-round. Pets are permitted with a deposit. Contact Dinkey Creek Inn, 53861 Dinkey Creek Road, Shaver Lake, CA 93664, 559/841-3435, website: www.dinkeycreek.com.

Directions
From Fresno, drive north on Highway 41 for six miles to the Highway 168/Clovis turnoff. Turn east on Highway 168 and drive 47 miles to the town of Shaver Lake. Turn right on Dinkey Creek Road and drive 13 miles. The resort is on the right side of the road.

8 CEDAR CREST RESORT
off Highway 168 on Huntington Lake

Luxury rating: ★ ★ ★ ☆ ☆   **Recreation rating:** ★ ★ ★ ★ ☆

Cedar Crest Resort has *old-fashioned* written all over it. It's obvious that this lakefront establishment has been around a long time, and that it knows how to do vacations right.

The cabins at Cedar Crest are beautifully situated on a steep hill above Huntington Lake. This is one of the few area resorts located far off the road that circles the lake; that guarantees a quiet atmosphere. Guarded by dense pines and firs, the cabins offer the rare gift of privacy.

Completely furnished for housekeeping, each cabin has a full kitchen, one or two bedrooms, and a private bathroom. For the ideal vacation, make sure you pay a few extra bucks for a cabin with a fireplace, kitchen, and lake view. If you are on a strict budget, you can settle for the tent cabins, which have beds, electricity, a woodstove for cooking, and a picnic table outside. Bathrooms are a short walk away.

The resort is full service; it has a restaurant, small store, and boat rentals at their marina. The boats are basic aluminum jobs with outboard motors. If you want something fancier, go to one of the larger marinas on the lake.

You probably won't want to do much but hang out on your cabin's deck, gaze at the lake, and listen to the wind in the pines. If you can tear yourself away, fishing and swimming are obvious options. For the energetic, some of the best hikes in the area begin at nearby Upper Billy Creek Campground. A strenuous 2,300-foot climb over five miles will take you to Nellie Lake, a beautiful subalpine lake. From the same trailhead, the easy Lower Kaiser Loop offers a look at Line Creek's cascades and stunning wildflowers in early summer. Another option is to walk the Coarsegrass Meadow Trail along Home Camp Creek (the trailhead is near Huntington Lake Resort's marina). It's five miles roundtrip to flower-lined Coarsegrass Meadow, or you can add on a steep two miles to Aspen Meadow.

Facilities

There are 14 cabins, ranging in size, that can accommodate up to six people. All cabins have fully equipped kitchens. Cabana units without kitchens, and tent cabins without baths and kitchens, are also available. A small general store, restaurant, and boat rentals are on-site. Linens and towels are provided except in tent cabins.

Reservations and Rates

Reservations are recommended. Fees are $95–150 per night for one-and two-bedroom cabins with kitchens. Cabanas with no kitchens are $100 per night. Tent cabins are $35–40 per night. The resort is open from late May to early September. Pets are permitted with a $5 fee per night. Contact Cedar Crest Resort, P.O. Box 163, Lakeshore, CA 93634, 559/893-3233, website: www.cedarcrestresort.com.

Directions

From Fresno, drive north on Highway 41 for six miles to the Highway 168/Clovis turnoff. Turn east on Highway 168 and drive 70 miles, past Shaver Lake and Sierra Summit Ski Area, to the left turn for Huntington Lake. Bear left on Huntington Lake Road and drive 3.5 miles to Cedar Crest Resort, on the left side of the road.

9 HUNTINGTON LAKE RESORT
off Highway 168 on Huntington Lake

Luxury rating: ★ ★ ★ ☆ ☆   **Recreation rating:** ★ ★ ★ ★ ★

Most cabins are rustic, plain, serviceable. Most cabins don't even try to be anything but . . . well, cabins. The cabins at Huntington Lake Resort are the exception. They're cute. They have a green-and-white gingerbread paint job on the outside, and a homey sweetness on the inside. Heck, they're adorable.

The cabins are set on Huntington Lake's west end, not far from the dam. Located across the road from the lake, but up high on the hillside, some are granted partial lake views. You can cook your catch of the day in your kitchen or on the barbecue by your front door, and then eat it outside on your deck.

Since you're staying at the lake's west end, you're in perfect position for a few day trips. One of the best is driving up scenic Forest Service Road 8S32 for 4.5 miles to Mushroom Rock Vista and Black Point Trail.

Mushroom Rock Vista delivers exactly what it promises—a big rock that looks oddly like a mushroom. Beyond the rock is the vista, a long-distance view of the forested slopes of the San Joaquin River Canyon and Shaver Lake. Black Point Trail, a half mile beyond Mushroom Rock, is a steep, half-mile hike to a spectacular overlook of Huntington Lake, Shaver Lake, Kaiser Ridge, and the San Joaquin River Canyon.

Anglers and sailors can rent a boat from the Huntington Lake Resort Marina. The marina provides sailboat and fishing boat rentals, plus tackle and supplies and a no-nonsense snack shop and café. Many anglers don't bother with a boat; instead, they fish from shore or the lake's dam. The usual catch is small stocked trout, plus occasional kokanee salmon. Home Camp Creek, which flows right next to the resort's cabins, is also a fair trout stream.

Although the western stretch of Huntington Lake Road is not plowed in winter, Huntington Lake Resort stays open year-round for those who are willing to snowmobile or ski in four miles. The resort owners will bring in your luggage and gear by sled. Once you're there, you can take your pick from miles of snow-covered roads and trails, then ski, snowshoe, or snowmobile to your heart's content.

Facilities
There are 10 cabins ranging in size and accommodating two to eight people. Most have fully equipped kitchens. Linens and towels are provided.

Reservations and Rates
Reservations are recommended. Fees are $65–110 per night. The resort is open year-round. Pets are permitted with prior approval and a $5 fee per night. Contact Huntington Lake Resort, P.O. Box 257, Lakeshore, CA 93634, 559/893-3226.

Directions
From Fresno, drive north on Highway 41 for six miles to the Highway 168/Clovis turnoff. Turn east on Highway 168 and drive 70 miles, past Shaver Lake and Sierra Summit Ski Area, to the left turn for Huntington Lake. Bear left on Huntington Lake Road and drive five miles to the west end of the lake. Huntington Lake Resort is on the right side of the road.

10 LAKEVIEW COTTAGES
off Highway 168 on Huntington Lake

Luxury rating: ★ ★ ★ ☆ ☆   **Recreation rating:** ★ ★ ★ ★ ☆

There's only one sensible choice at Lakeview Cottages: Rent the large two-bedroom cabins on the front of the property, facing the lake. Sure, they cost a little more, but as you spend day after day on your cabin's

© ANN MARIE BROWN

deck, gazing at azure Huntington Lake, you won't feel bad about the extra money.

Lakeview Cottages are similar to, and completely different from, other cabin resorts at Huntington Lake. They are similar in that they are set across the road from the five-mile long lake and are fully furnished with kitchens and bathrooms for vacation housekeeping. They are different in that their lake views are nearly unobstructed. And because they are near the end of a dead-end road, very few cars will pass by your cabin. This area of Huntington Lake is as quiet as it gets.

The cottages are rented by the week for most of the summer, but in the slower months (usually June and September), you can often get one for a shorter stay. They come with all the necessities of living except towels. Also, if you're the type who gets cold at night, bring a few extra blankets, because each bed only has one.

Rowboats and motorboats are also for rent by the week or the day, so you can fish to your heart's content. Plus, all of Huntington's other outdoor recreation options are yours to choose from: swimming, hiking, horseback riding, cycling, sailing, you name it.

Facilities

There are 11 cabins ranging in size and accommodating up to six people. All cabins have fully equipped kitchens. Linens are provided but not towels.

Reservations and Rates

Reservations are recommended. Fees are $400–450 per week for one-bedroom cabins and $595–685 per week for two-bedroom cabins. Shorter stays are sometimes available for $75–115 per night. The resort is open from June to September. Pets are permitted with a $6 fee per night. Contact Lakeview Cottages, P.O. Box 177, Lakeshore, CA 93634, 559/893-2330 (summer) or 562/697-6556 (winter), website: www.lakeviewcottages.net.

Directions

From Fresno, drive north on Highway 41 for six miles to the Highway 168/Clovis turnoff. Turn east on Highway 168 and drive 70 miles, past Shaver Lake and Sierra Summit Ski Area, to the left turn for Huntington Lake. Bear left on Huntington Lake Road and drive six miles to the west end of the lake, past the dam. Turn left on Huntington Lodge Road and drive one mile to Lakeview Cottages, on the right.

11 LAKESHORE RESORT
off Highway 168 on Huntington Lake

Luxury rating: ★ ★ ★ ☆ ☆   **Recreation rating:** ★ ★ ★ ★ ★

Rank: Best for Boating & Water Sports

Of all the big lakes in Sierra National Forest that are open for recreation, Huntington Lake is the most versatile of the lot. Although sailing is Huntington's big claim to fame, you'll find plenty of people fishing, boating, camping, hiking, picnicking, and sunbathing as well. The lake is big—five miles long and a half mile wide—so it almost never seems too crowded, even on summer weekends.

The cabins at Lakeshore Resort are about as versatile as the lake itself. With a grand total of 26 cabins, and no two exactly alike, you're bound to find one that suits your needs. They are behind Lakeshore's restaurant, store, and saloon, only a short walk from the lake (but with no lake views).

Lakeshore Resort is open year-round. In summer, spend your time hiking, boating, fishing, or waterskiing. In winter, try snowmobiling, snowshoeing, and downhill or cross-country skiing. Only 10 minutes away is Sierra Summit Ski Area, where you can tackle the slopes of Chinese Peak.

Serious hikers won't want to miss the chance to bag Kaiser Peak via a 10-mile round-trip trail. Not-so-ambitious hikers can walk the beautiful easy trails to Rancheria Falls or Indian Pools, or take a pleasant walk along the edge of Huntington Lake. A moderate six-mile hike leads to Twin Lakes via scenic Potter Pass. George Lake lies another 1.5 miles beyond the upper Twin Lake, requiring a nine-mile round-trip.

Of course, at this 7,000-foot elevation, some people find hiking a bit too strenuous. If you're in this camp, the sure-footed steeds at neighboring D & F Pack Station will escort you on two-hour trail rides, half-day rides, or longer fishing and pack trips.

© ANN MARIE BROWN

Many visitors opt to leave the landlubbers behind and spend all their vacation time on Huntington Lake. If you don't have your own boat, you can rent one at Rancheria Cove Marina, less than a quarter mile from your cabin. They have small fishing skiffs, large patio boats, skiing boats, various personal watercrafts, and canoes and kayaks. Trout fishing is decent from the shoreline but better while trolling; many anglers circle Big Creek Cove or work their way up and down the lake's long edges. Every few days someone catches a kokanee salmon, but most of the time, it's small planted trout.

Facilities
There are 26 cabins ranging in size from one to three bedrooms. Most have fully equipped kitchens. A general store, restaurant, and saloon are on-site. Linens and towels are provided; rates are discounted if you bring your own.

Reservations and Rates
Reservations are recommended. Fees are $85–170 per night. There is a two-night minimum on weekends and a three-night minimum on long holidays. The resort is open year-round. Pets are permitted with a $15 fee per night. Contact Lakeshore Resort, P.O. Box 197, Lakeshore, CA 93634, 559/893-3193, website: www.lakeshoreresort.com.

Directions
From Fresno, drive north on Highway 41 for six miles to the Highway 168/Clovis turnoff. Turn east on Highway 168 and drive 70 miles, past Shaver Lake and Sierra Summit Ski Area, to the left turn for Huntington Lake. Bear left on Huntington Lake Road and drive one mile. Lakeshore Resort is on the right side of the road.

12 MONO HOT SPRINGS RESORT
off Kaiser Pass Road near Huntington Lake

Luxury rating: ★ ★ ★ ☆ ☆   **Recreation rating:** ★ ★ ★ ☆ ☆
Rank: Most Unusual

Mono Hot Springs Resort is a place where it seems time has stood still. The road to reach it is long, narrow, and winding, with no gasoline or services along the way. Electricity is available only when the generator runs. The only telephone is a satellite cell phone, which will cost you a couple bucks per minute.

The resort's raison d'être is its natural warm mineral waters. A sign outside the communal bathhouse informs you how many parts per million of carbonates, bicarbonates, chloride, and sulfates are in the water. The bathhouse has six

private bathing tubs where you can soak away your cares for a few extra bucks. The tubs vary from old-fashioned claw-foot to modern fiberglass. All are rustic; don't expect the enamel to be sparkling white. If you prefer to bathe al fresco, there's a small outdoor mineral pool that's just big enough for about four bathers.

Be sure to reserve one of the resort's modern cabins or stone housekeeping cabins instead of one of the rustic ones. The modern and stone cabins are built of native cobblestone and come with bathrooms and full kitchens. Some even have their own showers and electricity. The rustic wood cabins cost half as much, but they are a tad too rustic. In addition to no electricity or heat, they have no cooking facilities (except an outside fire pit) and no bathrooms. You share a nearby outhouse and pay extra for showers or baths at the bathhouse. Overall, even the modern cabins suffer somewhat from a lack of upkeep; the owners need to sink a little money into these old buildings.

The resort store sells basic groceries if you want to cook in your cabin. If not, Mono's Indian Camp Fine Food Cafe serves buffalo steaks and buffalo burgers in addition to the regular kind, and the menu even offers a few veggie dishes. The restaurant is a friendly, casual place.

Hikers can set out from the resort and walk to Doris and Tule Lakes, both popular for swimming and fishing for trout and bass. Doris Lake is only one mile from the cabins, so even small children can make the trip. Other trails lead into the John Muir and Ansel Adams Wildernesses from nearby Edison and Florence Lakes.

Anglers, take note: Stream fishing is excellent in Mono Creek, Bear Creek, and the south fork of the San Joaquin River (all within hiking distance). Lake fishing is first-rate in nearby Edison and Florence Lakes. Boat rentals are at both lakes.

Facilities

There are 15 cabins ranging in size from studios to two bedrooms. The modern cabins have fully equipped kitchens and bathrooms; the rustic cabins do not. A bathhouse and outdoor mineral pool, plus restaurant, general store, and post office, are on-site. Linens and towels are provided in the modern cabins but not the rustic cabins.

Reservations and Rates

Reservations are recommended. Fees are $55–110 per night for modern and rustic cabins and $55–75 per night for tent cabins. The resort is open from late May to late October. Pets are permitted with a $5 fee per night. Contact Mono Hot Springs Resort, General Delivery, Mono Hot Springs, CA 93642, 559/325-1710, website: www.monohotsprings.com; Winter address: P.O. Box 215, Lakeshore, CA 93634.

Directions

From Highway 168 at the eastern edge of Huntington Lake, turn right on Kaiser Pass Road and drive 17 miles (narrow and winding) to a fork in the road. Bear left for Mono Hot Springs and Edison Lake, drive 1.6 miles and turn left again. You'll reach the resort in a quarter mile. (Note that trailers and motor homes are not recommended on Kaiser Pass Road.)

13 VERMILION VALLEY RESORT

off Kaiser Pass Road on Lake Thomas A. Edison

Luxury rating: ★ ★ ☆ ☆ ☆   **Recreation rating:** ★ ★ ★ ★ ☆

Let's get it straight: Before you make the trip to Vermilion Valley Resort at Lake Thomas A. Edison, make sure you are fully prepared. The place is 40-plus miles from the nearest town (Shaver Lake), and you won't want to make the trip more than once per vacation. It's 20 winding miles from Shaver Lake to Huntington Lake, then another 17 curving miles over 9,200-foot Kaiser Pass to Mono Hot Springs, then a final 6.5 twisting miles to Vermilion Valley Resort at Lake Thomas A. Edison.

When you reach the place, you find that it isn't exactly the Hilton, but it has all the basics. Vermilion Valley Resort's cabins are tent cabins—big tents with wood floors and twin bunk beds with mattresses, plus a table, chairs, and dresser. They have no heat, no kitchen facilities, and no electricity. Make sure you bring your sleeping bags and flashlights.

If you get tired of cooking meals on your camp stove or over a campfire, you can eat at the resort's café. It has an open kitchen, a few tables and chairs, trophy trout mounted on the walls, and some of the nicest people in the world working there. Breakfast is the café's claim to fame: big stacks of buttermilk pancakes, eggs, sausage, and bacon.

Edison Lake is a big trout producer, so the conversation at all meals usually revolves around who's catching what with which tackle. Unfortunately, the water level of the big lake fluctuates like most Nasdaq stocks. Up, down, up, down. It's not the most beautiful lake you've seen when it's drawn down, although it's a stunner when full, backed by the rugged 12,000-foot peaks of the high Sierra. The lake is at 7,700 feet in elevation.

Hikers can access the Pacific Crest Trail from Edison Lake, either by hiking the Mono Creek Trail along the lake's north edge or by taking the ferry across the lake. An excellent day hike is the Devils Bathtub Trail from the resort; it's five miles one-way to a rocky, beautiful alpine lake. Or hike the Mono Creek Trail south from Edison Lake to Mono Hot Springs, stopping to admire beautiful Mono Meadow and Doris Lake along the way. Hot springs lovers can drive to nearby Mono Hot Springs Resort and bathe in the soothing waters.

Facilities
There are 10 tent cabins, plus four motel rooms with kitchenettes. A café and general store are on-site. Linens and towels are not provided.

Reservations and Rates
Reservations are recommended. Fees for the tent cabins are $45–50 per night. Fees for the motel rooms are $75–95 per night. The resort is open from June to September. Pets are permitted. Contact Vermilion Valley Resort, P.O. Box 258, Lakeshore, CA 93634, 559/259-4000, website: www.edisonlake.com.

Directions
From Highway 168 at the eastern edge of Huntington Lake, turn right on Kaiser Pass Road and drive 17 miles (narrow and winding) to a fork in the road. Bear left for Mono Hot Springs and Edison Lake, and drive 6.5 miles to Vermilion Valley Resort. (Note that trailers and motor homes are not recommended on Kaiser Pass Road.)

MUIR TRAIL RANCH
off Kaiser Pass Road in John Muir Wilderness

Luxury rating: ★ ★ ★ ☆ ☆   **Recreation rating:** ★ ★ ★ ★ ★
Rank: Most Secluded

If you have a big family or like to vacation with a group of friends, you are in the perfect position for a fantasy-level high Sierra vacation at your own private mountain ranch. Where? In the John Muir Wilderness. How? By renting the Muir Trail Ranch for a week. Want to know more? Keep reading.

First, let's talk location. The Muir Trail Ranch is on 200 acres of private land near Florence Lake in Sierra National Forest, completely surrounded by the John Muir Wilderness. Getting to the ranch requires driving from Fresno to Huntington Lake, then following narrow and winding Kaiser Pass Road to Florence Lake, then taking the water taxi across the lake, then hiking or horse packing five miles from the taxi drop-off point to Muir Trail Ranch. Sounds remote and hard to get to? It is.

Next, let's talk money. Renting the ranch for one week will cost you $8,925. Yes, it sounds expensive, but that rate is for 15 to 20 people, which works out to less than $100 per person per night. Twenty people will not overcrowd the ranch; in fact, you'll be housed with room to spare in eight log cabins and five tent cabins. The tent cabins are set on the San Joaquin River and come equipped with electric lights and outlets; the log cabins are set along a stream and have wash basins and toilets, as well as electricity. The log cabins are cute and homey; the tent cabins are . . . well, tent cabin–rustic, but serviceable. The best of the lot is the Tenthouse Penthouse, which is perched on top of a big boulder and has a wooden deck overlooking the river. In addition to exclusive use of the cabins and surrounding land, guests who rent the ranch for a week also have access to the ranch's big kitchen and dining room for preparing all your meals. Most groups hire a caterer to do so. You must pack in all your groceries for the week.

What if you don't have 15 or 20 friends who are willing to make the trip? Well, you can take part in the Muir Trail Ranch's "short stay" program, available only in June or September, when open slots at the ranch are given to individuals or smaller groups who are willing to pay a per night fee. All of your meals are included in the nightly rate, and the meals are unforgettable.

So what do you do during your stay at your own private ranch in the Sierra? Well, here at 7,700 feet in elevation, the scenery is easy on the eyes, fly-fishing is excellent in the San Joaquin River, and hiking trails wind deep into the John Muir Wilderness. Thirty horses are available at the ranch, and one is always willing to hike to a pretty lake with you on its back.

A few staff members live and work at the ranch, under the leadership of owner Adeline Smith, an 89-year-old lady who is as smart and funny as anyone you'll ever meet in the Sierra. The staff takes care of basic facility maintenance, generating electricity, and keeping the horses fed and happy. They also run a small ranch store stocked with fishing supplies and other necessities, and they will guide you on horseback trips into the wilderness. Not only that, but by the time your stay is over, these people will have become your dear friends. That's just the way it is at Muir Trail Ranch.

One of the ranch's greatest features is its two enclosed hot springs, which everyone uses for bathing purposes as well as pure hedonistic pleasure. One bath is about 105°F; the other is a cooler 98°. The water pours into and then out of two beautifully constructed rock pools. The pools are continually refreshed by the bubbling spring, so the water is always kept clean without the use of any chemicals. If it's too warm outside for a hot bath, you can always go wash up in the San Joaquin River, about 100 feet away from the tent cabins.

Facilities
There are eight log cabins at Muir Trail Ranch, plus five tent cabins. The entire ranch accommodates 15 to 20 people. A kitchen is available. Horseback riding and hot springs are available. Linens and towels are not provided in the tent cabins; they are provided in the log cabins.

Reservations and Rates
Reservations are required. The fee is $8,925 for 15 to 20 people for one week. Horses are available for $65 per day, plus an additional fee for a guide. Individuals and smaller groups may rent the ranch on a nightly basis in June or September only. A tent cabin and all meals for two people is $125 per night; a log cabin and all meals for two people is $250 per night. The ranch is open from June to September. Pets are not permitted. Contact October to May: Muir Trail Ranch at P.O. Box 700, Ahwahnee, CA 93601-0700, 209/966-3195, website: www.muirtrailranch.com

Directions
From Highway 168 at the eastern edge of Huntington Lake, turn right on Kaiser Pass Road and drive 17 miles (narrow and winding) to a fork in

the road. Bear right for Florence Lake and drive six miles to the lake and store. From there, you will either hike to Muir Trail Ranch, ride a horse, or take the water taxi across the lake and hike the remaining five miles. (Note that trailers and motor homes are not recommended on Kaiser Pass Road.)

Summer address: P.O. Box 176, Lakeshore, CA 93634-0176, no telephone in summer.

15 CARDINAL VILLAGE RESORT
off U.S. 395 near Bishop

Luxury rating: ★ ★ ★ ☆ ☆   **Recreation rating: ★ ★ ★ ★ ☆**

Historic Cardinal Village Resort is a destination in itself. Part of an old mining claim, its buildings date back to the late 1890s, when miners settled here and worked the neighboring Cardinal Gold Mine. The original town of Cardinal Village boasted a post office, store, schoolhouse, and about 100 cabins. A few of those buildings still stand and can be rented for your vacation.

Each structure has been beautifully restored. The most popular cabin is Golden Trout, which was originally a stable. It is large enough for 8 to 16 people and is often reserved a year in advance. For smaller parties, there are one-, two-, and three-bedroom cabins, each one unique, though some are more modern.

All cabins at Cardinal Village have fully equipped kitchens, but if you don't want to cook, breakfast and lunch are served daily in the resort café. Saturday is Old West–style steak barbecue night. You're on your own for dinners the rest of the week.

Cardinal Village is set in a grove of aspens along Bishop Creek, where you can try your luck at trout fishing. The resort also has Cardinal Pond, a small natural pond that is stocked with trophy trout. Other fishing opportunities abound in Bishop Creek Canyon; the closest are those at Sabrina Lake and

© ANN MARIE BROWN

North Lake. Sabrina Lake has a full-service boat landing with rental boats and excellent fishing for rainbow, brown, and brook trout. Much smaller North Lake is reserved for shore anglers and those in float tubes and rafts. Both lakes feature a stunning backdrop of high mountain peaks, lodgepole pines, and quaking aspens.

In summer, guests can rent horses at Cardinal Village and take trail rides up the old road to Cardinal Mine. Little remains of the mine except a few building foundations and parts of its main shaft, but it's interesting to close your eyes and imagine the old days.

Hikers seeking a challenge should follow the Piute Pass Trail from North Lake Campground to Loch Leven Lake, Piute Lake, and spectacular Piute Pass. The scenic pass is six miles out, but the lakes are closer in, at 2.3 and 3.5 miles out. Alternatively, you can hike from the Lake Sabrina trailhead to photogenic Blue Lake in three miles. Each of these hike-in lakes is higher than 10,000 feet in elevation.

Facilities
There are 11 cabins plus two rental homes ranging in size and accommodating up to 16 people; all have fully equipped kitchens. A café and general store are on-site. Linens and towels are provided in all but two cabins, Golden Trout and Canter.

Reservations and Rates
Reservations are recommended. Fees are $100–300 per night, depending on cabin size. Pets are not permitted. Contact Cardinal Village Resort, Route 1, Box A-3, Bishop, CA 93514, 760/873-4789, website: www.cardinalvillageresort.com.

Directions
From Bishop on U.S. 395, turn west on Highway 168/West Line Street. Drive 17 miles on Highway 168 to Cardinal Village Resort. (Don't bear left at the South Lake fork; continue straight ahead.)

16 BISHOP CREEK LODGE
off U.S. 395 near Bishop

Luxury rating: ★ ★ ★ ☆ ☆   **Recreation rating:** ★ ★ ★ ★ ☆

Rank: Best for Fishing

The lodge dining room at Bishop Creek has a wagon wheel suspended from the ceiling, fishing lures hanging everywhere like Christmas ornaments, and a chainsaw-carved wooden cowboy propped up in the corner. Hunting and fishing trophies cover every inch of the walls—the heads of several long-departed deer, an antelope, a moose, an elk, and the lifelike bodies of a few big trout.

Bishop Creek Lodge makes no pretenses: It's a fish camp, a base for people heading to South Lake or Sabrina Lake to catch trout all day. Situated at the lofty elevation of 8,300 feet, the place also attracts hikers who want to traipse the myriad trails of Bishop Creek Canyon and the John Muir Wilderness.

The resort's cabins were built by pioneers in 1928. They're rustic, not fancy. Each cabin comes with a fully stocked kitchen and bathroom, plus electricity and heat. Because supplies are minimal at the resort store, you should buy your groceries in advance. (Either that or eat Power Bait for dinner.) If you don't want to cook, you can eat at Bishop Creek's café. The menu is limited—hamburgers and sandwiches served all day, steak and chicken for dinner. The service is delightfully informal.

A downer for some early-morning types is that hot breakfasts are not served at the lodge. However, there is a free continental breakfast (cereals, muffins, juice, and coffee), but it isn't served until 8 A.M.—late for most serious anglers.

The primary activity at Bishop Creek is fishing at South Lake (five

miles away), either along the shoreline or from a rented boat. If you don't catch anything at South Lake, head over to Sabrina Lake, just 10 miles away. Both lakes are known for their trophy brown trout. Many anglers also fish Bishop Creek; bring your fly-fishing gear.

Hikers head for the spectacular John Muir Wilderness. A

trailhead is near South Lake (try the six-mile loop hike to Ruwau, Bull, and Chocolate Lakes, or the shorter out-and-back trip to Long Lake). Another trailhead is found at the Bishop Creek Bridge (try the seven-mile round-trip to the four Tyee Lakes).

When you reserve your cabin at Bishop Creek Lodge, know that they are not all created equal. Five cabins are right on the road, which can be noisy in the early morning when trucks race up to the lake. If there are only two of you, cabin No. 6 is the best bet. It's up on a hill, far from the road, and set apart from the other cabins.

Facilities
There are 12 cabins ranging in size and accommodating up to eight people. All have fully equipped kitchens and private bathrooms. A café and general store are on-site. Linens and towels are provided.

Reservations and Rates
Reservations are recommended. Fees are $90–250 per night, with a two-night minimum. A continental breakfast is included. Pets are permitted with a $10 fee per night. Contact Bishop Creek Lodge, Route 1, South Lake Road, Bishop, CA 93514, 760/873-4484, website: www.bishopcreekresorts.com.

Directions
From Bishop on U.S. 395, turn west on Highway 168/West Line Street. Drive 14 miles on Highway 168 to the South Lake turnoff. Turn left and drive 2.5 miles to Bishop Creek Lodge.

17 PARCHERS RESORT
off U.S. 395 near Bishop

Luxury rating: ★ ★ ★ ☆ ☆   **Recreation rating:** ★ ★ ★ ★ ☆
Rank: Best for Fishing

Parchers Resort is owned and operated by the same folks who run Bishop Creek Lodge down the road, but Parchers is newer and just a little more posh than 70-year-old Bishop Creek.

Tucked in between two streams—Bishop Creek and Green Creek—and set among lodgepole pines and aspens, the cabins at Parchers Resort are pleasantly secluded and partially hidden from the road. They come in two styles: standard and rustic. The standard cabins house as many as four

© ANN MARIE BROWN

people. Each has a fully equipped kitchen and small dining area, separate bedroom with a queen or double bed, and a living area with a couple of extra twin beds. The rustic cabins are smaller but offer the same amenities, including a kitchen. A couple can save money by renting a two-person rustic cabin with no kitchen; they're half the price of the other cabins.

Parchers Resort is only 1.2 miles from big, beautiful South Lake (at 9,750 feet in elevation), which is well stocked with rainbow and brown trout. South Lake's marina has fishing boats for rent, or you can try your luck on the shoreline.

Hikers have access to numerous trails. To get a taste for the area, try the six-mile round-trip to the five Treasure Lakes. The route begins at South Lake on the Bishop Pass Trail; after an initial climb of nearly a mile, bear right on Treasure Lakes Trail. The first two lakes are easy to reach; the remaining three require some route-finding. Many people stop at the first Treasure Lake and are satisfied; it's a sparkling gem surrounded by jagged peaks. Be sure to pick up a trail map from the resort before you head out.

After a day of hiking and fishing, you might not have energy left for cooking, so eat at Parchers' South Fork Restaurant. Dinner is the main event; it's the most well-prepared grub you can find anywhere in Bishop Creek Canyon. Backpackers come off the Bishop Pass Trail and head straight for the restaurant; most of them have already decided what they will order 10 miles back.

Facilities

There are 10 one-bedroom cabins that can accommodate up to four people. Some have fully equipped kitchens. A restaurant and general store are on-site. Linens and towels are provided.

Reservations and Rates

Reservations are recommended. Fees are $80–170 per night and include a continental breakfast. The resort is open from May to October, depending on weather conditions. Pets are not permitted. Contact Parchers Resort, 2100 South Lake Road, Bishop, CA 93514, 760/873-4177, website: www.bishopcreekresorts.com.

Directions

From Bishop on U.S. 395, turn west on Highway 168/West Line Street. Drive 14 miles on Highway 168 to the South Lake turnoff. Turn left and drive six miles to Parchers Resort, on the left.

18 GLACIER LODGE
off U.S. 395 near Big Pine

Luxury rating: ★ ★ ☆ ☆ ☆   **Recreation rating:** ★ ★ ★ ★ ☆

Glacier Lodge suffered a devastating fire in May 1998 and has not yet been restored to its original splendor. The blaze, caused by a malfunctioning water heater, was a major financial setback for Glacier's owners, who have not rebuilt the historic 1917 lodge and restaurant building. Luckily, Glacier's cabins were untouched and are still for rent.

Despite this tragic turn of events, Glacier Lodge still offers one of the best access points for outdoor recreation in the eastern Sierra. The cabins are backed up against the mountains at 8,000 feet in elevation, just before the land becomes the John Muir Wilderness. The cabins are rustic in style, but they come with the critical luxuries: bathrooms, showers, electricity (from a generator), and tiny kitchens. The kitchens are nothing to brag about, but you can cook in them, which is important since the lodge's wonderful restaurant is gone.

What do visitors do at Glacier Lodge? Serious anglers fish Big Pine Creek, particularly the pools below First Falls. If you're willing to hike, fly-fishing is excellent farther up the canyon. If you have young kids with you, you can get them hooked on fishing at the small stocked pond right by the lodge.

Hikers head for the spectacular trails in Big Pine Canyon. An easy walk to First and Second Falls, on the North Fork Trail, begins right at the lodge. For a longer trip, head beyond the falls to Big Pine Lakes. If you take the left fork, you'll reach First Lake at four miles out. Try to make it all the way to Third Lake, five miles from

© ANN MARIE BROWN

the lodge and at 10,400 feet in elevation. The lake has a beautiful milky turquoise color caused by water flowing directly from Palisade Glacier, the southernmost glacier in the United States. The glacial silt is so fine that it does not settle out in the water, producing the lake's vivid, cloudy, blue-green color.

Hard-core mountaineers can make the trek all the way to Palisade Glacier, 8.5 miles from the lodge and at 12,400 feet in elevation. It's a long, hard hike, and when you near the glacier, you need climbing equipment and skills. Most people are happy if they get close enough to get a good look at it. The Palisade Crest is considered to have some of the finest alpine climbing in all of California, but it's not for the inexperienced.

Facilities
There are 10 one-bedroom cabins, all with fully equipped kitchens. A small store is on-site. Linens and towels are provided.

Reservations and Rates
Reservations are recommended. Fees are $80–100 per night. The resort is open from April to December, depending on weather conditions. Pets are permitted with a $15 fee per stay. Contact Glacier Lodge, P.O. Box 370, Big Pine, CA 93513, 760/938-2837, website: www.jewelofthesierra.com.

Directions
From Big Pine on U.S. 395, turn west on Crocker Street and drive 10.5 miles to the end of the road and Glacier Lodge. (The road becomes Glacier Lodge Road.)

19 SEQUOIA VIEW VINEYARD
off Highway 180 near Squaw Valley

Luxury rating: ★ ★ ★ ★ ☆   **Recreation rating:** ★ ★ ★ ☆ ☆

Jim and Debbie Van Haun retired from the urban life in Orange County and moved to a 20-acre vineyard just off the Blossom Trail in the Sierra foothills. Located 40 minutes from Kings Canyon and Sequoia National Parks, the Van Haun's farm has a separate guest house, where visitors too can pursue the dream of a life in the country.

The guest house, which is about 70 yards from the Van Haun's home and is partially hidden in the grape fields, is a 1948 farmhouse that has been lovingly restored with wide pine floors, an updated bathroom, and artistic touches such as country quilts and colorful wall stencils. With three good-sized bedrooms, the house could comfortably hold a family of six. The entire house is yours for the duration of your rental; you simply pay according to the number of people in your party and how

© ANN MARIE BROWN

many bedrooms you use. If there are only two in your party, you might consider renting the Winemaker's Suite, a separate one-bedroom unit that is built above the vineyard's wine-tasting room. It has a king sleigh bed and a balcony overlooking the vineyards.

The guest house and Winemaker's Suite are operated as a bed-and-breakfast, so a full gourmet meal is served each morning in the main house dining room. This is a chance for visitors to discuss the grape crop with Jim and Debbie, or test out the ripeness of the fruit from eight acres of nectarine trees. Debbie loves to cook, so expect an elaborate meal with entrées such as French toast cobbler, cast-iron breakfast pie, or sourdough pancakes. And of course you'll have freshly squeezed orange juice from the Van Haun's trees. You won't go away hungry.

Wine aficionados will be interested to know that the grapes on the Van Haun's vineyard are the rare Alicante Bouschet variety, one of the only red grapes that produces red juice (even without the skins). Most of the grapes are currently sold to premium wineries in Sonoma and Santa Cruz Counties, but step into the tasting room and you can sample some of the Van Haun's own vintages. The winery is currently producing nearly a dozen different wines. Local cheeses and olive oils are also for sale.

One of the best times to visit Sequoia View Vineyard is blossom season, from the end of February to mid-March. During this time, cyclists and drivers take to the area's back roads to witness the beauty of fruit tree orchards in bloom. The Blossom Trail is well signed, but brochures and maps are at the guest house.

Spring is also the season for white-water rafting on the nearby Kings River. Any time of year is just right for a visit to Kings Canyon and Sequoia National Parks, where a multitude of trails and one of nature's greatest wonders, the Giant Sequoia trees, await.

Facilities

There is one three-bedroom guest house with a kitchenette (microwave and refrigerator). Linens and towels are provided.

Reservations and Rates

Reservations are required. Fees for the guest house include breakfast and are $119 for two people, $169 for four people, and $219 for six people. The Winemaker's Suite is $139 per night, including breakfast. Pets are not permitted. Contact Sequoia View Vineyard, 1384 South Frankwood Avenue, Sanger, CA 93657, 559/787-9412 or 866/738-6420, website: www.svbnb.com.

Directions

From Fresno, drive east on Highway 180 for 19 miles to just east of Centerville and Minkler. Turn right on Frankwood Avenue and drive a quarter mile to Sequoia View Vineyard, on the left.

20 GRANT GROVE LODGE
off Highway 180 in Kings Canyon

Luxury rating: ★ ★ ☆ ☆ ☆   **Recreation rating:** ★ ★ ★ ★ ☆

Rank: Best for Hiking, Best Value

If you think there is no place left in California's national parks where you can rent a rustic cabin and partake in an old-fashioned nature experience, think again. Many of the cabins at Grant Grove Lodge in Kings Canyon National Park look and feel like a throwback to the 1930s, and some are only a small step above camping. Maybe that's the way it should be.

Here's the scoop on Grant Grove Lodge's cabins. The nine most luxurious "bath cabins" have electricity, propane heat, carpeting, and private baths. Some are duplexes, and some are stand-alone units. Twenty-four "rustic" and "camp" cabins are without private baths but have propane heat, an outdoor wood-burning stove, battery lamps, and a patio with a picnic table for outdoor cooking. Restroom and shower

© ANN MARIE BROWN

facilities are nearby. Grant Grove also has 18 barebones tent cabins without electricity but with battery lamps to light the way. The tent cabins are spaced quite close together; a stay in one is much like car camping.

None of the cabins have kitchens or any kind of indoor cooking facilities, so bring a camp stove and outdoor-cooking utensils and dishes, or plan to eat in the restaurant at Grant Grove. It's basically a large coffee shop, but the food is passable and affordable.

The cabins are open year-round, and it's hard to say which is the best season for a visit. If you like conifers covered in snow and cross-country skiing, plan on a winter trip. Some of the park's prettiest ski trails are in Grant Grove and Giant Forest, where you can see the cinnamon-colored Giant Sequoias crowned in snow. (The General Grant Tree, the third-largest tree in the world, is less than a mile from the cabins.) Rangers lead beginner-level guided snowshoe walks, and 75 miles of marked cross-country trails are available.

If you visit Grant Grove during the hiking season, a wide array of trails are nearby. Start with the 2.5-mile Sunset Trail, which leads from Sunset Campground downhill to two pretty waterfalls on Sequoia Creek then continues to Sequoia Lake. Don't miss Panoramic Point and Park Ridge Trail, which begins two miles from the cabins. The trail offers far-reaching views and a visit to an operating fire lookout tower.

Many more trailheads can be accessed by driving north or south into Giant Sequoia National Monument, or by taking Highway 180 to its end at Cedar Grove. The Grant Grove Visitor Center is a few steps away from the Grant Grove cabins, so you have easy access to all of the park and trail information you want.

Facilities

There are nine single and duplex one-room cabins with private baths, propane heat, and electricity; 24 rustic cabins without baths or electricity but with propane heat; and 18 tent cabins. In winter, only the cabins with bath are available. None of the accommodations have kitchen facilities, but outdoor cooking is possible. A restaurant, store, post office, and visitors center are on-site. Linens and towels are provided.

Reservations and Rates

Reservations are recommended. Fees are $110–117 per night for cabins with bath (available year-round), and $45–69 per night for cabins without bath and for tent cabins (available in summer only). All rates are based on double occupancy; there is an additional fee for extra people. Pets are not permitted. Contact Kings Canyon Park Services Company, 5755 East

Kings Canyon Road, Suite 101, Fresno, CA 93727, 559/335-5500 or 866/522-6966, website: www.sequoia-kingscanyon.com.

Directions
From Fresno, drive east on Highway 180 for 55 miles to the Big Stump entrance station at Kings Canyon National Park. Continue 1.5 miles and turn left for Grant Grove. Drive 1.5 miles to Grant Grove Village.

21 KINGS CANYON LODGE
off Highway 180 in Kings Canyon

Luxury rating: ★ ★ ☆ ☆ ☆   **Recreation rating:** ★ ★ ★ ☆ ☆

© ANN MARIE BROWN

There's nothing great about the cabins at Kings Canyon Lodge—no fireplaces, no extra amenities, and darn little in the way of decorative charm—but they do have a great location. They're situated right along Highway 180, the only road that runs deep into the spectacular canyon of Kings Canyon National Park.

Driving east on Highway 180, you know you're approaching the lodge when you see a hand-painted sign that reads "Caution: Ice Cream Ahead." Since there is little else on this stretch of highway, plenty of people slam on their brakes for some ice cream.

Kings Canyon Lodge makes a remarkably picturesque snapshot, with its rustic buildings and old-fashioned, gravity-fed gas pumps out front. But it's wise to know a few things before you stay there. Only a few of the rustic, wood-frame cabins have kitchens. Try to reserve one that does. If yours doesn't, be prepared to eat at the lodge's grill or to drive many miles for food. The grill serves little else besides hamburgers, but luckily the restaurant at Grant Grove (14 miles away) and the snack bar at Cedar Grove (18 miles away) have more extensive menus.

Also, make sure you avoid the one duplex cabin. Each side of the duplex is impossibly small and has paper-thin walls. Insist on a single unit; the best of the lot is cabin No. 4. Also, don't expect much customer service during your stay. The folks running the lodge do so on a laissez-faire basis.

The South Fork Kings River is across the highway from the lodge; the best access is via nearby Yucca Point Trail. It's a steep downhill path that leads to excellent wild-trout fishing early in the year and swimming later in the summer. Boyden Cave is down the road about six miles. There you can go on a tour of a fascinating limestone cavern or hike the Windy Cliffs Trail from the cave entrance. You'll gain marvelous views of the Kings River Canyon and its towering granite walls.

Many visitors stop at the picnic area at Grizzly Falls, a beautiful 80-foot waterfall right by the highway that rushes into the Kings River. It's a nice break on your way to Cedar Grove and the "End of the Road," where Highway 180 stops and the wilderness begins. Trailheads are plentiful in Cedar Grove, including the popular eight-mile round-trip to Mist Falls, or the incredibly scenic 1.5-mile Zumwalt Meadow Loop. Plenty of anglers try their luck in the South Fork Kings River from along this path.

Facilities

There are 12 cabins ranging in size from studios to two bedrooms. Some have kitchens. A café, bar, and gasoline are on-site. Linens and towels are provided.

Reservations and Rates

Reservations are recommended. Fees are $79–139 per night. The resort is open from late April to October. Pets are not permitted. Contact Kings Canyon Lodge, P.O. Box 820, 67751 Highway 180, Kings Canyon National Park, CA 93633, 559/335-2405. (The phone is not answered in the off-season, which is usually late October to early April.)

Directions

From Fresno, drive east on Highway 180 for 55 miles to the Big Stump entrance station at Kings Canyon National Park. Continue 1.5 miles and turn left for Grant Grove and Cedar Grove. Drive 17 miles on Highway 180 to Kings Canyon Lodge on the right.

Luxury rating: ★ ★ ★ ☆ ☆   **Recreation rating:** ★ ★ ★ ★ ★

Big Meadows Guard Station is one of four secluded Forest Service cabins for rent in Giant Sequoia National Monument. (For information on the others, see the listing for Mountain Home Guard Station in this chapter.) It's the only one that is near Kings Canyon and Sequoia National Parks, giving you the chance to explore the parks and surrounding national forest land from your own private rustic cabin.

Like most guard stations built in the 1930s, Big Meadows cabin is 900 square feet in size. It has a queen bed, twin bunk beds, and a double sofa sleeper, so six people can sleep comfortably. Up to 12 people are permitted with each reservation, but the extra six will have to spend the night on the floor or outside in tents. The cabin has electricity, running water, and a bathroom with a hot shower. Its kitchen has an adequate supply of dishes and utensils—even a coffeepot. All you need to bring are your clothes, food, and basic supplies.

Big Meadows' location couldn't be better. You drive through Grant Grove in Kings Canyon National Park to reach it, so that gives you a clue about the pleasure ahead. Set at 7,600 feet in elevation, the cabin is only a couple of miles from the Fox Meadow trailhead for Jennie Lakes Wilderness, from which pretty Weaver Lake can be reached in 1.5 miles. Larger, lovelier Jennie Lake can be reached in nine miles round-trip. The ambitious can hike to the summit of Mitchell Peak, elevation 10,365 feet, for rewarding views of the Great Western Divide and the Silliman Crest. It's a fine spot to catch your breath.

Anglers don't have to hike far to fish; Big Meadows Creek runs right across the street from the cabin.

For a quick thrill, take a drive over to Buck Rock Fire Lookout, about 10 minutes from the guard station. Climb the stairs to the tower, which is perched high atop Buck Rock, and have a chat with the lookout person while you admire the far-reaching view.

Facilities
There is one cabin that has beds for six people; up to 12 people are permitted. It has a fully equipped kitchen, electricity, and bathroom. Linens and towels are not provided.

Reservations and Rates
Reservations are required. The fee is $100 per night. The cabin is currently open from June 15 to October 15. Pets are not permitted. Contact Hume Lake Ranger District, Sequoia National Forest/Giant Sequoia National Monument, 35860 East Kings Canyon Road, Dunlap, CA 93621, 559/338-3222 or 559/338-2251, website: www.fs.fed.us/r5/sequoia.

Directions
From Fresno, drive east on Highway 180 for 55 miles to the Big Stump entrance station at Kings Canyon National Park. Continue straight 1.5 miles and turn right on the Generals Highway, heading for Sequoia National Park. Drive 7.5 miles and turn left at the sign for Big Meadows and Horse Corral. Drive 3.5 miles to Big Meadows Guard Station.

23 MONTECITO SEQUOIA LODGE
off Highway 198 in Giant Sequoia National Monument

Luxury rating: ★ ★ ★ ☆ ☆   **Recreation rating:** ★ ★ ★ ★ ☆

Rank: Best for Families

Montecito Sequoia Lodge is not for everybody. The place is run like a high Sierra Club Med, with a heavy emphasis on organized activities, especially for families. If you like to be left alone to do your own thing, you might find the atmosphere too obtrusive. But if you're looking for a way to keep your kids busy, active, and happy in the outdoors, you're in luck. In fact, with all the children's activities available, you might actually get some time alone with your spouse.

The lodge is at 7,500 feet in elevation in Giant Sequoia National Monument, and it bills itself as a "family vacation camp." That means in addition to all the great outdoor adventures possible in the surrounding area, there is also much to do right at the resort. Organized activities include tennis, archery, basketball, volleyball, canoeing, waterskiing, horseback riding, swimming, and cross-country skiing in winter.

The lodge is reached via a long driveway off the main road, so as you pull in, you feel like you are heading to your own private vacation retreat. At the driveway's end is a pretty little lake, a big lodge, and several cabins and motel-style rooms.

Many people like the simple payment plans at Montecito Sequoia Lodge. There are four- and six-night package deals that include all activities, meals, and accommodations. In the slow, off-season months of fall and spring, you can sometimes purchase accommodations-only packages.

Neither the 13 cabins nor any of the lodge rooms have kitchens; you eat all meals in the lodge dining room. Montecito Sequoia has developed a reputation for healthy, wholesome food served buffet style. One entrée at dinner is always vegetarian. Many diners take their food outside to the huge deck that overlooks the high peaks of the Great Western Divide.

The cabins at Montecito Sequoia house two to eight people. Each has a king- or queen bed, two or three bunk beds, a wood-burning stove, and electricity. For bathrooms and showers, you walk to the nearby bathhouse. (Private bathrooms are available only in lodge rooms, not cabins.)

In winter, visitors come to Montecito Sequoia to take advantage of excellent cross-country skiing and snowshoeing. Nearly 100 miles of groomed and backcountry trails lead from the lodge into surrounding national monument and park land. If you don't have your own equipment, you can rent everything you need, and lesson packages are available. Weather permitting, ice-skating is allowed on the lodge's small lake.

Facilities

There are 13 cabins that can accommodate up to eight people, plus 26 lodge rooms. The cabins do not have private baths; a central bathhouse is available. The cabins do not have kitchens; a restaurant is on-site. Linens and towels are provided.

Reservations and Rates

Reservations are required. Fees for the cabins are $110–140 per adult per night, including all meals; fees for the lodge rooms are more. Children's rates are discounted. Rates are discounted in spring and fall. Pets are not permitted. Contact Montecito Sequoia Lodge, P.O. Box 858, Grant Grove, CA 93633, 559/565-3388 or 800/227-9900, website: www.mslodge.com.

Directions
From Fresno, drive east on Highway 180 for 55 miles to the Big Stump entrance station at Kings Canyon National Park. Continue 1.5 miles and turn right on the Generals Highway, heading for Sequoia National Park. Drive 8.5 miles to the right turnoff for Montecito Sequoia Lodge. Turn right and drive a half mile to the lodge.

24 PEAR LAKE SKI HUT
off Highway 198 in Sequoia National Park

Luxury rating: ★ ★ ☆ ☆ ☆   **Recreation rating:** ★ ★ ★ ☆ ☆

Granite-backed Pear Lake

There isn't a cross-country skier or snowshoer alive who wouldn't enjoy a stay at Sequoia National Park's Pear Lake Ski Hut. But to make the trip, you need to accomplish two things: First, secure a reservation with the Sequoia Natural History Association; second, be in good enough shape so that you can cross-country ski or snowshoe six miles, much of it uphill. The total elevation gain is 2,000 feet from the trailhead at Wolverton to the ski hut north of Pear Lake, so it's not advisable for novice skiers or snowshoers. But with a few days of training and good aerobic conditioning, even intermediates can make the trip, especially if they start early in the day.

The ski hut is open to public use from mid-December to late April each year. To get a reservation, you must phone or make a written request by mid-November. A lottery is held, and dates are assigned accordingly. Usually everybody gets a reservation, although not always on the precise dates they want. Holiday weekends are the hardest to reserve; weekdays are easy.

The cabin houses 10 people in bunk beds; most people go with a group of friends so that they have the whole place to themselves. If your group is smaller than 10, you will probably share the hut with another group. No matter, you'll quickly make friends. If you don't, you can settle your differences with a rousing snowball fight.

The Pear Lake "hut" is an impressive stone building with huge wooden rafters. It serves as a backcountry ranger station in the summer and is heated by a wood pellet stove. Propane cooking stoves and lanterns are provided, as well as all cooking and eating utensils and a composting toilet.

The trail to reach the lake is a spectacular day hike in summer and an equally spectacular ski trip in winter. With your gear loaded on your back, you set out on the Lakes Trail from Wolverton Ski Area at 7,200 feet, heading east along Wolverton Creek. The trail starts climbing and keeps on climbing. The apex of your ascent is The Hump at 9,400 feet. After this high point, you have less than three miles of trail to cover, mostly downhill. You'll glide along the icy shores of Heather, Emerald, and Aster Lakes. When you reach Pear Lake Ski Hut at six miles out, you are less than a half mile from the shores of large Pear Lake.

The Sequoia Natural History Association makes your trip easier by sending you a suggested packing list. The list includes all the winter clothing and skiing equipment you might expect, plus some important essentials, like a sleeping bag (bunks are provided, but not bedding), propane fuel and matches (for the stoves and lanterns), enough food for your stay plus extra for emergencies, and water purification equipment. You must filter or boil all your water. The Association also insists that skiers carry survival equipment, just in case an avalanche, whiteout, or other snow emergency should occur.

Facilities
There is one ski hut that can accommodate up to 10 people. Propane cooking facilities are provided. There is a wood pellet stove for heat and a compost toilet. No drinking water is available. Linens and towels are not provided.

Reservations and Rates
Reservations are required. The fee is $22 per person per night ($18 for Sequoia National History Association members). Pets are not permitted. Contact Sequoia Natural History Association, HCR 89, Box 10, Three Rivers, CA 93271-9792, 559/565-3759, website: www.sequoiahistory.org.

Directions

From Visalia, drive east on Highway 198 for 40 miles, through the town of Three Rivers, to the Ash Mountain entrance station at Sequoia National Park. Continue 20 miles on the Generals Highway, past Giant Forest, to the Wolverton Ski Area turnoff on the right side of the road. The trail to Pear Lake begins at the far edge of the parking lot.

   BEARPAW HIGH SIERRA CAMP

off Highway 198 in Sequoia National Park

Luxury rating: ★ ★ ☆ ☆ ☆   **Recreation rating:** ★ ★ ★ ★ ☆

Rank: Best for Hiking

The tent cabins at Bearpaw High Sierra Camp, elevation 7,800 feet, make the spectacular backcountry of Sequoia National Park accessible to people who don't want to backpack but love to hike. To get there, you hike an easy, nearly level 11.5 miles through some of the most gorgeous high-country scenery you can imagine. When you arrive, you are spoiled by the opulence of tent cabins with

View from the High Sierra Trail en route to Bearpaw Meadow

clean beds and bedding, plus showers and home-style meals. Not only that, but you are treated to incredible vistas of the Great Western Divide.

You don't have to carry a tent. You don't have to plan your meals in advance. You don't have to pack a camp stove or pots and pans. All you need are your clothes and whatever personal items you want to bring— cameras, books, a day pack, fishing equipment, etc.

Your ticket to Bearpaw High Sierra Camp is the stunning High Sierra Trail, a popular trans-Sierra route that eventually leads all the way to Mount Whitney. In this section, the path travels along the north rim of the Middle Fork Kaweah River Canyon. Although 11.5 miles may sound like a long hike, the trail has a mere 1,000-foot elevation gain.

At Bearpaw Meadow, the campground is perched on the edge of a granite gorge. Once you're settled into your cozy tent cabin, you can spend a day hiking to Upper and Lower Hamilton Lakes. The lakes are set in a glacially carved basin at the base of 13,000-foot peaks. Many other excellent day hikes are available; the staff at Bearpaw can point you on your way.

One of the nicest things about Bearpaw is its small size. The maximum number of guests is 18, plus two staff members who work there.

So how do you get a reservation for this high-country paradise? It isn't easy. At 7 A.M. on January 2, the park concessionaire starts taking telephone reservations for the following summer at Bearpaw. Within a couple of hours, every date for the next season is booked.

If you're not one of the lucky ones to get through, it can seem disappointing, but it doesn't have to be. Although tons of people make reservations for Bearpaw, many of them never show up. The reservation office keeps a waiting list, and as people drop out, the wait-listers get in. Since there is a 30-day cancellation policy, wait-listers are usually phoned at least 30 days in advance to see if they want to fill an empty space.

Facilities

There are six tent cabins that can accommodate two to three people. Tent cabins do not have heat or electricity, but lanterns are provided. Showers and bathrooms are a few feet away. A backpacker's campground is also available. Linens and towels are provided.

Reservations and Rates

Reservations and a permit are required; call 559/253-2199 or 888/252-5757 as early as 7 A.M. on January 2 for the following summer. The fee is $350 per night for single or double occupancy, which includes breakfast and dinner (a third person is $75 extra). The High Sierra Camp is open from mid-June to mid-September. Pets are not permitted. Contact Delaware North Parks Services, P.O. Box 89, Sequoia National Park, CA 93262, 559/565-4070 or 888/252-5757, website: www.visitsequoia.com.

Directions

From Visalia, drive east on Highway 198 for 40 miles, through the town of Three Rivers, to the Ash Mountain entrance station at Sequoia National Park. Continue 16 miles on the Generals Highway to the Giant Forest area. Turn right on Crescent Meadow Road and drive 3.5 miles to the Crescent Meadow parking area. The High Sierra Trail begins near the edge of Crescent Meadow.

26 WICKY-UP RANCH
off Highway 216 in Woodlake

Luxury rating: ★ ★ ★ ★ ☆   **Recreation rating:** ★ ★ ★ ☆ ☆

Wicky-Up Ranch is an eclectic bed-and-breakfast and working orange ranch just 18 miles from the Ash Mountain entrance to Sequoia National Park. Its one cottage, Calico, is as fittingly quirky and charming as the rest of the ranch.

First, some background: Monica and Jack Pizura own and operate Wicky-Up Ranch, which has been in Monica's family for five generations. Their California Craftsman-style home was built in 1902 for Illinois State Senator Fred E. Harding, Monica's great-great uncle. The house is filled with antiques, Oriental rugs, and family heirlooms—each with its own story, which Monica will tell you if you ask.

The lush grounds surrounding the ranch house are a melting pot of interesting flora. Alongside the dark green acres of orange groves grow a multitude of roses, two giant deodar cedar trees, and a huge coastal live oak that was planted by Monica's mother. A trio of ringneck doves coo from a small aviary under the oak's wide canopy. The gardens are peppered with whimsical copper sculptures created by Jack.

The Calico Cottage is tiny (less than 100 square feet) but adorable. It has bunk-style stacked beds; the top is a twin, and the bottom is a full feather bed. A small bathroom with sink and toilet adjoins the main room. When it's time to clean up, guests head outside to a private patio and an intimate, enclosed outdoor shower.

Calico Cottage is so small that kitchen facilities are out of the question. But since Wicky-Up Ranch is operated as a bed-and-breakfast, your first meal of the day is prepared in fine style. Monica whips up a three-course, gourmet candlelight breakfast for her guests and serves it in the cedar-lined dining room of the main house. Freshly squeezed orange juice is de rigueur, of course. The food is a delight for the eyes as well as the stomach; Monica pays strict attention to presentation as well as taste.

© ANN MARIE BROWN

After breakfast, the Pizuras will take you on a Jeep tour of the orange groves, if you desire. Or, you can set out to Lake Kaweah for swimming and water sports, or to the Kaweah River for white-water rafting in spring. A few miles farther is the southern entrance to Sequoia National Park at Ash Mountain and the start of the long road to the spectacular Mineral King Valley. Hikers will find a wide array of trails at either location.

Facilities
There is one cottage that can accommodate two to three people. There are no kitchen facilities. Linens and towels are provided.

Reservations and Rates
Reservations are required. The fee for Calico Cottage is $90 for two people, including breakfast. A third person is $20 extra. Pets are sometimes permitted with prior approval. Contact Wicky-Up Ranch, 22702 Avenue 344, Woodlake, CA 93286, 559/564-8898, website: www.wickyup.com.

Directions
From Visalia, drive east on Highway 198 for 25 miles to Lemon Cove. Turn left (west) on Highway 216, which becomes Avenue 344. Drive 3.2 miles; Wicky-Up Ranch is on the right.

27 SEQUOIA MOTEL
off Highway 198 in Three Rivers

Luxury rating: ★ ★ ★ ☆ ☆   **Recreation rating:** ★ ★ ★ ★ ☆

Sequoia Motel is a peaceful oasis in the town of Three Rivers and has comfortable cabins and motel-style rooms. Located across the road from the White Horse Inn, a popular local restaurant, the motel features a relaxing swimming pool and colorful flower gardens.

Cabin No. 5 is a favorite of couples, with its private deck shaded by the canopy of a huge canyon oak. The one-room cabin has a fireplace, complete kitchen, full bath, cable television, queen bed, and sleeper sofa.

If you need more space, Cabin No. 4 has two bedrooms, plus a full bath, fireplace, kitchen, and deck. Four people can sleep comfortably in its two twin beds and one queen bed.

Located just four miles from the Ash Mountain entrance to Sequoia

National Park, Sequoia Motel is an obvious choice for people who want to explore the many wonders of the park. But there is also much to do in the Three Rivers area. In spring and early summer, the main activity is white-water rafting on the Kaweah River. Guided raft trips are available from put-in points between the national park entrance and Lake Kaweah.

Kaweah River by the Sequoia Motel

During the hot weather of summer, Lake Kaweah is a haven for water sports, including waterskiing, personal watercraft riding, sailing, and fishing. Boats are for rent at the Kaweah Marina. Anglers fish the rivers and streams that empty into the lake; the fishing season is open year-round in the Kaweah drainage.

When the weather cools in autumn and winter, cyclists take advantage of the quiet roads in the Three Rivers area. Both North Fork and South Fork Drives are quiet paved stretches suitable for long rides. The town of Three Rivers has bike lanes along both sides of the highway through the center of town. Plans are in the works to extend them all the way to the Sequoia National Park entrance.

Facilities

There are three cabins that can accommodate up to four people. Two cabins have fully equipped kitchens. Linens and towels are provided.

Reservations and Rates

Reservations are recommended. Fees are $115–195 per night for cabins. The resort is open year-round. Pets are not permitted. Contact Sequoia Motel, P.O. Box 145, 43000 Sierra Drive, Three Rivers, CA 93271, 559/561-4453, website: www.sequoiamotel.com.

Directions

From Visalia, drive east on Highway 198 for 40 miles, through the town of Three Rivers. Sequoia Motel is on the right (Highway 198), about two miles east of the center of town.

Other Cabins and Cottages Nearby

Cort Cottage, P.O. Box 245, Three Rivers, CA 93271, 559/561-4671, website: www.cortcottage.com.

Cinnamon Creek Ranch, P.O. Box 54, Three Rivers, CA 93271, 559/561-1107, website: www.cinnamoncreek.com.

28 SEQUOIA VILLAGE INN
off Highway 198 in Three Rivers

Luxury rating: ★ ★ ★ ☆   **Recreation rating:** ★ ★ ★ ☆

The cottages at Sequoia Village Inn have the three essentials for a perfect vacation: location, location, location. Situated at the Ash Mountain entrance to Sequoia National Park, they are ideally positioned for day trips into the remote southern areas of the park at Mineral King and South Fork, as well as the busier central areas of the park at Potwisha and Giant Forest.

The people who run Sequoia Village Inn have gone out of their way to make the place nice, with well-constructed buildings, private patios and verandas, and lovely gardens. The inn has six cottages, two large chalets, and one suite. Most of the cottages have full kitchens and views of either the Kaweah River or the mountains, plus special touches like claw-foot tubs, four-poster beds, and unique tile work. The large chalets are two stories high and have three bedrooms, fireplaces, full kitchens, and room for up to 12 people. A swimming pool and hot tub are on the premises.

With a one-minute drive from your cottage, you can be at the Ash Mountain entrance to Sequoia National Park. From there, your first stop should be Potwisha Campground, where you can pick up the trail to Marble Falls on the Marble fork of the Kaweah River. March, April, and May are the best months to visit, when the foothill wildflowers bloom and the air is comfortably cool.

From the same campground, you can take a five-mile loop hike to see Monache Indian historical sites, including some pictographs painted on the side of Hospital Rock. Along the route are many swimming holes in the Middle Fork Kaweah River.

If you want to reach higher elevations and cool mountain air, just continue up the park road for another 12 winding miles to the Giant Forest area. Hike the 380 steps to the top of Moro Rock and admire its dazzling views of the Great Western Divide. Then take a walk on any of a multitude of trails: Sunset Rock, Crescent Meadow, Huckleberry and Hazelwood Loop, or the

© ANN MARIE BROWN

Congress Trail. Up here at 6,000 feet, you're in the land of big Sequoias and cool, grassy meadows—an extreme contrast to the Three Rivers foothill country.

A longer drive from Sequoia Village Inn can take you into spectacular Mineral King in southern Sequoia National Park. It's 25 curving miles to the end of the road in Mineral King Valley, but if you get an early start on the drive and give yourself all day to hike and explore, it's worth it.

Facilities
There are six cottages, two three-bedroom chalets, and one small suite. Most have fully equipped kitchens. A swimming pool and hot tub are on-site. A restaurant is across the street. Linens and towels are provided.

Reservations and Rates
Reservations are recommended. Fees are $69–295 per night, depending on size of accommodations. Pets are permitted in some cottages with a $5 fee per night. Contact Sequoia Village Inn, 45971 Sierra Drive, P.O. Box 1014, Three Rivers, CA 93271, 559/561-3652, website: www.sequoiavillageinn.com.

Directions
From Visalia, drive east on Highway 198 for 40 miles, through the town of Three Rivers. Six miles past Three Rivers, you'll see Sequoia Village Inn on the left. If you reach the Ash Mountain entrance station to Sequoia National Park, you've gone a quarter mile too far.

Other Cabins and Cottages Nearby
Buckeye Tree Lodge, 46000 Sierra Drive, Three Rivers, CA 93271, 559/561-5900, website: www.buckeyetree.com.
The Gateway Lodge, 45978 Sierra Drive, Three Rivers, CA 93271, 559/561-4133, website: www.gateway-sequoia.com.

29 LAKE ELOWIN RESORT
off Highway 198 in Three Rivers

Luxury rating: ★ ★ ★ ☆ ☆   **Recreation rating:** ★ ★ ★ ☆ ☆

© ANN MARIE BROWN

Here's one to add to the "know before you go" category: Lake Elowin isn't really a lake. It's a large, artificially constructed pond with a single island and surrounded by a grassy lawn. The "lake" is located at Lake Elowin Resort, a complex of cabins just outside Three Rivers and Sequoia National Park.

If you're the type who likes to make your own rules, you won't be happy here. Lake Elowin Resort is policy intensive, and they ask you to agree to their terms before you reserve a cabin. For most visitors, the rules make good sense: no smoking anywhere on the premises, outside or inside; no car alarms; no littering; no stereos playing outdoors; no throwing rocks in the lake. If you break any of the rules, you pay a hefty fine. Fair enough.

In case you haven't figured it out, Lake Elowin Resort isn't a party place. It's a quiet, peaceful getaway, and the managers intend to keep it that way.

Although Lake Elowin is one of the oldest resorts in Three Rivers, you wouldn't know it from their cabins—all 10 are in excellent condition. In keeping with the quiet atmosphere of the place, they don't have televisions or phones, but they do have one or two bedrooms, comfortable queen beds, and fully equipped kitchens. Only one cabin has a fireplace.

People who come to Lake Elowin Resort pass their time in a variety of ways: swimming and canoeing in the large, pretty pond (or small lake, whatever you prefer), reading on the shaded lawn areas, dipping into the Kaweah River swimming hole on the resort's property, and fishing nearby stretches of the river. Many visitors drive into the southern part of Sequoia National Park to spend the day, then return in the evening to barbecue outside their cabin (or cook inside if the mood strikes them).

Facilities

There are 10 cabins ranging in size and accommodating up to six people. All cabins have fully equipped kitchens. Linens and towels are provided.

Reservations and Rates

Reservations are required. Fees are $80–220 per night with a two-night minimum on summer weekends. The resort is open year-round. Pets are not permitted. Contact Lake Elowin Resort, Dineley Drive, Three Rivers, CA 93271, 559/561-3460, website: www.lake-elowin.com.

Directions

From Visalia, drive east on Highway 198 for 40 miles, through the town of Three Rivers. Approximately three miles east of town, turn left on Dineley Drive. Cross the bridge and turn right; the resort is a quarter mile farther, on the right.

30 PARADISE CANYON CABINS
off Mineral King Road near Three Rivers

Luxury rating: ★ ★ ★ ☆ ☆   **Recreation rating:** ★ ★ ★ ★ ☆

Rank: Most Secluded

In the summer of 2001, a new resort opened near the Mineral King entrance to Sequoia National Park, and it's unlike anything anywhere else in the Sierra. The place is called Paradise Canyon, and it may forever change the meaning of the word *romance*.

Only two cabins are for rent at Paradise Canyon. They are behind a locked gate almost six miles from the town of Three Rivers, on the lonely, winding road to Mineral King. Perched on a oak-shaded slope above the east fork of the Kaweah River, the one-bedroom units have gas fireplaces, full kitchens, and comfortable queen beds. Their best features are screened-in porches (to keep the evening mosquitoes out) and wood-

burning hot tubs. To heat up the water, you simply add a few logs. Sure, it takes a while, but there's no reason to hurry in Paradise.

Although the canyon setting is very remote and rustic, the cabins do have electricity generated by solar panels and running water. (The bathroom is in a separate building and is

© ANN MARIE BROWN

shared by both units.) A caretaker lives on the premises to make sure everything operates smoothly.

The entire property is 14 acres in size. A hiking trail leads from the cabins downhill to the river, arriving at a remarkably deep, inky blue swimming hole fed by a small waterfall. It's a completely private spot; the only access is by kayak during the highest flows of spring, and even then, this stretch of river is considered to be unrunnable. Be sure to bring your hiking boots to negotiate the trail; it is steep and rough in places, but worth every footstep. The walk takes 10 to 15 minutes.

In addition to this fabulous swimming spot, your recreation options include the spectacular trails of Mineral King, less than an hour away on the circuitous road. But Paradise Canyon's owners strongly recommend that guests spend at least one day of their visit just relaxing on the property. Both cabins are serenaded by the music of a neighboring creek, enticing you to soak in the hot tub or read on the porch, accompanied by sweet water sounds.

The owners are marketing this lovely retreat specifically to singles or couples without children. Because of the rugged, isolated nature of the canyon, they do not allow anyone under 18. The cabins are perfectly sized for one to three people, and feature special "adult" touches, such as fine china instead of ordinary dishes.

Facilities

There are two one-bedroom cabins with fully equipped kitchens, fireplaces, and hot tubs. A shared bathroom is in a separate building. Linens and towels are provided.

Reservations and Rates

Reservations are required. Fees are $130–145 per night for two people, with a two-night minimum. The resort is open year-round. Pets are permitted with a $25 fee per night. Contact Paradise Canyon Cabins, P.O. Box 1150, 49215 Mineral King Road, Three Rivers, CA 93271, 559/561-4088, website: www.sequoiacabins.com.

Directions

From Visalia, drive east on Highway 198 for 38 miles to Mineral King Road, 2.5 miles east of Three Rivers. (If you reach the Ash Mountain entrance station, you've gone too far.) Turn right on Mineral King Road and drive 5.8 miles to the resort on the left side of the road.

31 SILVER CITY RESORT
off Mineral King Road in Mineral King

Luxury rating: ★ ★ ★ ☆ ☆   **Recreation rating:** ★ ★ ★ ★ ★

Rank: Best for Hiking

Silver City Resort in Mineral King is the kind of place you daydream about all winter long, when the southern Sierra is shut down by deep snow. The resort is in the beautiful Mineral King Valley in southern Sequoia National Park. Accessible by only one road—a 25-mile, winding thoroughfare that starts in the town of Three Rivers—Mineral King requires some serious effort to reach. But it's worth it.

Silver City Resort is the only commercial enterprise in Mineral King other than two park campgrounds. A lucky few own summer homes in Mineral King, but except for them and a few dozen campers, you won't find hordes of people. The road in is too long and slow for casual visitors.

The cabins at Silver City Resort come in a wide range of sizes and configurations, from a tiny one-room model to large three-bedroom chalets with a full kitchen, bathroom, outdoor deck, and woodstove. The chalets are so well built and cozy, you'll wish you could live in one year-round. Each cabin is different, so make sure you request the amenities you want. The resort's owners, Connie and Norm Pillsbury, are two of the nicest people you'll ever meet and will do their best to accommodate you.

While staying at Silver City Resort, you will want to sample some of Mineral King's trails. Hikers looking for an easy stroll should follow the first mile of Farewell Gap Trail along the East Fork Kaweah River. Some people cast a line into the water as they walk, hoping to catch a trout or two. Another pleasant easy hike is Cold Springs Nature Trail out of Cold Springs Campground. Like Farewell Gap Trail, the path parallels a babbling section of the Kaweah and offers fabulous views of Sawtooth Peak, Mineral Peak, and Rainbow Mountain. Hike either trail at sunset and you'll have plenty of memories to fuel your off-season Mineral King fantasies.

Hikers seeking more of a challenge can choose between several trails to spectacular high alpine lakes, including Eagle

Lake (6.8 miles round-trip), Mosquito Lakes (7.4 miles round-trip), Monarch Lakes (8.4 miles round-trip), and Crystal Lake (10 miles round-trip). Each is located above 10,000 feet in elevation, so expect classic high-country scenery with plenty of stark granite and deep blue water.

After so much hiking around, you'll be grateful for the good food at Silver City's café. It's simple fare—eggs and pancakes for breakfast, burgers and sandwiches for lunch and dinner—but it's consistently fresh and delicious. The resort serves its full menu Thursday through Monday. On Tuesday and Wednesday, they offer only beverages and homemade pies, so if you're staying over midweek, make sure you bring provisions to cook in your cabin's kitchen or outside on the barbecue. The variety of pies is surprising—apple, marionberry, blueberry, and so on—but eventually you'll have to eat something else.

Facilities
There are 10 cabins and four large chalets ranging in size from studios to three bedrooms. Most have fully equipped kitchens. Some cabins have private bathrooms; a central restroom and shower area is available. A restaurant and general store are on-site. Linens and towels are not provided.

Reservations and Rates
Reservations are recommended. Fees are $70–290 per night. Early June, late September, and October stays are discounted. The resort is open from late May through October. Pets are not permitted. Contact Silver City Resort, P.O. Box 56, Three Rivers, CA 93271, 559/561-3223 (summer) or 805/528-2730 (winter), website: www.silvercityresort.com.

Directions
From Visalia, drive east on Highway 198 for 38 miles to Mineral King Road, 2.5 miles east of Three Rivers. (If you reach the Ash Mountain entrance station, you've gone too far.) Turn right on Mineral King Road and drive 25 miles to Silver City Resort, on the left side of the road.

32 MOUNTAIN HOME GUARD STATION
off Highway 190 near Mountain Home State Forest

Luxury rating: ★ ★ ★ ☆ ☆   **Recreation rating:** ★ ★ ★ ★ ☆

Mountain Home Guard Station is one of four Forest Service cabins in Giant Sequoia National Monument available for public rental. These special facilities were once the residences of fire patrol officers keeping watch over the national forests, and today they can be the vacation home of families or small groups.

Hidden Falls at Mountain Home State Forest

If you want to achieve a feeling of wilderness with the comfort of a roof over your head, the Mountain Home Guard Station provides it. The cabin is 900 square feet in size and looks about the same as it did when it was built in the 1930s. Although it doesn't have electricity, it has running water and a working bathroom with hot showers. The heating system and kitchen appliances are propane. For light, you bring your own lanterns. Beds are provided for six people; if your group is larger, some people will have to sleep on the floor (or they can bring tents for outside).

The cabin is set at 6,000 feet in elevation in a small patch of national monument land surrounded by Mountain Home State Forest. The state forest is home to impressive stands of Giant Sequoias, including the odd Hercules Tree, which had a large room cut into its base in 1897. The guard station cabin is only four miles from two lovely waterfalls and swimming holes in the state forest—Hidden Falls and Galena Creek Falls—and two miles from the Adam and Eve Loop Trail. (Adam is a Giant Sequoia that is 27 feet in diameter and 240 feet tall.) The loveliest path for Sequoia viewing is the two-mile stretch of Moses Gulch Trail that runs between Shake and Moses Gulch Campgrounds.

Those eager to fish can find native rainbow, brown, and brook trout in the many miles of the north fork of the middle fork of the Tule River and its tributary streams. The state forest also has three ponds that are stocked with rainbow trout. Guide service and rental horses are at a pack station near Shake Camp.

One more note: If the Mountain Home Guard Station is booked for the nights you want, try renting one of the other guard stations in the Tule River Ranger District—Poso Station or Frog Meadow. Poso Station even comes with electricity—what luxury!

Facilities
There is one cabin that has beds for six people; up to 10 people are permitted. It has a fully equipped kitchen. There is no electricity, but propane heating is available. Linens and towels are not provided.

Reservations and Rates
Reservations are required; it is recommended to phone at least six months in advance. The fee is $75 per night. The cabin is open from May 15 to November 15. Pets are permitted. Contact Tule River Ranger District, Sequoia National Forest/Giant Sequoia National Monument, 32588 Highway 190, Springville, CA 93265, 559/539-2607, website: www.fs.fed.us/r5/sequoia.

Directions
From Porterville, drive east on Highway 190 for 18 miles to Springville. At Springville, turn left (north) on Balch Park Road/Road 239 and drive 3.5 miles, then turn right on Bear Creek Road/Road 220. Drive 14 miles to Mountain Home State Forest Headquarters, then continue beyond it for 2.5 miles to a T-junction. Turn left; the guard station is a half mile farther.

33 CAMP NELSON CABINS
off Highway 190 near Camp Nelson

Luxury rating: ★★★★☆　　　　　**Recreation rating: ★★★☆☆**

If you've never been here, it's hard to imagine how beautiful southern Tulare County is. I don't mean the section you see while driving Highway 99 around Visalia; I mean the landscape to the east, where the elevation rises, the temperature drops, and the Sequoias grow to enormous proportions.

Accessing the area takes some effort; the main road is the winding Highway 190 out of Porterville and Springville. The better the scenery gets, the more twisty the road becomes, so prepare to drive slow and take your Dramamine. Your destination is the town of Camp Nelson, at 5,000 feet in elevation, where a company called Mountain Real Estate will rent you a vacation cabin.

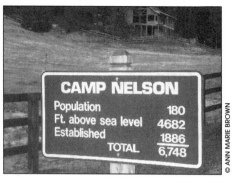

Each of Mountain Real Estate's cabins is someone's private home—vacation retreats that don't get used by their owners. The cabins vary in size and amenities, but all have fully equipped kitchens, plus fireplaces or wood-burning stoves. Many have laundry facilities, televisions, and VCRs. All you need to pack are sheets, pillowcases, and towels, plus your clothes and groceries (don't forget soap, toilet paper, and trash bags).

With Camp Nelson as your base, your nearby outdoor options include the Golden Trout Wilderness to the north and a multitude of trails to the south along Highway 190. One of the best trails leads to the Needles Lookout. Via an easy 2.5-mile walk, you reach a fire tower perched precariously on a granite spire, from which you have expansive views of the Kern River Basin, Lloyd Meadow, and the Golden Trout Wilderness.

Closer to home, be sure to pay a visit to the Amos Alonzo Stagg Tree, the sixth-largest Giant Sequoia in the world, at 243 feet tall and 29 feet in diameter. The tree is reached by a short walk from the parking area at Alder Drive in Camp Nelson. (Alder Drive is best accessed via Redwood Drive, 2.5 miles east of Camp Nelson on Highway 190.)

As if there wasn't enough to do in Giant Sequoia National Monument, another spectacular chunk of public land is nearby: Mountain Home Demonstration State Forest and Balch County Park. Expect to find Giant Sequoias, clean mountain air, and crystal clear streams.

Facilities

There are 12 cabins ranging in size from one to three bedrooms, all with kitchen facilities. Linens and towels are not provided.

Reservations and Rates

Reservations are required. Fees are $85–150 per night for four people, plus $5 for each additional person. There is a two-night minimum on weekends and holidays. Pets are permitted in some cabins with prior approval. Contact Mountain Real Estate, P.O. Box 95, Camp Nelson, CA 93208, 559/542-2822, website: www.slatemtn.com.

Directions

From Porterville, drive east on Highway 190 for 34 miles to Camp Nelson and the Pierpoint Springs Resort, on the right. Mountain Real Estate is located adjacent to Pierpoint Springs Resort; they will give you your keys and directions to your cabin.

34 GOLDEN TROUT WILDERNESS PACK TRAINS CABINS
off Highway 190 near Quaking Aspen

Luxury rating: ★ ★ ☆ ☆ ☆   **Recreation rating:** ★ ★ ★ ★ ☆

Rank: Best for Horseback Riding

If you like being around horses, you're going to like staying in the rustic cabins at Golden Trout Wilderness Pack Trains. Run by Dan Shew and his family since 1979, the cabins are a small part of Shew's much larger horse pack trip business. Some vacationers reserve the cabins the night before an early-morning start on a long horse trip into the Golden Trout Wilderness, while others come to stay for a few days and take shorter half- or full-day rides.

One thing is certain: If you aren't comfortable with the close proximity of dozens of horses, you won't be happy here. The cabins are within a stone's throw of the corral, so be prepared for plenty of equine sounds and

smells. It's part of the package.

Don't expect luxury, either. The cabins are basic, one-room jobs with no electricity. They do have private bathrooms and showers, which is fortunate, because you get awfully dusty riding horses all day. The cabins don't have kitchens; you take your meals at the main lodge, where the Shew family lives. (The nearest restaurant or store is 10 miles away, in Ponderosa.) You'll eat with the Shews and the ranch crew, which turns your vacation into an authentic Western ranch experience. Dan's wife, Kelly, does most of the cooking.

Visitors who choose to go on half- or full-day horseback rides will be taken to waterslides, swimming holes, secret trout-fishing spots, and Giant Sequoia groves. A popular destination is the summit of 9,100-foot Jordan Peak. Multiday pack trips usually center on fly-fishing in summer and deer hunting in autumn, but you and your family or friends can design any kind of trip you want. The Shews are happy to oblige.

If you want to bring your own horse with you, corrals are available for boarding. The pack station provides the water and hay. You and your trusty steed can spend the day loping around the wilderness and have a hot meal and a shower (for you, not your horse) waiting in the evening.

Facilities
There are four one-room cabins that can accommodate up to four people. The cabins have no kitchens or electricity. Meals are available at the main lodge. Linens and towels are provided.

Reservations and Rates
Reservations are recommended. Fees are $60 per night (meals not included). The resort is open from late May to late October. Pets are not permitted. Contact Golden Trout Wilderness Pack Trains, P.O. Box 756, Springville, CA 93265, 559/542-2816 (summer) and 559/539-2744 (winter), website: www.goldentroutpacktrains.com.

Directions
From Porterville, drive east on Highway 190 for 44 miles, past Camp Nelson, to Quaking Aspen. Just before the turnoff for Quaking Aspen Campground, turn left on Forest Service Road 21S50 and drive 7.5 miles to Golden Trout Wilderness Pack Trains.

35 MOUNTAIN TOP BED AND BREAKFAST
off Highway 190 near Quaking Aspen

Luxury rating: ★ ★ ★ ☆ ☆   **Recreation rating:** ★ ★ ★ ☆ ☆

Ponderosa is a small mountain community in Giant Sequoia National Monument, north of Kernville and south of Sequoia National Park and the Golden Trout Wilderness. Situated at 7,200 feet in elevation, Ponderosa is a

Nobe Young Falls near Mountain Top Bed and Breakfast

© ANN MARIE BROWN

blink-and-you'll-miss-it town. Its main enterprise is a café and saloon called Ponderosa Lodge.

Just down the road from the lodge is a place you can call your own for a few nights or a week. It's a mountain cabin that is rented out as part of a bed-and-breakfast business. Perfect for a family and longer stays, Mountain Pine Cabin has two stories; the 1st floor is a large studio area with full kitchen, living room, potbelly stove, and bathroom. Upstairs in the loft area is an open double bedroom (overlooking the downstairs) and an enclosed private bedroom. A barbecue and a picnic table are on the outside deck.

Although Mountain Pine Cabin is part of Mountain Top Bed and Breakfast, cabin guests don't receive a morning meal with the other bed-and-breakfast guests. Instead, you're on your own to cook in your cabin, or you can head to Ponderosa Lodge and order a plate of trout and eggs. So if you're set on the bed-and-breakfast experience, consider staying at the main house.

The cabin is for rent year-round. How you'll spend your time depends on what season it is. In winter, you can snowmobile, cross-country ski, or snowshoe. (Ponderosa Lodge rents equipment.) Once the snow is gone, you can fish in local streams, take a horseback ride at Golden Trout Wilderness Pack Station, go white-water rafting on the Kern River, or mountain bike on a labyrinth of Forest Service roads. Hikers should head to the spectacular grove of Sequoias on the Trail of 100 Giants. Other excellent trails include the hike to the peak of 9,300-foot Slate Mountain, the short walk to the top of granite Dome Rock, or the steep trek to see 100-foot-high Nobe Young Falls. If visiting fire lookout towers interests you, two of the finest are nearby: Jordan Peak and the Needles Lookout.

Facilities

There is one large two-bedroom cabin that can accommodate up to seven people, plus two guest rooms. The cabin has a fully equipped kitchen. A small general store and restaurant are nearby. Linens and towels are provided.

Reservations and Rates

Reservations are required. Fees are $110 per night for four people; each additional person is $10 per night. The resort is open year-round. Pets are not permitted. Contact Mountain Top Bed and Breakfast, 56816 Aspen Drive, Springville, CA 93265, 559/542-2639 or 888/867-4784, website: www.mountaintopbnb.com.

Directions

From Porterville, drive east on Highway 190 for 46 miles, past Camp Nelson and Quaking Aspen Campground, to Ponderosa (two miles beyond Quaking Aspen). Turn left at Aspen Drive (by the Ponderosa Lodge); Mountain Top is a quarter mile farther on the left.

36 WHISPERING PINES LODGE
off Sierra Way near Kernville

Luxury rating: ★ ★ ★ ★ ☆   **Recreation rating:** ★ ★ ★ ★ ☆

If the name Whispering Pines doesn't make you want to jump out of your chair and drive to Kernville right away, try this phrase: bed-and-breakfast cottages and bungalows on the Kern River.

That's the Wild and Scenic Kern River, of course, a celebrated favorite of rafters, anglers, and swimmers alike. A vacation cottage along its banks is the best way to take advantage of the Kern's many offerings.

Each of the four cottages at Whispering Pines has a river view, fireplace, king bed, full kitchen, and gas barbecue. Everything is beautifully decorated; they've spared no expense on draperies, furniture, and fabrics. Motel-style rooms are also available.

Breakfast is included in the price of your cottage, and it's more than your basic Danish and orange juice. Guests head to the dining room each morning for gourmet coffee, homemade breads and muffins, quiches, and fresh fruits. The owners go to great lengths to make things nice; they even hand out the local newspaper.

© ANN MARIE BROWN

If you want to swim or fish, all you need to do is walk 100 feet from your cottage down to the river. Bring your fly-fishing gear. For more water activities, take a drive to nearby Lake Isabella, one of the largest bodies of water in Southern California, with a capacity of 11,000 surface acres of water. (The average for the year is usually 8,000 surface acres.) It is an excellent lake for windsurfing, kayaking, and waterskiing; bass fishing is also popular. Trout fishers usually stick to the Kern River, although the Department of Fish and Game plants some rainbows in Isabella.

For hikers and mountain bikers, the Cannell Meadow National Recreation Trail begins less than a mile from Whispering Pines; it is a nine-mile trail that leads from the foothills, at 2,800 feet in elevation, to Cannell Meadow, at 7,500 feet. In spring, the lower stretches of this trail are lovely; in summer, you'll want to start at the upper end, or you'll bake in the heat.

A short drive to Wofford Heights and then up Highway 155 takes you into the richly forested Greenhorn Mountains. The area offers myriad hiking trails in summer and cross-country skiing trails in winter. Hikers shouldn't miss two easy, lovely trails: Unal Trail and Sunday Peak Trail. In the winter, cross-country skiers can glide to their hearts' content at Shirley Meadows Ski Area.

Facilities
There are four one-bedroom, duplex-style cottages with fully equipped kitchens. Motel rooms are also available. Linens and towels are provided.

Reservations and Rates
Reservations are recommended. Fees are $149–299 per night for two people, including breakfast. Each additional person is $20 per night. Pets are not permitted. Contact Whispering Pines Lodge, 13745 Sierra Way, Kernville, CA 93238, 760/376-3733 or 877/241-4100, website: www.kernvalley.com/inns.

Directions
From Kernville, drive north on Sierra Way/Road 99 for one mile to Whispering Pines Lodge on the left.

Other Cabins and Cottages Nearby
Chuck Richard's Falling Waters River Resort, 15729 Sierra Way, Kernville, CA 93238, 760/376-2242 or 888/376-2242, website: www.chuck-richards.com.

37 SIERRA GATEWAY COTTAGES
off Sierra Way in Kernville

Luxury rating: ★ ★ ★ ★ ☆   **Recreation rating: ★ ★ ★ ★ ☆**

© ANN MARIE BROWN

Considering that Kernville, the Kern River, and Lake Isabella are premier Southern California recreation destinations, you'd think the region would be loaded with cabin resorts. Instead, it's loaded with pedestrian-looking motels.

That's what makes Sierra Gateway Cottages special. These three newly remodeled one- and two-bedroom cottages are the real thing—not duplexes or motel units—with queen beds, full kitchens, fireplaces, patios, and gas barbecues. They're everything you need for a vacation in any season in the Kern River Valley.

Their location isn't perfect—they're set along the highway, not the Kern River. But you can walk to the river and also to the restaurants and shops of downtown Kernville. The cottages are set up on a hill next door to James Store, a busy, full-service grocery, tackle, and sporting goods store. Given all the activity around here, the cottages are surprisingly quiet, both inside and outside on their small landscaped patios.

Recreation options in the Kernville area are unlimited. In spring, rafting and kayaking trips are offered on the Upper Kern for every level of ability. Numerous local companies can get you set up with the kind of trip and equipment you want. Lake Isabella, which boasts sailing, boating, windsurfing, and fishing opportunities, is only a five-minute drive away. Fishing on the Kern River is only one minute away.

Hikers can explore the trails to the immediate north on Sierra Way, or, when the summer temperature heats up, drive 20 miles north to the turnoff for Sherman Pass Road. Following Sherman Pass to Big Meadow and Horse Meadow, you can choose from many cool-air, high-country trails, including Sherman Peak Trail, Salmon Creek Trail, and Manter Meadow Loop.

Mountain bikers take their pick from beginner rides like the Greenhorn Summit Loop and Forest 90 Fire Road, or advanced single-track trails like the Whiskey Flat and Wall Street rides. Check out the Forest Service visitors center in Kernville for bike trail maps and details.

Last but not least, don't forget winter recreation in the area. Shirley Meadows ski resort is less than a half hour away, with two double chairlifts, a family-oriented ski school, and a rental program. Both skiers and snowboarders are welcome. Near Shirley Meadows are several excellent cross-country ski and snowshoe trails.

Facilities

There are three one- and two-bedroom cottages, all with fully equipped kitchens. Stores and restaurants are nearby. Linens and towels are provided.

Reservations and Rates

Reservations are recommended. Fees are $125–145 per night. A two-night minimum is required. Weekly rates are discounted. The resort is open year-round. Pets are not permitted. Contact Sierra Gateway Cottages, 13432 Sierra Way, Kernville, CA 93238, 760/376-2533 or 800/888-8194, website: www.sierragatewaycottages.com.

Directions

From Kernville, drive north on Sierra Way/Road 99 for a quarter mile to Sierra Gateway Cottages, on the left.

38 OAK FLAT LOOKOUT TOWER
off Highway 178 near Bakersfield

Luxury rating: ★ ★ ☆ ☆ ☆   **Recreation rating:** ★ ★ ★ ☆ ☆
Rank: Most Unusual

Have you ever visited a fire lookout tower, perched high on a mountaintop amid miles of forested wild country? Have you ever stood at the lookout and gazed at the 360-degree panorama, dreaming of working as a fire scout and living alone in your mountain tower with only scenery, silence, and solitude?

If the answer is yes—or if it's no, but you've always wanted to—I know the perfect place for you to spend the night. It's the Oak Flat Lookout Tower in the Greenhorn Mountains near Bakersfield. Situated at 4,910 feet in elevation, the lookout was built in 1934 and used to detect fires until 1984.

This is how to book a stay. First, phone the Greenhorn Ranger District of Sequoia National Forest to make a reservation. Summer weekends can

© ANN MARIE BROWN

be tough; weeknights are easy. You'll fill out some paperwork and mail in a check for $35 per night, which goes directly to maintaining the lookout tower.

Next, start packing. Remember to pack light because everything must be hauled up to the tower, which means climbing 40 narrow, steep stairs or using a manual basket pulley system. (Acrophobes won't be happy here; the stairs can be daunting.) The heaviest thing you carry should be bottled water; none is at the tower.

Pack your sleeping bag and favorite pillow. (Two small beds are inside.) Flashlights and candles are a good idea, plus plenty of matches for lighting the propane appliances, which include an overhead light, heater, and stove. Bring an ice chest if you want to keep food or drinks cool (there's no refrigerator), and firewood if you want to have a campfire outside. Most important of all, take along plenty of trash bags for hauling out your garbage at the end of your stay.

Got your warm clothes for windy nights? Shorts and T-shirts for hot summer days? Hiking boots? Plenty of good food, plus cooking and eating utensils? Toilet paper for the outhouse? Okay, you're ready. The rangers at the Greenhorn District will give you a combination for the locks on the lookout road gate and tower. In winter, snow, rain, or ice can make the road impassable except for four-wheel-drive vehicles, but most of the year a passenger car is fine. Remember that you are 15 miles from the nearest pay phone or services, so if you have a need to stay in touch with the outside world, bring along a cell phone.

Passing the time on your visit is easy: Just sit and admire the view of the Kern River Valley. If you need some exercise, the Badger Gap Trail begins at the tower and heads downhill through sagebrush and oaks. It's a full 10 miles to its junction with Kern River Trail near Highway 178.

Facilities

The lookout tower can accommodate up to four people. Propane cooking and heating facilities are provided. There is no drinking water. Linens and towels are not provided.

Reservations and Rates

Reservations and a permit are required. The fee is $35 per night. Young children are not advised. Pets are permitted. Contact Greenhorn Ranger District, Sequoia National Forest, 4875 Ponderosa Drive, P.O. Box 3810, Lake Isabella, CA 93240, 760/379-5646, website: www.fs.fed.us/r5/sequoia.

Directions

From Bakersfield, drive east on Highway 178 for 12 miles to Rancheria Road. Drive 15 miles north on Rancheria Road (the pavement turns to dirt and gravel) to Forest Service Road 27S20. Turn right and drive a half mile (stay right at the fork) to the locked gate; open it and then continue the last quarter mile to the lookout.

39 RANKIN RANCH

off Highway 58 near Caliente

Luxury rating: ★ ★ ★ ★ ☆   **Recreation rating:** ★ ★ ★ ★ ☆

Rank: Best for Families, Best for Horseback Riding

Rankin Ranch is a taste of old California—the era of cowboys, cattle ranching, hay rides, and horseshoes. It is situated at 3,500 feet in elevation in Walker Basin, roughly midway between Bakersfield and Tehachapi. The land surrounding the ranch is a classic high mountain valley, with a mix of wide open meadows and forest. If you think this sounds like a good place to saddle up and ride into the sunset, you're right.

A man named Walker Rankin founded the original cattle ranch here in 1863, and the place has stayed in the family ever since. It is one of the oldest and largest family-owned ranches in California. Rankin family members still live on the 31,000 acres and raise Herefords.

The Rankins have also used their land to build a successful guest ranch business. For nearly 40 years, vacationers have come to Rankin Ranch to ride horses, fish, hike, and live the ranch life for a few days. It's especially popular with families; a long schedule of children's activities takes place daily.

The best season to visit may be spring, when Rankin Ranch offers its lowest rates of the year and the wildflowers bloom in Walker Basin. From late March to May, the mountain slopes and high meadows come alive with color. It's a sight to behold.

The ranch has seven duplex-style cabins that are on the modern side, with carpeting and wood paneling. Families rent both sides of the duplex and open the adjoining doors. (Couples will end up with half a duplex.) The fee for a night at the ranch includes three big meals in the dining room and all the horseback riding you can stand, plus a wide range of other activities: trout fishing in little Julia Lake, horseshoe tournaments, bingo, tennis, swimming, volleyball, hay rides, and so on. You pay noth-

A few of the residents at Rankin Ranch

ing extra for anything, including the organized children's programs, so you know in advance exactly what your vacation will cost.

Even if you've never been on a horse before, you'll have a good time at Rankin Ranch. Free riding instruction is provided, and each horse is carefully selected for each rider's abilities. Before long, even novices are riding out of the corral to check on the cattle or help bale the hay.

Facilities
There are seven cabins that can accommodate a total of 30 to 45 people; none have kitchen facilities. Meals are provided. Linens and towels are provided.

Reservations and Rates
Reservations are required. Fees are $155–190 per adult per night and include three full meals a day, horseback riding privileges, and all activities. Children under 12 stay for reduced rates. Discounts are available in April, May, and September. The ranch is open from April to September. Pets are not permitted. Contact Rankin Ranch, P.O. Box 36-HP, Caliente, CA 93518, 661/867-2511, website: www.rankinranch.com.

Directions
From I-5 just south of the I-5/Highway 99 split, take the Lake Isabella/Lamont/Arvin exit. Drive 15 miles north on Wheeler Ridge Road, then turn right (east) on Highway 223 (Bear Mountain Boulevard) and drive 16 miles. At the Highway 223 junction with Highway 58, drive east on Highway 58 for one mile and take the Caliente cutoff. Drive through Caliente and continue 2.5 miles until the road forks. Take the unsigned left fork up the hill; it's nine miles to Rankin Ranch from the fork.

Chapter 7

© ANN MARIE BROWN

Death Valley
and the Deserts

Death Valley
and the Deserts

The Death Valley and the Deserts region encompasses three of California's most spectacular national parks: Death Valley, Joshua Tree, and Mojave, plus the world famous oasis of Palm Springs and surrounding palm-lined villages of Desert Hot Springs and Twentynine Palms.

Although Death Valley, Joshua Tree, and Mojave are all considered desert parks, each is distinctly different. Death Valley is the largest U.S. national park outside of Alaska. Although its name is foreboding, the park comprises a vast landscape of desert beauty, from soaring sand dunes and mountain ranges to below-sea-level salt flats. In summer, the park is the hottest place in North America—greater than 120°F is common—but in winter, temperatures are cool and mild.

Death Valley is home to the lowest point in elevation in the Western Hemisphere: Badwater, at 282 feet below sea level. In stark contrast, it's also home to Telescope Peak, elevation 11,048 feet, which is snow-covered six months of the year.

You must plan ahead before making a trip to Death Valley. Accommodations, services, and towns are few and far between. Only three lodgings are available within the massive park's borders, and of those, only Furnace Creek Ranch has cabins.

In contrast to Death Valley's remoteness, Joshua Tree National Park is surrounded by small cities that offer a variety of lodging choices, including historic adobe bungalows at 29 Palms Inn and a stately stone mansion with cottages at Roughley Manor. One of the West's most unusual towns is found near Joshua Tree—Pioneertown, built in the early 1940s as a permanent Western "stage" for filming movies. A stay at Rimrock Ranch Cabins will give you the chance to explore this real but unreal Western town.

Once you're in the park, civilization is left behind. Joshua Tree is best known for its wide desert plains covered with strange-looking Joshua trees, amazing rock formations and boulder piles, rugged mountains, and gold mining ruins. The park is situated where the high Mojave Desert meets the low Colorado Desert, producing a wide variety of desert flora. Because much of the park is higher than 4,000 feet in elevation, the hiking and recreating season is somewhat longer than at Death Valley. Still, the most comfortable weather usually occurs from October to May; summer temperatures frequently soar past 100°.

Only 50 miles to the north, Mojave National Preserve is where the Mojave, Great Basin, and Sonoran Deserts join. As a result of this convergence, Mojave contains a wide diversity of plant and animal life, as well as interesting geological features. These include Cima Dome—a granite batholith covered with a dense forest of Joshua trees—and the volcanic-rock cliffs of Hole-in-the-Wall. The 500-foot-tall Kelso Dunes, the second highest in California after Death Valley's Eureka Dunes, are another of the preserve's attractions.

Like Joshua Tree, Mojave National Preserve is mostly high-desert terrain, with elevations ranging from 2,000 to 5,000 feet. Although summers can be hot, December to February is frequently windy and cold; higher elevations of the park are sometimes dusted in snow. There are no services to be found anywhere in the park; the closest cabins or cottages are in Randsburg at the historic Cottage Hotel.

Last but not least, the Death Valley and Deserts region includes the desert's most famous city, Palm Springs. This oasis was originally the home of the Agua Caliente band of the Cahuilla Indians, who still own major portions of the town's land. Not unlike today's Palm Springs visitors, the Agua Caliente worshipped the pure water flowing down the desert canyons, the natural hot springs, and the wind-sheltering curve of the San Jacinto Mountains.

Incorporated as a city in 1938, Palm Springs gained (and has never lost) an aura of glamour as a favorite retreat of movie stars and international celebrities. So many luminaries—from Ginger Rogers to Dinah Shore—made the desert their home that it is impossible to name them all. The stylish red-tile roofs and sparkling swimming pools of Palm Springs' cottage resorts reflect the glittering history of the area.

DEATH VALLEY AND THE DESERTS

NEVADA

Tonopah

Bishop

Death

Dry Mountain 8,726ft

Ubehebe Crater

Valley

Stovepipe Wells

Lone Pine

Funeral Mtns

1

National

Badwater -282ft

Telescope Peak 11,049ft

Park

Shoshone

Lake Mead

Coso Range

Argus Range

Quail Mtns

Kingston Range

see
Sequoia
and Kings
Canyon
page 246

Randsburg

2

Goldstone Dry Lake

Baker

Mojave

National

Preserve

Mojave

Barstow

Cady Mtns

Needles

Colorado River

Bullion Mtns

Amboy Crater

Old Woman Mtns

Twentynine Palms

3

4-5

Pinto Mtns

LOS ANGELES

see
Los Angeles
and Vicinity
page 78

Joshua

Tree

Palm Springs

6

7-9

National

Park

Long Beach

Blythe

ARIZONA

Santa Catalina Island

Salton Sea

Chocolate Mtns

San Clemente Island

see
San Diego
and Vicinity
page 132

El Centro

Yuma

PACIFIC OCEAN

0   20 mi

0   20 km

SAN DIEGO

Tijuana

M E X I C O

© AVALON TRAVEL PUBLISHING, INC.

Contents

1. Furnace Creek Ranch 320
2. The Cottage Hotel. 321
3. Rimrock Ranch Cabins. 323
4. 29 Palms Inn 324
5. Roughley Manor Inn 326
6. Two Bunch Palms 328
7. Korakia Pensione. 329
8. Casa Cody Country Inn 331
9. Orchid Tree Inn 332

1 FURNACE CREEK RANCH
off Highway 190 in Death Valley

Luxury rating: ★ ★ ★ ☆ ☆   **Recreation rating:** ★ ★ ★ ★ ☆

Don't confuse Death Valley's Furnace Creek Ranch with Death Valley's Furnace Creek Inn. The inn is everything the ranch is not. The inn stands for elegance; the ranch stands for economy. The inn defines service; the ranch defines serviceable.

But if you're on a budget and want to avoid staying in a cheap motel in Pahrump, Nevada, the cabins at Furnace Creek Ranch will serve you well. Located just one mile from the park's Furnace Creek Visitor Center, the ranch's cabins are perfectly situated for exploring Death Valley.

Furnace Creek Ranch is an entire little town, much like Curry Village in Yosemite National Park. Once the crew quarters for the Borax Mining Company, today Furnace Creek Ranch has a post office, a general store, three restaurants, a motel and cabins, a golf course, horseback riding facilities, a saloon, and the Borax Museum. The ranch's claim to fame, besides its Borax mining history, is that it has the world's lowest golf course, at 214 feet below sea level. How's that for a novelty?

The cabins are side-by-side duplexes and are fairly modern and pedestrian in appearance but adequate. They have telephones and televisions complete with pay-per-view movies and Nintendo; this contributes to their motellike ambience. Still, the cabins are quiet and peaceful, considering their density. Because they do not have kitchens, guests eat at the ranch café or neighboring steakhouse. Both seem overpriced, but the food is adequate.

It matters little if the cabins don't bowl you over, because you won't do much besides sleep and shower in them. There is a ton of exploring to do in

Death Valley, and because its landscape is so vast, you spend a lot of time just driving from place to place. One excellent day trip is to head north to Scotty's Castle (60 miles) to tour a fascinating 1930s desert mansion. Afterward, drive a few miles farther to Ubehebe Crater, then either hike down into its depths or follow its rim trail to two smaller volcanic craters.

Golden Canyon in Death Valley State Park

The ambitious can drive another 40 miles west to see Eureka Sand Dunes, the tallest sand dunes in California, at 680 feet. The drive is hell—a bumpy dirt road all the way—but the sand dunes are fabulous. Another day can be spent closer to the Furnace Creek area, hiking trails in Golden Canyon, Mosaic Canyon, the Keane Wonder Mine, and Salt Creek. Yet another day can be spent driving south in the park to visit Badwater, Wildrose Peak, and the Charcoal Kilns. Like I said, there's a lot to do.

Facilities
There are 24 duplex cabins that can accommodate up to four people, plus numerous motel rooms. None of the accommodations have kitchens. Several restaurants and stores are on-site. Linens and towels are provided.

Reservations and Rates
Reservations are recommended. The fee is $128 per night. Pets are not permitted.

Directions
From Barstow, drive east on I-15 for 60 miles to Baker and Highway 127. Turn north on Highway 127 and drive 80 miles to Death Valley Junction. Turn west (left) on Highway 190 and drive 30 miles, past the Furnace Creek Inn, to Furnace Creek Ranch on the left.

From U.S. 395 at Olancha, take Highway 190 east for 80 miles, past Stovepipe Wells Village. Turn right and drive 14 miles to Furnace Creek Ranch. Contact Furnace Creek Ranch, P.O. Box 1, Death Valley, CA 92328, 760/786-2345 or 888/297-2757, website: www.furnacecreekresort.com.

Other Cabins and Cottages Nearby
Delight's Hot Springs Resort, P.O. Box 368, Tecopa, CA 92389, 760/852-4343 or 800/854-5007.

2 THE COTTAGE HOTEL
off U.S. 395 in Randsburg

Luxury rating: ★ ★ ★ ☆ ☆   **Recreation rating:** ★ ★ ★ ☆ ☆

Do you feel like getting away? Far, far away, where nobody would ever think to look for you? The Cottage Hotel in Randsburg might be the place. The town, population 80, calls itself a living ghost town. It's south

© ANN MARIE BROWN

Exploring Owl Canyon below Velvet Peak

of Ridgecrest, northwest of Barstow, and northeast of Mojave. If you're getting a mental picture of dried-out cow skulls and vultures circling overhead, you're pretty close.

Even so, the Cottage Hotel at Randsburg is a wonderful place. A centerpiece of this historic gold-mining town, the Cottage Hotel was completely rebuilt and reopened in 1994. In its previous lives, it survived three fires, several flu epidemics, and a bevy of rough-and-tumble customers. Highlighted by cactus gardens and vintage oddities like an antique switchboard, the hotel displays photo albums and historic papers documenting the area's past.

The Cottage Hotel has only one cottage, plus four bed-and-breakfast rooms decorated in Gold Rush–era style. Located next door to the hotel, the cottage is just large enough for a couple or small family, with one bedroom, one bath, a living room, a kitchen, and a barbecue deck.

In addition to relaxing in the serenity of this way-out-there location in the Mojave Desert, you'll probably want to do some exploring. Several ghost towns are nearby: Garlock, Balarat, Skidoo, and Cerro Gordo. A few miles to the south and east is the Rainbow Basin Natural Area, run by the Bureau of Land Management (BLM). Take a driving tour through its colorful desert canyons, or park at Owl Canyon Campground and hike to the base of Velvet Peak.

Or drive northeast to Trona Pinnacles Natural Landmark and walk around its more than 500 giant tufa spires, which poke upward from the earth as high as 140 feet. It's one of the strangest landscapes in California. For more desert exploring, Red Rock Canyon State Park is nearby, as is the Desert Tortoise Natural Area. For the best chance of seeing a tortoise, show up in spring, when the elusive creatures leave their burrows to munch on wildflowers.

Facilities

There is one cottage that can accommodate up to four people. It has a fully equipped kitchen. A general store and restaurant are on-site. Linens and towels are provided.

Reservations and Rates

Reservations are recommended. Fees are $95 for two people, plus $10 for each additional person. Pets are not permitted. Contact The Cottage Hotel, 130 Butte Avenue, Randsburg, CA 93554, 760/374-2285 or 888/268-4622, website: www.randsburg.com.

Directions

From Kramer Junction at U.S. 395 and Highway 58, drive north on U.S. 395 for 26 miles to Johannesburg. Turn left and drive one mile to Randsburg and the Cottage Hotel.

3 RIMROCK RANCH CABINS
off Highway 62 in Pioneertown

Luxury rating: ★ ★ ★ ☆ ☆   **Recreation rating:** ★ ★ ★ ☆ ☆

The name Pioneertown sounds like a section of Disneyland, not a real town. But Pioneertown is real, and it's found north of Joshua Tree National Park near Desert Hot Springs and Yucca Valley.

Pioneertown not only sounds like Disneyland, it looks like Disneyland. The town was constructed by Gene Autry and Roy Rogers in the early 1940s as a permanent Western "stage" for filming movies (and later television serials). Classics such as *The Shootout, Cisco Kid,* and *Annie Oakley* were made in Pioneertown; the OK Corral is here too.

Today, the railroad-tie and adobe structures are inhabited by real people who own and operate a post office, bowling alley, motel, and the honky-tonk Pioneer Palace, where a four-generation family serves up good food, live music, and Western entertainment. Gunfights are staged on Mane Street (not Main Street) every Sunday afternoon.

If you want to see this surreal Old West town, your best bet is to book a stay at Rimrock Ranch. The ranch was built in 1947 as the first homestead in the Rimrock high-desert area. Set at 4,500 feet in elevation, it's just at the start of the snow line, so the temperature is 15–20°F cooler than in nearby Joshua Tree. This makes Rimrock ideal for summer visits to the park. You can spend all day hiking or rock climbing in the desert heat, then retreat to the cool tranquility of your mountain cabin.

The ranch has four barn-red cabins with green roofs, each furnished with antiques and Western-style decor (no surprises here). If you like knotty pine interiors, you'll like this place. Most everything is vintage, except that the largest cabin has an espresso machine in addition to its Wedgewood stove. Every cabin has a fully equipped kitchen and private patio with outdoor fireplace. You'll bathe in, and drink, natural mineral water from the ranch's well. A hot tub and hand-built barbecue pit are shared among the cabin guests, as are a large stargazing observation deck and swimming pool.

Rimrock Ranch borders on Pipes Canyon Wilderness Preserve, where you can take advantage of hiking, biking, and rock climbing opportunities. The myriad trails of Joshua Tree are only a short drive away. In addition, Big Morongo Canyon Preserve is easily accessible off Highway 62; more than 235 bird species have been identified at the preserve.

Facilities
There are four cabins that can accommodate up to four people. All have fully equipped kitchens. Linens and towels are provided.

Reservations and Rates
Reservations are required. Fees are $103–157 per night for two people, plus $25 for each additional person (up to four). Summer rates are discounted. Pets are permitted with a $10 fee and a $25 deposit. Contact Rimrock Ranch Cabins, P.O. Box 313, Pioneertown, CA 92268, 760/228-1297, website: www.rimrockranchcabins.com.

Directions
From Banning on I-10, drive east for 17 miles to the Highway 62 exit. Turn northeast on Highway 62 and drive 25 miles to Yucca Valley. Turn left (north) on Pioneertown Road and drive five miles to Pioneertown. Continue through town for four more miles (stay on the paved road) to Rimrock Ranch Cabins, on the left.

4 29 PALMS INN
off Highway 62 in Twentynine Palms

Luxury rating: ★ ★ ★ ★ ☆   **Recreation rating:** ★ ★ ★ ★ ☆

Rank: Best in the Desert

If you don't consider yourself to be an admirer of desert landscapes, a stay at 29 Palms Inn will convert you. Located just outside of the border of Joshua Tree National Park, 29 Palms is funky and charming and is the ideal base camp for enjoying the surrounding desert.

The inn has been around since 1928 and has been owned by the same family for five generations. It has 21 cabins, varying from adobe bungalows to old wood-frame buildings. Some of the cabins are duplexes, but they are private and quiet, with thick walls and fenced-in patios. Some units have fireplaces, some have woodstoves, and some don't have either, so be sure to ask for what you want. Only two buildings have kitchens; these are the three-bedroom Guest House and the one-bedroom Irene's Historic Adobe.

Joshua Trees near 29 Palms Inn

If you don't get a kitchen unit when you reserve, you won't be missing much. A complimentary continental breakfast is provided each morning. For lunch and dinner, you can eat at 29 Palms Inn's restaurant, which serves wonderful food in a friendly, casual atmosphere. The sourdough bread is to die for.

Other charms of 29 Palms Inn include a duck pond surrounded by pomegranate trees, an enclosed gazebo that shelters a large whirlpool tub, a big swimming pool, and a multitude of hand-carved signs scattered about the grounds bearing quirky messages. I won't give away what they say; you'll have to see for yourself.

When you're not in your 29 Palms cabin, you'll be out exploring Joshua Tree National Park. The best trails near the inn are those leading to Forty-nine Palms Oasis, Ryan Mountain, and Lost Horse Mine. If you have time, head to the Cottonwood Spring area in the south part of the park, where a terrific eight-mile round-trip trail leads to Lost Palms Oasis. If you don't want to hike that far, take the shorter left fork to Mastodon Peak and scramble to the top of its rocky pinnacle.

The main Joshua Tree visitors center is about two miles from 29 Palms Inn on Utah Trail Road. Rangers there can provide you with all the information you need for visiting the park.

Facilities

There are 21 cabins ranging in size from studios to three bedrooms. Two cabins have kitchens. A restaurant is on-site. Linens and towels are provided.

Reservations and Rates

Reservations are recommended. Fees are $95–295 per night. Discounted rates are offered from June 15 to September 15 and midweek year-round. Pets are permitted in some cabins for a $35 fee. Contact 29 Palms Inn, 73950 Inn Avenue, Twentynine Palms, CA 92277, 760/367-3505, website: www.29palmsinn.com.

Directions

From Banning on I-10, drive east for 17 miles to the Highway 62 exit. Turn northeast on Highway 62 and drive 45 miles to the town of Twentynine Palms. Continue east to the far end of town and National Park Drive (one block east of Adobe Road). Turn right on National Park Drive, drive a quarter mile, and turn right on Inn Avenue. You'll enter the grounds of 29 Palms Inn immediately.

5 ROUGHLEY MANOR INN
off Highway 62 in Twentynine Palms

Luxury rating: ★ ★ ★ ★ ★   **Recreation rating:** ★ ★ ★ ☆ ☆

When Bill and Elizabeth Campbell first settled in Twentynine Palms in 1928, they constructed a humble homestead from native materials. Not long thereafter, the Campbells inherited some big bucks, and they quickly decided it would be nicer to have a three-story stone manor house with leaded windows, five fireplaces, and Vermont maple floors. Who can blame them?

The Roughley Manor today is owned by Jan and Gary Peters, who have furnished the stately house with their antique collection. In addition to its nine guest rooms, the manor also has four cottages with private baths and kitchenettes. The buildings sit on 25 beautifully landscaped acres with a rose garden, palm and cypress trees, a hot tub under a gazebo, a five-tier fountain, and extensive stone walkways and patios. The overall effect is quite elegant.

Of the four cottages, Pinto and Sunrise are a duplex. Both have queen-size, four-poster beds and fireplaces. The separate Cottage has a sitting room, a bedroom with a queen bed, and an antique tub in the bathroom. Farmhouse has a breakfast bar that separates the living room from the kitchenette, and an antique four-poster bed.

Roughley Manor is operated as a bed-and-breakfast, and the morning

© ANN MARIE BROWN

Keys View, Joshua Tree National Park

meal is downright decadent. Jan Peters' twice-baked potatoes topped with eggs and bacon are legendary. Evening tea and dessert are served nightly at 6:30 p.m.

The manor is only a couple miles from the Oasis Visitor Center and the northern entrance to Joshua Tree National Park. If it's your first trip, be sure to drive to the overlook at Keys View, elevation 5,185 feet. On a clear day, the vista takes in Mount San Gorgonio, Mount San Jacinto, the Coachella Valley, and the Salton Sea. On a really clear day, Signal Mountain, in Mexico and more than 90 miles away, can be seen. Take the short walk from the overlook to the top of Inspiration Peak, just to the north of Keys View.

Many more hiking trails are found nearby, including the four-mile round-trip to Lost Horse Mine and its well-preserved gold stamp mill, and the three-mile round-trip to the summit of Ryan Mountain.

Facilities
There are four one-bedroom cottages, plus nine guest rooms. The cottages have kitchenettes (microwave and refrigerator). Linens and towels are provided.

Reservations and Rates
Reservations are recommended. Fees are $135–160 per night for two people; breakfast is included. Pets are not permitted. Contact Roughley Manor Inn, 74744 Joe Davis Road, Twentynine Palms, CA 92277, 760/367-3238, website: www.roughleymanor.com.

Directions
From Banning on I-10, drive east for 17 miles to the Highway 62 exit. Turn northeast on Highway 62 and drive 45 miles to the town of Twentynine Palms. Continue east to the far end of town and Utah Trail. Turn left (north) on Utah Trail and drive a half mile to Joe Davis Road. Turn right and drive a half mile to Roughley Manor, on the left.

6 TWO BUNCH PALMS
off I-10 in Desert Hot Springs

Luxury rating: ★ ★ ★ ★ ★   **Recreation rating:** ★ ★ ★ ☆ ☆

Rank: Most Luxurious, Best in the Desert

Two Bunch Palms is a 56-acre playground in the hot sun of Desert Hot Springs. Two Bunch Palms is a serious health spa, offering mud baths, massages, skin treatments, and the like. It's also a hot springs oasis, where water rushes out of the ground at more than 150° and flows into an assortment of beautiful rock pools. And even more, it's a country club with tennis and racquetball courts, artificially constructed lakes, lush landscaping, and a gourmet restaurant.

The variety of accommodations at Two Bunch Palms is as diverse as the resort itself. There are modern, spacious casitas and villas, luxury spa suites, older bungalows with Victorian antiques and Art Deco accessories, and even the House on the Hill—a very secluded two-bedroom house with dramatic desert and mountain views. Plus, there are smaller, less-expensive guest rooms.

Far and away the most interesting lodging is the Rock House. As the story goes, in 1928 the Miami police gave Al Capone 24 hours to get out of town. The increasingly paranoid Capone wanted a hideaway where any enemy could be spotted for miles around; he chose Two Bunch Palms. He built the first permanent structures at the oasis: an enclave of bungalows made of solid rock, complete with stained-glass windows and a sentry turret. He and his gangster buddies supposedly hid out at Two Bunch Palms until the early 1930s, and then one day, perhaps out of fear of being discovered, everyone just got up and walked away. Not long after, Capone was sentenced to federal prison in Georgia.

Capone's Rock House is in the heart of Two Bunch Palms, alongside its "grotto," where rock-lined mineral water pools are shaded by towering palm trees. The main activity at the resort is soaking in its many pools. Bicycles are available if you'd like to ride around the grounds, and walking and running trails crisscross the property.

Two Bunch Palms is not a budget-minded place, but it becomes substantially more affordable from June to September, and also in the first three weeks of December. The best rates are available in July and August; ask about their combined resort and spa packages, which include taxes and gratuities.

Facilities

There are 45 guest rooms, suites, villas, and bungalows, ranging in size from studios to three bedrooms. Some have fully equipped kitchens. A restaurant is on-site. Linens and towels are provided.

Reservations and Rates

Reservations are required. Fees are $355–675 per night for villas and $175–305 per night for guest rooms. Substantial discounts are available in summer. Children and youth under 18 are not permitted. Pets are not permitted. Contact Two Bunch Palms, 67425 Two Bunch Palms Trail, Desert Hot Springs, CA 92240, 760/329-8791 or 800/472-4334, website: www.twobunchpalms.com.

Directions

From I-10 in Banning, drive east for 23 miles and take the Palm Drive/Desert Hot Springs exit. Drive north on Palm Drive for five miles. Turn right (east) on Two Bunch Palms Trail and drive one mile to the gated entrance to Two Bunch Palms, on the right.

◼ KORAKIA PENSIONE
off Highway 111 in Palm Springs

Luxury rating: ★ ★ ★ ★ ☆   **Recreation rating:** ★ ★ ★ ☆ ☆

Korakia Pensione is Palm Springs at its most stylish. The bed-and-breakfast inn consists of two adjacent historic villas, each encompassing a passel of bungalows, guest houses, gardens, and pools. Its beautifully appointed accommodations have been written up in *Travel & Leisure, Condé Nast Traveler, Architectural Digest,* and the *New York Times.*

Korakia's freestanding bungalows are either in what is called the Mediterranean villa, across the street from the main inn, or the Moroccan villa. Both villas were built in the 1920s. Decorative details are perfect in every way: handmade feather beds, wood accents, antique furnishings, whitewashed walls, and stone and tile floors. My favorite units are the South Pool Bungalow, a one-bedroom with a Japanese stone bath, and the North Pool Bungalow, with eight glass doors opening out from its living room to the pool. The grounds of the villas consist of 1.5 acres of fruit trees, mosaic tile fountains, stone waterfalls, and bougainvillea.

For all this luxury, prices at Korakia are fairly reasonable. A gourmet

© ANN MARIE BROWN

continental breakfast is included in the price, and there are kitchens in most units.

It's unlikely, but if you are willing to drag yourself away from the sparkling swimming pools of this oasis, you can visit the nearby shops, restaurants, and attractions of Palm Springs. Most of the downtown is within walking distance.

A short drive will take you to newly opened Tahquitz Canyon. Named for an Agua Caliente shaman who abused his powers and was banished from his tribe, Tahquitz Canyon is a spectacular outdoor museum of desert flora and fauna. Entry is by guided hike only; preserve rangers lead groups on an easy, two-mile trek through the canyon to the base of its 65-foot waterfall. Tahquitz's other treasures include plentiful birdlife, Native American rock art, and lush stands of desert lavender, mesquite, and creosote.

If you seek a longer, more solitary desert adventure, head over to neighboring Murray Canyon, where you can hike unescorted. A delight for photographers, the colorful canyon is filled with nearly 1,000 leafy *Washingtonia* fan palms, 100-foot-high red-rock outcrops, a multitude of rotund barrel cactus, and a series of small waterfalls (called the Seven Sisters) at two miles out. Bighorn sheep are often spotted standing guard on the high canyon walls.

Facilities
There are 20 guest houses, bungalows, studios, and rooms, ranging in size from studios to two bedrooms. Most have fully equipped kitchens. Linens and towels are provided.

Reservations and Rates
Reservations are recommended. Fees are $129–395 per night and include a continental breakfast. Pets are not permitted. Contact Korakia Pensione, 257 South Patencio Road, Palm Springs, CA 92262, 760/864-6411, website: www.korakia.com.

Directions
From I-10 in Banning, drive east for 12 miles and take the Highway 111 exit for Palm Springs. Drive southeast for 10 miles; Highway 111 becomes Palm Canyon Drive. Turn right on Arenas Road, and head west four blocks. Turn left on Patencio Road; Korakia is on the left.

8 CASA CODY COUNTRY INN
off Highway 111 in Palm Springs

Luxury rating: ★ ★ ★ ★ ☆   **Recreation rating:** ★ ★ ★ ☆ ☆

Casa Cody, the oldest operating hotel in Palm Springs, is a wonderful historic hideaway. Although it is located in the midst of Palm Springs Village, Casa Cody offers far more seclusion than neighboring lodgings. Once you pass through its gates, you feel as if you've entered your own private desert compound.

The most impressive (and private) unit at Casa Cody is its 1910 two-bedroom adobe villa, where Charlie Chaplin once stayed. The villa has open-beamed ceilings, tile and wood floors, and extensive rock work in its kitchen and bath—counters, shower, and tub. It's tempting to move right in and never leave.

Even the smaller cottages have private patios, fireplaces, fully equipped kitchens, cable television, and private phones. Casa Cody's decor is Southwestern in style, bringing to mind the colorful resorts of Santa Fe. Its grounds are a mix of flowering vines and shrubs, and huge citrus and fig trees. In season, you can pick your own grapefruit. Two swimming pools and a hot tub are also on the property.

No trip to Palm Springs is complete without a ride on the world-famous Aerial Tramway, and no tram ride is complete without a hike at its high terminus. During the 15-minute, two-mile ride, you are whooshed from the Palm Springs' desert floor (at 2,643 feet in elevation) to Mount San Jacinto State Park (at 8,516 feet). Palm trees suddenly transform into conifers, and the air temperature drops 30°.

At the top, hiking opportunities abound. A good introductory hike is the four-mile round-trip to Round Valley. The trail meanders past huge granite boulders, old-growth white firs, and Jeffrey pines to a pretty alpine meadow. There's nothing quite like the experience of walking among desert cactus in the morning, then hiking among mountain conifers in the afternoon.

The ambitious can get an early start on long summer days and head for the summit of

© ANN MARIE BROWN

10,804-foot San Jacinto Peak, a 12-mile round-trip. Just be sure to make it back in time for the last tram of the day—or bring your backpacking gear.

If you ride the Aerial Tramway from November to April, you have a good chance for a winter wonderland at the top. Cross-country skis and snowshoes are for rent; visitors glide around the snow-covered hiking trails.

Facilities
There are 23 guest houses, bungalows, and rooms, ranging in size from studios to two bedrooms. Most have fully equipped kitchens. Linens and towels are provided.

Reservations and Rates
Reservations are recommended. Fees are $109–349 per night in winter and $69–229 per night in summer; a continental breakfast is included. Pets are permitted with a $10 fee. Contact Casa Cody Country Inn, 175 South Cahuilla Road, Palm Springs, CA 92262, 760/320-9346, website: www.casacodypalmsprings.com.

Directions
From I-10 in Banning, drive east for 12 miles and take the Highway 111 exit for Palm Springs. Drive southeast for 10 miles; Highway 111 becomes Palm Canyon Drive. Turn right on Tahquitz Canyon Way, drive two blocks, then turn left on Cahuilla. Casa Cody is on the right.

9 ORCHID TREE INN
off Highway 111 in Palm Springs

Luxury rating: ★★★★☆   **Recreation rating:** ★★★☆☆

The Orchid Tree Inn is quintessential Palm Springs: a 1930s desert garden retreat with a cluster of red tile–roofed, Spanish-style bungalows set amid swimming pools, palm trees, cactus gardens, citrus trees, and bougainvillea. Once seven separate smaller properties, the inn now has a total of 50 units, including 10 one-bedroom bungalows large enough for a small family, plus three swimming pools and two hot pools.

In season (November to April), a complimentary breakfast is served daily. The rest of the year, you're on your own to cook in your bungalow, or you can walk a few blocks into downtown Palm Springs to order your eggs at a restaurant.

Orchid Tree is only a short walk from many of Palm Springs' attractions, including the Palm Springs Desert Museum and the Cahuilla Indian Museum. Within a couple miles are the Palm Springs Aerial Tramway (where you can ride to the top and hike in the cool shade of conifers at Mount San Jacinto State Park) and the

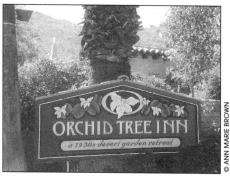

Agua Caliente Indian Reservation (where you can explore the waterfalls and desert flora and fauna of spectacular Murray, Andreas, Palm, or Tahquitz Canyons). Smoke Tree Stables is nearby for those who prefer to take a guided horseback ride through the desert. Bicycle rentals are in town, and Bighorn Bicycle Adventures leads guided tours.

One of the most unusual local attractions is the giant wind farm at the northern entrance to Palm Springs. Palm Springs Windmill Tours takes visitors on a 90-minute electric-cart ride through thousands of 80- to 300-foot-tall wind turbines. During the tour, you learn how windmills make electricity, why some blades are turning while others stand still, and why the popularity of wind farms is increasing.

And as if there weren't enough to do right in Palm Springs, a one-hour drive will take you to Joshua Tree National Park, Anza-Borrego Desert State Park, or Idyllwild, in San Bernardino National Forest.

Facilities

There are 50 rooms, suites, and bungalows that can accommodate up to four people. All have fully equipped kitchens. Linens and towels are provided.

Reservations and Rates

Reservations are recommended. Fees are $119–249 per night in winter and $69–189 per night in summer. Pets are not permitted. Contact Orchid Tree Inn, 261 South Belardo Road, Palm Springs, CA 92262, 760/325-2791 or 800/733-3435, website: www.orchidtree.com.

Directions

From I-10 in Banning, drive east for 12 miles and take the Highway 111 exit for Palm Springs. Drive southeast for 10 miles; Highway 111 becomes Palm Canyon Drive. Turn right on Baristo Road; the inn is on the right, at the corner of Baristo and South Belardo Roads.

Index

Page numbers in **bold**
indicate maps.

A

Adam and Eve Loop
Trail: 301
Adventure in Camping
Travel Trailers: 134–135
Aerial Tramway: 331–332,
333
Agnew Lake: 202
Agnew Meadows: 225
Agua Caliente County
Park: 148
Agua Caliente Hot
Springs: 148–149
Agua Caliente Indian
Reservation: 333
Agua Caliente Indians: 317
Ahwahnee: 249–250
Alisal Guest Ranch & Re-
sort, The: 10, 54–56
Aliso Canyon Loop Trail:
59
Alpers Owens River
Ranch: 7, 211–212
Alpine Pedal Path: 98
Amos Alonzo Stagg Tree:
303
Ancient Bristlecone Pine
Forest: 242
Andreas Canyon: 333
Andrew Molera State
Park: 22, 25, 27
Angeles National Forest:
76
Angelus Oaks: 106–110
Annett's Mono Village
Resort: 175–176

Ansel Adams Wilderness:
267
Anza-Borrego Desert
State Park: 130, **132**,
139–141, 142, 147–148,
152, 333
Apple Tree Inn: 221–222
Aquarium of the Pacific:
115
Arrowhead Pine Rose
Cabins: 88–89
Arroyo Grande: 50
Ash Mountain entrance,
Sequoia National Park:
291, 292, 294
Aspen Meadow: 261
Aster Lake: 288
Aurora: 178
Avalon: 111, 112–114

B

Badger Gap Trail: 311
Badger Pass: 164, 200,
215
Badwater: 316, **318**, 321
Bakersfield: 310–312
Balarat: 322
Balboa Park: 131, 160
Balch County Park: 303
Banner Peak: 223
Barney Lake: 175, 177
Bass Lake: 245, 249,
250–255
Bass Lake Realty: 253
Bass Lake Vacation
Rentals: 253
Bayside Trail: 160
beach activities: best cab-
ins for 12–13; Big Sur

21–30; Cambria 43–44;
Carmel 20–21; Catalina
Island 110–114; Cayucos
48–49; Chula Vista
160–161; Gorda 31–34;
Laguna Beach 117–121;
Long Beach 114–116;
Morro Bay 46–48; ;
Newport Beach
116–117; Pacific Beach
154–156; Paso Robles
45–46; Pismo Beach
51–52; Rancho Santa
Fe 135–136; San Diego
134–135, 157–158;
Santa Barbara 56–57,
61–69; Temecula
121–122; Ventura 70–71
Beach Cottages, The: 13,
155–156
Beachfront Vacation
Rentals: 52
Bear Canyon Trail: 84
Beardsley Reservoir: 165
Bear Manor Cabins and
Lakeview Lodge:
101–102
Bearpaw High Sierra
Camp: 6, 289–290
Bearpaw Meadow:
289–290
Bennettville: 187
Bertha Peak: 96, 98
Big Bear: 95–106
Big Bear Frontier Lodge:
98
Big Bear Lake: 91, 94–108
Big Bear Mountain Re-
sort Rentals: 100

Big Falls: 50, 106, 108–110
Big Meadow: 309
Big Meadows Guard Station: 284–285
Big Morongo Canyon Preserve: 324
Big Pine: 277–278
Big Pine Canyon: 277
Big Pine Creek: 277
Big Pine Lakes: 277
Big Pines: 76, 82
Big Rock Creek: 82
Big Rock Resort: 209–211
Big Sur: **18**, 21–30
Big Sur Campground and Cabins: 24–26
Big Sur Lodge: 26–27
Big Sur Retreat Cabins: 29
Big Virginia Lake: 183–184
biking: Ahwahnee 249–250; Angelus Oaks 106–110; Bass Lake 252–254; Big Bear 95–106; Big Pine 277–278; Big Sur 21–30; Bishop 241–242, 272–277; Borrego Springs 140–141; Bridgeport 175–181; Cambria 43–44; Carmel 20–21; Catalina Island 110–114; Cayucos 48–49; Chula Vista 160–161; Crestline 86–87; Desert Hot Springs 328–329; Devils Postpile National Monument 224–226; Edison Lake 268–269; Fish Camp 219–222; Giant Sequoia National Monument 284–285; Gorda 31–34; Greenhorn Mountains 310–312; Green Valley Lake 94–95; Hetch Hetchy Valley 191–193; Hollywood 80–81; Huntington Lake 260–268; Idyllwild 123–127; Julian 141–147, 149–150; June Lake 201–211; Kernville 307–310; Kings Canyon National Park 280–283; Laguna Beach 117–121; Lake Arrowhead 89–92; Lake Nacimiento 41–43; Lake San Antonio 40–41; Lee Vining 181–186, 188–189; Long Beach 114–116; Los Padres National Forest 72–73; Mammoth Lakes 211–212, 222–224, 226–236; Mono Hot Springs 266–268; Morro Bay 46–48; Mountain Home State Forest 301–302; Mount Baldy 83–85; Mount Laguna 151–154; Newport Beach 116–117; North Fork 255–257; Oakhurst 250–252; Ojai 69–70; Pacific Beach 154–156; Palm Springs 329–333; Paso Robles 45–46; Pioneertown area 323–324; Pismo Beach 51–52; Rancho Santa Fe 135–136; Running Springs 92–93; San Diego 134–135, 157–159; San Luis Obispo 49–50; Santa Barbara 56–69; Santa Ysabel 137–138; Shaver Lake 257–260; Solvang 52–56; Squaw Valley 278–280; Strawberry 173–175; Temecula 121–122; Three Rivers 292–297; Tioga Pass 186–187; Tom's Place 236–241; Twentynine Palms 324–327; Twin Peaks 88–89; Ventura 70–71; Warner Springs 138–140; Wrightwood 81–83; Yosemite National Park 198–200, 215–216, 218–219
Birch Aquarium: 160
Bishop: 241–242, **246**, 272–277
Bishop Creek: 272, 274–275
Bishop Creek Canyon: 274
Bishop Creek Lodge: 7, 274–275
Black Forest Lodge: 104
Black Point Trail: 262
Blossom Trail: 278–279
Blue Jay Lodge: 151–152
Blue Lake: 184, 273
Boat and Breakfast Newport: 116–117
boating: Ahwahnee 249–250; Bass Lake 252–254; best cabins for 8; Big Bear 95–106;

Bishop 272–277; Bridgeport 175–179; Campo 161–162; Catalina Island 110–114; Edison Lake 268–269; Giant Sequoia National Monument 285–287; Huntington Lake 260–268; Julian 141–147, 149–150; June Lake 201–211; Laguna Beach 117–121; Lake Arrowhead 91–92; Lake Nacimiento 41–43; Lake San Antonio 40–41; Lee Vining 183–186, 188–189; Long Beach 114–116; Mammoth Lakes 226–232, 234–236; Mono Hot Springs 266–268; Mount Laguna 151–154; Newport Beach 116–117; Ojai 69–70; Paso Robles 45–46; San Luis Obispo 49–50; Santa Barbara 58–59; Santa Ysabel 137–138; Shaver Lake 257–258; Sonora 172–173; Strawberry 169–171, 173–175; Temecula 121–122; Three Rivers 292–297; Tioga Pass 186–187; Tom's Place 236–237; Twin Peaks 88–89; Ventura 70–71; Woodlake 291–292
Bodie State Historic Park: 179, 181–182, 188
Bonnie B Ranch: 7, 255–257
Borax Museum: 320

Borrego Palm Canyon: 141
Borrego Springs: 140–141
Boulder Creek Resort: 100
Boulder Flat: 179
Boyden Cave: 283
Bracken Fern Manor: 89–90
Bridgeport: 175–181
Buckeye Creek: 177, 178
Buckeye Hot Springs: 179, 180
Buckeye Tree Lodge: 295
Buck Rock Fire Lookout: 284–285
Burst Rock: 169
Butler Peak Lookout: 96
Buzzards Roost Trail: 26

C

Cabins at Strawberry, The: 170–171
Cabrillo Inn Spanish Vacation Cottages: 66
Cabrillo National Monument: 157, 160
Cahuilla Indian Museum: 333
Cahuilla Indians: 317
Caliente: 312–313
Cal-Pine Chalets: 102
Cambria: 36, 43–44
Cambria Pines Lodge: 43–44
Cambria Vacation Rentals: 44
Camp Nelson: 302–304
Camp Nelson Cabins: 302–304
Campo: 161–162
Camp Seeley: 87

Cannell Meadow National Recreation Trail: 308
Canyon Oak Loop: 144, 147
Cardinal Gold Mine: 272–273
Cardinal Village Resort: 272–273
Carlon Falls: 192
Carmel: 20–21
Carmel River Inn: 20–21
Carpinteria: 36
Carson Peak: 203, 206, 208
Casa Cody Country Inn: 331–332
Casa Laguna Inn: 117–119
Castle Rock: 101–102
Castle Rock Trail: 96
Castlewood Theme Cottages: 11, 102–104
Catalina Cottages and Hermosa Hotel: 114
Catalina Island: 110–114
Cayucos: 37, 46, 48–49
Cayucos State Beach: 47
Cayucos Vacation Rentals: 12, 46–48
Cedar Creek Trail: 72
Cedar Crest Resort: 260–262
Cedar Grove: 281, 282
Cerro Gordo: 322
Chalet for Two: 221
Champion Lodgepole Pine: 101
Channel Islands National Park: 37, 71
Charcoal Kilns: 321
Chateau Marmont: 12, 80–81
Chesire Cat Inn & Cottages: 64–66

Chilnualna Falls: 218
Chinese Peak: 265
Chuck Richard's Falling Waters River Resort: 308
Chula Vista: 160–161
Chumash Wilderness: 72
Cienaga Creek Ranch: 97
Cima Dome: 317
Cinnamon Creek Ranch: 294
Circle Bar B Guest Ranch: 7, 56–57
Cleveland National Forest: 122, 130–**132**, 137, 139, 142, 145–146
Coachella Valley: 327
Coarsegrass Meadow Trail: 261
Cold Springs Nature Trail: 299
Congress Trail: 295
Convict Lake: 234–235
Convict Lake Resort: 7, 234–236
Cooney Lake: 184
Corlieu Falls: 220
Coronado Island: 160
Cort Cottage: 294
Cottage Hotel, The: 321–323
Cottontail Creek Ranch: 48–49
Cougar Crest Trail: 96, 98
Country House Inn: 46
Creek Runner's Lodge: 97
Crescent Meadow Trail: 294
Crestline: 86–87
cross-country skiing: Big Bear 99; Dodge Ridge Ski Area 173; Giant Sequoia National Monument 306; June Mountain Ski Area 206, 210; Kings Canyon National Park 281; Los Padres National Forest 72–73; Mammoth Mountain Ski Area 226–227; Montecito Sequoia Lodge 286; Mount San Jacinto State Park 332; San Bernardino National Forest 94; Sequoia National Park 287–288; Shaver Lake 258, 260; Tom's Place 239–241
Crowley Lake: 236–237, 238, 241
Crystal Cove State Park: 118, 120
Crystal Crag Lodge: 228–229
Crystal Lake: 185, 230, 300
Crystal Pier Hotel: 13, 154–155
Curry Village Cabins: 198–200
Cuyamaca Mountains: 130–131
Cuyamaca Rancho State Park: 130, 142, 149–150, 152
Cuyamaca Rancho State Park Cabins: 149–151

D
Dana Point: 118
Darlene's Vacation Cabins: 171
Davis Lake: 238
Dawson Saddle trailhead: 82
Death Valley National Park: 316, **318**, 320–321
Deep Creek Hot Springs: 90
Deer Springs Trail: 123
Deetjen's Big Sur Inn: 27–29
Delight's Hot Springs Resort: 321
Del Mar: 136
Desert Hot Springs: 316, 328–329
Desert Tortoise Natural Area: 322
Desert View Loop: 144, 147
Desert View Nature Trail: 152
Devils Bathtub Trail: 269
Devils Postpile National Monument: **166**, 223–226
Devils Slide Trail: 123, 125
Dewey Point: 215
Dinkey Creek: 259
Dinkey Creek Inn: 259–260
Dinkey Lakes Wilderness: 259
Doc & Al's Resort: 178–179
Dockside Boat and Bed: 114–116
Dodge Ridge Ski Area: 169, 171–173
Dome Rock: 306
Doris Lake: 267, 269

Double Eagle Resort: 12, 207–209
Duna Vista Trail: 50

E

Eagle Creek: 178
Eagle Lake: 299–300
Eagle Mine: 142
East Fork Kaweah River: 299
Edelweiss Lodge: 224
Edison Lake: 267, 268–269
El Capitan: 164
El Encanto Hotel & Garden Villas: 61–62
Emerald Iguana Cottages: 69–70
Emerald Lake: 228, 288
Emigrant Wilderness: 169, 171–172, 174
Emma Wood Beach: 70–71
Ernie Maxwell Scenic Trail: 123, 125
Eureka Dunes: 317, 321
Evergreen Lodge: 191–193
Ewoldsen Trail: 24

F

Falls Recreation Area: 106, 108–109
family friendly destinations: Adventure in Camping Travel Trailers 134–135; Alisal Guest Ranch & Resort 54–56; Annett's Mono Village Resort 175–176; Beach Cottages 155–156; Bear Manor Cabins and

Lakeview Lodge 101–102; best cabins for 10; Big Meadows Guard Station 284–285; Bishop Creek Lodge 274–275; Bonnie B Ranch 255–257; Cabins at Strawberry 170–171; Camp Nelson Cabins 302–304; Cardinal Village Resort 272–273; Castlewood Theme Cottages 102–104; Cedar Crest Resort 260–262; Chula Vista 160–161; Circle Bar B Guest Ranch 56–57; Convict Lake Resort 234–236; Crystal Crag Lodge 228–229; Curry Village Cabins 198–200; Cuyamaca Rancho State Park Cabins 149–151; Dinkey Creek Inn 259–260; Forks Resort 252–253; Furnace Creek Ranch 320–321; Giant Oaks Lodge 92–93; Golden Trout Wilderness Pack Trains Cabins 304–305; Grant Grove Lodge 280–282; Green Valley Lake Cozy Cabins 94–95; Hounds Tooth Inn 250–252; Hunewill Guest Ranch 179–181; Huntington Lake Resort 262–263; KOA Santa Margarita Lake 49–50; KOA Yosemite-Mariposa 213–214; Laguna Moun-

tain Lodge 153–154; Lake Elowin Resort 296–297; Lake Henshaw Resort 137–138; Lake Nacimiento Resort 41–43; Lake San Antonio South Shore Resort 40–41; Lakeshore Resort 265–266; Lakeview Cottages 263–265; Lodge at Angelus Oaks 107–109; Mammoth Mountain Chalets 222–224; Miller's Landing 254–255; Mono Hot Springs Resort 266–268; Montecito Sequoia Lodge 285–287; Mountain Home Guard Station 301–302; Mountain Top Bed and Breakfast 305–307; Mountain View Motel 81–83; Mount Baldy Lodge 83–84; Pacific Beach 154–156; Parchers Resort 275–277; Pinecrest Chalet 173–175; Pinecrest Lake Resort 172–173; Quail Cove Lodge 95–96; Rancho Oso Guest Ranch & Stables 58–59; Rankin Ranch 312–313; Redwoods Cabins 218–219; Rivers Resort 169–170; San Diego Metro KOA 160–161; Sequoia Motel 292–293; Sequoia View Vineyard 278–280; Sequoia Village Inn 294–295; Seven Oaks Mountain Cabins 106–107; Shaver Lake Lodge 257–258; Shore Acres Lodge 97–98; Sierra Gateway Cottages 309–310; Silver City Resort 299–300; Snowcrest Lodge 84–86; Stagecoach Trails Resort 148–149; Tamarack Lodge Resort 226–227; Vermilion Valley Resort 268–269; Virginia Creek Settlement 181–183; Whispering Pines 109–110; Wildwood Resort 99–100; Yosemite Lakes 190–191

Farewell Gap Trail: 299

Fern Creek Lodge: 204–205

Ferndell Nature Museum: 81

Fern Lake: 203

Fern Valley Inn: 124–125

First Falls: 277

First Lake: 277

Fishbowls: 72

Fish Camp: 219–222, 250

fishing: Ahwahnee 249–250; Angelus Oaks 106–110; Bass Lake 252–254; best cabins for 7; Big Bear 95–106; Big Pine 277–278; Bishop 241–242, 272–277; Bridgeport 175–181; Cambria 43–44; Camp Nelson 302–304; Campo 161–162; Catali-

na Island 110–114; Cayucos 48–49; Crestline 86–87; Devils Postpile National Monument 224–226; Edison Lake 268–269; Fish Camp 219–222; Giant Sequoia National Monument 284–287, 305–306; Golden Trout Wilderness 304–305; Green Valley Lake 94–95; Groveland 190–191; Hetch Hetchy Valley 191–193; Huntington Lake 260–268; Idyllwild 123–127; John Muir Wilderness 270–272; Julian 141–147, 149–150; June Lake 201–211; Kernville 307–310; Kings Canyon National Park 280–283; Laguna Beach 117–121; Lake Arrowhead 89–92; Lake Nacimiento 41–43; Lake San Antonio 40–41; Lee Vining 181–186, 188–189; Long Beach 114–116; Mammoth Lakes 211–212, 222–224, 226–236; Mariposa 213–214; Mineral King Valley 299–300; Mono Hot Springs 266–268; Morro Bay 46–48; Mountain Home State Forest 301–302; Mount Baldy 83–85; Mount Laguna 151–154; Newport Beach 116–117;

North Fork 255–257; Oakhurst 250–252; Ojai 69–70; Paso Robles 45–46; Pismo Beach 51–52; Rankin Ranch 312–313; Running Springs 92–93; San Diego 134–135, 157–158; San Luis Obispo 49–50; Santa Barbara 56–59; Santa Ysabel 137–138; Sequoia National Park 289–290; Shaver Lake 257–260; Solvang 54–56; Sonora 172–173; Squaw Valley 278–280; Strawberry 169–171, 173–175; Temecula 121–122; Three Rivers 292–297; Tioga Pass 186–187; Tom's Place 236–241; Twin Peaks 88–89; Ventura 70–71; Warner Springs 138–140; Woodlake 291–292; Wrightwood 81–83; Yosemite National Park 191–200, 215–216, 218–219

Florence Lake: 267, 270

Forest 90 Fire Road: 309

Forks Resort, The: 8, 252–253

Fortynine Palms Oasis: 325

Four Seasons Biltmore: 12, 67–69

Four Seasons, The: 206–207

Fox Meadow trailhead: 284

Franklin Canyon: 81
Frazier Park: 72–73
Fresno: 270
Fresno Dome: 220, 250
Frog Lakes: 184
Fuller Mill Creek: 124–125
Furnace Creek Ranch:
    320–321

G
Galena Creek Falls: 301
Garlock: 322
Garnet Peak: 152
Gateway Lodge, The: 295
Gaviota State Park: 53
Gaylor Lakes: 187
Gem Lake: 202
General Grant Tree: 244,
    281
ghost towns: 178–179,
    181–182, 321–322
Giant Forest: 281, 294
Giant Oaks Lodge: 9,
    92–93
Giant Sequoia National
    Monument: 245–**246**,
    281, 284–287, 301–302
Giant Sequoias: Kings
    Canyon National Park
    244–245, 279; Mariposa
    Grove 218, 221; McKin-
    ley Grove 259; Moun-
    tain Home State Forest
    301, 303; Nelder Grove
    220, 250; Sequoia Na-
    tional Park 244–245,
    279; Yosemite National
    Park 164
Glacier Lodge: 277–278
Glacier Point: 164, 215
Glacier Point Ski Hut:
    200–201

Glenborough Inn Bed
    and Breakfast: 64
Glen Oaks Motel: 23–24
Goat Mountain Trail: 254
Golden Bear Cottages:
    105
Golden Canyon: 321
Golden Trout Wilderness:
    303
Golden Trout Wilderness
    Pack Trains Cabins: 7,
    304–305
Goldmine Lodge: 104
Goleta: 37
Gorda: **18**, 31–34
Gorda Springs Cottages:
    32–34
Grant Grove: 282, 284
Grant Grove Lodge: 6,
    11, 280–282
Grant Lake: 203
gray whales: 16, 43, 118
Great Western Divide:
    284, 286, 289, 294
Greenhorn Mountains:
    308, 310–312
Greenhorn Summit Loop:
    309
Green Valley Lake: 94–95
Green Valley Lake Cozy
    Cabins: 11, 94–95
Grey Squirrel Resort: 100
Griffith Park: 81
Grizzly Falls: 283
Grout Bay trailhead: 96
Groveland: 190–191
Gull Lake: 203, 205
Gull Lake Lodge: 207
Gunsight, The: 101

H
Half Dome: 164, 199, 200

Hamilton Lakes: 290
Happy Isles trailhead: 199
Harbor Island: 158–159
Harbor Vacations Club:
    158–159
Harden Lake: 194
Harden Lake Trail: 194
Hat Creek: 230, 231, 235
Hazelwood Loop: 294
Heaps Peak Arboretum
    Trail: 90
Hearst Castle: 37, 43, 45,
    47, 48
Hearst Memorial State
    Beach: 44
Heart Rock Falls: 87
Heather Lake: 288
Hercules Tree: 301
Hetch Hetchy Valley:
    191–193
Hidden Falls: 301
High Peak Mine: 142
High Sierra Camps:
    195–196, 289–290
High Sierra Trail: 289
hiking: Ahwahnee
    249–250; Angelus Oaks
    106–110; Bass Lake
    252–254; best cabins for
    6–7; Big Bear 95–106;
    Big Pine 277–278; Big
    Sur 21–30; Bishop
    241–242, 272–277; Bor-
    rego Springs 140–141;
    Bridgeport 175–181;
    Cambria 43–44; Camp
    Nelson 302–304;
    Campo 161–162;
    Carmel 20–21; Catalina
    Island 110–114; Cayucos
    48–49; Chula Vista
    160–161; Crestline

86–87; Death Valley National Park 320–321; Desert Hot Springs 328–329; Devils Postpile National Monument 224–226; Edison Lake 268–269; Fish Camp 219–222; Giant Sequoia National Monument 284–287, 305–306; Golden Trout Wilderness 304–305; Gorda 31–34; Greenhorn Mountains 310–312; Green Valley Lake 94–95; Hetch Hetchy Valley 191–193; Hollywood 80–81; Huntington Lake 260–268; Idyllwild 123–127; John Muir Wilderness 270–272; Julian 141–147, 149–150; June Lake 201–211; Kernville 307–310; Kings Canyon National Park 280–283; Laguna Beach 117–121; Lake Arrowhead 89–92; Lake Nacimiento 41–43; Lake San Antonio 40–41; Lee Vining 181–186, 188–189; Long Beach 114–116; Los Padres National Forest 72–73; Mammoth Lakes 211–212, 222–224, 226–236; Mariposa 213–214; Mineral King Valley 299–300; Mono Hot Springs 266–268; Morro Bay 46–48; Mountain Home State Forest 301–302; Mount Baldy 83–85; Mount Laguna 151–154; Newport Beach 116–117; North Fork 255–257; Oakhurst 250–252; Ojai 69–70; Pacific Beach 154–156; Palm Springs 329–333; Paso Robles 45–46; Pioneertown area 323–324; Pismo Beach 51–52; Rancho Santa Fe 135–136; Randsburg 321–322; Rankin Ranch 312–313; Running Springs 92–93; San Diego 134–135, 157–159; San Luis Obispo 49–50; Santa Barbara 56–69; Santa Ysabel 137–138; Sequoia National Park 289–290; Shaver Lake 257–260; Solvang 52–56; Sonora 172–173; Squaw Valley 278–280; Strawberry 169–171, 173–175; Temecula 121–122; Three Rivers 292–298; Tioga Pass 186–187; Tom's Place 236–241; Twentynine Palms 324–327; Twin Peaks 88–89; Ventura 70–71; Warner Springs 138–140; Woodlake 291–292; Wrightwood 81–83; Yosemite National Park 191–200, 215–216, 218–219

Hilton Lake: 238

Historic Gas Lamp District: 157
Hole-in-the-Wall: 317
Hollywood: 80–81
Home Camp Creek: 261
Homestead, The: 249–250
Hoover Wilderness: 175, 177
horseback riding: Anza-Borrego Desert State Park 148; best cabins for 7–8; Bonnie B Ranch 256; Convict Lake Resort 235; Golden Trout Wilderness Pack Trains 304–305; Hunewill Guest Ranch 179–181; June Lake Loop 206; Red's Meadow Resort 224–226; Santa Barbara 56–59; Yosemite Lakes 190; Yosemite National Park 199
Horse Meadow: 309
Horseshoe Lake: 231
Hospital Rock: 294
Hot Creek: 223, 232–233, 238
Hot Creek Geologic Area: 233
Hot Creek Ranch: 7, 232–234
hot springs: Agua Caliente Hot Springs 148–149; Bridgeport 175–181; Desert Hot Springs 328–329; Edison Lake 268–269; John Muir Wilderness 270–272; Lake Arrowhead 90; Lee Vining

181–183; Mammoth
Lakes 211–212,
222–224, 226–236;
Mono Hot Springs
266–268; Palm Springs
329–333; Pioneertown
area 323–324; Solvang
53; Warner Springs
138–140
Hot Springs Mountain:
139
Hounds Tooth Inn:
250–252
Huckleberry Trail: 294
Humber Park: 124–125
Hump, The: 288
Hunewill Guest Ranch: 7,
179–181
Huntington Lake: 245,
257, 260–268
Huntington Lake Resort:
262–263

I

Ice House Canyon: 83
Icehouse Canyon Trail: 84
ice-skating: 88, 91, 171,
173, 199
Idyllwild: **78**, 123–127, 333
Indian Pools: 265
Inn at Rancho Santa Fe,
The: 135–136
Inspiration Peak: 327
Inyo National Forest: 224

J

Jackson Lake: 82
Jade Cove: 30
Jenks Lake: 106–107
Jennie Lake: 284
Jennie Lakes Wilderness:
284

Jesusita Trail: 62
John Muir Trail: 197
John Muir Wilderness:
238, 241, 267, 270–272,
274–275
Jordan Peak: 305, 306
Joshua Tree National
Park: 316–**318**, 323–325,
327, 333
Julia Lake: 313
Julian: 131, **132**, 141–151
Julian Bed and Breakfast
Guild: 141–143
Julian Gold Rush Hotel:
147
Julia Pfeiffer Burns State
Park: 22, 24, 27
June Lake: 165, 201–211
June Lake Loop: 201,
204, 206, 208, 210
June Lake Motel and
Cabins: 207
June Lake Pines Cot-
tages: 207
June Mountain Ski Area:
205, 206, 210

K

Kaiser Peak: 265
Kaiser Ridge: 262
Kaweah River: 244–245,
289, 292–294, 296–297
Keane Wonder Mine: 321
Kelso Dunes: 317
Kern River: 244–245,
306–309
Kern River Basin: 303
Kern River Trail: 311
Kernville: 307–310
Keys View: 327
Kings Canyon Lodge:
282–283

Kings Canyon National
Park: 244–**246**, 278–283
Kings River: 244, 279,
283
Kings River Canyon: 283
Kirk Creek trailhead: 33
Knapp's Castle: 60
Knotty Pine Cabins:
123–124
KOA Santa Margarita
Lake: 49–50
KOA Yosemite-Mariposa:
11, 213–214
Korakia Pensione:
329–330

L

La Casa del Zorro Desert
Resort: 11, 140–141
Laguna Beach: **78**, 117–121
Laguna Mountain Lodge:
153–154
Laguna Mountain Recre-
ation Area: 151–153
Laguna Mountains:
130–131, 151–152
Lake Arrowhead: 88–92,
94
Lake Cachuma: 55
Lake Casitas: 70
Lake Dorothy: 235
Lake Elowin Resort:
296–297
Lake Front Cabins: 207
Lake Fulmor: 123–125
Lake George: 229–230,
265
Lake Gregory: 86–87, 88
Lake Henshaw: 131,
137–138
Lake Henshaw Resort:
137–138

Lake Isabella: 308–309
Lake Kaweah: 292, 293
Lake Mamie: 231
Lake Mary: 228
Lake Morena: 161–162
Lake Morena County Park Cabins: 161–162
Lake Nacimiento: 36, 45
Lake Nacimiento Resort: 41–43
Lake Sabrina: 241
Lake San Antonio: 36, 45
Lake San Antonio South Shore Resort: 7, 8, 40–41
Lakeshore Resort: 8
Lakes Trail: 288
Lake Thomas A. Edison: 267, 268–269
Lakeview Cottages: 263–265
Lakeview Forest Resort: 106
Lakeview Lodge: 101–102
La Paloma Cottages: 13, 112–114
La Purisima Mission State Historic Park: 53
Lee Vining: 181–186, 188–189
Lembert Dome trailhead: 195, 197
Lewis Creek National Recreation Trail: 220, 250
Lightning Ridge Trail: 152
Limekiln Creek State Park: 30
Line Creek: 261
Little Falls: 50
Little Green Valley Trail: 95

Little Lakes Valley: 238
Little Valley Inn: 214
Little Virginia Lake: 183–184
Lloyd Meadow: 303
Loch Leven Lake: 273
Lodge at Angelus Oaks, The: 107–109
Log Cabin Resort Rentals: 104
Long Beach: **78**, 114–116
Lopez Lake: 50
Lopez Lake Recreation Area: 50
Lord Mayor's B&B Inn: 116
Los Angeles: 76–**78**
Los Padres National Forest: Gorda 33; Mount Pinos 72–73; Santa Barbara area 36, 58–60, 63, 70; Solvang 53
Los Penasquitos Canyon Preserve: 136
Lost Horse Mine: 325, 327
Lost Palms Oasis: 325
Love Valley: 139
Lower Doane Valley: 122
Lower Falls: 223, 225
Lower Hamilton Lake: 290
Lower Kaiser Loop: 261
Lower Rock Creek: 241–242
Lower Twin Lake: 176–177
Lucia: **18**
Lucia Lodge: 13, 29–31
Lukens Lake: 194
Lundy Canyon: 185–186
Lundy Lake: 185

Lundy Lake Resort: 185–186

M

Madera Sugar Pine Lumber flume: 220–221
Mammoth Crest: 230
Mammoth Lakes: 164–**166**, 208, 211–212, 222–224, 226–236
Mammoth Mountain: 209
Mammoth Mountain Bike Park: 222–224
Mammoth Mountain Chalets: 9, 222–224
Mammoth Mountain Ski Area: 222–224, 226–227
Mammoth Mountain Summit Trail: 227
Manter Meadow Loop: 309
Manzanita Cottages: 13, 119–121
Marble Falls: 294
Mariposa: 213–214
Mariposa Grove: 218, 220, 221
Masonic: 178
Mastodon Peak: 325
May Lake trailhead: 195
McGee Creek: 238
McKinley Grove: 245, 259
McLeod Lake: 231
McWay Falls: 24
Meadow Creek Ranch: 214
Middle Fork Kaweah River: 294
Middle Fork Kaweah River Canyon: 289
Mildred Lake: 235

Mill Creek: 185
Miller's Landing: 8, 254–255
Mineral King entrance, Sequoia National Park: 297–300
Mineral King Valley: 245, 292, 294–295, 299–300
Mineral Peak: 299
Mission Bay Park: 131, 134, 157, 160
Mission Creek: 62
Mist Falls: 283
Mitchell Peak: 284
Mojave Desert: 98, 316–**318**, 322
Monache Indian historical sites: 294
Monarch Lakes: 300
Mono Basin National Forest Scenic Area: 189
Mono Creek Trail: 269
Mono Hot Springs: 266–269
Mono Hot Springs Resort: 11, 266–268
Mono Lake: 188–189
Mono Lake County Park: 189
Mono Lake Tufa State Reserve: 189
Mono Meadow: 269
Mono Pass Trail: 238
Montana de Oro State Park: 48
Montecito: 66–67
Montecito Sequoia Lodge: 10, 285–287
Monterey: **18**
Moraines and Meadows Trail: 187
Morena Reservoir: 161–162

Moro Rock: 294
Morro Bay: **38**, 46–48
Morro Bay State Park: 47
Morro Strand State Beach: 47
Mosaic Canyon: 321
Moses Gulch Trail: 301
Mosquito Flat trailhead: 238
Mosquito Lakes: 300
Moss Point: 118
Mountain Home Demonstration State Forest: 303
Mountain Home Guard Station: 301–302
Mountain Home State Forest: 245, 301–302
Mountain Pine Cabin: 306
Mountain Properties Vacation Rentals: 72–73
Mountain Top Bed and Breakfast: 305–307
Mountain View Motel: 81–83
Mount Baden-Powell: 82
Mount Baldy: 76–**78**, 83–86
Mount Baldy Lodge: 83–84
Mount Hollywood: 81
Mount Laguna: 131, 151–154
Mount Morrison: 234–235
Mount Pinos: 72–73
Mount Ritter: 223
Mount San Gorgonio: 77, 107, 108, 327
Mount San Jacinto: 77, 327

Mount San Jacinto State Park: 331–333
Mount Whitney: 244, **246**, 289
Muir Trail Ranch: 13, 270–272
Murray Canyon: 330, 333
Mushroom Rock Vista: 262

N
Needles Lookout: 306
Nelder Grove: 220, 245, 250
Nellie Lake: 261
Nevada Falls: 199
Newport Beach: 116–117
Newton B. Drury Peak: 123
Nobe Young Falls: 306
Nojoqui Falls County Park: 53
North Fork: 255–257
North Fork Trail: 277
North Lake: 241, 273

O
Oak Flat Lookout Tower: 11, 310–312
Oakhurst: 250–252
Ocean Beach: 157–158
Oceanside: 122
Ojai: 36, 69–70
Olaine Lake: 225
Old Town, San Diego: 157–158
Old Town State Historic Park: 157
Oneida Lake: 185
Orchard Hill Farm: 45–46
Orchid Tree Inn: 332–333
Oriole Lodge & Cottage: 83

Ostrander Ski Hut: 216–217

Our Secret Garden Mountain Retreat: 9, 104–105

Owens River: 212, 238, 241

Owens Valley: 241–242

Owl's Nest Cabins: 219–220

P

Pacific Beach: 154–156

Pacific Crest Trail: 90, 98, 139, 162, 197, 269

Pageant of the Masters: 120

Painted Cave: 60

Palisade Crest: 278

Palisade Glacier: 278

Palm Bowl: 148

Palm Canyon: 333

Palm Springs: 317, **318**, 329–333

Palm Springs Desert Museum: 333

Palomar Mountain: 137–138

Palomar Mountains: 130, 131

Palomar Mountain State Park: 122, 131, 137

Palomar Observatory: 122, 131, 138

Panorama Dome Trail: 227

Panoramic Point: 281

Paradise Canyon Cabins: 13, 297–298

Paradise Resort: 241–242

Parchers Resort: 7, 275–277

Park Ridge Trail: 281

Paso Robles: 36, **38**, 40–43, 45–46

Pear Lake: 288

Pear Lake Ski Hut: 287–288

pets permitted: Adventure in Camping Travel Trailers 134–135; Apple Tree Inn 221–222; Arrowhead Pine Rose Cabins 88–89; Big Rock Resort 209–211; Big Sur Campground and Cabins 24–26; Bishop Creek Lodge 274–275; Camp Nelson Cabins 302–304; Carmel River Inn 20–21; Casa Cody Country Inn 331–332; Casa Laguna Inn 117–119; Cayucos Vacation Rentals 46–48; Cedar Crest Resort 260–262; Convict Lake Resort 234–236; Crystal Crag Lodge 228–229; Cuyamaca Rancho State Park Cabins 149–151; Dinkey Creek Inn 259–260; Doc & Al's Resort 178–179; Double Eagle Resort 207–209; Fern Creek Lodge 204–205; Forks Resort 252–253; Four Seasons Biltmore 67–69; Glacier Lodge 277–278; Green Valley Lake Cozy Cabins 94–95; Huntington Lake Resort 262–263; Knotty Pine Cabins 123–124; KOA Santa Margarita Lake 49–50; Laguna Mountain Lodge 153–154; Lake Henshaw Resort 137–138; Lakeshore Resort 265–266; Lakeview Cottages 263–265; Lodge at Angelus Oaks 107–109; Lundy Lake Resort 185–186; Miller's Landing 254–255; Mono Hot Springs Resort 266–268; Mountain Home Guard Station 301–302; Oak Flat Lookout Tower 310–312; Paradise Canyon Cabins 297–298; Paradise Resort 241–242; Pinecrest Chalet 173–175; Pine Hills Lodge 145–146; Quail Cove Lodge 95–96; Rancho Oso Guest Ranch & Stables 58–59; Red's Meadow Resort 224–226; Redwoods Cabins 218–219; Rimrock Ranch Cabins 323–324; Rivers Resort 169–170; Rock Creek Lodge 239–241; San Ysidro Ranch 66–67; Sequoia Village Inn 294–295; Seven Oaks Mountain Cabins 106–107; Shore Acres Lodge 97–98; Snowcrest Lodge 84–86; Stagecoach Trails Resort 148–149; Tom's Place Resort 236–237; 29

Palms Inn 324–326; Twin Lakes Resort 176–178; Vermilion Valley Resort 268–269; Virginia Creek Settlement 181–183; Virginia Lakes Resort 183–184; Wilder Cabins 126–127; William Heise County Park Cabins 146–147; Woods Lodge 229–230; Yosemite Lakes 190–191
Pfeiffer Beach: 22, 25
Pfeiffer Big Sur State Park: 22, 24–25, 26, 28
Pfeiffer Falls: 26
Pierpont Inn, The: 70–72
Pine Cliff Resort: 224
Pinecrest Chalet: 9, 173–175
Pinecrest Lake: 165, 169, 172
Pinecrest Lake Resort: 10, 172–173
Pine Hills Lodge: 145–146
Pine Knot Guest Ranch: 98
Pine Mountain Club: 72–73
Pine Rose Inn: 252
Pines Resort, The: 253
Pioneer History Center: 218
Pioneertown: 316, 323–324
Pipes Canyon Wilderness Preserve: 324
Pismo Beach: **38**, 51–52
Piute Lake: 273
Piute Pass: 273
Piute Pass Trail: 273
Point Lobos State Reserve: 20–21, 27

Point Loma Lighthouse: 160
Ponderosa: 305–306
Ponderosa Lodge: 306
Ponderosa Vista Nature Trail: 107
Porterville: 302
Potter Pass: 265
Potwisha: 294
Powell Lake: 169
Pygmy Grove: 148

Q
Quail Cove Lodge: 95–96
Quaking Aspen: 304–307
Queen Mary: 115
Quiet Creek Inn, The: 127

R
Rainbow Basin Natural Area: 322
Rainbow Falls: 223, 224–225
Rainbow Falls Trail: 224–225
Rainbow Harbor: 114–115
Rainbow Mountain: 299
Rainbow View Lodge: 93
Rancheria Falls: 265
Rancho Oso Guest Ranch & Stables: 10, 58–59
Rancho Santa Fe: 135–136
Randsburg: 321–323
Rankin Ranch: 8, 10, 312–313
Rattlesnake Canyon: 62
Razor Point Trail: 156
Red Rock Canyon State Park: 322
Red Rock Falls: 220
Red's Meadow: 231

Red's Meadow Resort: 7, 224–226
Redwoods Cabins, The: 218–219
Reverse Creek Lodge: 203–204
Reversed Creek: 203, 208
Rim of the World Scenic Highway: 108–109
Rimrock Ranch Cabins: 323–324
Ripplewood Resort: 21–23
Riverside Campground and Cabins: 29
Rivers Resort, The: 169–170
Robinson Creek: 178
Robinson Creek Trail: 177
Rock Creek Canyon: 238, 239, 241
Rock Creek Lake: 238, 241
Rock Creek Lakes Resort: 6, 238–239
Rock Creek Lodge: 9, 239–241
Roughley Manor Inn: 326–327
Round Valley: 331
Ruby Lake: 238
Running Springs: 92–93
Rush Creek trailhead: 202
Ryan Mountain: 325, 327

S
Sabrina Lake: 272–273, 274
Saddleback Inn: 91–92
Saddlebag Lake: 187
Salmon Creek Trail: 33, 309

Salt Creek: 321
Salton Sea: 147, 327
San Antonio Falls: 85
San Bernardino: **78**
San Bernardino Mountains: 76–77, 94
San Bernardino National Forest: Big Bear 99; Falls Recreation Area 108–109; Idyllwild 123, 333; Lake Arrowhead 90–91; San Bernardino Mountains 76–77, 94; San Gorgonio Wilderness 108–109; San Jacinto Mountains: 77
San Buenaventura Beach: 70
Sand Dollar Beach: 30, 33
San Diego: 130–**132**, 157–159
San Diego Metro KOA: 160–161
San Diego Wild Animal Park: 122, 136
San Diego Zoo: 131, 157
San Elijo State Beach: 134–135
San Gabriel Mountains: 76
San Gorgonio Wilderness: 108
San Jacinto Mountains: 77, 125, 317
San Jacinto Peak: 123, 332
San Jacinto Wilderness: 123
San Joaquin River: 224–225, 267, 270–271
San Joaquin River Canyon: 262

San Joaquin Valley: 72
San Luis Obispo: **38**, 49–50
San Luis Rey River: 138
San Onofre State Beach: 134
San Simeon: 37, **38**, 40, 43, 45
San Simeon State Beach: 43
Santa Ana River: 106, 108
Santa Barbara: **38**, 54, 56–69
Santa Barbara Mission: 62
Santa Cruz: **18**
Santa Cruz Mountains: 17
Santa Cruz Trail: 60
Santa Lucia Mountains: 17
Santa Lucia Wilderness: 49–50
Santa Margarita Lake: 49–50
Santa Rosa Mountains: 125
Santa Ynez Mission: 54
Santa Ynez Mountains: 36, 52–53
Santa Ynez Recreation Area: 58–59
Santa Ysabel: 137–138
Santa Ysabel Mission: 138, 142
San Ysidro Ranch: 12, 66–67
Sawdust Art Festival: 120
Sawtooth Peak: 245, 299
Sawtooth Range: 176–177
Scott's Cabin: 122
Scotty's Castle: 320

Seal Beach Inn and Gardens: 116
Sea World: 157, 160
Second Falls: 277
Secret Garden Inn & Cottages: 64
Seeley Creek Trail: 87
Sentinel Dome: 215
Sentinel Rock: 164
Sequoia Lake: 281
Sequoia Motel: 292–293
Sequoia National Park: 244–**246**, 278–279, 287–292
Sequoia View Vineyard: 278–280
Sequoia Village Inn: 294–295
Seven Lakes Point: 227
Seven Oaks Mountain Cabins: 13, 106–107
Seven Pines Trail: 125
Shadow Lake: 225
Shadow Mountain Ranch: 143–144
Shadow of the Giants National Recreation Trail: 250
Shaver Lake: 245, 257–260, 262
Shaver Lake Lodge: 8, 257–258
Shaver Lake Vacation Rentals: 259
Sherman Pass: 309
Sherman Peak Trail: 309
Sherman Tree: 244
Shirley Meadows: 245
Shirley Meadows Ski Area: 308, 310
Shore Acres Lodge: 8, 97–98

Siberia Creek Trail: 101
Sierra Gateway Cottages: 309–310
Sierra National Forest: 219–220, 245, 252, 265, 270
Sierra Nevada: 72, 85, 164–**166**
Sierra Summit Ski Area: 258, 260, 265
Sierra Vista National Scenic Byway: 249–250
Sierra Way: 307–310
Signal Mountain: 327
Silliman Crest: 284
Silver City Resort: 7, 299–300
Silver Lake: 201–202, 203, 205
Silver Lake Resort: 201–202
Silver Peak Wilderness: 17, 33
Silver Strand State Beach: 160
Silverwood Lake: 87, 88
Simpson House Inn: 12, 63–64
Skidoo: 322
skiing: Big Bear 94–106; Dodge Ridge Ski Area 169–173; June Lake 203–211; Kernville 308, 310; Lake Arrowhead 91–92; Mammoth Lakes 222–224, 226–227, 233, 235; Mount Baldy 83–85; Shaver Lake 258, 260; Snow Valley Ski Resort 88; Tom's Place 239–241; Wrightwood 81–83; Yosemite

National Park 187, 200–201, 215–219
Sky Meadows Trail: 228
Slate Mountain: 306
sledding: 171, 173, 210
Sleepy Hollow Cabins: 86–87
snowboarding: 91–92, 99, 173, 210, 222–224, 226–227
Snowcrest Lodge: 9, 84–86
snowmobiling: 173, 210, 258, 260, 306
snowshoeing: Big Bear 99; Dodge Ridge Ski Area 173; Giant Sequoia National Monument 306; June Mountain Ski Area 206, 210; Los Padres National Forest 72–73; Mammoth Mountain Ski Area 226–227; Mount San Jacinto State Park 332; Sequoia National Park 287–288; Shaver Lake 260
Snow Valley Ski Resort: 91–92
Soda Springs Trail: 33
Soda Springs trailhead: 197
Solvang: 37, 52–56
Solvang Inn & Cottages: 54
Sonora: 172–173
Sotcher Lake: 224
South Carlsbad State Beach: 134–135
South Fork: 245, 294
South Fork Kings River: 283

South Lake: 241, 274–275
Spanish Mountain: 244
Spring Cove Trail: 254
Springville: 302
Squaw Valley: 278–280
Stagecoach Trails Resort: 148–149
Stanislaus National Forest: 169, 171–172
Stanislaus River: 169–170
Starkweather Lake: 224
Strawberry: 169–171, 173–175
Strawberry Creek Inn: 126
Suicide Rock: 123
Sunday Peak Trail: 308
Sunrise trailhead: 195
Sunset Inn Yosemite Guest Cabins: 191
Sunset Rock Trail: 294
Sunset Trail: 281
swimming: Angelus Oaks 106–110; Bass Lake 252–254; Big Bear 95–106; Big Pine 277–278; Big Sur 21–30; Bishop 241–242, 272–277; Borrego Springs 140–141; Bridgeport 175–181; Camp Nelson 302–304; Campo 161–162; Carmel 20–21; Catalina Island 110–114; Cayucos 48–49; Chula Vista 160–161; Crestline 86–87; Death Valley National Park 320–321; Desert Hot Springs 328–329; Edison Lake 268–269; Fish Camp

219–222; Giant Sequoia National Monument 284–287, 305–306; Golden Trout Wilderness 304–305; Gorda 31–34; Green Valley Lake 94–95; Groveland 190–191; Hetch Hetchy Valley 191–193; Hollywood 80–81; Huntington Lake 260–268; Idyllwild 123–127; John Muir Wilderness 270–272; Julian 141–147, 149–150; June Lake 201–211; Kernville 307–310; Kings Canyon National Park 280–283; Laguna Beach 117–121; Lake Arrowhead 89–92; Lake Nacimiento 41–43; Lake San Antonio 40–41; Lee Vining 181–186, 188–189; Long Beach 114–116; Los Padres National Forest 72–73; Mammoth Lakes 211–212, 222–224, 226–236; Mariposa 213–214; Mineral King Valley 299–300; Mono Hot Springs 266–268; Morro Bay 46–48; Mountain Home State Forest 301–302; Mount Baldy 83–85; Mount Laguna 151–154; Newport Beach 116–117; North Fork 255–257; Oakhurst 250–252; Ojai 69–70; Pacific Beach 154–156; Palm Springs 329–333; Pioneertown area 323–324; Pismo Beach 51–52; Rancho Santa Fe 135–136; Rankin Ranch 312–313; Running Springs 92–93; San Diego 134–135, 157–159; Santa Barbara 56–69; Santa Ysabel 137–138; Sequoia National Park 289–290; Shaver Lake 257–260; Solvang 54–56; Sonora 172–173; Squaw Valley 278–280; Strawberry 169–171, 173–175; Temecula 121–122; Three Rivers 292–298; Tioga Pass 186–187; Tom's Place 236–241; Twentynine Palms 324–326; Twin Peaks 88–89; Ventura 70–71; Warner Springs 138–140; Woodlake 291–292; Wrightwood 81–83; Yosemite National Park 191–200, 215–216, 218–219

T

Taft Point: 215
Tahquitz Canyon: 330, 333
Tahquitz Peak: 123, 125
Tamarack Lodge Resort: 9, 226–227
Tamarack Winter Sports Area: 258
Tehachapi: 312
Telescope Peak: 316, **318**
Temecula: 121–122

Templeton: 46
tent cabins: Bearpaw High Sierra Camp 289–290; Big Sur Campground and Cabins 24–25; Catalina Island 111; Grant Grove Lodge 281; Muir Trail Ranch 270–272; Yosemite National Park 193–194, 196–198, 199
Theodore Woolsey House: 70
Third Lake: 277–278
Three Rivers: 292–298
Three T's Trail: 84
Tides Motel, The: 12, 51–52
Timberline Lodge: 97
Tioga Lodge: 188–189
Tioga Pass: 186–188
Tioga Pass Resort: 9, 186–187
Toiyabe National Forest: 176, 178
Tom's Place: 236–241
Tom's Place Resort: 236–237
Torrey Pines State Reserve: 156, 157
Trail of 100 Giants: 306
Trail of the Gargoyles: 169
Transverse Range: 36
Travertine Hot Springs: 179, 180
Treebones Resort: 31–32
Trona Pinnacles Natural Landmark: 322
Trumbull Lake: 183–184
Tule Lake: 267
Tule River: 301

Tunnel Trail: 62
Tuolumne Lodge: 6,
    197–198
Tuolumne Meadows: 195,
    197
Tuolumne River: 172, 174,
    190, 192
20 Lakes basin: 187
29 Palms Inn: 11,
    324–326
Twentynine Palms: 316,
    318, 324–327
Twin Falls: 226
Twin Lakes: 226, 265
Twin Lakes Recreation
    Area: 176–178
Twin Lakes Resort:
    176–178
Twin Peaks: 88–89
Two Bunch Palms: 11, 12,
    328–329
Two Harbors Cabins: 11,
    110–112
Two Waters Trail: 50

U

Ubehebe Crater: 320
Unal Trail: 308
Upham Victorian Hotel
    and Garden Cottages,
    The: 64
Upper Hamilton Lake:
    290
Upper Twin Lake:
    175–177

V

Valley of Enchantment: 87
Valley View Loop: 26
Velvet Peak: 322
Ventana Wilderness: 17,
    33

Ventura: 36, **38**, 70–72
Vermilion Valley Resort:
    268–269
Vernal Falls: 199
Vicente Flat trailhead: 33
Victoria Beach: 118
Vincent Gap trailhead: 82
Vincent Tumamait Trail:
    72
Virginia Creek Settle-
    ment: 10, 11, 181–183
Virginia Lakes Resort:
    183–184
Visalia: 302
Vista de la Cruz: 53
Vivian Creek Trail: 107

W

Walker Basin: 312
Wall Street Trail: 310
Wapama Falls: 192
Warner Springs: 138–140
Warner Springs Ranch:
    138–140
Washington Tree: 244
Wawona: 218–219, 220
Weaver Lake: 284
Weir Trail Loop: 122
Whiskey Flat Trail: 310
Whispering Pines:
    109–110
Whispering Pines Lodge:
    307–308
Whispering Pines Motel
    and Cabins: 207
Whispering Pines Trail:
    107
White Lotus Foundation:
    11, 59–61
White Mountains: 242
White Wolf Lodge:
    193–194

Wicky-Up Ranch:
    291–292
Wilder Cabins: 126–127
Wildrose Peak: 321
Wildwood Resort: 99–100
Wildyrie Resort: 231–232
William Heise County
    Park: 130–131, 142,
    144–147
William Heise County
    Park Cabins: 11,
    146–147
Windy Cliffs Trail: 283
Wine Valley Inn & Cot-
    tages: 52–54
winter sports: Ahwahnee
    249–250; Angelus Oaks
    106–110; best cabins for
    9; Big Bear 95–106;
    Fish Camp 219–222;
    Giant Sequoia National
    Monument 285–287;
    Green Valley Lake
    94–95; Huntington
    Lake 262–263; Julian
    141–147, 149–150; June
    Lake 203–211; Kernville
    307–310; Lake Arrow-
    head 91–92; Lee Vining
    188–189; Los Padres
    National Forest 72–73;
    Mammoth Lakes
    222–224, 226–227,
    234–236; Mount Baldy
    83–85; Mount Laguna
    151–154; Running
    Springs 92–93; Sequoia
    National Park 287–288;
    Shaver Lake 257–260;
    Sonora 172–173; Straw-
    berry 169–171, 173–175;
    Tioga Pass 186–187;

Tom's Place 236–237, 239–241; Twin Peaks 88–89; Wrightwood 81–83; Yosemite National Park 198–201, 215–219
Wolverton Creek: 288
Wolverton Ski Area: 288
Wooded Hill Nature Trail: 152
Woodlake: 291–292
Woodland Park Manor: 124
Woods Lodge: 229–230
Wrightwood: 81–83

XY
Yosemite High Sierra Camps: 6, 195–196
Yosemite Lakes: 10, 190–191
Yosemite Mountain Sugar Pine Railroad: 221, 250
Yosemite National Park: 164–**166**, 186, 190–201, 215–219, 250
Yosemite Pines RV Resort: 191
Yosemite Riverside Inn: 193

Yosemite Valley: 192, 213
Yosemite West: 215–216
Yost Creek Trail: 203
Yost Lake: 203, 210
Yost Meadows: 210
Yucca Point Trail: 283
yurts: 31–32, 60, 190

Z
Zaca Lake Resort: 56
Zosa Ranch & Gardens: 121–122
Zumwalt Meadow Loop: 283
Zwart House: 224

Notes

Notes

Notes

Notes

Notes

Notes